T0284773

Praise for *Build*

"In *Build*, Sadek Wahba makes a compelling case for greater private sector involvement in America's infrastructure investment. This book is essential reading for anyone who cares about our long-term success in the twenty-first century and beyond."—President Bill Clinton

"Using insights from his years in academia, business, and policy, Wahba offers a compelling answer: the private sector and government must work together, each doing what it does best. Urgent reading for anyone who wants answers to one of the most vexing problems of our time."—Rajeev Dehejia, professor of public policy, co-director of the Development Research Institute, New York University

"Wahba's important new book could not have come at a better time. Using a case-by-case approach, Wahba provides what is easily the most comprehensive analysis of the problems facing US infrastructure available today. He also lays out an actionable plan to better include private investment in our infrastructure that would address many of those endemic challenges."—Rick Geddes, founding director, Cornell Program in Infrastructure Policy (CPIP)

"Wahba makes an excellent case for why America needs to invest more in its crumbling infrastructure and suggests the funding model itself needs an update. He thoughtfully illustrates how and when to leverage private capital to ensure we have sufficient investment dollars to do so, including where this has worked, where it has failed, and possible paths forward."—Heidi Crebo-Rediker, adjunct senior fellow, Council on Foreign Relations

"A remarkable work, both scholarly and accessible, written by an infrastructure leader. Wahba both diagnoses and prescribes a cure for America' chronic and debilitating underinvestment in critical infrastructure such as bridges, roads and water systems. In today's fiercely competitive world, with adversarial nation-states, *Build* is essential to America, and even to freedom itself."
—Terence C. Burnham, Chapman University, coauthor of *Mean Genes*

"An indispensable book for regulators, long-term investors, and policymakers as it provides a roadmap for public-private partnership to deliver more efficient infrastructure outcomes. Wahba successfully provides constructive alternative solutions to America's infrastructure deficiencies from a global perspective."
—Michael Pascutti, Yale University

"Whether you're a policymaker or investor, *Build* is an invaluable guide and comprehensive resource to better understand the complex history, vast opportunities, and great challenges facing America's infrastructure. *Build* is a compelling case for the United States to aggressively invest in infrastructure to remain competitive and secure its future."—L. Felice Gorordo, US Alternate Executive Director, World Bank

"In *Build*, Wahba invites the reader to consider global infrastructure through a multiplicity of lenses: economic, geopolitical, socioeconomic, and ideologic. Wahba has a unique understanding of the challenges facing infrastructure stakeholders. He offers pragmatic solutions based on case studies of global best practices and a frank, data-driven 'lessons learned' approach. *Build* is a must have on any infrastructure investor's bookshelf."—Tara Higgins, global co-leader of Energy, Transportation, and Infrastructure Group, Sidley Austin LLP

"A detailed, comprehensive review of the battle to get sufficient funding to rebuild the American infrastructure. Despite the excellent bill the Biden Administration passed into law, the fight is an ongoing one that will require continuing focus."—Ed Rendell, former governor of Pennsylvania

To read more, please visit BuildBySadekWahba.com

BUILD

BUILD

INVESTING IN AMERICA'S INFRASTRUCTURE

SADEK WAHBA

GEORGETOWN UNIVERSITY PRESS   WASHINGTON, DC

© 2024 Sadek Wahba. All rights reserved. No part of this book may be reproduced or utilized in any form or by any means, electronic or mechanical, including photocopying and recording, or by any information storage and retrieval system, without permission in writing from the publisher.

The publisher is not responsible for third-party websites or their content. URL links were active at time of publication.

Library of Congress Cataloging-in-Publication Data

Names: Wahba, Sadek M., 1965– author.
Title: Build : investing in America's infrastructure / Sadek Wahba.
Description: Washington, DC : Georgetown University Press, 2024. | Includes
    bibliographical references and index.
Identifiers: LCCN 2024008535 (print) | LCCN 2024008536 (ebook) | ISBN
    9781647124960 (hardcover) | ISBN 9781647124977 (ebook)
Subjects: LCSH: Infrastructure (Economics)—United States. | Public-private sector
    cooperation—United States.
Classification: LCC HC110.C3 W343 2024 (print) | LCC HC110.C3 (ebook) |
    DDC 388.0973—dc23/eng/20240612
LC record available at https://lccn.loc.gov/2024008535
LC ebook record available at https://lccn.loc.gov/2024008536

♾ This paper meets the requirements of ANSI/NISO Z39.48-1992 (Permanence of Paper).

25 24   9 8 7 6 5 4 3 2 First printing
Printed in the United States of America

Cover design by Ryan Boser
Interior design by Classic City Composition, Athens, GA

Cover image: "Spokane, Washington and Falls." Postcard. Northern Pacific, Yellowstone Park Line, [ca. 1930–1945]. *Digital Commonwealth*, https://ark .digitalcommonwealth.org/ark:/50959/pko2cm52h.

*To the memory of the ninety-eight people who died in the collapse of
the Champlain Towers in Miami Beach, Florida,
on June 24, 2021*

*To Victoria and Charles
may they live in a safer and better America*

CONTENTS

PREFACE

"Please call me urgently! Where are you?" This was the message I received from my daughter, Victoria, on the morning of June 24, 2021. I was heading home after a morning walk and didn't react immediately; I was used to messages like this one, and typically the crises were not what I would describe as "urgent." This time, though, I was wrong.

When I got to the house, my daughter stared at me through reddened eyes and asked me if I had seen the news. "No, no idea what you are referring to," I said. A twelve-story condominium on Miami Beach had collapsed, she told me, and most of the people living in the building were missing. That took me by surprise. In fact, I couldn't quite comprehend what she was telling me at first. As someone who has spent decades investing in infrastructure around the world—in structures like bridges and power plants—I understood the potential dangers, but I could not believe a building in the United States had just disintegrated. My mind quickly went to the fateful day of September 11, 2001. I was working in Manhattan, New York, that terrible morning and similarly could not fathom that the World Trade Center, where many of my colleagues at Morgan Stanley worked, had collapsed. Was this a terrorist attack, too?

What I had missed in my daughter's anxious voice, as I tried to wrap my head around the event, was that this was not just any condominium to her. She had friends in the building. As events unfolded over the following days, I wanted to help but felt powerless. I reached out to Mayor Daniela Cava Levine, a formidable woman who showed her leadership and humanity in this disaster, but all I could offer was a fervent message of support for the mayor, the early responders, the firefighters, and the city. My daughter attended a vigil while the rescuers searched through the rubble. In the end, tragically, her friend was one of the ninety-eight people who perished in the collapse.

Over the ensuing days and weeks, my daughter would ask me: "How could this have happened? We're in the United States of America! What went wrong?"

Indeed, how *could* this have happened? How can it be that in the greatest economy in the world, buildings are collapsing? How can it be that bridges are falling, and thousands of children are drinking lead-tainted water? Why are American roads so congested that the trucking industry loses over $74 billion a year on idling drivers? How is it that the United States has invested less than 2 percent of its GDP in infrastructure in the last several decades, while China has poured in over 8 percent? How is it that in November 2021, the greatest power in the world could only barely pass an infrastructure bill that promised only a third of the funding needed just to restore its systems? While Americans complain that China is winning the race for the twenty-first-century economy, the country seems unable, or unwilling, to undertake the work to make the United States more efficient and more productive, and to prepare its people for the strategic competition of the coming decades. The consequences of US inaction are global, but also—as my family learned that June day—extremely immediate.

This book grew out of a desire to answer the question: What went wrong? Not just in that Miami condominium, but across the country. How can America rebuild its infrastructure? While the causes of US infrastructure failures may be complex, the solutions don't have to be, and there are many more options available than have so far been tried seriously. America must find a way to ensure, as best as it can, that similar tragedies do not happen in the future. This book is dedicated to those ninety-eight people who died in the collapse in Miami, to the many thousands who have died through negligence and poor infrastructure management in the country, and to the belief that Americans can prevent such deaths in the future.

In the wake of the most significant infrastructure bill in a generation, an enormous amount of work remains to be done. The funds allocated under the 2021 Infrastructure Investment and Jobs Act will help refurbish existing infrastructure assets and build some new ones, but the bill was far short of what was needed despite President Joe Biden's best efforts. More important, there is urgent need to reform US methods of infrastructure investment. If the country is to meet the challenges of the twenty-first century, it needs to break out of the cycle of short-term, stop-gap solutions and come up with a plan to maintain and grow American infrastructure in a permanent and sustainable way.

In *Build*, I argue that rather than rely principally on federal and state tax revenues to finance its infrastructure, or ever-increasing budget deficits, the United States should encourage a larger role for the private sector in infrastructure investment, as private sector involvement can bring in much needed capital and greater efficiency in the delivery of infrastructure services. There are many ways this might be accomplished, all of which are hotly debated, and this book will attempt to understand the many sides and facets of the discussion.

The first chapter surveys the state of infrastructure in the United States and lays out in broad strokes the challenges the country faces and why a pragmatic approach to infrastructure investment should include the private sector. Chapter 2 walks through the history of infrastructure investment in Europe and the United States to remind the reader that the current way of investing in infrastructure has not always been the norm, and that the Great Depression, the New Deal, and World War II profoundly changed the delivery of infrastructure by creating a greater role for the state. (A clear exception is the power sector, which embraced a private approach.) The following chapters review particular cases of infrastructure development through real examples and try to demonstrate why things fail and how they succeed. And though the private sector has a larger role to play, it is not always the best answer. Chapter 3 looks at the water sector and dives into the details of the crisis in Flint, Michigan, providing comparisons with water regulation schemes in other countries. Chapter 4 examines US bridge infrastructure and the efforts in Chicago to involve the private sector in the operation of the Chicago Skyway, drawing lessons from Chicago's privatization experience for other cities and infrastructure sectors. Chapter 5 takes up roads, explores the failed effort to privatize the Pennsylvania Turnpike and the privatization of the Indiana Toll Road, and compares their regulatory structures to other models, such as those in India and Italy. Chapter 6 investigates the situation at US airports and asks why government programs aimed at stimulating private investment in airports have stumbled, focusing on the withdrawn proposal to privatize Lambert International Airport and the success of Puerto Rico's airport. Chapter 7 offers a more upbeat story of private involvement in infrastructure delivery by analyzing the structure and history of US seaports through a discussion of the Port Authority of New York and New Jersey. Chapter 8 delves into debates surrounding the expansion of broadband access and the challenge of financing emergent technologies, arguing that government will always have an important role to play in infrastructure delivery. Finally, in chapter 9 I review the debate that has dominated US infrastructure policy, analyze the performance of privatized infrastructure in the last decade compared to public infrastructure, and consider a handful of policy recommendations, including different forms of public-private partnerships and broader policy recommendations such as creating an infrastructure bank.

Public debates rarely capture the complexity of infrastructure investment, and many of the common assumptions about how infrastructure ought to be managed go without serious critical examination. As I argue in this book, investment in US infrastructure is essential to America's economic and political success, both domestically and internationally. The United States needs innovative, large-scale thinking about how infrastructure assets should be administered, managed, regulated, and funded. By drawing on decades of literature dedicated to this topic, as well as discussions with infrastructure experts, regulators, and politicians, this book hopes to elucidate the challenges and options the country faces. I hope it can make a small contribution to the ongoing debate.

one

THE CASE FOR A NEW OLD APPROACH

The Challenges Facing US Infrastructure

PHIL: "What would you do if you were stuck in one place and every day
was exactly the same, and nothing you did mattered?"
RALPH: "That about sums it up for me!"

—*Groundhog Day* (1993)

In Beijing, a private company manages the city's water infrastructure.[1] This
is true also in Chengdu, Guangzhou, and Macau, where the private sector
operates water systems through long-term concessions from municipal governments.[2] It's a remarkable fact: in an economy overseen by the Chinese
Communist Party, in the largest cities of the second largest economy in the
world, privately owned utility operators manage municipal infrastructure.
All across China, in fact, private investors and private operators participate
in the development and management of not only the nation's water systems,
but also its toll roads, wastewater facilities, ports, and telecommunications
infrastructure. The firm I am part of, I Squared Capital, owns and operates wastewater concessions in Henan, Shaanxi, and Heilongjiang; a data
center in Nanjing; solar plants in Shandong; and district energy plants in
Chongqing, Zhejinag, and Shandong. To be sure, many of the publicly listed
companies operating Chinese infrastructure are ultimately government-
controlled firms, and many of the country's infrastructure assets are owned
by municipalities, but many municipal-owned infrastructure assets are also
leased to wholly private companies. The fact is that China has adopted a
multilayered system to run its infrastructure. As Deng Xiaoping, the leader
who opened China to the world starting in the 1980s, stated in explaining his fundamental rationale for economic reforms in China: "Black cat or
white cat, as long as it catches the mouse, it's a good cat."[3]

1

China is not alone in this approach. Around the world, regardless of political orientation or stage of economic development, governments are learning to invest in infrastructure through alternative methods of ownership, management, and regulation. Often this means partnering with the private sector. The United Kingdom enlisted the private sector in the 1980s to own and operate its waterworks. So did Chile. In Australia, private institutions own and operate many of the major airports, from Sydney to Perth. India, which has embraced private investment and private operators in its network of toll roads since 1996,[4] is currently using a massive public-private partnership to expand its toll roads by fifteen thousand miles, with $2.4 billion in investment coming from the private sector for those projects alone—one of many India has undertaken with private sector participation.[5]

In recent decades the United States has also experimented, in fits and starts, with modern forms of private participation in infrastructure investment. There have been a few remarkable triumphs, but on the whole the nation has experienced a greater number of missed opportunities. It seems to be unable to move beyond the existing model of investing in infrastructure, a model that this book will argue is wholly inadequate for the long-term sustainability of the country's critical systems. Decades after London privatized Heathrow Airport, and long since Paris publicly listed Charles de Gaulle Airport (with the French government remaining the controlling shareholder), almost no major airports in the United States today are truly operated by a private entity. In some of the cases examined in this book, even when cities and states cannot afford to repair their lead-contaminated water systems, local officials reject privatization proposals. In July 2023 state attorneys challenged and won from federal courts a temporary hold on a new Biden administration Environmental Protection Agency (EPA) rule designed to better protect public water systems from cybersecurity attacks. While the issue revolved around whether the EPA was using the right tools, it was also about the question of who would pay for those new regulatory requirements.[6] American infrastructure is in a state of decline, so why is there such resistance to solutions that have been adopted around the world? Why is the United States so flatfooted on infrastructure development? How can the country spur itself to rebuild its once preeminent infrastructure?

These are the questions this book explores, and answering them will take us deep into the inner workings of city halls and statehouses across the country, as well as into the decision-making processes of many economies around the world. The book will bring us through the households, neighborhood streets, and utility companies in American towns from Florida to

Alaska. Along the way we'll hear directly from some of the world's most experienced policymakers, regulators, and asset managers. This is a book about American infrastructure: how it is financed, operated, and regulated. It is a study of the challenges faced by infrastructure managers in the United States today, but most importantly, it is an exploration of the many options available when it comes to operating and investing in critical systems. For a glimpse into these other options, and to see the United States more objectively, it is helpful to look at the ways other countries around the world handle infrastructure investment, particularly to examine the models of privatization and the public-private partnerships that have been successful—*and* those that have not. The book draws comparisons between the managerial crisis in US infrastructure and the experience of countries that employ alternative strategies of infrastructure investment, like the United Kingdom, India, France, Australia, and many others. American policymakers generally don't like to compare the nation's systems to the rest of the world, but in this case it is inevitable. The United States is far behind other countries and needs to catch up.

China presents a particularly important comparison. Its massive domestic infrastructure investment program and its Belt and Road Initiative, which has taken China's infrastructure industry global, highlight the strategic significance of infrastructure investment and its critical contribution to economic growth. Launched by President Xi Jinping in 2013, the Belt and Road Initiative demonstrates that infrastructure can play a central role in generating economic and political influence and opens new paths for economic development around the world. Investing in infrastructure is not just about economic growth in the United States, but also about ensuring in the long run the nation's ability to succeed in strategic competition—a competition that will dominate its foreign and, in many ways, domestic policies in the coming decades. As Antony Blinken stated in his first major speech after being appointed secretary of state, "More than at any other time in my career—maybe in my lifetime—distinctions between domestic and foreign policy have simply fallen away. Our domestic renewal and our strength in the world are completely entwined."[7] China's investments in infrastructure have powered its economic rise and now, increasingly, define its global ascendancy as well. In terms of investment levels, especially investment in twenty-first-century technologies, the United States lags behind China. However, as I have argued elsewhere,[8] by revolutionizing our methods of managing and funding infrastructure, the United States can still modernize its infrastructure. In an age of strategic competition, a vibrant domestic infrastructure sector made up of many actors—including construction companies, manufacturing, engineering schools, and research and development in technologies with direct application to infrastructure services—will contribute to a stronger United States, one that can increase productivity, increase sustainable growth rates, and ensure its competitive edge globally.

The dilemmas caused by its failing infrastructure investment model have plagued the country for generations, outlasting economic ups and downs, wars, and numerous changes in government. As we will see, the effects of large-scale infrastructure investment strategies are felt directly in local budgets, local systems, and institutions, and therefore by the people who use them. This is a challenge that elected officials ought to do everything in their power to fix, and yet any discussion of alternative infrastructure investment strategies quickly descends into political battles. My hope is that this book will encourage policymakers and the general public to change that.

I have been involved in infrastructure for over three decades, beginning at the World Bank in Washington, DC, where I came to understand deeply the role infrastructure plays in economic and societal development. My first encounter was working on the social dimensions of structural adjustments in Côte d'Ivoire in 1990. The 1980s were dominated by structural adjustment programs pushed by the World Bank and the International Monetary Fund (IMF), which often included radical policies for developing countries, such as removing subsidies, devaluing currencies, slashing government deficits, and entering into massive privatization programs. These policies created economic distress across all levels of society in many countries, but especially among the poorest households, which did not have the ability to adjust to these rapid changes. In response the World Bank, grudgingly at first, established a unit called Social Dimensions of Adjustment. I started my career thinking through how to ensure positive social outcomes, avoiding political rhetoric and focusing on the data. We conducted multiyear surveys to understand the impact of these economic adjustments on households, then devised improved reforms and targeted plans to support them.

I visited Côte d'Ivoire many times. A country of spectacular, rugged mountains, savannah grasslands, and tropical growth alongside sprawling beaches in the south, it is one of the most beautiful countries in the world, with a diverse population all trying hard to build their country. It is one of the largest exporters of cocoa and coffee in the world, developing from a practically nonexistent economy in the 1950s to become the richest country in the region by the 1970s. Its extraordinary people have gone through suffering and, in recent decades, civil war, but have never ceased striving for a better life. On one of my visits to an education project outside Abidjan, the country's economic capital, I saw a group of young girls and boys, impeccably dressed, walking along a muddy road. They were going to school. With no public transport system, these children walked two hours every day on an unpaved, swampy road to get a basic education that would allow them to better themselves and compete in the world. Later on I realized that this scene was not unique to Côte d'Ivoire but repeated itself in developing countries everywhere, where the lack of basic transport and infrastructure was an impediment to education, health, and commerce. Infrastructure is truly essential to furthering quality of life and economic development.

The work I did in Côte d'Ivoire on the social dimensions of structural adjustments has guided my thinking about infrastructure ever since; I have never looked back from those children trudging to school. Later, after I left the World Bank, I moved to Morgan Stanley, the investment bank in New York, where I helped finance numerous infrastructure projects in the United States and internationally, then started investing in infrastructure assets on behalf of institutional investors such as US pension funds.

Through these experiences I have come to care deeply about the best way to deliver infrastructure services, and I have learned quite a bit about the many ways to invest in and manage assets. While I no doubt have a bias toward the involvement of private capital in infrastructure, what I have learned is that there is no one-size-fits-all answer. Each country, each state, and each infrastructure sector may require its own approach. In many cases, a public-private partnership (P3 or PPP) or outright privatization can offer an indispensable tool if properly structured; in others, participation by the private sector may not be necessary or may simply not be adequate. Sometimes the political climate may only allow a suboptimal solution, which is still better than none.

There is a growing literature, historically hampered by the lack of data, that evaluates infrastructure privatizations and P3s. The most recent studies (discussed in detail in chapter 9) point to the net positive effect of involving the private sector in infrastructure but also indicate that, in other respects, there is much work to be done to improve the contractual structure by which the private sector can operate efficiently in the provision of public services such as highways, airports, and water supply. The issue of how to invest in infrastructure inspires strong opinions on both sides of the US political divide. The deadlock has led to inaction. Without attempting to sidestep this debate, I argue that at the least, the United States has failed to seriously examine alternative methods of funding and developing its infrastructure.

This is not good common sense. When it comes to developing and maintaining infrastructure, we ought to be open to every possibility. Pragmatism is the watchword. "All of the above" is the operative mantra.

However, US infrastructure policy has tended toward the dogmatic rather than the pragmatic. Over the past fifty years the United States has hardly diversified its approach to infrastructure investment. The country remains trapped in an outmoded and, in many instances, ideologically doctrinaire model. There is an irony to the American resistance to private sector involvement in the infrastructure arena. In the United States, reputedly the freest market in the world, privatization of infrastructure is still often regarded as unacceptable. China, meanwhile, which is still—and increasingly—a state-controlled economy,[9] accepts the expediency of P3s and privately owned infrastructure assets. The dogmatism of US policy lies in the belief that the state (in this case defined as federal, state, or municipal government, or a state agency) ought to own and manage "public" infrastructure. This belief stems in part from a state bureaucracy that goes back to the Great Depression and Roosevelt's New Deal in the 1930s, when many assets that were originally in private hands were transferred to government. Public infrastructure was already expanding prior to the New Deal, but Roosevelt's policies firmed up the political philosophy that promoted government ownership and management. As recent literature demonstrates, the advent of World War II accelerated the process whereby industries and infrastructure were taken over by the government in the interest of the war effort. After the war, with no incentive to return operations to private hands, much of that infrastructure stayed with the state.[10]

Until policymakers learn to embrace more pragmatic approaches to infrastructure investment, the country will continue to miss out on opportunities, and its infrastructure will remain in a state of deterioration. In his book *A Nation of Wusses*, Ed Rendell, former Democratic governor of Pennsylvania and staunch union supporter, asks:

> How is it that we've come to this state of affairs in our infrastructure? Why have we let this happen? The answer lies with the elected officials. First because they've made the allocation of infrastructure spending political. The funds aren't distributed where they're needed, where they'll get the best return for the investment. They have been, in great part, allocated by who has the most powerful congressman or senator. Hence we have the "Big Dig" or the "bridge to nowhere." This lack of accountability and transparency has eroded the public's confidence in infrastructure spending.

Second[,] my friend Mika Brzezinski, the co-anchor of "Morning Joe," says that infrastructure "is the least sexy word in the English language." By that she means that it's hard to get people riled up about infrastructure. People understand it is important, but it takes a backseat to what are perceived as more immediate and pressing needs. It's easy to say that we'll get to that next year.[11]

He is darn right.

There is nothing inevitable or necessary about current US infrastructure investment strategies. There are many ways to invest in the upgrading and expansion of infrastructure, from greater federal or state funding to increased participation from the private sector; from straightforward privatization to the creation of one of many forms of P3; and from the establishment of a national infrastructure bank to the deregulation of public utilities, as done in the power market. At the very least, the country might increase user fees for toll roads or raise the gasoline tax, which has not changed since 1993!

The reasons to reform US systems of infrastructure management are many—as many as there are reasons to invest in infrastructure in the first place. Infrastructure is the fabric that holds a society together, the grease that keeps the gears turning. Behind every banana I buy at the grocery store is a network of roads, bridges, cold storage facilities, ports, airports, operators, regulators, investors, policymakers, and more, all of which allow me to buy my snack without giving any of these factors a second thought. The enormous importance of our infrastructure systems came into focus during the 2020 pandemic, when the phrase "supply chain" became part of our everyday vocabulary. The reason to fix the US infrastructure and reimagine the systems for investing in it is that infrastructure has an immediate effect on the quality of life and productivity of citizens every day, in ways both small and large. More concretely, investment in infrastructure has been shown repeatedly to boost economic growth.

It is important to digress a little here to review the economic literature on the causal relationship between infrastructure and economic growth, since this underpins my premise about investing in infrastructure in the first place. Economic theory has established a link between public spending on infrastructure and economic growth, starting with the work of Kenneth Arrow in 1970 and revisited by Robert Barro and others in 1990.[12] The basic premise is that public spending on infrastructure has a positive effect on economic growth, but the extent of that impact will depend on a series of factors, including the relative size of public spending and the state of economic development. To summarize the argument briefly, higher spending has a positive effect, but too much spending starts to have a diminishing effect. When too much spending occurs, capital is deployed in less productive assets and crowds out other sources of capital, slowing economic growth.

The result is that measuring the effect of infrastructure investment on economic growth becomes an empirical question, dependent on the country's stage of economic development, the mechanism by which infrastructure is funded (whether through taxes or private or foreign investment) and delivered, the institutional decision-making process at play, and the regulatory and legal frameworks, to name just a few of the parameters. This points beyond the initial link between growth and public infrastructure investment to the importance of an empirical analysis of investment models and a case-by-case evaluation of which model of ownership, regulation, and funding is best suited to the task.

A report by the IMF published in 2020 reaffirms the importance of public investment in economic growth and the case for scaling up investment, especially during a recovery period.[13] In the United States the relationship between infrastructure and economic growth has been extensively studied. The early, pioneering work conducted by economist David Aschauer, and followed by Alicia Munnell and others, demonstrated a clear positive link between public spending and economic growth.[14] Aschauer's work in turn generated a new area of empirical research to capture the exact causal link between economic growth and infrastructure spending (see Valerie Ramey's chapter in the excellent volume *Economic Analysis and Infrastructure Investment*, edited by Ed Glaeser and Jim Poterba).[15] A 2017 study by Josh Bivens, the director of research at the Economic Policy Institute, reaffirms that infrastructure investment can boost US economic growth.[16] He suggests that every $100 billion in infrastructure spending can boost gross domestic product by up to $150 billion. Furthermore, he found that this growth in GDP could increase employment by up to one million additional workers.

Recently, researchers in this space have also examined the role infrastructure investment plays in reducing income inequality and absolute poverty.[17] Another 2017 study, published by the Central Bank of France, shows that across US states, as the rate of infrastructure investment increased, income inequality lessened. The impact varied sharply by project type; greater investment in highways, for instance, resulted in greater access to jobs and education and thus disproportionately benefited lower-income households.[18]

This is compelling empirical evidence for the importance of infrastructure investment to economic development; in general, these studies provide strong evidence that infrastructure investment can spark the engine that will reboot the American economy for the twenty-first century.

There has been particular attention to the impact of infrastructure investment on China's economic growth. Studies have shown a positive correlation between infrastructure and GDP growth, as well as a positive effect on poverty reduction and income inequality.[19] However, it is a fact that too much investment in infrastructure becomes less productive. While there is no question that the early investment in infrastructure in China was vital for the country's economic development (there was essentially no infrastructure to speak of when China opened up to global markets in the 1980s), after forty years of continued large spending on infrastructure, the results are mixed. Kurt Campbell's book *The Pivot: The Future of American Statecraft in Asia* reviews China's infrastructure investments in the context of its pivot strategy toward Asia and notes that while impressive, many of China's investments have come at considerable expense and could ultimately "destabilize the country's financial system and stunt China's growth."[20] A study published in 2017 found that "more infrastructure is not always better, [and] too much investment in infrastructure can even be detrimental to growth."[21]

There is little doubt that the United States needs to take infrastructure more seriously as an engine of economic growth as well as for addressing income inequality. Yet as important as infrastructure investment and development are to economic growth, they must be done right to achieve optimal impact. The United States can draw both encouraging and cautionary lessons from China's investment, and the nation ought to approach its own investment by relying on the economic data rather than political rhetoric.

The United States should be on the verge of a new *infrastructure decade*. In November 2021 I had the honor of attending the signing ceremony for the Infrastructure Investment and Jobs Act (IIJA) at the White House. It had been a long road to the signing, and it represented a milestone accomplishment. In the bill, initially introduced as the Build Back Better Plan in 2021, the Biden administration sought a total of $4 trillion in federal spending to fund physical infrastructure; climate change mitigation; and a slate of "soft" infrastructure programs, including initiatives to invest in home health care, eldercare, and paid family leave. The agenda was divided into two plans: the American Jobs Plan, oriented toward infrastructure, climate investments, and research and development, and the American Families

Plan, aimed at eldercare and childcare services, among other things. As opposition mounted to the soaring price of Biden's agenda, these two parts of the Build Back Better Plan were officially separated into distinct legislative proposals when a bipartisan coalition of lawmakers adopted an alternative plan, based only on physical, "traditional" infrastructure. The American Jobs Plan then became the Bipartisan Infrastructure Bill, championed by senators Kyrsten Sinema (I-AZ) and Rob Portman (R-OH). After months of bitter negotiations between Republicans and Democrats, as well as between progressives and moderates in the Democratic Party, the Bipartisan Infrastructure Bill was signed into law as the IIJA. Progressive lawmakers, led by Pramila Jayapal (D-WA), voted "no" on the bipartisan bill in protest against the abandonment of climate measures and elements from the American Families Plan, along with thirty Republicans. But with enough Republican support, Democrats nevertheless managed to pass the bill, delivering $550 billion in desperately needed new spending on infrastructure.

Though the significantly scaled-back law excluded many of the key provisions of the original Build Back Better Bill, more laws were in the wings. The research and development portion of the Biden administration's plan became the Creating Helpful Incentives to Produce Semiconductors and Science Act (or the CHIPS and Science Act), which allocated $280 billion to the National Science Foundation, the US Department of Energy, and the US Department of Commerce for research and development,[22] particularly in semiconductors, which are strategically important but also key to every element of infrastructure investment. The progressive agenda did not die in the water, either. The following summer, after applying continued pressure on Democratic holdouts (especially West Virginia Democratic senator Joe Manchin), progressives reanimated the American Families Act in the form of the Inflation Reduction Act (IRA). Nominally aimed at addressing the inflation crisis of 2022, the IRA directed $250 billion to the energy sector, another $46 billion toward the environment, and $23 billion to transportation and electric cars, in what is probably the largest effort in the world to support a push for renewables infrastructure.[23]

The ambitious agenda outlined by the Biden administration has, to an impressive extent, been fulfilled—largely thanks to pragmatic, bipartisan compromises. Throughout the process I did what I could to contribute to the debate and to advocate for an open-minded approach to alternative models of investment. In September 2022 I was honored to accept President Biden's nomination to the National Infrastructure Advisory Council

(NIAC), which advises the White House on the security and resilience of American infrastructure systems.

I believe the administration's efforts to rescue US infrastructure have been absolutely necessary and monumental. The reality, however, is that government spending will not get the whole job done, and as long as the state maintains its monopolistic power over US infrastructure, some of the nation's foundational issues will go unsolved. To fully realize the infrastructure decade that is coming, the country will need more than just federal and state investment.

At the start of the 2020s, US infrastructure was in a state of collapse. In its 2021 Infrastructure Report Card, the American Society of Civil Engineers (ASCE) gave US infrastructure a C– grade and estimated that the country required $4.6 trillion in total spending over ten years to address the problem. It stipulated that $2.6 trillion of this spending must be new investment.[24] The Biden administration used this report widely during its campaign for the Build Back Better Bill. As praiseworthy as IIJA was, it was still well short of the ASCE's recommendation. Of the $1.2 trillion the IIJA provided in total spending, only $550 billion was new investment, less than a fifth of what the United States needs. In the wake of the IIJA, the IRA, and the CHIPS and Science Act, it would be easy to let infrastructure slip from our minds, but the country needs a more thoroughgoing kind of intervention. There is so much more the nation can achieve by unleashing its potential through private sector participation and by reforming the state agencies responsible for managing its infrastructure by giving them more resources and investing in human capital, by looking, for example, at new pricing mechanisms to address congestion issues (which have been on the table since the 1950s), or by integrating technology into the delivery of infrastructure services.

In each of the sectors discussed in this book, the United States underperforms. There are many sectors in which the country outperforms every other economy in the world. Great. It should, with its resources, ingenuity, and entrepreneurial spirit, outperform in almost every sector. In 2022 two million Americans did not have access to safe drinking water. In a more widespread failure, 40 percent of American roads were in poor or mediocre condition.[25] Congestion costs the trucking industry over $74 billion a year from idling drivers,[26] well over half the total amount allocated for road repairs in the IIJA.[27] Between thirty-three and forty-six bridges in the United States fail annually,[28] over 6 percent are in poor condition,[29] and 78,800 should be replaced entirely.[30] There are 2,300 high-hazard-risk dams across the country at risk of failure.[31] The list goes on.

The failures of American infrastructure policy are brought into relief when we compare the United States to other countries. Take roads: between 2000 and 2020, traffic fatalities were on the decline worldwide. In the United Kingdom, mortalities fell from 6.9 to 3.2 per 100,000 people; in France, the drop was even more pronounced, from 13.4 to 5.1. In the United States, however, deaths have only dropped from 15.7 per 100,000 people to 12.7.[32] In 2021, fatalities rose 10 percent from the previous year, accounting for 42,915 deaths on US roads in a single year.[33] Our road fatalities are roughly double those of most other advanced economies. These fatalities may not all be directly caused by road quality, of course, but it is not unrelated that across the country, states and municipalities have struggled to keep up with road maintenance or to expand roadways to address congestion. Broadband, a quintessentially twenty-first-century technology, tells a similar story. In Canada, 92 percent of people have access to broadband service; in the United Kingdom that figure is 94 percent.[34] But in the United States, only 90 percent of people can access high-speed internet. Or we can look at water quality. Since 1992, in the United Kingdom, France, and Australia, along with the majority of the developed world, 100 percent of residents have had access to safe drinking water. In the United States, only 99.2 percent had safe water until 2018, leaving 2.6 million people without clean water.[35]

Meeting these challenges demands creative problem-solving and the full scope of the country's resources. The tectonic plates that support the American way of life are on the move. The shift toward green energy has begun in earnest, and the world is beginning to realize that climate change requires us to radically transform our energy and transportation systems. Additionally, technological advances are opening new possibilities for infrastructure, from broadband networks to smart roads and data servers. New technologies require new forms of infrastructure, and to invest in these transformations the United States will need to overhaul and reimagine its methods of financing, too. These revolutions in infrastructure will impact the lives of millions. It is essential, as the country progresses further into this infrastructure decade, that policymakers, businesspeople, and voters alike understand how these systems function.

A Simple Framework for Analyzing Infrastructure Assets

Definitions of infrastructure vary. The word *infrastructure* is relatively new, having come into the mainstream only in the 1970s, so some confusion is understandable. As Margaret Thatcher famously quipped in 1985, "You and I come by road or rail, but economists travel by infrastructure."[36] Indeed, a survey I conducted in 2022 found that nearly four in ten Americans "aren't sure they know what politicians are talking about when they talk about infrastructure."[37] Infrastructure covers a wide variety of services and structures, from water delivery and power generation to roadways and cell towers. Depending on one's legislative priorities, the word infrastructure might also be extended to include drug pricing, day-care facilities, or elderly care facilities. In this book, infrastructure is limited to its conventional categories, including roads, bridges, waterworks, power generation and electricity transmission and distribution, communications systems (including broadband and internet), ports, airports, and public transit. While after-school and health-care centers certainly count as vital systems, they involve an entirely different kind of investment, management, and maintenance than the sectors associated with "traditional" infrastructure. The physical systems that facilitate transportation, water delivery, communication, and power generation require enormous capital investment, construction, and careful regulation and management. The sectors highlighted in this book—waterworks, bridges, roads, airports, ports, and broadband—were also chosen because these sectors have seen fewer creative solutions than other sectors like power and utilities. One puzzle addressed in this book is why American households and local policymakers are comfortable paying regulated prices to get their electrons from private companies (some of them directly or indirectly owned by Canadian and Chinese pension funds) but cannot accept that our water molecules could ever be controlled by similar entities.

For too long the United States has been stuck in a false debate about whether privatization is a legitimate means for investing in and expanding our infrastructure, while the rest of the world has gone beyond the United States in not only resolving that debate but establishing the most pragmatic and efficient ways to use capital through P3s. That isn't to say that this debate is not ongoing in the European or other economies, but simply that industrial economies, as well as high-growth economies such as China, have adopted the view that whoever is able to deliver efficiently and productively over a long period of time should manage infrastructure, whether in the waterworks, roads and bridges, or airports sectors. That is what we need to do in the United States: go beyond the rhetoric and take the actions that will allow us to not only catch up but become a leader in infrastructure development and management on a global scale.

At this stage it is useful to provide a more explicit framework for understanding what I mean by privatization. *Privatization* in this context is defined as the involvement of the private sector in an infrastructure asset through ownership and/or management under a regulatory framework established either independently by the government or jointly with the private entity, which results in the transfer of significant risk over the long term from the state to the private operator. Privatization, then, revolves around three parameters: (1) ownership, (2) management, and (3) regulation. The projects discussed in the next eight chapters can be analyzed by looking at

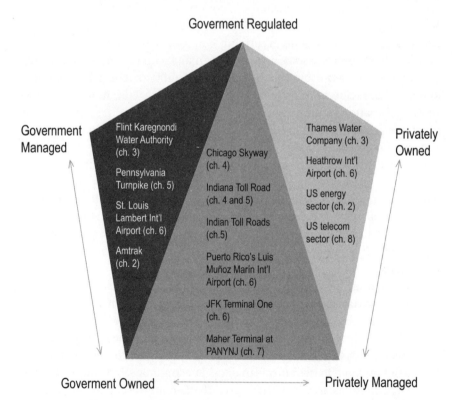

Figure 1.1. Configurations of infrastructure ownership, management, and regulation, with examples.

these three parameters. Figure 1.1 presents the different ways these parameters can be adapted, illustrating the heart of the debate about infrastructure procurement. Each face of the pyramid represents a different configuration of ownership, management, and regulation, with each point in the pyramid representing an owner, manager, or regulator in the public or private sector. As one can see, government regulates in each configuration.[38] On each face are examples of each configuration, all of which are discussed in detail in the following chapters.

The first parameter, "ownership," refers to the entity that ultimately owns the asset: the legal owner of the right to provide a particular service, such as a wastewater plant, and/or the owner of the physical assets, whether that means physical land or equipment or something intangible, such as monopoly rights. For example, the US container ports discussed in chapter 7 are owned by the state through a state agency, the Port Authority of New York and New Jersey. The state may lease a port under a long-term concession to a third party, but it nevertheless owns the asset and is the ultimate shareholder, and when the lease ends it will regain control of the asset. This is no different than owning a house and renting it out. The deed holder owns the house, but the renters live in the house and benefit from it. If the renters leave, the owner gets back the use of the house and can rent it again or decide to live in it or sell it. Assets might be owned in whole or in part by the private operator; in the case of the UK water sector, reviewed in chapter 3, the government sold 100 percent of the water companies. If the United Kingdom would like to reclaim ownership, it would need to renationalize them by buying the companies back from their current owners. By contrast, in the case of the French airport company Aéroports de Paris, the French state owns 51 percent of the company, and the remaining 49 percent is owned by public shareholders, since the company is listed on the French stock exchange. Similar to many Chinese companies that are controlled by the state but are listed on the stock exchange, anyone can buy shares, but no one can buy control over the company because the state has the majority ownership.

The second parameter is the management of the assets. Management can be undertaken by the owner or by a third party. In the case of the US container ports, while the Port Authority owns the asset, the management of the container port itself is undertaken by a private operator through a long-term lease that is referred to as a P3. The same is true for toll roads that involve the private sector. The Indiana Toll Road, for example, is 100 percent owned by the state of Indiana via its agency, but for the period of its concession contract (seventy-five years), it is managed by a private operator. If that operator files for bankruptcy, the creditors can take over the management of the concession but not the ownership. The state incurs no loss and keeps the original amount it received at the time it entered into the P3. Let's say the operator had no creditors but violated certain terms of the P3; the state would have the right to take over the asset and lease it to another party and get paid once again. This, again, is no different than leasing commercial real estate: if a commercial tenant pays the full rent for the coming ten years up front and the tenant defaults, the landlord may keep the money and lease the property again.

The third parameter is the regulation of the asset. Generally, regulation is specific to each sector and crafted to deal with that sector only, unlike a contract to build a road, which is subject to a "standard" contractual agreement and for which disputes are generally regulated by a judiciary process. The regulation can be implemented either by a state authority, for example a public utility commission in the case of regulated utility companies, or else directly by the state itself through the relevant department or through a P3 specific to that asset that specifies the overall regulatory framework, or through some combination. In a P3, regulation can be jointly established and negotiated through the terms of the concession. This is necessary because the concession might extend for many years, in which case both the private operator and the state will want to account for unanticipated contingencies in the future. Typically, concession agreements must be approved by state or city authorities and elected bodies. In many cases, the state will develop the regulatory framework of a concession and ask companies to bid on it as a take-it-or-leave-it deal. Every infrastructure sector that has clear monopoly rights is regulated by the state. Even in the case of the fully privatized infrastructure in the United Kingdom, airports are regulated by an airport authority, the water sector is regulated by a water authority, and so on.

If the municipality owns and manages an infrastructure asset, it still relies on the private sector. As operator of a wastewater facility, for instance, the state would contract various operations to the private sector, no different than how one would contract a plumber or electrician for one's home. This is the way most states procure activities such as capital expenditure and maintenance (capex). States often administer private contracts for new projects through a design-bid-build (DBB) process, in which private entities plan and construct an asset, but the state operates it and takes on most of the risk.

In public-private partnerships, in contrast to simple contracts, the private entity takes on the most risk, not only designing and building the asset but also operating and managing it long term, generally paying up front for the right to do so. There are various models of P3s that structure the relationships among owner, operator, and regulator. Most common are build-operate-transfer or build-transfer-operate (BOT/BTO) models, in which a private entity builds, for example, a wastewater plant, and transfers ownership of it to the state upon completion, but operates it for a period of time afterward. Similarly, a P3 could also be designed on a build-own-operate (BOO) model, whereby the state grants a private entity the right to build an asset, own it, and operate it, but keeps the right to regulate the asset and determine, for example, an acceptable rate of return on the private entity's investment.

Public-private partnerships therefore are normally defined, according to the World Bank, as long-term contracts between a private party and a government entity for providing a public asset or service in which the private party bears significant risk and management responsibility and in which remuneration is linked to performance. How does that definition fit with our simple framework for privatization? Let's review the World Bank definition in the context of the three parameters. In the case of ownership, this definition of P3s implies that the ownership remains squarely in the hands of the state since it emphasizes that it is a contract between a private party and a government entity for providing a public asset or service and is related only to the *management* of that public asset or service. In the World Bank's definition, a P3 fits into the category of management only because it involves neither ownership nor regulation. The difference between a P3 management contract and a management service contract is about *duration* (long term rather than short term). The manager needs to bear *significant* risk. Another distinguishing factor is that remuneration is linked to *performance* rather than determined beforehand. The third element, regulation, is not addressed in this definition explicitly, but the implication is that the regulatory framework lies squarely in the hands of the government entity; as noted earlier, the regulatory function is almost always undertaken by the government. Those interested in reviewing every form of P3 contract and the many intricacies therein may refer to the World Bank's *Public Private Partnerships: A Reference Guide Version 3*,[39] published in conjunction with ten multilateral organizations, including the African Development Bank, the Asian Development Bank, the Inter-American Development Bank, the European Bank for Reconstruction and Development, and various UN organizations. This reference guide is part of a sustained effort by the World Bank to identify best practices and came out of a World Bank P3 Lab that eventually became the Public-Private Partnership Legal Resource Center.

The guide includes everything a municipality might want to know about P3s but was afraid to ask, and most of the critics of P3s in the United States can find answers in the work done by these international agencies. In addition, the Federal Highway Authority has also developed the Center for Innovative Finance Support, which has made huge strides in providing as much information as possible for municipalities interested in P3s for road development, including examples of basic financial models to enable state entities to start evaluating projects.[40]

Figure 1.2 provides an illustration of the continuum associated with risk and funding, which acts as a guide across the various alternative models. The x axis represents the degree of risk taken by the private or public sectors, and the y axis shows the amount of funding needed from the public or private sectors. At one extreme, most of the risk is borne by the private sector, and most of the funds come from the private sector. Conversely, at the other extreme all the risk is assumed by the public sector, and all the funds are provided by the public sector, too. At the extreme left is the standard

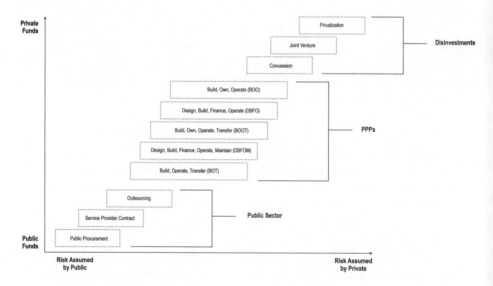

Figure 1.2. Methods of procurement from least to most private involvement across risk. *Source:* Adapted from Joaquim Miranda Sarmento and Luc Renneboog, "Anatomy of Public-Private Partnerships: Their Creation, Financing and Renegotiations," *International Journal of Managing Projects in Business* 9, no. 1 (2015): 94–122.

DBB process, and at the extreme right is full privatization. In the middle would be various forms of P3s: BTO or BOT; design-build-finance-operate (DBFO); build-own-operate-transfer (BOOT—a BOT that involves owner-ship prior to transfer); design-build-finance-operate-maintain (DBFOM); and BOO.

Including the Private Sector

In comparison to many other countries, the United States has been quite slow to adopt privatization models. Let's begin again with roads. In the United States, a few privatized (P3) roads have appeared in the last decades, but the idea of privatizing roads still strikes most American policymakers as impractical.[41] In Europe, by contrast, privatization of roads and high-ways has been relatively common since the 1970s. In Sweden, a country often described as a social democratic haven, two-thirds of road networks are owned by private companies.[42] In Italy, the privately owned company Autostrade per l'Italia owns the majority of the country's highways: 1,864 miles.[43] In France, 5,729 miles of motorway are leased as concessions to private companies—that's just under half of the 12,427 total miles of motor-way in the country.[44] Airports paint a starker picture. Some of the largest airports in the world are privately owned; throughout Europe, 30 percent of airports are owned wholly or in part by private investors.[45] In the United States, by contrast, only 1 percent of airports are privately owned, either in part or in full.[46]

There are nuances to these numbers, of course, but in principle in the United States, states, municipalities, and government agencies have a mo-nopoly on the ownership, management, and regulation of infrastructure assets. Since the 1970s, federal infrastructure spending as a share of GDP has steadily fallen. As demonstrated in figure 1.3, between 1971 and 2019, the ratio of nondefense infrastructure spending to total GDP fell from 0.85 percent to 0.61 percent, a sharp drop.[47]

The decline in federal spending resulted first in an increase in state spending and then, as states also pulled back their infrastructure budgets, a sharp rise in municipal spending as local governments took responsibil-ity for management of their infrastructure almost completely. This has cre-ated an impossible situation for infrastructure investment. In the twentieth century, the United States built its infrastructure using large federal invest-ments; as these investments dried up over time, the infrastructure they built

Nondefense Structures/GDP (NS/Y)
1950–2019

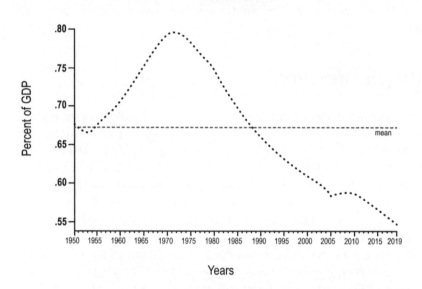

Nondefense Highways and Streets/GDP (NS4/Y)
1950–2019

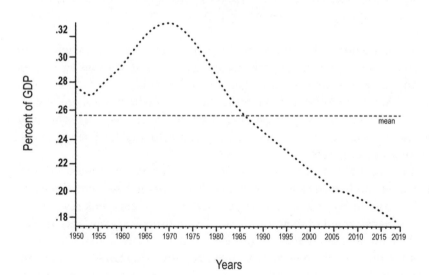

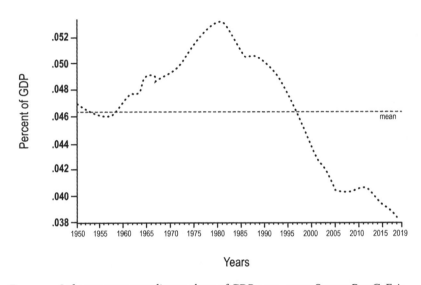

Figure 1.3. Infrastructure spending as share of GDP, 1950–2019. *Source:* Ray C. Fair, "U.S. Infrastructure: 1929–2019," Discussion Paper No. 2187, Cowles Foundation, July 2019, 6–7, https://fairmodel.econ.yale.edu/rayfair/pdf/2019d.PDF.

could no longer be maintained with local government budgets alone. After decades of deterioration, the system has stopped working.

To contrast our ailing infrastructure with a robust and growing infrastructure market, we can turn again to China. Since the 1980s, China has maintained the highest rate of infrastructure investment as a share of GDP in the world. To put this in more concrete terms, between 1992 and 2018, the number of wastewater facilities in China increased from 100 to 4,436, treating fifty-five billion cubic meters of discharged water.[48] Over the same period, the number of facilities in the United States fell from 15,613 to 14,581.[49] To be sure, China began in 1992 with many fewer treatment plants than the United States had, and the latter still has considerably more, but what is astonishing is the rate of expansion. It is a rate that will be difficult to match with funds provided solely by the federal or state government.

The water sector is not the only one that offers an unflattering comparison. Let's consider hydropower, a critical feature of sustainable energy.

Between 1972 and 2018 the United States increased its hydropower capacity by 14 percent. In Canada, capacity rose by 47 percent. In India it was 104 percent, and in China 270 percent.[50] The situation is similar in the renewables sector, too. In 2021 the share of energy produced through renewable sources was 20.5 percent in the United States, up from 11.5 percent in 1990.[51] In the United Kingdom it was double that, 40 percent, increased from 2.4 percent in 1990. The United States even lags behind the global average, which rests at 28 percent.[52] Across the board, US investment rates do not measure up to those of other countries and more importantly to the country's own needs.

When I spoke with former governor Jeb Bush from my home state of Florida about the IIJA and the future of infrastructure investment, he lamented that the Biden administration's bill did not include an explicit role for the private sector.[53] A former governor of Florida and a candidate for president in 2016, Bush intimately understands the frustrations of funding infrastructure. While governor, Bush oversaw enormous infrastructure improvements to the state of Florida, notably the I-395 connector tunnel. He has also been a champion of expanding broadband access to underserved areas. He explained that the difficulty facing infrastructure is not simply raising funds, but the processes of government infrastructure procurement, which involve miles of red tape and is structurally inefficient. "I think the infrastructure bill that passed is great, but we have to see how easy it will be to take advantage of all that money. How prescriptive are the requirements for states to accept federal money? Instead of just using the federal government money to lever state and local monies, it is equally important to bring in private sector funding to be able to accelerate projects." Bush compares the bill to the American Recovery and Reinvestment Act of 2009, which the Obama administration passed in the wake of the Great Recession. States issued bonds under new, favorable conditions instated by the legislation, often with the intention of investing in infrastructure, but because of the state procurement model, the large influx of capital was largely squandered. "It was an unmitigated disaster," Bush says, "because the private sector wasn't involved, and no one had skin in the game." With short-term officeholders making decisions about long-term infrastructure assets, there is little incentive, Bush argues, for politicians to ensure the long-term financial solvency of such deals. "We need to accelerate the ability to build," Bush told me, "and we need to start planning long-term. And there are very few rewards for politicians to do long-term projects. There is not a lot of leadership. As a country, we are in stasis." This is not a question of the right or the left, but a pragmatic and sobering assessment of the state of our infrastructure. Leadership is a recurring theme with many policy analysts when it comes to implementing infrastructure policy at the federal or state levels. The Biden administration and the members of Congress who supported the IIJA, Republicans and Democrats alike, showed leadership. Governor Rendell showed leadership, as did many others across the United States. The infrastructure attorney Marc Gravely begins a chapter dedicated to the topic in his book *Reframing America's Infrastructure* with an apt quote by Albert Einstein: "The measure of intelligence is the ability to change."[54] There is no doubt that without leadership, little can be achieved.

Transferring responsibility of infrastructure management to the private sector could address our shortcomings, but privatization of infrastructure remains mysterious and controversial to many, even as the potential advantages of privatization become clearer. It can be difficult to reach a conclusion about privatization in itself because so many variables are at play in the analysis of any infrastructure asset, including the independence of the government institutions doing the privatizing, the strength of public regulatory bodies, the stability of the acquiring company, the structure of the laws governing privatization, and the sector being privatized.[55] Over the last several decades, however, analysts have identified a number of benefits associated with private sector involvement in infrastructure. The most recent studies published in the last ten years generally conclude that privatization and public-private partnerships result in positive outcomes (as chapter 9 explains in detail).

First of all, the private sector *can* be a more efficient operator of infrastructure assets than government. Private managers hold specialized know-how about infrastructure operation, whereas government officials can walk into infrastructure management positions with little to no experience or simply without sufficient resources or personnel. The increased efficiency generated by such specialized knowledge produces higher profits, which can be shared with the state. In my conversations conducted with colleagues for this book, infrastructure managers from both the public and private sector, as well as politicians, lawyers, and consultants, said that private sector expertise added value to infrastructure management. David Gadis, the CEO of DC Water, the state-owned but independently managed water authority in Washington, DC, explained that in his experience, municipally run water utilities "really, truly need help from the private sector. They just don't have the full set of competencies to run the utility the way it needs to be run."[56] Gadis's family worked in the water industry in Indianapolis for three generations. His father was employed by the Indianapolis Water Company, laying the city's waterpipes. Gadis understands the industry from all sides. While he does not believe privatization of water infrastructure is always the answer, he is confident that municipal ownership is not the best solution either.

Macky Tall, partner and chair of Carlyle's Global Investment Group, also emphasized the importance of private sector expertise. Macky was born in Bamako, Mali, and lived for many years in Haiti before arriving in the United States. Before moving to Carlyle, he was the founding chair and CEO of CDPQ Infra, the infrastructure arm of Caisse de Dépôt et Placement du Québec, the second largest pension fund investment firm in Canada. Tall warned against underestimating the abilities of government-run utilities but suggested that the job may often simply be too big for government. "By definition, municipal or state and provincial governments have to manage limited resources, financial but also technical. And so that's where private investors really have a meaningful role to play, because they can help fill the gap and accelerate the build-out and rollout of investment by, yes, bringing capital in a meaningful way—that's been demonstrated in a number of countries—but also by bringing expertise, best practices, execution capability, accountability, and with accountability, financial discipline."[57]

In addition to private sector expertise, there are many reasons to look beyond state funding in infrastructure delivery. Opening infrastructure development to private participation allows the government, whether local or federal, to introduce competition into the market, pushing costs of construction down and increasing the total value of the asset for the state. By bringing in private operators, government can focus on regulation and monitoring of private operator performance. This removes the conflict that arises from the government acting as both operator and regulator at the same time. By transferring maintenance costs, the government can also inoculate itself against fluctuations in the market that could impact infrastructure revenue and against transformations in technology that could make infrastructure obsolete. By transferring initial and upkeep costs to private industry, the government can redirect capital to other, more critical areas in which the private sector plays a more limited role, such as public education, health care, eldercare, and policing. And last, with the underfunding of local resources, it is simply not possible for a small-town administration with resource constraints to manage existing challenges and at the same time undertake large-scale projects with costs that run into the hundreds of millions. What we are asking of the people who have been working hard to maintain our systems as well as they can is a near-impossible task.

Questions of political conviction and ideological commitment often also factor into decisions about infrastructure. The global trend of the last decades toward privatization is most commonly traced to British prime minister Margaret Thatcher, whose dedication to private infrastructure sprang from both pragmatism and idealism. During her time in office, from 1979 to 1990, Thatcher privatized England's water delivery and wastewater treatment systems, its railroads, many of its roads, and its electric and gas energy systems. Reflecting on this politically charged, bureaucratically Byzantine undertaking in her 2010 autobiography, Thatcher offers an impassioned defense of privatization, not only on the basis of her successes in transforming British infrastructure, but also on philosophical grounds. "The state should not be in business," she writes.[58]

Prior to Thatcher, the British state was very much in business, acting as a monopoly in the different infrastructure sectors, owning and managing assets worth hundreds of billions of dollars without market competition or, as she writes, the "discipline of bankruptcy" that trains the private sector. If assets do not turn a profit, that's not a problem for a state operator. For Thatcher, government management of infrastructure constituted an improper extension of state power:

> Privatization, no less than the tax system, was fundamental to improving Britain's economic performance. But for me it was also far more than that: it was one of the central means of reversing the corrosive and corrupting effects of socialism. Through privatization—particularly the sort that leads to the widest possible share of ownership by members of the public—the state's power is reduced and the power of the people is enhanced. . . . [P]rivatization is at the centre of any programme of reclaiming territory for freedom.[59]

At the time, privatization of British infrastructure seemed unthinkable to many in the United Kingdom, and the speed at which the Thatcher government transitioned infrastructure management into the private sector took many by surprise. This was the experience of Jonson Cox, the chair of Ofwat, the British water regulator, between 2015 and 2022. In the 1970s, as a young student in economics, Cox could not imagine privatizing British water, but he has since become one of the key figures in the private water sector of the United Kingdom. Cox has had a storied career in both the water and energy sectors, having served as managing director of Yorkshire Water and then CEO of Anglian Water, after beginning his career at Shell Group. Throughout his career, he has stood at the center of some of the most heated controversies surrounding infrastructure, from the management of environmental violations in the water sector to the decision to shut down British coal production. Over his tenure, he has earned a reputation as a problem-solver with a knack for salvaging utilities that are struggling with the transition from state ownership to private management.[60] In 2022 he became chair of the Port of London Authority. The authority is one of the key infrastructure assets of the city of London, and in his role as chair, Jonson was invited to attend the state funeral of the late Queen Elizabeth II in full regalia!

I have known Jonson since 2012, and have always found him a keen observer, a straight shooter, a man of enormous intelligence. Cox was born in the picturesque countryside of Devon, in the south of England (where I spent many summers in childhood); his mother was an artist, and his father was the principal of the Dartington College of Arts. His father was progressive in his vision of combining arts with the community and in the 1960s ran a program on culture and music in India, joining forces with Rabindranath Tagore University in West Bengal. At his retirement, faculty and students brought an elephant to the university, and Jonson's parents climbed on its back to ride around the campus.

When Margaret Thatcher came to power, Cox was reading economics at Cambridge, and he and his cohort were not sure what to expect from the new government. "There was a lot of fear about Thatcher," he said, "and her reputation didn't help. I don't think anybody foresaw what was going to come in terms of privatization. Personally, I think there was some radical stuff that was necessary but also some hardship that was quite avoidable."[61] Even after Thatcher privatized British Telecommunications and British oil and gas, Cox still didn't imagine the water system could be privatized as well.

> In 1979, and for the 10 years that followed until it [water sector privatization] actually happened, it was inconceivable. It was nowhere near discussion. Our economics classes that related to what we would think of as state industries at the time were all about efficiency of allocation and investment decisions. I can't remember a single moment of anyone opening their mind or thinking in the way we would today about what it might look like if you put infrastructure management in private hands.

And he was himself skeptical that wastewater and water distribution *ought* to be in private hands. Once he was further inside the sector, and after witnessing what had been accomplished in terms of privatization in other areas, though, Cox began to believe privatization might work for the water sector, too.

> The factor that most convinced me that it was right to privatize it, once I got closer to see it, was the scale of investment and change that was needed. And in an asset-based industry that had to invest massively on the water side to meet emerging EU standards for drinking water, and on the wastewater side had to clean up its disgraceful act of polluting rivers, I came to realize that you couldn't make the change that was necessary— both make the investment and make the capital planning that was necessary—if you didn't have a really long-term horizon for the assets.

Cox puts his finger on exactly the problem.

If in England privatization of the water system seemed unthinkable at the start of Thatcher's term but had been accomplished by the end of it, it is possible to imagine that the United States might see such a fast transition, as well. Minds can be changed, as Cox proves.

Of course not everyone agrees with Thatcher's approach. In the United Kingdom the Labour Party has traditionally backed the continued involvement of the public sector in infrastructure investment, and a vocal slice of the political spectrum on the left has continually argued for renationalizing England's water and energy sectors. The poor performance of the privatized rail system and the continued underperformance of Thames Water, the water company for the greater London area, have been used as examples of why UK privatization has not been successful.[62] Jeremy Corbyn, the leader of the Labour Party at the time, outlined an agenda for England in his 2019 party manifesto, "It's Time for Real Change." He expressed the will of many in both the United Kingdom and the United States who advocate that states and municipalities should continue to control basic infrastructure. "We will put people and planet before profit by bringing our energy and water systems into democratic public ownership," the Labour agenda promised: "In public hands, energy and water will be treated as rights rather than commodities, with any surplus reinvested or used to reduce bills. Communities themselves will decide, because utilities won't be run from Whitehall [the seat of the UK government] but by service-users and workers. Public ownership will secure democratic control over nationally strategic infrastructure and provide collective stewardship for key natural resources. In the case of energy, it will also help deliver Labour's ambitious emissions targets."[63]

In short, if you want the punch line between two drastically different ideological concepts on how infrastructure should be run, here you have it. But the defeat of the British Labour Party in the 2019 general election delivered a clear verdict on this program, and the Labour Party has since dropped this key aspect of its policy. Nevertheless, it remains the opinion of many on both sides of the Atlantic, and in many other countries around the world, that the state, not the private sector, should run key infrastructure assets. Whether one agrees with the position or not is one thing; a more pertinent question is whether such a position is feasible. From a practical point of view, it seems unlikely. At least in the United States, this model has demonstrably failed to provide adequate infrastructure services over the last few decades.

In the United States a similar dynamic played out during roughly the same time period. In 1987, toward the end of his second term, President Ronald Reagan appointed a presidential commission on privatization. By then privatization in the United Kingdom had taken off, and the World Bank and IMF were recommending the outright sale of national assets as part of the structural adjustment reforms that were needed by emerging economies. This would be followed by the mass privatization that occurred in eastern Europe and the former Soviet Union after 1991. While Reagan's commission achieved very little (Reagan did not have control of Congress, and most of the assets were in the hands of states, not the federal government), the rationale for the commission is interesting nevertheless. The Reagan administration wrote:

> The Commission will help fulfill the commitment I made in my Economic Bill of Rights to end unfair government competition and return government programs and assets to the American people. Privatization follows in the great tradition of free enterprise and private ownership of property that has long been a part of American history, from the initial sale of government lands under the Northwest Ordinance to the homestead program that brought the pioneers to the American West over 100 years ago.
>
> There are many activities that are not the proper function of the Federal Government and that should simply be left to the private sector. The American people know that in many cases the Government is less efficient than private enterprise in providing certain services. Government agencies do not have the same incentives and interests that allow the private market to provide goods and services more efficiently and effectively.

Privatization programs have the potential for bringing enormous benefits to all members of society. Workers can be given part ownership in the newly created private company and often receive a pay raise. The public receives better services. Managers are free to respond to the proper incentives to build a successful business, and competition in the free market allows others to share in the prosperity. As recent experience in Great Britain shows, privatization also increases the public participation in the market system: By selling government-owned enterprises, the number of families owning stock increased dramatically.[64]

Privatization of the sort Reagan imagined did not really materialize in the United States, and perhaps consequently, the Democratic Party has never made nationalization of infrastructure assets a part of its platform. However, since the 2016 and 2020 presidential campaigns of democratic socialist senator Bernie Sanders (I-VT), Democratic politicians have moved closer to this message. Along with Senator Elizabeth Warren (D-MA), Sanders called for the nationalization of the US health-care sector. Sanders's plan was to increase the power of the federal government, proposing $16 trillion in spending overall, which would be funded through new taxes on the highest earners. Among the most aggressive elements of his spending plan was the "Green New Deal," which, among other things, would have returned to government a near-monopoly power over the electricity sector:

Currently, four federal Power Marketing Administrations (PMAs) and the Tennessee Valley Authority generate and transmit power to distribution utilities in 33 states. We will create one more PMA to cover the remaining states and territories and expand the existing PMAs to build more than enough wind, solar, energy storage and geothermal power plants. We will spend $1.52 trillion on renewable energy and $852 billion to build energy storage capacity. Together with an EPA federal renewable energy standard, this will fully drive out non-sustainable generation sources. The renewable energy generated by the Green New Deal will be publicly owned, managed by the Federal Power Marketing Administrations, the Bureau of Reclamation and the Tennessee Valley Authority and sold to distribution utilities with a preference for public power districts, municipally- and cooperatively-owned utilities with democratic, public ownership, and other existing utilities that demonstrate a commitment to the public interest. The Department of Energy will provide technical assistance to states and municipalities that would like to establish publicly owned distribution utilities or community choice aggregation programs in their communities. Electricity will be sold at current rates to keep the cost of electricity stable during this transition.[65]

Between Reagan and Sanders, Thatcher and Corbyn, there is plenty of room to maneuver. But in both countries, each extreme has strong support, meaning bold movement in any direction is likely to cause an outcry.

Where does this book stand in this ideological debate? I completed my PhD in economics at Harvard in the mid-1990s under the late Gary Chamberlain and Guido Imbens. My work was about understanding the causal relations between, say, a government policy and income level. Would training programs help increase income for those who benefited from that training?[66] Unlike the medical field, in which one can conduct simple experiments, in the social sciences that is not possible. Guido Imbens, Joshua Angrist, Don Rubin, and others developed a new econometric framework that can measure more efficiently that causality; Guido and Joshua Angrist received the Nobel Prize in Economics for it in 2021.[67] Gary and Guido, along with the entirety of Harvard's economics department, maintained very open minds, focusing principally on what the data would suggest rather than trying to impose a particular ideological model. To quote Virgil, as I did in the introduction to my thesis, "Felix qui potuit rerum cognoscere causas" (happy is he who knows the causes of things). That isn't to say that some of the Harvard professors at different ends of the political spectrum did not have divergent views on the most equitable way to manage the economy. Coming out of this environment, my perspective has been principally grounded in empirically based and pragmatic solutions. My pool of data comes from my real experience investing in and managing infrastructure assets across fifty countries and leading over sixty thousand employees that serve millions of customers every day, whether by providing clean water in China, safe roads in India, efficient logistics systems or waste management in the United States, or power generation in a variety of countries.

Whenever it is possible and realistic to have a strong regulatory framework, government should be more in the business of regulating infrastructure assets, as opposed to operating them. Joseph Stiglitz, who obtained the Nobel Prize in Economics in 2001 for his work on asymmetric information, has been a leading economist on public economics and the role of the state in economic development. In *The Economic Role of the State*, published in 1989, Stiglitz expounds a theory that revolves around the question: "In what does the government have a comparative advantage?" While his theoretical model goes beyond the scope of this book, ultimately he makes a set of compelling arguments. There are inherent characteristics in both the state as an economic player and the private sector as an alternative economic player that determine the efficiency of each, apart from questions of redistribution and equity. He highlights key fallacies in the traditional conception of the state. One is the idea that nationalized industries act in the public interest—that is, that a water company owned by the state will always act in the public interest compared to a water company operated by the private sector. That is simply not true. It is also a fallacy, though, to assume that government is everywhere and at all times inefficient. Stiglitz summarizes his view thus:

> I am advocating . . . an eclectic position. Doctrinaire positions of the right, saying that government intervention at all times and in all circumstances is welfare-decreasing, that governments are inherently wasteful, that attempts at redistributions simply give rise to rent-seeking activities, are both wrong and unhelpful. . . . Similarly doctrinaire positions of the left, calling for increased government intervention, idealizing the government, anthropomorphizing it as a single individual (a benevolent despot), and attributing the successive failures of governments to correct the market failures to the particulars of the situation (e.g. to the particular leader of the government) without recognizing the limits of government are also not very helpful.[68]

This "eclectic," nuanced approach is exactly what is needed in the infrastructure arena. Ideological commitments to public or private infrastructure management are misguided. As John Maynard Keynes, the father of Keynesian economics and a highly pragmatic economist, wrote:

> As soon as anyone comes to consider the facts it becomes evident that every sane and sensible person regards a great deal of public enterprise as unavoidable, necessary, and even desirable, and on the other hand, there is an enormous field of private enterprise which no one but a lunatic would seek to nationalize. The line of demarcation between the two is constantly changing in accordance with the practical needs of the day. As to where precisely this line should be drawn *no great question of principle is involved* [emphasis added].[69]

What is the essential role of government, then? In a famous article, "The Lighthouse in Economics," Ronald Coase describes the economic role of government through the lens of the lighthouse.[70] John Stuart Mill first deployed the example of the lighthouse in his *Principles of Political Economy*, and later economists have adopted it.[71] According to Mill, the lighthouse symbolizes an infrastructure asset that represents a public good. The lighthouse saves lives, ships, and cargo, providing a public service for the larger social benefit. Such service would not be available without government investment and cannot be left to private enterprise. If it were left to the private sector, the thinking goes, the lighthouse would never be built because there is no incentive. Of course, in those days there was no way to collect fees from ships passing by.

Coase, who received the Nobel Prize in 1991, takes a different approach. In his article he returned to Mill's argument and analyzed exactly how the system at lighthouses in England worked all the way back to the sixth century. Coase discovered that lighthouses were in fact developed by private companies, and they charged a user fee. The concept of the lighthouse was used to demonstrate that government should provide services for the public good. That may have been true at some point, but with the evolution of P models, the private sector has stepped in. Today, many operators' lighthouses are developed privately and operated privately, paid for with user fees. The lighthouse as public good argument no longer seems entirely persuasive.

Throughout history, what constitutes the public and private spheres has changed, and today the practical needs of society call for the line demarcating public and private arenas to shift once again. In the United States the state monopolizes markets for water delivery, wastewater treatment, and air and rail travel; that cannot be the only answer.[72] It is time to investigate new solutions, time to seriously look at incorporating more participation from the private sector. This is not a radical departure from US convention or tradition; in fact, it is a return to the roots of American infrastructure investment. As we will see, private sector ownership and public-private partnerships are not a new solution to an old problem, but rather an old solution to a permanent problem. What the United States needs to do is dust off that old approach and update it, creating a "new old" approach to the problem of infrastructure investment that has confronted governments for millennia. This chapter has laid out the bones of the argument for such an approach; my hope is that in the following chapters this argument will come to life as we see the challenges of infrastructure management in closer detail.

But something more remains to be said about the history and ideology that directs US infrastructure policy. Before diving into case studies that illustrate the difficulties facing US systems, the next chapter explores in greater detail why the United States has its current system and where US bias against privatization comes from. It wasn't always so. Indeed, in its early history, and in some of its greatest endeavors, American infrastructure relied on the private sector. What was the rationale behind the private management of infrastructure in the early United States, and how did the country end up in the twenty-first century with a system of state-owned, -managed, and -regulated assets?

two

FROM BOOM TO BUST

The History of Infrastructure Management

JEREMY: "It's what I've always dreamed about, Glyn . . . a new country where we can make things grow. We'll find a valley where the earth is rich . . . where the mountains shelter us from the north winds. We'll use the trees that nature has given us . . . cut a clearing in the wilderness. We'll put in roads . . . and use the timber to bridge the streams where we have to. Hah! Then we'll build our homes, Glyn, build them strong to stand against the winter snows."

—*Bend of the River* (1952)

For most of history, both in the United States and around the world, infrastructure was owned and/or operated by a combination of the private sector and the public sector. In the eighteenth and nineteenth centuries, private entities managed America's water services, toll roads, electricity infrastructure, railroads, and later airports. How did ownership and operation of these systems transfer to the US government? Largely, the answer lies in the US response to the Great Depression and World War II. Though more public funds were already being allocated for infrastructure in the 1920s, President Franklin Roosevelt's New Deal explicitly established a new course for US infrastructure and set up the structures through which infrastructure is still managed today. In the heyday of privately managed infrastructure, however, the country accomplished some of its greatest feats of engineering and logistics. The long history of infrastructure, going back to medieval Europe and even ancient Rome, shows that it has always been necessary to include private entities in infrastructure delivery.

Perhaps the most emblematic example of early private American infrastructure is the transcontinental railroad, completed in 1869. With 1,912 miles of track that cut through mountains and desert, it was among the most ambitious and transformative projects ever undertaken in the United States. The railroad opened the American West to industrialization, expanded opportunities for commerce everywhere, and not least of all, sparked the American imagination. In American culture, railroads have come to occupy a central place, from Mark Twain's experiences on the transcontinental railroad described in *Roughin' It*, to standard folk songs like "I've Been Working on the Railroad" and "Casey Jones," to Alfred Hitchcock's classic film *Strangers on a Train*. All of this sprang from the vision of private investors and entrepreneurs. Yet the methods used to finance the transcontinental railway would hardly be entertained in debates about rail today.

In the twenty-first century, with the exception of commercial rail, US passenger rail has been owned by the federal government. Amtrak, which is a federally chartered corporation, was created in 1971 with Richard Nixon's Rail Passenger Service Act and today operates all the major passenger train routes around the country. Amtrak draws funds from user fees (ticketing accounts for around 76 percent of its recovered costs), as well as state, local, and federal subsidies.[1] The system isn't working well. In its fifty years of operation, Amtrak has never turned a profit.[2] It has been criticized for exorbitant prices, delays, limited range, and slow speed compared to its European and Asian counterparts. More seriously, the rail operator has a poor record of accidents and derailments. Since the late 1990s, it has seemed to many that Amtrak's days are numbered. In *Derailed*, an influential study of the transportation system published in 1997, the author Joseph Vranich made the argument bluntly: "Regardless of the future shape of federal transportation policies, my view is that there is no useful role for Amtrak. Amtrak has failed in what it was set up to accomplish. A fitting action to take on Amtrak's thirtieth anniversary . . . would be to put Amtrak to rest, passing the baton to private-sector and state-agency successors."[3] Vranich proposed that Amtrak's assets could be sold to regional or state transportation authorities or to private investors.

Of course this has not happened. Instead, federal funding for Amtrak increased under the administrations of both George W. Bush and Barack Obama.[4] Through the IIJA, the Biden administration provided Amtrak with $22 billion over five years.[5] Additional federal dollars were seemingly a good thing for the railroads, and in the first decade of the twenty-first century, Amtrak ridership rose and derailments declined. But this improvement concealed a deeper crisis. There were still 136 derailments between 2000 and 2010,[6] and even today Amtrak ridership accounts for only a minuscule portion of everyday traffic in the United States, about .6 percent of all commuters.[7] Furthermore, as the Cato Institute has argued for decades, Amtrak funding is routinely mismanaged and inefficiently spent.[8]

Vranich's argument remains relevant because Amtrak is still struggling to be relevant itself. There will likely always be a place for government in the operation of US rail lines, particularly in financing routes to sparsely populated areas that are unlikely to turn a profit. But the government monopoly on trains is hurting the country, and a majority of Americans know it. A poll by the Rail Passengers Association in 2022 found that 78 percent of Americans favor increased federal spending on trains,[9] and according to some polls a majority of people would prefer that high-speed rail be built by private enterprise.[10] Rail may (or may not) present the United States with an opportunity to expand public-private partnerships, with a combination of increased federal investment and participation from the private sector. There are many models this process might follow, but there are so many vested interests, political and economic challenges, practical issues such as permitting, costs of construction, and a whole litany of problems, that it may very well not happen. The country may remain stuck with the status quo, in which taxpayers subsidize an inefficient infrastructure system used by a very small number of people. The point of reviewing the history of the rail system is to remind ourselves that, at least, it is not impossible that the private sector could play a key role in the development of the country's twenty-first-century infrastructure—it has done so in the past and could do so again.

In the first half of US history, infrastructure was by and large owned by private operators. The delivery of water, for example, which is today typically controlled by public authorities and financed through user fees and state and federal subsidies, was mostly private in early American history, or else managed through public-private partnerships. From the earliest days of the colonies and into the nineteenth century, many communities relied on private wells, cisterns, and private delivery systems.[11]

In 1652 Boston officials granted the first corporate charter for a water transportation company, which allowed James Everill and Joshua Scottow to install pipes throughout the city and transport water from Scottow's private well.[12] This prerevolutionary water company operated in the Boston area until 1817. The system of granting water delivery rights to owners of private wells spread to other cities in New England, as a series of similar charters in Providence shows.[13] In Providence, city records indicate these private companies didn't merely build the systems and transfer them to the government in a BOT structure. Rather, companies were granted the indefinite right to levy user fees, in a BOO contract.[14] Such utility corporations proliferated across the country in the nineteenth century. Some became the water utility companies that still exist today, while others were later bought out by state governments.

This arrangement was common to roadways, as well. Prior to the twentieth century, and especially before the expansion of railroads, most American roads were privately constructed and owned.[15] In the early 1800s efforts to federalize road funding were repeatedly beaten back in Congress in favor of private toll roads.[16] This attitude toward infrastructure investment naturally carried over into railroads when they first began to appear in the nineteenth century. The first railway systems were all privately owned and operated.[17] Why wouldn't they be? Transregional wagonways were private, as were urban tramways. It was only logical that railroads would be privately owned, too. The development of the railway sector followed a similar path to the organic evolution of private water services. Those with the ingenuity and resources to create an infrastructure system were granted rights to exclusive ownership of those systems.

In 1825 John Stevens became the first person to demonstrate that the steam engine could power a locomotive. A New Jersey resident, Stevens was an inventor and lawyer and had been a captain in the Revolutionary War. His vision for the railroad, though, was inspired by his work as a steamship captain in New Orleans. So certain was Stevens that his railroad invention would work that he filed to establish his corporation in 1815, a decade before he could prove his design viable, the same year Napoleon was defeated at Waterloo.[18] Stevens's confidence paid off in the end, and his charter corporation, Camden and Amboy, would grow into the profitable United New Jersey Railroad and Canal Company by 1830.[19] At the time he filed his corporate applications, however, railroads appeared a risky bet. It was unclear how the endeavor might be financed. The state of New Jersey accepted Steven's charter, and he was granted what amounted to monopoly rights to railroad operations in the New Jersey area. But what the government would not offer was funding.

It was not that Stevens didn't want federal or state subsidies. In fact, he sent a near constant stream of letters to legislators in his home state of New Jersey, as well as to lawmakers from Maine to Florida. Knowing that railways were the future, Stevens implored the government to invest in his company. "I am aware that today there are no Steam Rail Roads anywhere in the world," he wrote to the New York Canal Commission, "but that is not to say that they will not surely come. . . . We must, sooner or later, have railways— why not expend a small amount, now, to experiment."[20] But legislators and public transportation commissions were not interested in the sort of public-private partnership Stevens sought. The development and implementation of the first railroad, and the first rail company, were thus left entirely to the private sector. Other local lines opened shortly after Camden and Amboy, including the Mohawk and Hudson Railroads, servicing upstate New York, and the Baltimore and Ohio Railroad, all of which followed the same model pioneered by Stevens. For a time, private rail was organized rather like the modern-day electricity sector, being divided into quadrants in which each company operated without competition. But regional rail had, by its nature, limited range, and demand for more comprehensive networks was growing.

Theodore Judah, an engineer and entrepreneur, had a vision that would meet this demand and in the process transform the American landscape: a transcontinental railroad. The project promised not only to revolutionize the railroad industry but also to inaugurate a new era in American life. As John Stevens had dreamed, the railway might finally "permit a man at one extreme of the country to visit a man on the other end and ask his real opinion . . . and lay unbreakable bounds of union across our States."[21] Like Stevens, Judah believed that in addition to bolstering trade, the transcontinental railroad would unify the country. His idealistic vision attracted one of the most popular politicians of his day: Abraham Lincoln. In the 1850s, before becoming president, Lincoln corresponded with Judah, encouraging him in his quest to build the longest rail line in the world. Lincoln had defended railroad companies as a lawyer and was personally enthusiastic about trains.[22]

Judah was a trustworthy ambassador for such a project, having earned his spurs as an engineer for the Lewiston Railroad, which ran from Lewiston, New York, to Niagara Falls, and later helping to construct the first railroad in California, the Pacific Coast. He had an innovative plan for construction and estimated the transcontinental line would cost around $150 million (roughly $5.6 billion in 2023 dollars).[23] It was a staggering sum at the time; the only public expenditure that exceeded it was the Louisiana Purchase. But Judah's plan was prudent—everyone agreed, even if they weren't willing to participate. There were obvious financial benefits to the train at a time when commercial traffic to California went by way of boat, with a brief stop to travel the Panama Railroad (before the canal was built), which levied hefty surcharges. Moreover, Judah's strategy for construction was sound, hinging on the creation of two separate railroad companies to share costs and labor and to decrease building time.[24] When it was finally enacted, the plan was virtually unchanged; the Central Pacific Railroad Company began construction in Sacramento, working east, while the Union Pacific Railroad Company began at Council Bluffs, Iowa. As it turned out, the construction and engineering posed fewer problems than the funding.

Despite his reputation, his powerful friends, and a convincing business plan, for years Judah's proposal languished on the desks of both politicians and private investors. From 1857 to 1863 Judah tirelessly crossed the country in search of investors to fund his railroad. He gave speeches, met with business and political leaders, and even wrote a manifesto, *A Practical Plan for Building the Pacific Railroad*. By the 1860s his single-minded devotion to his project had earned him the nickname "crazy Judah,"[25] but he had yet to persuade anyone to give him the capital he needed to begin construction.

With the election of Lincoln, his old supporter, to the presidency in 1860, the tide began to turn. Yet even Lincoln, who believed fervently in the plan, would not directly invest in the project using federal funds. He did, however, promise to argue for land grants, tax incentives, and direct loans from Congress. On the basis of these guarantees, Judah finally began to find start-up funding among a group of Sacramento investors known as "the Big Four," or "the Associates," which included the governor of California at the time, Leland Stanford. These principal investors pooled resources and drew on their networks—particularly in the mining sector, which especially stood to benefit from more efficient shipments back east and better access to the mines in the West.

By 1862 the Pacific Railway Act was passed, and a version of Judah's plan became law. The foundation of the plan relied on private investors and private operators, but it required significant accommodations from the federal government as well. Unlike the private water systems and private roads, which had only needed formal concessions from government, the Pacific Railway Act was more substantially a public-private partnership, one in which the private sector took the lead—and assumed the risk. As the investment banker and diplomat Felix Rohatyn writes, "[The Pacific Railway Act] was a revolutionary bill. Cash incentives, competing companies, government bonds based on performance—nothing like it had ever been proposed on such a vast and expensive scale."[26]

Construction began in 1863. Before the year was out Theodore Judah had died of yellow fever, without knowing if his dream would in fact be realized. And there were times during construction when it appeared it might not be. The following year the Central Pacific was staring down bankruptcy; construction costs had ballooned (in part due to fraud on the part of the construction company, a concern critics of private investment like to point out), and a number of government loans were held up as the Civil War raged on. Without their firebrand, "crazy" Judah, the Big Four returned to Congress, hat in hand, to request additional support. Seeing the progress that had already been made, Congress assented. Among other reasons, Congress may have recognized the increased importance of the railroad in light of the 1862 Homestead Act, which promised 160 acres of land on the western frontier to anyone who had not taken up arms against the government; growing populations demanded growing infrastructure. Perhaps the legislators finally saw the wisdom of John Steven's prediction that the railroad was inevitable, or perhaps they were happy that the private sector had already done the difficult work of organizing the project. In any event the timing was right, and Congress approved the second Pacific Railway Act of 1864, doubling the federal government's land grants. Critically, the act also allowed the Union and Central Pacific companies a new revenue stream. After 1864 the companies were permitted to issue their own bonds, borrowing against their (still uncertain) future profits. Though issuances were slow to start, by 1868 they had sold $25 million worth of bonds and were making a healthy profit.[27]

In May 1869 the two rail lines finally united, at Promontory Summit, Utah, in the western foothills of the Rocky Mountains, and Leland Stanford hammered in the final ceremonial railroad spike, made of 17 karat gold. The railroad was finished. By the completion of the project, government loans had reached $37 million, and land grants amounted to 5.5 million acres.[28] From beginning to end the railroad was a private venture, though it could not have been completed without significant support from the government. It was a culminating event in early American infrastructure investment strategy, driven by Judah's entrepreneurial zeal and the know-how of the private sector, and supported with federal loans, grants, and incentives. The nation had gained a major piece of infrastructure without accruing much debt, raising taxes, or putting much capital at risk.

From what we've seen so far, it might appear that this arrangement was a consequence of the historical time period, when government bureaucracy was small and major systems could still be pioneered by private financiers. But the US infrastructure investment strategy in the eighteenth and nineteenth centuries was not an accident, nor was it merely a function of the stage of the country's development. Similarly, the choice to allow private investment to manage and build infrastructure was not simply a continuation of the Jeffersonian model of enterprising landowners unhampered by federal intervention. In fact, the early US attitude toward infrastructure investment grew out of a long tradition, going back all the way to ancient Rome.

A Brief History of European Infrastructure

In 334 BCE, in the earliest days of its power, Rome set out to construct one of its first major paved roads in the world, the Via Latina, which ran south past Naples. Costs, however, overran expectations (as they tend to do), and public funds were running out. Rather than raise taxes, the senate decided to supplement public resources with private investment. From then on, wherever public monies ran short, Rome would draw from what it called the *fiscus*, or "prince's coffer," supplied by the personal fortunes of Roman statesmen, generals, and wealthy private citizens.[29] Eventually the Roman Empire created the *aerarium*, a reserve fund used to consolidate resources of this kind for rainy day infrastructure investments. This system was instrumental in building the sprawling roads and aqueducts that served Europe into the medieval period and that still cross the European countryside from Constantinople to Londinium (or Istanbul and London today).[30] Rome discovered early in its long history that private capital was required to achieve large-scale growth. It institutionalized a system of partnering private capital and public funds using what we might think of today as an infrastructure bank.

Though we may not envy the fate of the Roman Empire, we can certainly admire the legacy of its infrastructure, which laid the foundations for European infrastructure. I have driven many times on another ancient Roman road, the Via Aurelia, which runs north into France across the mountainous western coast of Italy. Every time I travel on the road, built in 241 BCE, I admire the longevity of Roman construction. But it's not only the remnants of Roman roads, aqueducts, and sewer systems that remain with us. Many of Rome's techniques for financing infrastructure have also lasted into the present day. The kingdoms of Europe inherited earmarked tax revenue, user fees, and partnerships with private financiers from Roman antecedents. As the historian Hugh Goldsmith writes in the magisterial *Economics of Infrastructure Provisioning: The Changing Role of the State*, "The basic elements of urban, water, sanitation, transportation and communication systems were well developed by the late Roman Empire."[31]

Roman infrastructure was maintained by governments and communities throughout the Middle Ages, during which period monarchs claimed sole ownership of the inherited infrastructure. By the sixteenth century, however, Western Europe was growing in population and wealth and outgrowing the remnants of Rome's systems, which were deteriorating as a result of poor upkeep and lack of investment. The problem of investing in infrastructure befuddled monarchical governments, which wanted to maintain control of infrastructure assets but could not afford, or organize, decent management of the assets. As a result, vital systems fell into disrepair, and governments failed to create new infrastructure to serve Europe's growing population and expanding townships and cities. In the unmaintained Roman roads still used in much of Europe's countryside and the underserved new communities cropping up everywhere, some of the earliest entrepreneurs in Europe saw an opportunity to develop their own system of roadways, creating better service and offering an alternative to the toll roads maintained by governments. In 1582 the London Bridge Waterworks Company, the first private British waterworks, opened its doors. A second water company in London, the New River Company, opened in 1619, funding for which was raised by selling sixty "adventurer" shares to private investors. In 1707 the first toll road was established by private entities without connections to the government.[32]

The economic historian Marcella Lorenzini has highlighted the example of Thomas Massner as emblematic of this age of private infrastructure construction in the era of dominant monarchies. A merchant and city councilor from what is today Switzerland,[33] Massner won a concession from the local authorities in 1708 to build a new road over the alps to connect the eastern burgh of Coire with the Swiss interior. Not only did Massner's government, known as the Three Leagues, grant its permission, it also partnered with Massner, creating a new export tariff to provide direct funding for the road.[34] This might have been an example of an equal partnership between the state and the private sector, but instead, reflecting the confused role of the private sector at the time, the Three Leagues absorbed Massner's enterprise, making him treasurer and enveloping his enterprise as their own.[35] The kind of public-private coalition assembled by Massner and the Three Leagues eventually developed into more formal arrangements across Europe. States continued to incorporate private investors into government offices, creating enormous, centralized infrastructure systems under the control of the sovereign.

In the monarchies of both France and England, the relationship between private entities and the government became clearer when state treasuries began issuing monopoly rights in different infrastructure sectors to joint-stock companies, led by England.[36] But these monopolies also proved risky. In its earliest days of royal charters and monopoly grants, joint-stock companies had little regulation, exposing them to speculative bubbles and manipulation.[37] After the first major stock crash, investment approaches diverged across Europe. In the "South Sea Bubble" of 1720,[38] speculative excesses inflated the price of stocks in the Compagnie des Indes, chartered by John Law, a Scottish economist based in French Louisiana,[39] and the South Sea Company in England, both major joint-stock companies on the Paris and London stock exchanges. Both companies were also heavily invested in the African slave trade, and when fighting between Britain and Spain in the Spanish War of Succession between 1701 and 1714 disrupted trade routes, prices plummeted. In the aftermath, London passed the "Bubble Laws," introducing regulations on monopoly grants, and France stopped granting new monopolies to companies entirely.[40]

After the 1789 French revolution and by 1848, nation-states adopted a variety of infrastructure investment models, with some privatizing infrastructure and others attempting to maintain the centralized systems developed earlier. After 1789 the new French Republic hoped to maintain control of the monarchy's central bureaucracy and even to take back direct ownership and operation of assets from holders of monopoly rights.[41] The country quickly reverted to an imperial government under Napoleon, but the French continued to view the state's infrastructure as the public's assets.[42] After seventy years of volleying between republicanism and monarchy, the prince-president Napoleon III, who came to power in 1848, set out to renovate Paris, and he would do so using private investment. Under the direction of Georges-Eugene Haussmann, Napoleon's chief urban planner, the Second Empire (1852–70) began a massive expansion of the city's roads, bridges, and water system. To undertake the large-scale demolition and reconstruction of major avenues, such as the glamorous Rue de Rivoli, the French government began to privatize infrastructure, at first by offering tax exemptions and other incentives, including large subsidies to the private companies that would do the construction. In 1853, one year after Napoleon declared himself emperor, the Compagnie Général des Eaux was created to provide Paris with water. By 1880 the company had won concessions for water distribution in Venice and Istanbul, the capital of the Ottoman Empire. Eventually Napoleon III also offered railroad concessions to private entities, allowing the private sector to construct and operate railroads around

Paris.[43] Napoleon's reforms outlived his reign. Most of these private enterprises lasted until World War II, when they were ultimately nationalized and only privatized again in the 1980s.

The English, by contrast, never fully turned away from the privatization of infrastructure, as the French did in the late eighteenth and early nineteenth centuries. During the seventeenth and eighteenth centuries, England developed a system of maintaining infrastructure that left control to municipalities, churches, and landowners. Within this loose system, plenty of space was afforded for entrepreneurs to build and operate infrastructure systems. Private roads and bridges became standard, typically funded with tolls,[44] and as Hugh Goldsmith writes, "by 1750, virtually all of the main roads from London were turnpiked."[45]

It was the English system that colonial American settlers inevitably established in Virginia in 1607 and the Massachusetts Bay Colony in 1629. When the town clerk of Braintree, Massachusetts, a man named Captain William Tyng, granted Everill and Scottow exclusive rights to build a private waterworks for Boston, he was not creating a novel method of financing infrastructure based on colonial conditions, but was instead following a strategy that had been adopted by the English for generations. Today the US system looks quite different.

American Municipalities and the Debt Markets

One of the keys to understanding the infrastructure crisis in the United States today lies in the precarious finances of municipalities. Today, municipalities are struggling. Saddled with infrastructure costs they cannot keep up with, cut off from federal and state investment except in cases of emergency, and managed by politicians without incentive to make politically risky decisions, municipalities are cutting back on infrastructure investment, the unsexy investment, in order to finance other critical services.

Let's look at Chester, Pennsylvania, as an indicative example. Chester is not a typical town, but the financial difficulties it faces are typical. The oldest township in Pennsylvania and a safe haven for the state's Quakers, until the early twentieth century the town was a bustling industrial center on the outskirts of Philadelphia, alongside the Delaware River. Since the 1950s and the exodus of manufacturing from American towns, however, Chester has seen stark economic decline.[46] Today, 28.5 percent of Chester's population lives below the poverty line,[47] and between 1960 and 2010 the population was nearly halved.[48] During a financial crisis in 1995 the town issued an official "Determination of Municipal Financial Distress," resulting in $1.3 billion in grants from the state, delivered through Pennsylvania's Municipalities Financial Recovery Act (known as Act 47). The municipality remained in a state of financial distress until 2018, when Pennsylvania issued the town an exit plan, allowing it to raise the income tax rate and refinance its debt. More significantly, the plan called for Chester to abandon the majority of its capital growth expenditures, effectively calling a halt to further infrastructure development.[49] The subsequent introduction of a casino at Chester boosted the economy, but the strain of debt and state obligations, like pension and postemployment benefits, continued to leave Chester in financial hardship.[50] Only two years after approving an exit from financial distress, Chester had once again to declare a financial emergency with the onset of the COVID-19 pandemic, and this time it entered into a receivership with Pennsylvania. In a receivership, the local municipal government forfeits its control over financial decisions and receives direction from state officials. Receiverships are one of the most aggressive forms of intervention the central government can take. In many cases they are absolutely necessary in order to keep a city functioning, but as they are employed with greater frequency across the country, they increasingly weaken local governments.

Chester's budget offers a glimpse into the desperate state of municipal finance. In 2022 federal and state grants constituted 51 percent of Chester's total revenue.[51] Its total revenue from income taxes covered just over half the cost of human services, not including spending for water delivery or sewerage, parks, libraries, or public safety and correction, which are separate categories. Meanwhile, debt service made up 9 percent of the 2022 municipal budget, or $54 million. The town spent more on debt service than on general government, public safety, corrections, and judicial costs combined.[52]

Chester's debt derives from its sale of bonds, and its aggressive debt service plan is designed to maintain the town's AAA bond rating,[53] which allows it to continue selling bonds more easily and at lower interest rates. Bond credit ratings play an enormous role in municipal decision-making, and failure to service bond debt can be a death knell for credit ratings and thus further loans to develop and grow the city's economy. With little capital to invest in economic growth and income levels that limit possible tax increases, there are few options for Chester to escape the cycle of bond sales, debt repayments, and state and federal bailouts.

In its current receivership, state officials pressured Chester to privatize its infrastructure, particularly its water delivery and sewer system. As of 2022

Chester received no revenue from its water service, as is common among municipalities. Nevertheless, the municipality fought the push to privatize; it was opposed by the Water Authority itself, which was controlled by the municipality. In 2022 the Pennsylvania Supreme Court began deliberations over the state's stipulation that Chester, in its receivership, must privatize its water systems. The town has no other infrastructure to speak of, since the largest infrastructural assets, the Beaver Creek Dam and the Commodore Barry Bridge, are controlled by intercounty and state authorities and therefore cannot unilaterally be sold or leased by Chester.[54] With no other options, and no potential revenue loss, why would one reject privatization? One explanation is that some municipal leaders do not want to lose control over a valuable asset, even if doing so would benefit their municipality's finances. The belief is that municipalities have an obligation to own infrastructure assets.

This belief that municipalities have an obligation to manage infrastructure assets—ignoring the long history of states doing otherwise since colonial times—began in the United States after the Great Depression, in the wake of the reforms enacted by Franklin Roosevelt as part of the New Deal. Roosevelt initiated the first sweeping government infrastructure program, organized through the Public Works Administration (PWA). The motivating idea behind the grand expansion of publicly funded infrastructure was to create jobs, and by some measures as many as twenty million people benefited from Roosevelt's work relief programs. Between 1932 and 1940 the unemployment rate fell from 22 to 9 percent.[55] Following the famous adage of John Maynard Keynes that in a recession the government should pay workers to dig holes in the ground and fill them up again,[56] Roosevelt bet that large-scale infrastructure spending would jolt the economy back into activity. With massive injections of new federal investment, the nation built some of its most ambitious projects, including the Hoover Dam, the Lincoln Tunnel, the Bay Bridge, the Triborough Bridge, and others. Much better than holes in the ground. Not only was the New Deal in the business of megaprojects, but it also encouraged municipal infrastructure. By and large, the plan to create jobs and stimulate the economy through spending succeeded—at least while the spending lasted. The PWA was closed in 1943 to focus on the war efforts; by the end of World War II spending levels had dropped precipitously, and the program of large-scale infrastructure spending began to recede. President Dwight Eisenhower's 1956 National Interstate and Defense Highways Act was the last great national infrastructure project taken on in the tradition of the New Deal, at least until President Joseph Biden's infrastructure bill.

In many ways the New Deal was what the country needed to pull out of the Great Depression. Much as the 2021 Infrastructure Investment and Jobs Act was required to address the collapsing American infrastructure, the government spending of the 1930s was an important factor in addressing the economic crisis. But Roosevelt's reforms also created the conditions that led to the current predicament of municipal governments. Not only did they establish the expectation that infrastructure was the responsibility of government, but in more concrete ways they set up local governments for their ongoing financial struggles.

The New Deal ushered in an era of government spending, but also one of increased government regulation and taxation. In order to empower municipalities to invest in and operate their infrastructure, Roosevelt needed to regulate that power away from businesses. One of the key mechanisms driving Roosevelt's economic vision was the income tax, which would in theory both constrain businesses and bolster municipal budgets. As the economist Joseph Stiglitz notes about the era: "Government regulation of business did not take on the pervasive role it plays today until the New Deal, part of the aftermath of the Great Depression. The income tax (both the individual and the corporate tax) became of central importance, both in individual and corporate decision making, only during the past half century."[57]

Prior to the New Deal, public works authorities had principally been tasked with maintaining local infrastructure using a pay-as-you-go method, rather than with large up-front investment.[58] During the New Deal, however, municipalities were expected to participate in the program of job creation by increasing spending on local systems. Municipal authorities became extensions of Roosevelt's newly established PWA and Works Progress Administration (WPA), which were created to execute the New Deal reforms and which poured capital into local infrastructure across the country. But Roosevelt knew such levels of federal spending would not and could not last—they were designed to be a temporary measure to stem the economic bleeding from the Depression. As a result, a significant portion of federal infrastructure investment came in the form of bond-buying. Roosevelt explicitly directed municipalities to ramp up their own infrastructure investment potential by more aggressively engaging the bond market, which he had adjusted to favor municipal bond issuances by offering tax exemptions on their purchase. In order to extend more loans to municipalities, though,

Roosevelt needed to reverse a long-standing law limiting the amount of debt that a local government could accrue.[59] Debt ceilings had first been imposed after the bond crisis of 1837, after a spate of state defaults on debt obligations, but Roosevelt believed he had found a way to circumvent the limits.[60]

One of the key features of Roosevelt's plan to help municipalities was to allow commercial banks to sell municipal bonds to private or state investors, who would provide an immediate capital injection to municipalities with the expectation of interest on repayment. To incentivize investment in local infrastructure, Roosevelt made the sale of municipal bonds tax exempt but stipulated that creditors must keep interest rates low, usually about 1 percent. The 1933 Banking Act, often referred to as Glass-Steagall, imposed strict limitations on how banks could invest, but in the case of municipal bonds, it actually expanded the role of commercial banks and outside investors in funding local infrastructure. The intention was that through newly empowered public authorities, issuing larger and more frequent bonds, municipalities could build their infrastructure, own it outright, and operate it at a profit. Through a combination of government ineptitude, the realities of managing infrastructure, and the fear of increasing unpopular user fees, this is not what happened, and profits never really materialized.

As the 1 percent cap established by Roosevelt expired, and once the worst effects of the Great Depression had subsided, interest rates offered to municipal bondholders began to rise, and repayment windows shortened. The result was that municipalities were increasingly saddled with greater amounts of debt, and larger shares of municipal budgets were dedicated to servicing debt as quickly as possible—all leading to the sort of predicament that Chester County faces today.

The total amount of outstanding debt held by municipal and state governments has increased since the 1950s, when current trends began. In 1950 the total amount held by state and local governments in debt securities and loans was $21 billion, and by 1975 it had ballooned to $219 billion. In 2020 total state and local debt reached over $3.2 trillion.[61] Consequently, taxes steadily hiked upward during this period as well. Total tax revenue from state and local governments rose from $17 billion in 1950 to $2.2 trillion in 2020.[62] Comparing debt securities and loans issued by states as a percentage of state and local government receipts, that ratio went from 112 percent in 1947 to over 145 percent in 2021.[63] When compared to total GDP, that percentage jumps from 6.5 to 13.6 percent for the same period. As cities, townships, and states labor to pay off their outstanding debts, still more debt must be taken on to continue funding infrastructure assets that are already not realizing their full revenue potential, creating a never-ending cycle. In addition to the cost of servicing debt, the bond market also comes with related fees. These fees, levied by bond issuers, financial advisers, and legal advisers, are not insignificant. Analyzing the costs of 812 bond issuances, the University of California, Berkeley, found that municipalities spend between 1 and 9 percent of their budgets just on the issuance of bonds.[64]

The difficulties of debt financing were compounded by the fact that as interest rates were going up, federal spending on infrastructure was steadily decreasing. In 1943, when the PWA closed, all the infrastructure assets developed during the Depression were transferred to states and municipalities, along with the obligation to maintain them.

At the federal level, spending on highways fell from 1.58 percent in 1952 to 0.9 percent in 2017. Spending on water delivery fell from 0.2 to 0.15 percent.[65] As federal spending has contracted, so has state spending.[66] The combination of reduced federal and state spending has put the onus almost entirely on municipalities. As of 2017 the ratio of municipal and state to federal spending stood at 3:1, with municipalities shouldering the brunt of it.[67]

The tight budgets and short-term fixes of municipal infrastructure have led to what David Gadis calls a "break/fix situation": "You break it and you fix it, but you don't invest in it." So why does the United States still rely on the debt market to fund its critical systems? Kent Rowey, a partner at the law firm Allen and Overy who specializes in P3s, believes the reason has to do primarily with historical entrenchment. I have worked through infrastructure privatization negotiations with Rowey in the past and have found his perspective on public-private partnerships to be thoughtful and unique. Rowey has practiced in both the United States and United Kingdom and advised on P3s in a variety of infrastructure sectors. Discussing the bond markets that emerged after the Eisenhower administration's highway boom (featured in chapter 5), Rowey comments, "You had an entire cottage industry that grew up around funding transportation infrastructure through the tax-exempt bond market."[68] As Rowey points out, the problem is not exactly that the municipal system of management excludes the private sector entirely; instead, the issue is that it incorporates the private sector in an inefficient and roundabout way. Rowey articulates the situation well: "You have private investment, but you have private investment in the form of tax-exempt debt, and then a whole ecosystem around the issuance of tax-exempt debt, which then becomes entrenched." This entrenchment leads to US reliance on the debt market and the country's reluctance to grant a larger role to the private sector. In such an entrenched system, many parties rely on the status quo for their career, position, or livelihood and are thus incentivized to defend it, regardless of how inefficient it might be when considered objectively. "You have the public sector engineering unions, which have political power within state departments of transportation. You have a group of banks that are making a lot of money with their lobbyists protecting the tax-exempt debt markets. All of these entrenched interests perceive that they would either lose jobs or lose business if we went to a different method for financing transportation and other types of infrastructure."

In order to maintain the cycle of bond issuances and debt service, municipalities turned to tax increases early on. When this final resort led to political backlash from residents, attempts to fund infrastructure beyond basic maintenance largely petered out. The tax hikes required to satisfy bond contracts met with strong public resistance even in the 1960s. After protests in San Francisco against new taxes to fund the issuances of bonds for infrastructure, a 1966 proposal for a large tax increase in the city was voted down, setting off a national trend. The discontent with bond issuances and debt payment in turn ushered in an era of decreased municipal spending across the country.

By tolerating the crippled debt market after the tax protests, municipalities condemned portions of the population to live with deteriorating infrastructure and accepted a system that would eventually constrain the power of those same local governments. As the historian Destin Jenkins argues in his study on municipal debt in San Francisco, *Bonds of Inequality*, the influence of bondholders and the credit rating companies that advise them has contributed to the unequal distribution of infrastructure funding across the United States. Bondholders invest in local infrastructure because they trust that municipalities will have stable tax revenue. When a neighborhood suffers a unique economic hardship, as was the case in Detroit when the automotive industry moved out, or experiences social unrest, as San Francisco did the 1970s and 1980s, credit rating agencies often downgrade the municipality's creditworthiness.[69] In turn, bondholders are less inclined to invest. From the perspective of those holding bonds, political turmoil promises disruptions in leadership, controversy over spending, and ultimately the possible termination of any contract that might be entered into. From the perspective of bond issuers, however, it appears that bondholders are punishing municipalities for pursuing political change. As Jenkins points out,

When Moody's downgraded San Francisco bonds in the spring of 1980, it revealed how even this ostensibly exceptional city, insulated as it had been from deindustrialization and white flight, and buttressed by a relatively strong tax base, could be penalized, not for missing quantitative targets but due to a supposed climate of uncertain voter support. It wasn't that too much democracy was a bad thing, but the uncertainty of democracy itself was brought to bear on the city's credit standing.[70]

If financial responsibility for infrastructure were transferred, in part or in whole, to private operators, local governments would no longer have to double as infrastructure management corporations and could focus more on the work of running a government accountable to the people. Separating government from infrastructure operations would also create an opportunity to strengthen regulatory bodies. As we'll see in the next chapter, one of the key problems with government ownership of infrastructure is that it must then self-regulate. When government is responsible for both identifying failures and paying to address those failures, there is a major conflict of interest.

The problem may not lie in the bond market itself, but rather in how excessively it is relied upon by local government. Even those who advocate for the municipal debt market know the system is stretched too thin. Ultimately, whether it is high debt or high taxation, the root of the problems facing local governments lies in the original New Deal assumption that municipalities ought to own and manage their infrastructure.

Over the last decade more municipalities have explored public-private partnerships, and privatization of municipal infrastructure has gained a degree of acceptance in the United States. Public-private partnerships reemerged after the financial crisis of 2008 as an efficient and plausible means of addressing municipal infrastructure needs and have been building some steam across the country.[71] Renewed interest is in part due to the fact that the model addresses two primary needs of average municipalities: to stave off additional bond service and to maintain a degree of control over infrastructure. There are many ways to involve the private operators, and in this moment of crisis, it is time to dust off old strategies of investment and find a larger role for the private sector. One way to advance this process might be to follow the example set by the dramatic but incrementalist partial deregulation of the wholesale electricity sector initiated four and a half decades ago.

Structured Partial Deregulation of the US Power Sector

For the first sixty-five years of the regulated American electric utility industry, electric utilities functioned as vertical monopolies in all three of the
core asset classes required within the business: generation, transmission,
and distribution. The historical origins of this system lie in the lobbying of
Samuel Insull, Thomas Edison's protégé and the nation's first utility mag-
nate.[72] In 1913, at Insull's urging, the Illinois General Assembly replaced the
Railroad and Warehouse Commission with the State Public Utilities Commission, consisting of five appointed members. In addition to its existing
authority over railroads, the new commission was given broad powers over
all of the investor-owned public utilities within the state. This was Insull's
dream come true, as it created the first and foundational "regulatory compact" for electric utilities, which was quickly replicated across all of North
America. The quid pro quo was simple: the utilities commission told the
utilities how much they could charge customers and determined the authorized return on capital that the companies could earn. In return, the utility
was granted an exclusive monopoly over a defined geographic jurisdiction,
in which all residents and industries could only be served by that single
utility.[73] This regulatory compact led to the successes of today's industry because it instantly created the creditworthiness under which the monopoly
utilities, waving their exclusive franchises in the faces of Wall Street bank-
ers, could finally achieve long-term, low-cost financing for their massive
program of capital investments.

The business model of vertically integrated electric utility monopolies
worked quite well for many decades. With technological evolution, each
new investment in generation was more efficient than the last. Consistent
and compounding load growth resulted in downward pressure on rates in
both real and nominal terms. Fuel prices were stable in nominal terms and
declining in real terms, supporting the virtuous cycle that underpinned the
preservation of the status quo. Competitive forces had no place within the
industry because neither consumers nor policymakers saw any need to dis-
turb a model that was clearly working.

But that model was bound to break eventually. Lacking the challenge
of competitive friction, by the 1970s the electric utility sector had become
complacent and insensitive to customer needs. Why would a utility be sensitive to customer needs if it were literally the only game in town? And
then, at mid-decade, everything that had created the multi-decade virtuous
cycle of declining costs was turned on its head. Inflation across all sectors

of the economy took a toll on an industry whose rates were set for many years at a time. Fuel costs exploded as a result of the 1973 oil crisis and its effects across the fossil fuel ecosystem. The economy turned sharply south during this period, drastically reversing load growth projections and their otherwise positive impact on customer rates. The final blow to the utilities came with a historically unprecedented spike in the cost of capital and a corresponding decline in the availability of capital, which not only had a material impact on a utility's legacy return on capital equation, but more importantly, made new capital investments massively more expensive and dilutive to existing shareholders.

This set of events came to a head during the administration of President Jimmy Carter, a Democrat—and as it happened, a nuclear engineer by training who knew a thing or two about how power plants run and what they cost. The history books talk about how the Carter administration deregulated the electricity sector by opening the monopoly-dominated market to private competitors.[74] This isn't quite what happened. The Public Utility Regulatory Policies Act of 1978, best known by its acronym PURPA, involved a highly structured and regulated *partial* opening of the capital formation process within the generation sector of the electric utility market. What PURPA accomplished was far more constructive and societally beneficial than simple "deregulation" suggests. It is PURPA's careful, structured method of deregulation that makes its approach potentially expandable into other infrastructure sectors. Because of the potential for PURPA-like policy initiatives in other sectors of the infrastructure space, it is worth a deeper dive into this transformational legislation, and in particular, the concept of "avoided cost."[75]

PURPA has many sections and addresses a range of topics that incrementally reshaped the industry, but perhaps the single most impactful concept within PURPA is that of a utility's avoided cost. Simply stated, avoided cost is what a specific utility evaluated as the total cost—including capital recovery, fuel, operations and maintenance, overheads, property tax, insurance, and ongoing capital improvement—associated with what it would cost that utility to build, own, and operate the next generation asset that it intends to build or buy. Until 1978 there was nothing avoided or avoidable about avoided cost. No two ways about it, the utility was going to build that plant, and its cost was going to be imposed on its monopoly-bound customers. Suddenly, thanks to PURPA, any nonutility contender that wanted to put its own capital at risk could now come in and get paid by the utility an amount equal to what the utility's own avoided cost would have been for the same power commodity. However, under PURPA the country got a far better result. First, PURPA dictated that the only way to actually get the utility to pay an independent nonmonopoly the avoided cost was to build something far more efficient and cleaner than the utility had in mind. For plants using fossil fuel, PURPA contracts were only available to cogeneration plants that used fuel efficiently in both generating power and taking the waste heat and supplying steam to industrial customers, thus reducing societal fuel use and resulting in far better environmental performance. PURPA contracts were also available to renewable plants having much more benign environmental externalities, including hydro, solar, wind, biomass, and geothermal projects.

Thus, under PURPA regulated utilities faced real competition for the first time ever, but only in the generation part of their business and only under a highly structured and regulated paradigm. As a result, utilities were forced to become more efficient and cost focused. Beyond that, the benefits to ratepayers were clear: a utility's avoided cost was what it thought the cost would be to build and run the next crop of generation assets with all model inputs being perfectly executed. Under PURPA the risk of cost escalation, bad investments, poor plant performance, and runaway fuel costs was for the first time in the industry's history shifted from ratepayers to the PURPA plant owners, whose contracts with the utilities were based on a pay-for-performance rather than a cost-pass-through model, which allowed utilities to collect costs from their customers as long as they adhered to prudent utility practices. Finally, society as a whole benefited, as cleaner, more efficient plants took the place of the avoidable utility units, which were typically large-scale, power-only, fossil-fueled generators.

Prior to PURPA and its avoided cost standard, regulated utilities in the United States operated like monopolies because they were monopolies on the wholesale generation development and ownership front. They predictably, in many cases, delivered wasteful and inefficient service because they could perform in that manner and not be challenged by loss of customers or margins—until Carter introduced the concept of structured, regulated competition from the private sector. Immediately after PURPA's enactment, not only did novel renewable sources of electricity begin to gain a foothold, such as wind, solar, and geothermal power, but the hydroelectric sector also saw rapid expansion. In the twelve years after PURPA's deregulation, electricity generation by nonutilities tripled. Perhaps the most important outcome of PURPA is one that we cannot quantify: avoidance of the scores of billions of dollars of cost overruns and failed projects that would have likely resulted from the continued stranglehold that the regulated utilities would have had over the development and ownership of new generation resources. This powerful tool is readily available to policymakers globally to adapt and deploy in a range of other infrastructure industry segments.[76]

For many, the structured competitive opening of the wholesale generation aspect of the electricity sector was an eye opener. Kent Rowey, the specialist in public-private partnership law, said the foundation of his interest in private sector participation in infrastructure delivery began with Carter's partial deregulation of the electric power industry. "I came of age around the time when the energy crisis was in full swing. During the Iranian hostage crisis, energy prices went just through the roof. Gasoline was being rationed. So, there was a lot of scrutiny and people started to ask: are we really approaching energy policy in the right way?" As Rowey points out, the United States in fact led the way on infrastructure privatization; the United Kingdom privatized much of its infrastructure only after the US experiment with the electricity sector. "The US was definitely a lab of innovation to bring private investment into the energy utility markets. The UK played catch up." But that dynamic was soon reversed. "The UK then started their own independent power program, which I was involved in. But then the UK government took it a step further, bringing the innovation that came from the US power markets and using the tools from those markets to expand private investment into other infrastructure sectors. And that was really the game changer." As Rowey reminds us: "That happened in the UK but did not happen in the US." The consequence has been uneven quality in infrastructure. "The US remained a two-speed country in terms of infrastructure delivery, private on the energy side, but public sector-dominated on the transportation, water and sewer utilities," he said. Having once led the way, the United States recoiled from a revolution in infrastructure delivery that ended up playing out in the United Kingdom and many other countries instead.

The larger lesson of thoughtful, structured deregulation extends beyond electricity generation. There will always be a push and pull in infrastructure investment between, on the one hand, the need for centralized government investment and regulation, and on the other, the need for private and independent entities to fill in the holes; pick up the slack; or invest in bold, risky endeavors that government naturally shies away from. In many infrastructure areas, public utilities still operate as functional monopolies. Water utilities, for instance, have many of the same protections and privileges that were afforded to the electric utilities before PURPA, and arguably the water sector has had even worse outcomes than the 1970s energy crisis. As a counterbalance to the regulations of the Progressive Era and the centralization of industry controls and oversight imposed during the New Deal, PURPA helped to mitigate the worst tendencies of monopolistic infrastructure companies in a way that provides a "proof of concept" for other sectors.

Power generation lends itself to an integrated system; it may be more challenging to open roads and water systems to competition from the private sector and establish a nationwide regulatory model. Yet at the state level, introducing competition and private participation through deregulation can and should happen, with each state developing regulatory bodies, such as public utilities commissions for water, roads, and so forth, as the transportation expert Robert Poole has suggested for the highway sector.[77] Striking a balance between comprehensive, federally guaranteed service and the efficiency and innovation of the private sector is what every infrastructure sector needs. Meeting our infrastructure challenges may not require full privatization, but only the creation of a fair playing field on which government services are forced by competition and the "discipline of bankruptcy" to either improve or stand aside.

Every situation requires its own approach, and there are many avenues to explore. To examine the possibilities in more concrete terms, let's move on to our case studies.

three

PLUGGING THE LEAKS

Municipal Waterworks and the Flint Water Crisis

MORTY: "Isn't that something? Middle of a drought and the water commissioner drowns."

—*Chinatown* (1974)

In early May 2014, residents of Flint, Michigan, noticed that the water coming out of their taps was different: it had a murky, yellowish color and a metallic taste. For years Flintites had complained about their dysfunctional water system, and so, inured to their failing infrastructure, many simply let the water run until the discoloration cleared and continued to use it. But that summer it became obvious something terrible had gone wrong. The people of Flint began losing hair while showering. They started to break out in rashes after bathing. Children across the city complained of debilitating stomach pain and an inability to concentrate. Then there was an outbreak of Legionnaires' disease that summer, which killed twelve people.[1] Something was happening with Flint's water, but city leaders promised that it was safe to drink.

Throughout the following year, as public outrage mounted, city and state officials continued to deny that anything was amiss. Such assertions may have been politically imperative, but as court documents would later show, they were not just wishful thinking but rather outright falsehoods.[2] Officials had been warned directly, by the private inspector Veolia,[3] about the dangerous lead levels in Flint's water but had suppressed the findings.[4] As the world eventually learned, some fifty thousand people, and as many as nine thousand children, were then being exposed to toxic lead levels in Flint's water.

As a symbol of water contamination in the United States, Flint stands in for municipalities across the country that suffer from lead-tainted or otherwise unsafe drinking water. The United States falls behind every other advanced economy in terms of water quality, from Finland to Australia.[5] According to the Centers for Disease Control, seven million Americans are sickened by water contamination each year.[6] More startlingly, in an analysis of 17,900 water systems around the nation, a study in the *Proceedings of the National Academy of the Science* found that every year as many as forty-five million people in the United States were exposed to unhealthy or dangerous water contaminants between 1982 and 2015.[7] In 2015 alone, twenty-one million people were served by water systems in violation of quality standards. In the same study, researchers found that systems under private ownership were more likely to comply with safety protocols, and recent studies based on cross-sectional data across countries show clearly that privatized water companies have fared better than nonprivatized assets. The case of Flint gives us some insight into the root causes of this epidemic and why private operators should play a more important role in the water sector over the coming decades.

The poisoning of Flint and the city's malfeasance and cover-up have been well covered in the media and in a number of books.[8] And yet in all this coverage we find very little discussion about two central causes of the crisis. The first is that the state of Michigan and the municipality were acting as owners, operators, and regulators all at once. It's true that the EPA played a role as well, but as we will see, federal regulatory bodies are ill-equipped to prevent such crises and often defer to state-run offices that are ultimately controlled through the state house. The tragedy that occurred in Flint might have been avoided if the city, or the state of Michigan, had not insisted on retaining operational control of its water authorities and had instead focused on developing a strong, independent system of regulation that would have allowed operators to do their work and be accountable. In addition to the conflict of interest inherent in the state acting as both operator and regulator, there is another, even more foundational cause of Flint's crisis: as owner-cum-operator, the system becomes subject to municipal funding and federal funding, which, as discussed in the previous chapter, has been reduced over the last several decades. Without long-term, stable funding for infrastructure assets and expert, sector-specific oversight programs, the sort of catastrophe we saw in Flint is destined to repeat itself. To pay for improved services would inevitably require user-fee increases, which the state was politically unwilling to undertake, so instead it let water quality deteriorate. A report issued by President Biden's National Infrastructure Advisory Council (NIAC) in 2023 stated:

The true costs of supplying and treating water are often not reflected in the price the consumer pays. Water utilities have resisted increasing the price of water until recently, and instead covered the cost through reductions in operations and maintenance (O&M). Due to deferred maintenance, about one-sixth of finished water in the U.S. never reaches customers but leaks out of storage and distribution systems. This loss of revenue is borne by the utilities because leaked water cannot be billed since it never reached the user.[9]

The Flint crisis ended roughly in 2019. After several rounds of emergency congressional funding, as well as emergency capital from the state of Michigan, the streets of Flint were excavated, and its lead pipes were replaced. Emergency spending eventually steered the city out of disaster, and the rescue of Flint succeeded. But the underlying causes of the crisis still remain, and so far nothing has been done to fix them. Nothing structural prevents Flint, or a similar city, from falling into crisis again, and just as importantly, policymakers have done little to provide an alternative means of addressing such crises besides emergency spending. Moreover, it is still extremely common in the United States for states and municipalities to both own and regulate their infrastructure assets, and the systems of financing discussed previously are still very much in place.

It should not come as a surprise, then, that the scale of the crisis of Flint continues to spread to other cities around the country. Pittsburgh, Pennsylvania, has dealt with lead contamination as a result of aging pipes since at least 2016,[10] as has Newark, New Jersey.[11] And lead is not the only difficulty facing our aging and insufficient water systems. In 2022 Jackson, Mississippi, found itself without clean water for seven weeks after water was contaminated with bacteria; in addition, extremely low water pressure meant that many home faucets in Jackson produced no water at all.[12]

As David Gadis, who runs DC Water, told me, "I think a lot of the trouble is because these water entities operate as a municipal structure. I think if it were run differently, you would not see the Jacksons, you would not see the Flints—and there's a number of other water utilities that are in trouble as well across this country that could benefit from a different model." He added, "I'm not knocking mayors or council members or any of them." As Gadis implied, it is the municipal management structure itself that is at the heart of the difficulty.

American water delivery and sewerage, in fact, face a host of challenges. Lead is a major issue, and not just in Flint. Much of the current US water system, which was built primarily in the early twentieth century, uses lead pipes. President Biden promised a complete overhaul of the system as part of the IIJA, which allocated $30 billion in direct funds for lead remediation.[13] But as the draft report on water infrastructure produced by the president's NIAC suggests, while the IIJA will close the deficit gap, all water pipes will need to be replaced or repaired by 2040, which will perforce increase the cost to users substantially.[14] Unless new sources of funding are identified, or user fees are increased, or private operators step in to participate in the upgrade and maintenance of this critical sector, the problem will continue to worsen.

Climate change also presents growing challenges. Climatologists predict that extreme flooding will become more frequent as global temperatures rise, straining the capacity of sewer systems around the country and threatening the safety of water supplies.[15] Poor sewerage can lead to bacterial contamination, as happened in Jackson, and poses a slew of other health risks. And then there is the water shortage in the American West. In California and swaths of the Southwest, drought has reduced water supplies, forcing unprecedented efforts at conservation. According to experts, the drought is not a passing phenomenon but a new normal.[16] As reservoirs begin to dry up, we will need bold, transformative action to keep people hydrated and keep cities running. A worrying example of the evaporating water is Lake Mead, the largest reservoir in the country, located outside Las Vegas in the Colorado Basin. Since 1980 the lake's elevation has fallen by 130 feet, according to NASA.[17] The reservoir was created during the infrastructure boom of the 1930s as a result of the construction of the Hoover Dam on the Colorado River, and it supplies the drinking water (and, through the dam, the electricity) for as many as forty million people.[18] We will need long-term solutions to store and transport more water to key hubs like Los Angeles in the near future, which will likely require the creation of new regional providers.

Other types of issues exist in Florida, for example, where the Everglades, which provide 90 percent of the drinking water for the southern part of the state, have been contaminated and otherwise impacted by the sugar industry. Over $10 billion is slated to be spent on infrastructure projects to save the Everglades and ensure water flow in the region. That could hardly be undertaken by the private sector. In fact, it is the private sector, in the form of the sugar industry, that has in large part been responsible for the environmental disaster and the water contamination.[19]

It is time to reinvest and reinvent—but where can such heavy investment come from? When it comes to water infrastructure, the country seems unable to muster the necessary commitments. For instance, the city of Jackson requested $47 million from Mississippi to provide immediate fixes to its sewer and water delivery systems, but the state allocated only $3 million.[20] In a more dire sign of our underinvestment, the IIJA dedicated only $75 million to improvements for Mississippi's water systems,[21] but Jackson's mayor, Chokwe Lumumba, estimated Jackson alone would need $1 billion for a complete system overhaul. Who will fund the difference?

Even setting aside transformative projects like hauling new water to California, simple maintenance of water systems is costly. In 2022 there were roughly 240,000 water main breaks in America. According to the American Water Works Association, the cost of fixing every pipe that needs replacement could reach up to $1 trillion in the coming years. The EPA estimates that bringing the entire US water system up to par will require investment of $743 billion over twenty years.[22]

The upside is that more federal *spending* is not the only answer. Rather than await the next knock-out congressional fight over spending, we should begin the process of reforming our infrastructure management models to ensure the most efficient use of federal spending and find ways to incorporate more long-term *investment* models that include the private sector. In our discussion about privatization, former governor Bush identified the water sector as one of the most promising avenues of privatization, if only voters would give it a fair hearing. "One place where there is huge potential and the need is phenomenal, even more than in roads or transportation infrastructure, is in the water sector," he said. However, as he knows firsthand, the public backlash for even considering privatization of water can be fierce. "When I was governor," he said, "I had a meeting on my schedule to discuss privatizing the water in some county, and the attacks I received just for listening to a proposal were incredible—it wasn't even a specific plan." If we are unwilling even to consider alternatives, nothing will ultimately improve. "We're stuck in the past," Bush concluded.

Before delving further into these alternatives, let's look more closely at what really went wrong in Flint to understand why the manner in which our infrastructure is managed and funded needs fundamental reform.

The Origins of the Flint Water Crisis

For the entirety of the twentieth century, Flint had purchased its water from the Detroit Water and Sewerage Department, a company controlled by the city of Detroit, which sourced water from Lake Huron and delivered it to Flint and other regional centers via its own network of pipelines. Like most water providers, the Detroit Water Department began as a private operation in the nineteenth century.[23] In the early 1820s Detroit posted advertisements for an operator to pump water for the city from the Detroit River, but no suitable bids were tendered. Then, in 1825, a man named Bethuel Farrand arrived unexpectedly at city hall, having walked eighty-three miles from his home in Aurelius, Michigan, to announce his plan for a city waterworks. The town granted him the concession, and in 1829, with his partner Rufus Wells, Farrand established the Detroit Hydraulic Company, the first citywide water source. Soon after, a group of investors, E.P. Hastings, Lucins Lyon, and P. Davis Jr., purchased the company and developed it as the city grew.[24] During the Progressive Era it became regulated by the state, and in the 1930s, following the national trend, the authority was purchased by Michigan and came under direct management of the city of Detroit.[25] By the 1960s, the utility had grown to serve surrounding towns and cities, including Flint.

At the end of April 2014, however, Flint broke off its long-standing relationship with the Detroit utility and switched to the recently opened Karegnondi Water Authority—owned by the state of Michigan—which would source water from the Flint River. This may have been the proximate cause of the disaster, but the trouble began long before the switch. Why did Flint want to leave the Detroit system in the first place?

Residents were suspicious of the change from the beginning. There were protests against the plan to change providers even when it was first announced in 2012. For decades, General Motors had used the Flint River as a waste depository and the river water had failed EPA inspections since the 1960s.[26] The pollution of the Flint River played only a small role in the disaster, as we will see. But residents were not only wary of drinking from a former dumping site, they were also suspicious of the politicians who were managing the water utility.[27]

Their fears were borne out. Ignoring the protests, officials went ahead with the change anyway. It is difficult to assign blame concretely for the disaster; charges were brought against eight of the officials involved in the disaster, including former governor Rick Snyder, but they were dropped a year later by the courts. Assigning final responsibility is about as difficult as knowing who was ultimately in charge of Flint's water system at the time. Was it the city? The state? The water authority? The EPA?

To appreciate the full web of responsibility, it's necessary to go back further than the switch from Detroit Water to the Flint River, back to the financial crisis in Michigan in 2011. The story of Michigan's economic woes is well known, but the case of Flint is especially dramatic. In the 1930s Flint was the headquarters of GM and the home of Buick and Chevrolet. It was a bustling city that for a time rivaled neighboring Detroit. In the 1960s, however, Flint automakers started to move manufacturing out of the city and into the suburbs, where land and taxes were less expensive. Between 1960 and 2011 the population of Flint fell from 200,000 to 90,000. Between 1978 and 1990, the number of Flint area residents employed by GM dropped from 80,000 to 23,000.[28] Today, the city has an average household income of $39,500, significantly below the per capita income for the United States, which is over $60,0000. According to the 2020 census, 40 percent of Flintites live below the poverty level.[29]

In 2011, in the aftermath of the 2008 financial crash, the city of Flint declared a financial emergency. Flint was a bellwether; cities across Michigan soon faltered, too, reaching a climax two years later when Detroit declared a financial emergency, and soon thereafter, bankruptcy. In the chaos of these financial emergencies, Michigan's infrastructure was put on the chopping block. As the state and municipalities explored ways to cut costs, they often looked to slash infrastructure funding. Both Flint and Detroit switched water providers in an effort to reduce civil expenditures. In both cities, municipal insolvency opened the door to state interventions—just like in Chester, Pennsylvania. In the case of Flint, this state intervention was a decisive factor in the start of the water crisis.

One of the key conflicts in the early stages of the Flint water crisis was between the administration of Michigan governor Rick Snyder, a technocratic Republican elected in 2011 as a budget hawk, and the local elected officials in Flint, including city councilors and the mayor, Dayne Walling, a Democrat. The tension circled around one question: Did the city own its infrastructure, or did the state? This controversy first mounted when Governor Snyder introduced Public Act 4, a piece of legislation that would be among his most hotly debated.[30]

Public Act 4, or PA 4 as the bill was known, extended the powers of emergency managers. In Michigan, when a city declares a financial emergency it enters a state of receivership, and the state sends an emergency manager to take charge of the city's recovery. PA 4 increased the power of emergency managers to include the ability to terminate any contract the city holds with trade unions, nongovernmental organizations (NGOs), and any other entity—with the important exception of bondholders.

At the time PA 4 was introduced, many activists argued that the bill allowed state officials to usurp power from elected local representatives. Initially, the Michigan State House voted PA 4 down, but near-identical legislation, PA 436, was passed by lawmakers soon after. On their face, PA 4, PA 436, and the expansion of the powers of emergency managers did not seem to suggest a dramatic change. Yet in Flint, emergency managers continually deepened the crisis by using their powers to veto community decisions about infrastructure contracts at key moments. It was emergency managers who first initiated the change in Flint's water suppliers.[31]

In 2011 Mike Brown, a former interim mayor of Flint, was named the first of four emergency managers to bring the city out of crisis. At the time of his arrival, there was already a proposal to switch water providers circulating in City Hall, but it was Brown who fast-tracked the plan. Working closely with Mayor Walling and Jeffrey Wright, the drain commissioner, Brown ordered a financial study and found that, by leaving the Detroit Water and Sewage Department and buying water instead from the newly opened Karegnondi Water Authority, the city of Flint could save $5 million over two years, a relatively small portion of Flint's budget.[32] (Typically, water services make up less than 1 percent of municipal budgets.)[33] But Brown seized every opportunity for savings. Before the decision to switch providers, the state first tried to force raising the price of water. Between 2011 and 2014, prices rose by 200 percent.[34] The increase was so much that some residents were paying more than $100 a month for water. Under these conditions, the prospect of saving $5 million on water and finding a more efficient authority was irresistible.

Overall, Brown's financial strategy involved relaying the costs of infrastructure to the users without any benefit to the municipality of Flint. This approach reflected the infrastructure funding strategies of the state of Michigan at large and indeed the rest of America. For decades, the state of Michigan had increasingly been placing infrastructure costs on local governments and decreasing state funds that help cities with maintenance and building.[35] State cuts reflected larger trends. The federal government itself had been passing off the costs of infrastructure to states since the 1970s, when federal infrastructure spending began steadily decreasing as a share of GDP.[36] The upshot has been that the burden placed by the federal government on the states ultimately falls on local governments.

The fundamental question here is whether the municipality is the right entity to manage the water needs of cities like Flint. The management of these infrastructure assets has only become more complex, with higher populations, new technologies, more extensive regulations (including EPA standards), and new technologies for treatment that offer higher quality and efficiency, which did not exist when the Flint water system was built. Nonexpert bodies and elected officials may have potential conflicts of interest when it comes to managing vital assets. Research has shown that local leaders and municipal governments are averse to taking on complicated restructuring techniques, especially involving public-private partnerships. Sometimes this aversion is not so innocent. Sometimes, as in the case of Flint, the conflicts of interest animating municipal managers could amount to possible corruption.[37]

Many experts suggest that political influence plays a significant part in municipalities' desire to own water infrastructure. Mark Kennedy, who served Minnesota's second and sixth districts in Congress between 2001 and 2007, understands the motivations and incentives of elected officials, especially concerning infrastructure. Kennedy sat on the Transportation and Infrastructure Committee as well as the Energy and Commerce Committee and introduced legislation that increased the number of highway lanes by expanding cashless tolling technology. The Fixing America's Surface Transportation Act (or the FAST Act) authorized $305 billion for the underresourced Federal Highway Authority, guaranteeing funding between 2016 and 2020. As Kennedy emphasizes, even if municipalities do not accrue considerable revenue from an infrastructure asset, it nevertheless endows its operator with considerable influence.

> Amongst the people who are most anxious to court the favor of a member of Congress are members of coalition groups that are advocating for a specific road expansion, transit, water, whatever. And a House member will partner with some of these coalitions and help either with an earmark or advocate with the state or the federal government on their behalf. The state is filled with people who have multi-year plans as to what they want to do with infrastructure, and they come up with a prioritization scheme as to how they are going to prioritize which projects. So, these coalition groups are constantly lobbying with the state, but since the state makes the ultimate decision, they are reticent to go against it. Since the state has so much invested in this strategic planning, unless they have a politician

that will step out and take the risk of doing a public-private partnership, they are likely to stay in their lane.[38]

After Brown took charge of the city, Flint announced its plans to switch from Detroit to the Karegnondi Water Authority, the newly opened facility drawing water from the Flint River. The City Council had voted to sign a contract with the Karegnondi Water Authority, but only *after* it had finished construction of a pipeline to Lake Huron. The council had rejected the idea of using the Flint River for any period. Yet in conjunction with Flint mayor Dayne Walling, Emergency Manager Mike Brown vetoed the city council's decision and determined that the Flint River would serve as an interim water source while the pipeline was completed. In the long run, this decision would end up costing the state of Michigan $350 million—a staggering figure when put beside the $5 million Flint hoped to save.

It seems there was more than hasty government incompetence or reckless austerity at work in the decision to leave the Detroit system, however. Several Flint officials may have had a personal stake in the success of Karegnondi, which had been in development since the 1980s. The CEO of the Karegnondi Authority, Jeffrey Wright, was also the drain commissioner for Genesee County, home of Flint. Flint's mayor, Dayne Walling, was himself the chair of the Karegnondi Board of Trustees. With the Karegnondi Authority, municipal leaders hoped to consolidate power over water services. It might not have been a bad plan, at least in principle. But the state and city's rush to connect Flint to the new authority was reckless. The Karegnondi Water Authority was not yet ready to service a city of such size; it had primarily supplied water to commercial customers. The treatment facility was missing essential technology and materials. Nevertheless, Flint officials chose to jump the gun.

It is important to understand Karegnondi. Like the majority of water providers in the United States, it is a government-owned corporation, controlled directly by the State of Michigan and managed on a day-to-day basis by local drain commissioners from Flint and other surrounding towns. The company, however, still had to compete for city contracts, despite being state run. A state-owned utility is not always guaranteed state contracts, because generally each municipality can independently choose how to procure the services it needs. As government officials and, simultaneously, senior leadership at a state-owned corporation, Walling and Wright were in a position to self-deal using public funds. As mayor and drain commissioner, they were able to secure a contract for a company they each had a personal financial stake in. The problem was not that there was competition in the water sector—that is generally beneficial—but instead, as suggested, the competition was rigged.[39] Where there is a choice between water providers, it is often between state-owned utilities, often between a regional or local provider. This is not because there are no private water services in the United States—there are—but rather because local government has historically wanted to retain tight control over infrastructure.[40] In Flint, control of infrastructure meant personal economic opportunity for government officials. There are other ways for politicians to exploit control over infrastructure, too, whether simply by campaigning on improving services or by influencing which neighborhoods and townships get development projects.

In Flint, these opportunities for self-dealing and selective dealing were taken advantage of to the fullest. In 2011 the Karegnondi pipeline to Lake Huron needed additional funding, and only a contract with the City of Flint would provide the authority with enough capital to complete the long-awaited project. The predicament was that Flint City Council wouldn't sign a contract with Karegnondi until it completed its pipeline, but the Karegnondi Authority couldn't complete the pipeline until Flint signed its $81 million contract. With the expanded powers of Emergency Manager Mike Brown, however, this deadlock could be broken, and Brown took the side of the officials and the new water authority over the city council. Brown declared that Flint would override the city council and take a gamble on the Karegnondi Water Authority. In the summer of 2012 Flint announced that it had signed the agreement, and Karegnondi moved full speed ahead on its new pipeline to Lake Huron, which was scheduled for completion in 2016. In the meantime, Flint would drink its river water. In April 2014, Mayor Dayne Walling, along with a new emergency manager, Darnell Earley, flipped the switch that connected Flint to the Karegnondi Water Authority, two years before the Huron pipeline would be finished.

The fundamental challenge arose because ownership, management, and regulation were all intertwined. Whether this was outright corruption or not, the investment framework must minimize those conflicts of interest. City officials overrode the decisions of local government in order to secure a project that may have helped them personally, and the state intervened on behalf of city officials. Government operators committed every sort of mistake a skeptic of privatization might fear from a private infrastructure operator. In fact, the mistake in part escaped regulators because the operator *was* governmental and the regulator was also a local governmental entity.

Had Flint contracted a private operator with *strong* regulatory oversight, if there had been a well-structured public-private partnership in place, those same regulators would have had fewer incentives to look the other way when they discovered violations, as they did in this case. The ultimate failure in Flint, then, might have occurred in the process of regulation and oversight. Jonson Cox has always insisted regulatory bodies need to be highly competent and well compensated in order to be effective.

The Price of Poor Regulatory Systems

In late February 2015, an EPA official named Miguel Del Toral conducted water testing on the tap water at the home of LeeAnne Walter, one of the most vocal residents at Flint town hall meetings. Del Toral found her drinking water had twenty-five times the maximum lead content allowed by the EPA. As any lead warning will tell you, no amount of lead is safe, but the EPA considers lead concentrations above 15 parts per billion (ppb) to be actionable. LeeAnne Walters's water tested at 400 ppb. Del Toral, who was a regional groundwater and drinking water regulations manager at the EPA, sent a memo to the chief of the Michigan Department of Environmental Quality (MDEQ), spelling out the health hazard of Flint's lead-tainted water and calling for an immediate review. MDEQ ignored Del Toral's warnings.[41]

Why were Del Toral's warnings dismissed at the EPA? At first, it seemed to many to be a case of bureaucratic incompetence, but as documents revealed at the trial of Emergency Manager Darnell Earley showed, MDEQ and city officials were aware of the problem and attempted to cover it up.[42] It wasn't only Dayne Walling and Flint officials who wanted to ignore the tainted water, though. Rick Snyder and state leaders, including Flint's emergency managers, also insisted on sticking with Karegnondi and its financial savings. The self-dealing of Walling and Wright, taking place under the umbrella of the municipality and the Karegnondi authority, was accompanied by conflicts at the state level. The governor and his administration were committed to economic austerity and were in the process of managing the bankruptcy of Detroit and the restructuring of the Detroit Water and Sewerage Department.[43] Flint could be spared no additional state funding; compared to Detroit water, the safety of Flint water was not a priority.

As the news of tests on LeeAnne Walters's water spread, however, pressure mounted on Flint to act. The City Council agreed to hold a vote on whether to abandon its contract with Karegnondi and switch back to the

Detroit system and back to Lake Huron. But once again, a new emergency manager, Gerald Ambrose, intervened. Arguing that switching back to the Detroit authority would bankrupt the city, Ambrose vetoed the vote, ensuring the city would stay with Karegnondi and the Flint River.[44]

Once again, an official with little expertise in water management took control over the drinking water of eighty thousand people. It simply does not make sense for vital infrastructure to be at the whim of municipal budgets and austerity-minded state politicians. Managing infrastructure requires attention to detail and a healthy supply of capital. During the financial crisis in Michigan, both of these were in dangerously short supply.

On his own initiative, Del Toral continued to investigate the issue. Spurred by his anger at the EPA's inaction, the next month he made one of the most damning discoveries in the Flint water crisis. While examining the Karegnondi Water Authority, Del Toral found that it wasn't adding the proper chemicals to treat Flint's water, having changed the requirements after taking over from the Detroit system. Specifically, Karegnondi was not adding enough anticorrosion agents. The Flint River is an unstable water source, but this was not the problem. Everything that happened to Flint stemmed from Karegnondi's failure to treat the water correctly.

To be potable, Flint River water requires large amounts of polyphosphates, specifically a kind called orthophosphates. This treatment is needed not because the river is toxic, as so many in Flint believed, but because it prevents the corrosion of the sealant on lead pipes in Flint's old water and sewage system. When pipes corrode, lead leaches into the water, and once the sealant is worn through, the pipes typically must be replaced. The lack of anticorrosives was also responsible for the outbreak of Legionnaires' disease. When lead was introduced into Flint's water, it began to break down another part of the water treatment: chlorine. Once lead had dissolved the chlorine compounds in Flint's water, bacteria were able to bloom in the drinking water unimpeded.[45]

In July 2015, Del Toral's findings were released to the press and for the first time, the Flint water crisis began to receive national attention. In a matter of months, things changed. That October, Governor Snyder sent $9 million to Flint to reconnect it to the Detroit system; the switch happened the following day. In November, Mayor Walling was replaced, and Nick Lyons resigned as director of MDEQ. By January 2016, President Obama had declared a national emergency in Flint and sent $5 million to alleviate the crisis. National Guard troops moved into the city to distribute water bottles and keep the peace.

Immediately after the switch back to the Detroit Water Department, lead levels dropped in Flint water, but only in parts of the city and only for a time. The untreated water that had flowed for eighteen months from Karegnondi had done irreparable damage to Flint's water infrastructure. The phosphate coating had completely eroded, leaving raw, exposed lead seeping into the water.

By the summer of 2016 lead levels were again on the rise, and it soon became clear that Flint's entire water system would need to be replaced, including the pipes in approximately twelve thousand homes. In December Congress approved $100 million to overhaul Flint's water system. The EPA contributed an additional $100 million grant, and Michigan promised $200 million. What had initially been estimated, in 2016, as a $55 million effort had ballooned into one that, in total, would cost nearly $450 million in federal and state spending.[46]

In addition to ignoring Del Toral's reports, the EPA had turned a blind eye to the insufficient water treatment at Karegnondi. As documents show, officials at the EPA were explicitly directed by Governor Snyder and his administration not to pursue evidence of treatment problems at Karegnondi.[47] In 2014, just before the switch took place, a water quality inspector at Karegnondi named Mike Glasgow raised a red flag about the treatment, putting the grand opening on hold for nearly two months. According to testimony he delivered to Congress in 2022, Glasgow's warnings were dismissed because officials at the state level wanted to push it through.

What ought to be done about such failures at the EPA? There is no question that the case of Flint indicates the need for a stronger oversight body for the water sector. This might mean the creation of a new federal or state entity, or an expansion of the EPA, perhaps to create a series of sector-specific agencies.

There is no question that better regulation is needed. But the failure in Flint wasn't simply that regulatory bodies were insufficient, or that regulators were incompetent. Two separate regulators did notice the problem and reported it to their supervisors, just as they are expected to do. The regulators did their job. It was the state that the regulators answered to that neglected their duty. Their superiors should have brought in state authorities to force the municipality into compliance, but instead they swept complaints under the rug. In the end, what undermined the process in Flint was the fact that infrastructure was regulated, owned, and operated by related parties, viz., the government. If it is the state itself that is mismanaging infrastructure, there is no body, outside the federal government, with the

power to force it into compliance. The upshot is that with state-owned and
-managed infrastructure, there is a weaker incentive structure to comply
with regulations, even though technically the state itself creates those regulations. If infrastructure safety is not a priority for the state, there is nothing
a state regulator like MDEQ can do.

If one part of the infrastructure ecosystem performed well in the Flint
crisis, it was the users—the citizens of the city. The response of Flint residents to their predicament eventually secured Flint not only clean water but
also the city's first large-scale infrastructure overhaul in decades, albeit one
administered under the worst possible conditions. One lesson from this is
that poor infrastructure management will not go unnoticed by users, and
in a free market democracy, the people still have the ability to challenge a
system that is not working.

But where did this clean water come from? When Flint switched back to
the Detroit system, in 2016, it was itself undergoing a radical transformation. The Detroit Water and Sewerage Department had just filed for bankruptcy (at the same time as the city of Detroit), and the state and city were
in the midst of deciding what should be done with it. In an article published
in the *Journal of Law and Society* during the decision-making process, Anna
Rossi outlined the variety of options Detroit considered, from outright privatization, to a diversity of P3 models, to the creation of a regional state
authority.[48] The decision involved delicate negotiations between state and
city. According to the Michigan constitution, privatization and the creation of regional authorities require consent from both state and city officials. The emergency manager assigned to Detroit, Kevyn Orr, explored all
these possibilities, including the possibility of privatization: either offering
an outright sale or else following an operation, maintenance, and management (OMM) model. But city officials would not agree to privatization. The
Detroit City Council opted instead for the creation of a regional authority,
holding on to state control of infrastructure. The creation of a regional authority, as Rossi argued in 2016, would allow the city to retain a greater degree of community control over infrastructure, but it would not offer the
same financial benefits that Detroit would have won from privatization.
Those against privatization argued that after years of belt tightening and
streamlining as a result of poor performance, there was little a private company could still do to improve the efficiency of the provider. That meant
the only benefit for the city would be the influx of capital, which opponents, including Rossi, asserted was less important than community oversight of the water system. Though the logic is sound, one has to wonder:

How reassuring is community oversight really? Under a regional authority, those in control of infrastructure are not immediately elected but rather appointed by the mayor and other participating county officials. City officials still have the power to use infrastructure control for their own ends and, more importantly, the state remains both operator and regulator. It is true that a regional authority establishes a greater balance of power between local officials, who must all agree to decisions, but the fundamental problem of state management remains. As long as the new water authority acts independently from the state authorities and the regulatory oversight is overseen by a different body, these structures can work well, especially if they have their independent balance sheet and ability to raise debt outside of the municipal or state guarantee.

The city negotiated a transition from the Detroit Water and Sewerage Department to a newly created regional water authority, the Great Lakes Water Authority (GLWA). A joint venture between the State of Michigan and assorted municipal leaders, the Great Lakes Water Authority now provides 40 percent of the state with drinking water. According to Detroit's bankruptcy deal, the Great Lakes Water Authority assumed the Detroit Water Department's outstanding debts and took over responsibility for its key operations.[49] The regional water authority has a corporate structure, operating with more independence than the Detroit Water Department, or Karegnondi, and has more direct oversight by state EPA officials. Its capital funding is not directly tied to any municipal budget, nor are its operations subject to takeover by emergency managers. Certainly a better model would be closer to the structure of DC Water, which is the gold standard for public water authorities.

While Flint switched to a somewhat improved regional model, municipally owned utilities still manage water delivery in most of the country. Regional providers are not uncommon, but the default method of investment mirrors the one that led to the crisis in Flint. Of course there are several exceptions, most notably in Indianapolis, Indiana, which never claimed control of water systems and has been served by private operators since the nineteenth century. The Water Works Company of Indianapolis opened for business in 1871, founded by Thomas Morris, a civil engineer who settled in Indianapolis during its founding in 1821. Morris sold his company to a group of local investors soon afterward, and it became the Indianapolis Water Company, which in the twentieth century grew into the largest privately held water company in the country. It changed hands again in the early twentieth century, at a time when many private operations were transferred to the state and wound up in the control of a Philadelphia-based utility investor, Clarence Geist. Over the course of the century, the Indianapolis Water Company undertook tremendous improvement projects for the Indianapolis community, including the construction of Geist Reservoir and Morse Reservoir (also named for a manager of the water company), as well as the expansion of the treatment facilities to keep pace with a growing population.[50] In 2002 the City of Indianapolis finally purchased the Water Company itself but immediately turned around and licensed it to Veolia on a twenty-year lease, which was transferred in 2010 to a nonprofit corporation.[51] Veolia paid the city $1.5 billion for the contract.[52]

It was the Indianapolis Water Company that employed David Gadis's father to lay the city's waterpipes, and it was during the transition to Veolia that David became CEO. On the city's decision to lease the asset so quickly after purchasing it, Gadis said, "The city of Indianapolis realized very quickly that they did not have the capability to run the utility, and that it had been successful because it had been privately held. As a result, they made a decision very quickly—they wanted to own it, but they did not want to run it. They wanted to keep it privately run and that's when Veolia won that contract, which I would describe as a great public-private partnership." It is interesting that a municipality that had the opportunity to take over operations chose not to because it had experienced the benefits of private management. Ownership is one thing; operations are another.

Several other cities in Indiana have also maintained privatized water systems, including Fort Wayne and Lake Station,[53] and other cities such as Newark, New Jersey, and Cincinnati, Ohio, also leased their water infrastructure to private or nonprofit companies in the wake of the 2008 financial crisis.[54] Bayonne, New Jersey, situated between Jersey City and Staten Island on the Graveseed and Newark Bays, is another exception. In 2012 the city was in financial distress after failing to meet budget projections. New Jersey warned the city it was in danger of being taken over by the state. To avoid that fate, the city licensed its waterworks on a forty-year lease to a private company owned by KKR, a private equity firm listed on the New York Stock Exchange, raising $150 million to cover the city's budget gaps and avoid a receivership. The private operator also promised to invest in the assets and replace dilapidated infrastructure, some of which dated to the 1880s.[55] Yet the privatization caused an outcry. Water rates rose by 28 percent after the lease began, and for years residents complained about prices, leading a new mayor, Jimmy Davis, to pursue canceling the lease. To do so, the city would be required to repay the $150 million, but those funds were already spent. Locked into an agreement, then, there is little the city can do to change its water rates. But as KKR points out, the rate changes were outlined in the original P3 deal, and "three state agencies and the rate-payer advocate reviewed the transaction and the predetermined rate formula with the needs of the city and the ratepayers in mind."[56] In other words, the rate hikes were built into the agreement and approved by the city. With the improvements to infrastructure, the change in rates may be a shock and a public relations problem, but it reflects the true cost of providing clean water and ensuring long-term viability. If the municipality wishes to support low-income households, it can do so by developing targeted subsidies, which are more efficient than keeping water rates flat for decades, which ends up being a form of regressive tax. Still, controversy over privatization in cases like Bayonne's discourages other cities, from a political perspective, from pursuing it themselves. Municipalities more typically fight any effort to transfer control of infrastructure to the private sector. In 2022, for instance, the Pittsburgh City Council blocked a $1.1 billion deal to privatize its sewerage with the American water company Aqua, which would have been the largest privatization of a water system in US history.[57] In 2018 Baltimore voted to make privatization of water infrastructure illegal![58]

In a recently published book, *Plunder: Private Equity's Plan to Pillage America*, Brendan Ballou mounts an attack on the role of private equity in the American economy, devoting a chapter to the privatization of public infrastructure. He refers to the Bayonne case as well as another one in Middletown, Pennsylvania, where the water and sewer system entered into a P3 also managed by KKR. Ballou cites these two cases as examples in which, according to him, private operators outwitted the city managers by entering into highly beneficial P3s that gave little leeway to the cities to change the agreement or control price increases. "The disasters in Middletown and Bayonne are part of a much larger story about how the basic facets of government are increasingly being privatized, with the aid of private equity firms."[59] The author is, as you can deduce from the title of his book, no supporter of private equity firms. It is unclear, however, whether the issue is private capital per se, the city's lack of ability to manage such P3 contracts, or (presumably) a combination of both. Careful design of P3s followed by implementation and monitoring can prevent private equity or state officials taking advantage of municipalities and can lead to superior outcomes. In its report NIAC suggests, among a long list of concrete proposals, removing "barriers to privatization, concessions, and other nontraditional models of funding community water systems; allow[ing] access of privately owned water providers to Water Infrastructure Finance and Innovation Act (WI-FIA) and federal grant programs; and [supporting] regionalization of water systems."[60] It also recommends to the president, in what may be a first, creating a federal Department of Water:

> The regionalization of water will require federal action. We need to elevate water as a national priority. The People's Republic of China (PRC) has the Ministry of Water Resources as a department within China's Central People's Government responsible for managing water resources in PRC, an $800 billion annual water budget, and a Five-Year National Water Security Plan. The U.S. has an outward facing Global Water Strategy, but no five-year or long-term national strategy. Water resources are managed by a variety of federal agencies, with little coordination among them. EPA enforces water quality requirements through the Clean Water Act and the Safe Drinking Water Act; the Department of Interior has oversight of the data-gathering U.S. Geological Survey and the Bureau of Reclamation, which is responsible for large water infrastructure and hydropower in the western U.S.; the Department of Defense, through the U.S. Army Corps of Engineers, manages the inland waterways east of the Rocky Mountains with a focus on flood control and navigation. The Departments of Energy (DOE), Transportation (DOT), and Commerce have varying water related programs and interests. Examples include DOE's Water Conservation Program and DOT's Water Management Policy. This fragmentation of responsibility at the federal level makes it difficult to ascertain the country's water needs and strategically prepare the nation for a water-secure future.[61]

The UK Water Sector Privatization

Like the United States, for most of its history England left infrastructure investment to entrepreneurs and private companies. Beginning in the early twentieth century, though, and especially in the years immediately following the end of World War II, Britain centralized its infrastructure through the creation of national regulating authorities.[62] One of the first nationalizations was called for in the Water Act of 1945, which established a stable water supply and delivery system. This was quickly followed by nationalizations in the airline industry, the coal mines, the electricity sector, railroads, telecommunications, and the steel industry.[63] As in the United States, responsibility for infrastructure investment landed primarily on municipalities. Like the United States again, by the 1970s English infrastructure had fallen into disrepair and municipalities into stifling bond debt, and Parliament could not be moved to establish a long-term means of funding national infrastructure. In 1974 the government did make an attempt when it consolidated municipal systems into larger regional water authorities—not unlike the Great Lakes Water Authority that came to service Flint. These regional authorities made gains in efficiency, in part because they were no longer tied to municipal political machinations.[64] But regional authorities experienced significant setbacks in the planning of water resources and forecasts for future demand.[65] Moreover, large investment gaps persisted, and service quality remained poor. This, for the most part, ends the similarities between US and UK infrastructure.

Upon coming to power in 1979, Margaret Thatcher reversed many of the nationalizations of the 1940s, privatizing railroads, roads, airports, and telecommunications.[66] In a suitable symmetry, the water sector was one of the last privatizations of Thatcher's term. In 1989 the British Parliament voted to approve the new Water Act, creating ten private regional water and wastewater authorities in England and Wales, along with twenty-four existing small, statutory, water-only companies, consolidating existing municipal and regional authorities into a *manageable* number of providers. (The United States, in contrast, has 148,000 water authorities, the smallest of which, the Loving County Water District,[67] serves fewer than 100 people.) The method of privatizing such a complex network of assets involved bundling regional and municipal infrastructure together into groups and floating the bundles on the London Stock Exchange. Today, all ten of the original private water and wastewater companies still operate in England and Wales (nine in England, one in Wales), and a new wastewater-only company has been created. As figure 3.1 indicates, close to 40 percent of the water companies' value is publicly traded, with investors coming from all over the world, including the United States, Europe, China, Hong Kong, Australia, and the Middle East, to name a few.[68]

The Thatcher revolution had a dramatic effect. From 1982 to 1991 the public production of goods as a share of GDP fell from 6.6 to 1.9 percent.[69] Thatcher's program for taking government out of business made enormous strides, and with government operators removed from the picture, private investors poured capital into the water sector. In the first twenty-five years following the Water Act, private companies invested £100 billion in water infrastructure.[70] The investment reaped rewards in both the long and

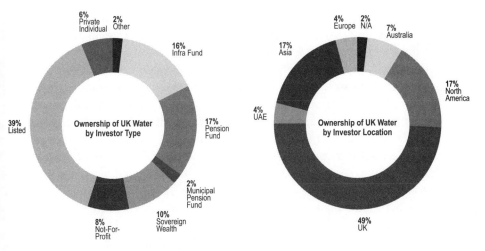

Figure 3.1. Ownership of the UK water sector by type. *Source:* Adapted from Water Services Regulation Authority (Ofwat).

short term. The quality of drinking water improved, with almost a fifth the number of incidents of water contamination compared to pre-privatization. British waterways rebounded dramatically, and riverways and canals improved as well. Privatization brought wastewater treatment into line with the 1991 (and later) European directives, with particularly notable effects on coastal bathing waters and discharges from all urban areas. The number of treatment plants in compliance with European standards increased by more than 10 percent. In addition, the proportion of water customers vulnerable to low water pressure fell one-hundred-fold to nearly zero by 2010.[71]

Many of the benefits were not easily perceptible to all users, and not all the obvious consequences pleased them. After privatization, user fees increased—as private companies forecasted they would. Still, the change was a shock to many consumers. In the first ten years, prices rose 46 percent in real terms, sparking outrage in the press.[72] Fee and toll increases very often accompany privatization; this is in part because government operators fail to make reasonable rate hikes out of fear of political retribution, which is one of the reasons state-run infrastructure assets often operate at a financial loss. It isn't that water tariffs went up because of privatization, but that water tariffs never reflected the true cost before privatization. In the case of England, in the following ten years after privatization, the initial increases leveled off, falling 15 percent. Users inevitably react when rates go up, and unfortunately one of the reasons some have encouraged privatization is precisely that politicians do not want to take the blame for rate hikes and can transfer that blame to a third-party private operator.

In the end, it was more important that the UK water crisis had subsided. By the early 2000s, the success of Britain's system had become a hotly debated topic in academic infrastructure circles, and curiosity about private water providers grew around the world. The United States, China, Germany, Finland, Argentina, the Philippines, and many other countries began experimenting with private water providers to differing extents. At least eighteen countries implemented some form of privatized water between 1989 and 2009.[73] In the 1990s Buenos Aires privatized 30 percent of its water infrastructure through a twenty-year lease to the company Aguas Argentinas, led by the French water investor Suez (the successor to one of the most famous concessions in modern history, the Suez Canal), resulting in $200 million in new investment. Evidence from a study published in the *Journal of Political Economy* suggests that the reduction of bacteria and parasites in drinking water after privatization had an impact on the 31 percent drop in child mortality rates that Argentina experienced in the 1990s.[74] However, the Aguas Argentinas story did not end well. With the massive currency devaluation, the company was unable to pass that cost on to users and faced financial challenges. Coincidentally, a report by the auditor general found that the company was treating only 12 percent of wastewater, and in the words of then president Nestor Kirchner, had "put the public's health at risk." As part of a wave of nationalizations (some would describe it as expropriation), Kirchner rescinded the lease for the water system and promised AR$144 million ($838 million) to address the contamination that had resulted from poor treatment.[75] The terms of the lease allowed the government to retake control of the asset to protect public health. What ensued instead was a series of lawsuits between the government and the private operators, which only ended in 2019.

One of the keys to the success of the UK water privatization was investment from pension funds. From the beginning, both UK pension funds and foreign pension funds invested heavily in water. These funds are a good match for infrastructure investment because of their large size and long investment horizons. Macky Tall, now at the Carlyle Infrastructure Group, was formerly a leading investor with Caisse de Dépot et Placement du Quebec (CDPQ), one of the largest managers of Canadian state pension funds. Tall has described such deals, between state governments and pension fund managers, as "public-public partnerships." As Tall says, the mandate of CDPQ is to manage the retirement savings of millions of Quebecers. So, in that way, it has a very public nature, in the fact of managing for the public interest monies for so many people in Quebec. There is really a virtuous circle between that public mandate of private investment and putting that mandate in place through a partnership with the government of Quebec to lead, develop, build, own, and operate a major public transit system, for instance. That would significantly improve the daily lives of millions of commuters, have an economic impact by creating key corridors to improve mobility, and have an impact on reducing congestion for commercial traffic.

As I have argued, pension funds can play a significant part in infrastructure investment, if they can only be persuaded to do so.[76]

But it was not simply a matter of investment that led to success in England and Wales. There were also innovations in regulation that were critical to securing the benefits of privatization. Under the English framework, private investors both own and operate assets under a license policed by the regulator. In its incentives-based structure, it is in the asset owners' interest to provide cost-effective and high-quality servicing of assets, avoiding underperformance and striving for outperformance. In this model, most importantly in the context of Flint, the regulator and the owner are separated. After the passage of the 1989 Water Act, the United Kingdom created three new regulatory bodies: an independent economic regulator known as Ofwat, an environmental regulator, and a drinking water quality regulator more closely tied to the environmental ministry.[77] Ofwat only handles water sector regulation—not all environmental regulation, as is the case with the EPA and its state branches in the United States. Ofwat is an independent water regulator, structured with a board of directors and CEO, but it is state managed and accountable directly to Parliament. As such, it also works closely with a variety of other state regulatory bodies, such as the Environment Agency, the equivalent of the EPA, as well as the Drinking Water Inspectorate from the Food and Rural Affairs Department.[78] As the lawyer and P3 expert Kent Rowey explains, the emphasis on regulatory bodies independent of political governance paved the way for privatization with the British public and created clear roles for both public and private sectors.

I think that's why the UK government progressed much further and faster than the US. It recognized that if you want private capital, you can't let it go unregulated. You have to make sure people don't make undue profits and that service delivery and safety is addressed. The UK's thinking from a policy point of view was, let's bring in the private sector—because we need capital investment—but then let's regulate it so that we make sure that it's safe, that service is provided in a professional, top-quality way, and that you're not having private companies making a killing, gouging people through high tariffs.

Removed from the difficulties of operating the water system, England and Wales were able to pay greater attention to regulation. Ofwat has twin statutory duties to ensure that customers are protected and that efficient firms can raise capital and is highly effective at enforcing an incentives-based framework to promote ethical, financial, and operational excellence in water companies. Its independence in decision-making, particularly on prices and cost allowances, has given great confidence to consumers and investors alike. By contrast, the Flint regulators had no oversight—or, rather, those with oversight were the ones operating the asset.

The system of public water authorities in Flint also offered no incentives to prioritize safety. Karegnondi feared neither direct legal nor financial punishment for flouting regulations so long as government officials were on its side. Ofwat has no stake in the financial success of the private owners of water companies and can levy hefty fines and penalties if regulations are violated. It can fine up to 10 percent of annual revenues, as it has done to some of the largest water companies, with these fines payable by shareholders, not consumers. Where a water company persistently fails, Ofwat has the powers, informally or formally, to bring in and license new owners. If a local state authority fails in their regulatory duty, there is no statewide impact. By contrast, many regulators will exclude private operators from continuing to participate in bids if they have failed in other P3s. (See figure 3.2 for a complete picture of the actors involved in the British water sector.)

I asked Jonson Cox, the former Ofwat chair, whether he thought an independent water regulator like Ofwat, separate from the EPA, would help the US system. "I think there's very good reason why, in its abstraction of water from the environment or control of pollution coming from wastewater, you want a single regulator like an EPA that's also regulating every other industrial discharge into the environment," he said. Because pollution of the land and air can impact water pollution, it makes sense to have one agency monitoring them all. States should have economic regulators like Ofwat, but Cox commented that one of the biggest challenges facing water regulators is finding good leaders willing to work under high-pressure conditions.

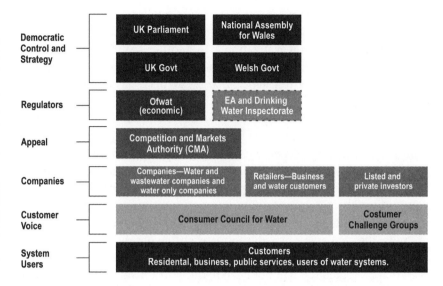

Figure 3.2. Structure of the British water sector. *Source:* Jonson Cox, "Speech at Water Industry City," Water Services Regulation Authority (Ofwat), March 2018.

The bold and difficult bit, and I don't think the US has cracked this on the power distribution side either, is how do you get regulatory offices, regulators, who know how to tackle business. And this is another reason to maintain larger regulatory bodies: "If you did it on any less than a state-level basis, you're never going to get anybody of any caliber. And you need people of some caliber to do it. And you need people who understand how businesses operate. But you need people also able to be quite single-mindedly difficult when they need to." What makes the job especially difficult is attempting to balance short-term and long-term effects of regulation, which Cox described as a kind of business acumen. Your decisions are either too soft or too hard. Sometimes they appear too hard in the short term and in the long term you realize you weren't tough enough. It's a really challenging job of essentially business judgment.

In 2022 all the British water regulators came under fire after a series of violations was brought to light by UK water authorities. Some of the complaints pertain to the depletion of reservoirs in the United Kingdom or the increase in flood waters, forces outside the control of both providers and regulators.[79] Other violations are more serious. It was reported, for instance, that certain providers were dumping illegal quantities of sewage off the English coast and into waterways, undoing some of the original benefits that came with privatization.[80] In another scandal trumpeted by the British papers, it was discovered that the monitoring systems requiring Ofwat to regulate wastewater discharge had been turned off by companies, sometimes at strategic moments when high volumes of waste would have been dumped.[81] Private operators were also criticized when the media publicized that as much as 515 million gallons of drinking water were lost during delivery due to leaky pipes.[82] Finally, columnists, labor union leaders, and various political parties complained that the price hikes imposed had not gone toward infrastructure improvements, but instead toward bonuses for executives.[83]

In some cases these criticisms were valid. No one expected privatization to remove the challenges of water infrastructure entirely. The violations of environmental regulations were inexcusable, and Ofwat leadership acknowledged that its regulation had not been perfect. As Ofwat CEO David Black stated at the time, some private water companies needed to "up their game."[84]

On average, the ten major water providers still had a strong record on quality of drinking water, the environmental health of rivers and other bathing waters, and water pressure. To the extent the overall performance has lagged over the past ten years, it was largely a result of two underperforming providers: Thames Water, which supplied London and surrounding suburbs, and Southern Water, which serviced southeast England, including Sussex and Kent. Ofwat lobbed hefty fines at both these companies: Thames Water faced £196 million in penalties over three years, and Southern Water was fined £126 million by Ofwat for mismanagement of wastewater and another £90 million by the environmental regulator. In 2023 Ofwat had ongoing enforcement investigations against six companies for potential wastewater failures related to monitoring. In the case of Thames Water, the company could be at risk of being taken over by the government until a new buyer is found. To be clear, the equity holders, in this case a group of Canadian and UK pension funds, would lose their investment, not the state; bondholders may not get back 100 percent of the principal (not the state); and no taxpayer monies would be involved.

Within the Ofwat regulatory regime, comparative competition prevails such that companies that set new frontiers of performance (which then set higher targets for other companies) can receive annual performance rewards, and laggard performers are penalized—thus preserving incentives. On the whole, the regulator and the private companies succeeded in meeting both British and European Union regulatory standards to a greater extent than the central government did prior to privatization. Water quality, river health, and water pressure all stayed at higher levels throughout privatization than in the period before it.

Other criticisms of the private water system have typically been motivated by ideology, rather than data, or based on understandable but misguided perceptions about the real cost of water delivery. An example is the outcry over leakage. With a few notable exceptions (again at struggling companies like Thames Water), leakage generally met or came close to meeting regulatory targets. As Robert Colvile, journalist and director of the Centre for Policy Studies, wrote in response to the uproar:

> The way everyone thinks of the water industry is as, well, an industry. The private companies running it get up to whatever mischief they like, while the hapless regulator tries in vain to stop them. But the reality is that the water companies are essentially contractors. They are running the water network on behalf of the state, in a fashion agreed with the state, to targets laid down by the state. . . . The reason that just over 20% of Britain's water is lost to leaks (although drought is pushing that number up) is because that is the level set *by* the regulator [emphasis added].[85]

In 2018 the UK leakage was better than the European average, with the English and Welsh private companies performing even better than the state-run companies of Scotland and Northern Ireland. But particularly in droughts, when restrictions may be mooted, there can be public outrage. Ofwat has progressively ramped up the targets for leakage control; new requirements from 2019 brought leakage to its lowest level in 2023, with about one-fifth overall lost in distribution.

The same was true for the treatment of waste: much of the anger was over dumping that was within legal limits. This was also true of executive pay and price hikes. Ofwat, as an independent economic regulator for water, uses its economic powers to cap the price of water and uses its license powers to ensure that dividends and executive pay reflect the performance of the company for customers. The public complaints about the UK system stemmed not so much from the fact of privatization itself, but rather from the nature of the contracts written by government administrators during the 1989 Water Act, which, according to critics, provided too many financial incentives to raise water prices and restrained Ofwat's ability to punish companies with more than fines.[86]

Cox agreed there is room for improvement at Ofwat, but also noted that the ups and downs of water supply, and consequent price spikes experienced by the UK water sector, inevitably create a volatile relationship with customers. "When the industry doesn't perform very well—as we saw in the UK during the summer of 2022—the public loses confidence in privatization. Under the Corbyn years we saw how easily people are whipped into the nationalization debate." When it comes to regulatory violations, Cox suggests the problem is primarily a question of creating incentives and penalty regimes that ensure that rewards to companies only come with stretching performance for customers. "In my view, when there is criticism of the regimes, it has often come about because the original powers in the privatized model weren't strong enough. So, we have seen a few periods where companies have not performed well enough and yet extravagantly outperformed financially." The regime has evolved over the last decade, with new legal powers to change licenses and create tougher economic tools that incentivize stability and improve performance, which are the most important virtues in a utility company. Stability helps not only to avoid regulatory violations but also to attract investment. "One of the issues that has run through my whole tenure in Ofwat has been the fact that you need to make sure capital retains incentives. You need to make sure that you continue to attract capital, but you are attracting capital that is looking for stable returns. So, let's have some error correction mechanisms that make sure you won't have wild results."

The privatized British system has experienced growing pains in its fourth decade of existence. One of the largest benefits of privatization is the independence that comes to public regulators as a result, but these benefits need to be carefully managed through correction mechanisms and careful planning. The benefits may not have been fully realized yet by Ofwat and the UK system, but that doesn't mean that they can't be in the future. As conditions change, public regulatory standards can be shifted, and the terms of privatization can be amended. One of the criticisms of privatization schemes like P3s is that they require an up-front planning and specification of all possible outcomes, including possible regulatory changes, because otherwise private operators become concerned about risk and may protect themselves with high prices for services or will simply not participate in any P3 programs. According to critics, this is why private capital is simply not suited to public infrastructure.

The UK system has served as a model to the world, but its particularities are not set in stone. In many other countries, water systems have been only partially privatized, and independent regulatory bodies have been given more or less power.

Learning from China?

One such country is China. Counterintuitive as it may be, as part of its enormous expansion of water infrastructure, China has developed innovative solutions to funding and regulating water services. This includes the creation of a water ministry with substantial and guaranteed state funding, but also extensive use of public-private partnerships and privatization. Since 1992 China has increased its water production more than sixty-fold,[87] and much of that work has been accomplished through the inclusion of private firms, both domestic and international.

My first visit to China dates to the winter of 1987, as a student at the American University in Cairo. Tim Sullivan, a China expert, professor of political science, and later provost, had organized student visits to China since 1977. China has changed quite dramatically since 1987. In the last decade I have invested in a variety of infrastructure assets, including hydropower, wastewater treatment, data centers, cogeneration facilities for industrial parks, and solar power generation. The shift toward more market-based economics during the 2000–2010 period was remarkable, and one cannot understand why the United States would not adopt similar approaches, while a communist country was eager to bring in private capital.

In 2015 I visited China Cube Water, a water company headquartered in Nanjing. One of the oldest sites of human habitation on earth (a subspecies of *Homo erectus*, "Nanjing Man," was active in the area 500,000 years ago),[88] Nanjing is an ancient capital of China, established during the Zhou dynasty between the sixth and third centuries BCE.[89] It was the seat of power during the Ming dynasty in the fourteenth and fifteenth centuries,[90] and under the Republic of China and the anti-communist leader Chiang Kai-shek, Nanjing again became the center of state power—only to be brutally devastated by Japanese troops during World War II in what has famously been called the rape of Nanjing.[91] Located on a strategic bend in the Yangzi River, the city still holds a central position in Chinese governance and commerce and, merging modern skyscrapers and ancient pagodas, testifies to China's rich and diverse history.

In the 1980s China reasoned that the only way to sustain a high economic growth rate was to quickly develop a large funding base for infrastructure.[92]

With a population of one billion people in 1985, many living in poverty, and great regional diversity, China faced a steep uphill battle to develop its infrastructure. Nevertheless, it concluded that infrastructure had to be a central part of its planned economy, and from the beginning of its modernization, the country invested in it heavily. The Chinese started with the water industry, just as the English had. The first private infrastructure enterprise in the People's Republic of China was a water treatment plant that opened in 1992.

In the early years of its modernization, the Chinese government did not have the resources required to undertake the infrastructure development it envisioned. As it began modernizing China's economy, the government saw that outside capital would be needed to jump-start growth, and premier Deng Xiaoping invited private investors to participate in China's water infrastructure development. After the initial opening of the economy to the private sector in 1988, China pursued other, more aggressive methods to drive infrastructure development. In 1991 China's leaders decided to invite foreign capital into the water sector as well. Soon companies such as Veolia, Suez, and others were investing billions of dollars to build wastewater plants or take over management of existing assets.[93] The expansion of the water sector was the very first large-scale infrastructure investment program undertaken by China and paved the way for the country's ambitious infrastructure development thereafter. China has not become a free market economy as a result of private investment, but nevertheless, private enterprise has become a foundational element of its economic growth.

To get more insight into the structure and motivations behind China's P3 programs, I spoke with an adviser to China's Ministry of Finance on P3s who has practiced in the infrastructure sector for twelve years. He oversees a team of thirty people who conduct financial analysis and feasibility studies in consultation with local Chinese officials to bring P3 projects to a close. China is engaged in a variety of privatization and public-private partnerships. Across all sectors, it has encouraged private firms to construct infrastructure assets following a BOT model, in which the state reclaims operations after a certain period. In other cases, China has sold infrastructure assets by floating them on the Shanghai stock market.[94] Figure 3.3 illustrates the portion of investment undertaken through P3s in the crucial period between 1990 and 2014.

After the privatization of the early 1990s, China began developing more public-private partnerships throughout the early 2000s; the rate of P3 projects dipped in the wake of the 2008 crisis, but after 2014 it climbed higher than ever before. "When China started P3s nationwide," the adviser said, "they really wanted to set up a framework in terms of policy. So, they

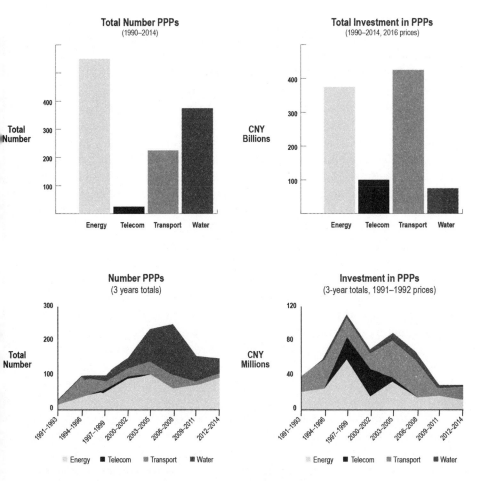

Figure 3.3. Public-private partnership activity in China, 1990–2014. *Source:* Xiaoting Zheng, Yi Jiang, and Craig Sugden, "People's Republic of China: Do Private Water Utilities Outperform State-Run Utilities?," Asia Development Bank, August 2016, https://www.adb.org/sites/default/files/publication/190682/eawp-05.pdf.

brought the global experts to help the Ministry of Finance set up the China based policies." The motivation, he said, was primarily financial. Estimates of the amount of spending China has directed to infrastructure vary, but in most, it runs into the trillions. In the process, China has incurred debts:

One of the major incentives for China to develop P3s is financial. As you may have heard, China spent quite a few trillions of US dollars on infrastructure in the early days, before 2015. The good thing is that China built up a remarkable infrastructure network, from high-speed rail, power generation, water, and many other sectors. But the consequence is that, at that time, local governments accumulated huge debts in order to have sustainable investment in infrastructure. So, I think the trigger point for governments nationwide to push forward P3s, in 2015, was that they wanted to use the private sector's money to invest in the infrastructure.

But, the adviser continued, "the second point is to increase the operational efficiency and effectiveness levels." The Ministry of Finance "will expect [private investors] to bring in the know-how, the IP, the operational experience to help build and operate good infrastructure that will benefit the end users." P3s really took off in 2014 when China began releasing guidelines for establishing P3 frameworks and more aggressively courting private investors.[95] In other words, the financial situation in China resembled the one in the United States, but the People's Republic took a different route.

Currently there are 10,331 public-private partnerships operating in China, representing $2.2 trillion in investment, overwhelmingly in municipal works and transportation.[96] It is necessary when accounting for China's infrastructure growth to remember the contribution the private sector has made. Considering the positive links between infrastructure investment and GDP growth discussed in chapter 1, the effects of private investors on infrastructure should be part of China's miraculous growth story over the last twenty years, too.[97]

The majority of wastewater infrastructure in China is operated by private entities: 55 percent of the market consists of private, foreign, and other types of operators. To be clear, that number includes government-owned entities that are run as independent commercial operations with their own management and board. It is as if DC Water were to invest in water assets across the United States (which it isn't allowed to do, unfortunately) with the objective of maximizing returns within the regulatory framework. The contrast to the United States never ceases to amaze me: here, only 15 percent of the water sector is private, and most of these private systems are private wells in rural areas. Given its management model and the size of its investment, it should not surprise us that China has made enormous strides.

In the process of its impressive, celeritous growth, China's water sector has dealt with issues of water quality that go well beyond what Flint experienced. At the beginning of his tenure, Xi Jinping captured the mood of the people when he joked in 2013 that "the standard that [people] apply for lake water quality is whether the mayor dares to jump in and swim." China also

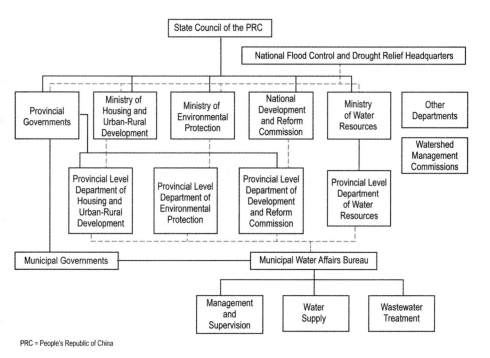

Figure 3.4. Structure of Chinese water management and regulation. *Source:* Xiaoting Zheng, Yi Jiang, and Craig Sugden. "People's Republic of China: Do Private Water Utilities Outperform State-Run Utilities?," *Asia Development Bank*, August 2016, https://www.adb.org/sites/default/files/publication/190682/eawp-05.pdf.

suffers the worst water scarcity of any major economy in the world. With 20 percent of the world's population, China has barely 6 percent of the global supply of fresh water. And after the industrial boom of the last decades, it is estimated that 80 percent of the aquifer system is polluted.[98] When he came to power, Xi Jinping took an aggressive stance on regulation. The environmental standards regulating China's water are overseen by the Ministry of Ecological Environment, which inspects groundwater, surface water, and ocean water, and the Ministry of Water Resources, which oversees drinking water quality and quantity. As in the United Kingdom, water in China is regulated by two separate entities, each providing a check on the other. The results have already begun to show. Figure 3.4 shows the importance of water as a key economic and strategic resource for China by establishing an extensive set of national and regional authorities.

Regulatory practices in some cases are more advanced than those in the United States. Most water facilities in China have remote measurement technology that sends data on the quality of water directly to municipal authorities. These technologies are now slowly being adopted in the US.[99] By releasing operational control of its infrastructure assets to private investors, China availed itself of the most cutting-edge technology in water delivery and regulation.

Could Privatization Succeed in the United States?

The example of China is provocative, in part because it indicates the potential for alternative infrastructure investment models. If the Chinese can privatize their infrastructure and maximize their regulatory oversight, why can't the United States at least explore in a serious and systematic way how the private sector can help with American water? In the United States, privately owned or operated water utilities serve a vanishingly small percentage of the population. A sector that provides an essential service, and which is underfunded, ought to be the perfect place to overcome the country's resistance to privatization. It has worked for the British and for the Chinese. Why not try it? It is critical to highlight that by private sector we do not mean just private operators but also US state pension funds as well as labor union pension funds that would be willing to invest in such assets so long as they can generate adequate long-term returns, on the model of the public-public partnerships described by Macky Tall.

According to Kent Rowey, the simple reason the United Kingdom embarked on privatization was that "it made financial sense to do so." But the same could be said about the United States—so what made the situation different here? In the first place, the issue was less politicized in the United Kingdom. "On both sides of the aisle there was a recognition that the infrastructure situation in the UK was not good enough, that private capital was needed to improve it. I think there was a very high degree of non-politicization of the policy," Rowey noted.

Putting aside the logistics and political dynamics of privatization, the American people at least are willing to entertain involving the private sector to a greater extent. Based on polling I have conducted of American attitudes toward infrastructure,[100] it's clear there is an appetite for, or at least a definite openness to, private companies managing US infrastructure. When asked if their "state or local community could be run like England, where all water systems and airports are privately run," 49 percent were in favor, 14 percent were against, and 38 percent expressed no opinion.

The difficult part lies in describing the mechanism by which privatization would happen. A key element of this involves regulation, as Kent Rowey pointed out. For starters, at least, the US system of regulation could benefit from following the lead of Ofwat. This might pave the way for more experiments with the private sector. In 1970 the United States created the Environmental Protection Agency under the presidency of Richard Nixon, a Republican. According to its charter, the president appoints the EPA director, who must be confirmed by the Senate, and its funding comes directly from Congress.[101] In 2022 it had an operating budget of $35.5 billion.[102] This is a sizable budget, but it is used to cover an enormous number of issues. As mentioned, the EPA oversees a wide array of sectors, not just water. It regulates pesticides on farms, tracks landfills, measures air quality, regulates toxic chemicals in industrial manufacturing, and oversees buildings for scourges like mold and bedbugs. Not only does it investigate environmental violations, but it also looks into fraud and waste. In short, it is an enormous agency that attempts to address nearly every facet of US environmental well-being. With such a full slate, one might expect the EPA to have a presence in every state, perhaps even every municipality. In fact, it manages only ten regional branches.[103] With approximately 152,000 public water systems in the United States,[104] it's no wonder the country has so much difficulty monitoring them all.

The more entities one controls, the more difficult it is to monitor and regulate them. The fragmentation inherent in a network of independent municipal and regional providers—like the current system in the United States—decreases efficiency, transparency, and ease of monitoring. The UK water companies each serve a large customer base of 7.6 million people on average, or 3 million households. When such large systems are in play, there is less room for hiding and greater scrutiny from the press (although, as we saw, even with fewer authorities, UK regulators missed some key violations). Compare this to the Karegnondi Authority, which served only 80,000 residents.

In addition to the federal EPA, every state has its own environmental agency that oversees local infrastructure. These agencies draw funding from state governments, as well as from EPA grants, loans, and fellowship programs. The EPA spends a large amount of its budget on research and action for long-term programs—in 2022, for instance, it allocated $1.8 billion to address climate change preparedness[105]—but much of the EPA budget is diverted to states and municipalities on the basis of need. For example, in

2022 the EPA awarded $147 million in grants to 277 communities across the country to clean up and rehabilitate brownfield projects—land or building sites contaminated by pollutants or otherwise in need of environmental treatment.[106] It granted another $50 million for air quality control through 132 grants and similar numbers for each of its main areas of concern: land, water, and air.

To a great extent, the immediate work of regulating infrastructure is left to state agencies, while the federal EPA exists to fill in the gaps and help address major disasters. Findings from a study of regulatory efficiency and drinking water quality violations published in the *Proceedings of the Academy of National Sciences* suggest that the EPA could benefit from increased communication across sectors such as land and water.[107] If the EPA served as a point of centralization for independent, specialized agencies, it could better focus on the bigger picture. Consolidation of authorities is a good starting point. But these new, more powerful authorities must be paired with oversight bodies of comparable power.

The United States needs a sector-specific regulator that works with municipalities and investors to develop long-term water strategies. Given how divisive the EPA has become in the last years, it is difficult to imagine such a broad expansion of its powers. Since 2011 the Republican Party has tried to reduce considerably the scope of the EPA,[108] and President Trump proposed abolishing the EPA altogether.[109] Though Trump did not succeed, in 2020 the Supreme Court, in *EPA v. West Virginia*, ruled to strike key powers of the EPA.[110] And the Supreme Court further limited the role of the EPA when it ruled in *Sackett v. EPA* in 2023 that the federal government has much narrower jurisdictional protection of wetlands than in the past. Wetlands play a critical role as filters for major pollutants dumped in the water system. This will further complicate the regulatory framework for water management across the United States.[111]

Perhaps if infrastructure investment were in part handled by the private sector, the calculus on this front would change. After all, if government came to view its job as primarily regulatory, Congress might be more enthusiastic about diverting funds to regulation. If states encouraged greater private sector participation, then the need for a statewide regulator such as Ofwat, or "EPA Water," would be critical. The United States needs to seriously analyze what other countries have developed in this area. Not surprisingly, most of the research on funding the water sector, and in particular P3s, has been conducted in Europe and emerging markets rather than the United States.[112]

The United States is at a turning point in the history of its infrastructure. Its urgent needs call for a massive transformation of infrastructure. The Biden administration launched the IIJA and has followed up with fundamental actionable recommendations. The solutions are known. The country just needs to implement them. Privatization of water infrastructure makes sense in many cases, though not all, especially if accompanied by a strong independent regulatory office, as the Biden administration has recommended. But as we will see in the next chapter, introducing privatization is much easier said than done.

four

ABOVE AND BEYOND

Investing in Bridges and the Chicago Privatization Efforts

COLONEL SAITO: "One question: can you finish the bridge in time?"
— *The Bridge on the River Kwai* (1957)

In 2002, on the campaign trail for his fifth term as mayor of Chicago, Richard M. Daley expounded the necessity of involving the private sector in the city's finances. Daley promised private participation would both relieve the city's debt and secure the best services, a message he had advanced since his first election in 1989.[1] The scion of one of Chicago's most prominent political families, Daley wielded enough influence to broach an idea that many US politicians feared would provoke public backlash. But with city expenses outpacing revenue and bond service costs soaring,[2] Daley insisted Chicago needed to try bold, novel solutions. In the 2002 election, voters agreed, delivering Daley a landslide victory (he took 78.5 percent of the vote) and a mandate to pursue his technocratic agenda.[3] "Private and corporate contributions are more important than ever, in light of the serious budget problems facing our state and local governments," he proclaimed in his 2003 inaugural address.[4]

The motivations behind involving the private sector are many, including efficiency, large-scale investment programs that a state budget cannot undertake, expertise, and various other objectives. The most controversial argument for privatization, though, has always been couched in terms of a financial crisis and the urgent need to close a budget deficit. Critics see such a response to crisis as akin to selling the family jewels in order to make it to another day.

The idea of selling the family jewels to pay off debt is familiar to many Americans, and so it is logical that government actions would be understood in this way, too. The American middle class is not as prosperous as

94

one might think. In a survey conducted by the Federal Reserve Bank in 2016, 47 percent of Americans said they would need to sell something or borrow money if they were faced with a $400 emergency expense.[5] This sense of fear about debt and living in a state of constant precarity is integral to the American psyche going back to the founding of modern America. After all, this country is made up of immigrants, many of whom left their homelands with little means to start a new life. American literature is full of references to the plight of the American household finding itself indebted, from Ben Franklin's dictum that he would "rather go to bed without dinner than to rise in debt," to John Steinbeck's *The Grapes of Wrath* and Arthur Miller's *Death of a Salesman*. One should remember that one of America's favorite authors, Washington Irving, became the author of "Sleepy Hollow" and other favorite stories because his family went bankrupt, and he could not stand the humiliation. The theme of debt and bankruptcy runs through American movie culture, too, from Frank Capra's *It's a Wonderful Life* to the Coen brothers' *Fargo* and the Safdie brothers' *Uncut Gems*.

Though municipalities may resemble indebted American households, this narrative gets projected onto municipalities in somewhat misleading ways. Whenever mayors or governors propose privatization of infrastructure assets, the first question is always: Why are we "selling" the family jewels? But this question is the wrong one to ask. To the extent a state faces a deficit, the question is how to address it. Will it be through an increase in taxes, a reduction in expenditures, or both? When looking at selling assets, the next question to ask is: How would the proceeds be used? To pay down the deficit to avoid raising taxes, or to rebuild the economy? Municipalities do not need to "sell" anything. A long-term concession on an asset could raise funds that would allow the state to improve the operation of what may be a poorly managed asset, starved for maintenance and capital improvement. The state can then retake control of the asset at the end of the concession term. Municipalities may face debt woes familiar to American families, but they have many more options and powers at their disposal.

These were the questions and issues, in any event, that Mayor Daley had to navigate in addressing the concerns of his constituency. Daley's strategy for including the private sector in city services eventually developed into a pathbreaking plan. In coordination with the city council, the mayor announced that Chicago would privatize the Chicago Skyway, an elevated, six-lane highway that cuts diagonally through the south side of the city, making it the first toll bridge and toll road in the United States to be leased to private operators in a long time, certainly since World War II.[6] This approach is not new in the United States, as previously discussed. The first US toll bridge was built in 1785 across the Charles River in Massachusetts, connecting Boston with Charlestown. It had a forty-year concession, and a special purpose company was created to manage the bridge.[7] A collection of prospective buyers quickly emerged, and in 2004 a private consortium led by the development firms Cintra and Macquarie took control of the Skyway under a ninety-nine-year lease, paying the city $1.83 billion in return.[8]

The story of Daley's intervention in Chicago's infrastructure, in particular the privatization of the Chicago Skyway, reveals some of the inefficiencies and limitations that come with infrastructure management by public bureaucracy and the challenge of explaining the long-term objectives of private involvement and getting a buy-in from the majority of the public. The Skyway privatization effort faced several limitations, including interstate discoordination, legislative roadblocks, and mounting bond obligations. These issues arise for nearly all large-scale infrastructure assets, from the electricity grid to wastewater systems to railroads. It isn't surprising then that Chicago's decision to privatize the Skyway spurred debate about private infrastructure across the country and served as a model for the long-term privatization of other state infrastructure for some—most notably in Indiana, which privatized its toll road in 2006—but also as a warning to anyone who would dare to think of involving the private sector in managing our infrastructure assets. Indeed, some of the later P3 projects undertaken by the city—such as the Chicago parking meter system—were mired in public controversy. Though not all agree that Chicago's privatization of the Skyway has been a success, it undoubtedly provided essential lessons for subsequent privatizations, especially concerning the question of how to manage tolls. The experience of Chicago offers a road map for responding to concerns about selling the family jewels and how municipalities should think about P3s.

Economists often lump bridges together with roads (they are after all extensions of the roadway), but bridges deserve special attention, especially in the context of P3s. The case of bridges is unique and, perhaps more than any other infrastructure sector, calls for innovative and aggressive solutions. The problem of financing and maintaining bridges poses a fundamentally different and more daunting challenge than that of roads. In the first place, bridges entail considerably more serious risks than roads—the catastrophe of a bridge collapse doesn't compare to the dangers of worn or pothole-filled roads. Bridges require a different, more expert kind of oversight and regulation, which is why within the Federal Highway Administration, unique and elaborate regulations that differ markedly from road and tunnel inspections govern the inspection of bridges.[9]

Second, and more significantly, the construction and maintenance of bridges involves an entirely different category of investment in comparison to roads and highways. The cost of constructing a new mile of roadway in 2023 has increased substantially.[10] For many municipalities, this is already prohibitively expensive, but compared to the average price of bridge repairs and construction, it is a drop in the bucket. Consider the $1.5 billion price tag for the replacement of the Goethals Bridge in New York in 2018,[11] or the $6.5 billion reconstruction of the Oakland Bay Bridge, which was completed in 2013.[12] The Hong Kong-Zhuhai-Macau Bridge, which spans the South China Sea and is the longest bridge in the world, cost $20 billion to construct.[13] The upshot is that while municipal and state governments typically finance their own road repairs and even expansions, the capital requirements for replacing and repairing bridges lie outside the scope of most local governments.

Federal spending often makes up for what states and cities cannot afford, but the scope of the crisis confronting bridges in the United States exceeds even the most substantial federal allocations. The 2021 Infrastructure Investment and Jobs Act (IIJA) provided an essential increase in investment in bridges—it was the largest federal commitment to bridges since the creation of the national highways system in the 1950s.[14] However, the $110 billion set aside for roads and bridges by the Biden administration still left a yawning investment gap. To restore all US bridges to good condition would take $22 billion annually (for bridges alone!) over as many as fifty years, and that excludes any new ventures or investments in new technology.

According to the American Society of Civil Engineers, in 2021 there were 231,000 bridges in need of repair and maintenance; 46,154 were in "poor" condition, requiring overhaul or replacement. More concerning, engineers typically plan that bridges will require reconstructive repair or outright replacement after fifty years of use. Some 42 percent of US bridges are over fifty years old, with the vast majority rapidly approaching that cut off.[15] Bridge collapses are already far too common. Between 1987 and 2011, 103 bridges across the United States failed, either collapsing or requiring closure for repairs.[16] As time continues to wear away these assets, the risk of such collapses increases dramatically. The IIJA should help over the coming years, but this is only to make up for the lack of serious investment in the last decades. It will be possible to reduce these risks, but not if we continue with our traditional funding strategies. In June 2023 a stretch of Interstate

I-95 collapsed. The I-95 is one of the most important freight corridors in the United States, carrying twenty-one million tons of freight worth over $100 billion. The repair under normal procurement process would have taken months if not a full year. As Eric Goldwyn of New York University's Arron Institute of Urban Management stated in *Bloomberg*: "In our system we have both a problem of diffuse power where we don't know exactly who is in charge, but we also have these moments of incredible centralized power where a governor, a mayor, a president whatever can act and enact things quickly."[17] Repairing the stretch of the bridge that collapsed in just two weeks was unheard of. The principal reason it was done so quickly seems to be that the governor was able to sign an emergency declaration that allowed the state to overrule the usual bidding rules and mobilize all the necessary resources.

The United States is not the only country to have bridges collapse. In 2022 the Morbi Bridge collapse in India killed 141 people. In 2018 the Morandi Bridge in Genoa, Italy, collapsed, resulting in 43 fatalities. How do other countries repair and replace bridges? How do they invest in them? In the United States, investment in repairs and replacements does not match the rate of deterioration, meaning that even as we fix those bridges that are already in poor condition, an even greater number will become dangerously old in the meantime.[18] As more bridges fall into poor condition, we should review the model of privatization adopted by Chicago for its Skyway and other states that have managed to privatize infrastructure.

Throughout its history, Chicago's economic vibrancy depended on embracing the newest forms of transportation infrastructure, from canals to railroads to expressways, and hence also the newest ways to finance transportation infrastructure. With this in mind, Chicago's privatization strategy under the Daley administration deserves serious consideration.

The Chicago Skyway: An Emergency

The story of Chicago's Skyway originates in a larger story about roads and the patchwork manner in which our networks of roads are built. It ends, however, with new attitudes toward privatized bridges in the United States. In the first half of the twentieth century, Chicago aggressively pursued the infrastructure transformations ushered in by the age of the automobile. Well before the United States acted to dramatically expand the National Highway System in the 1950s, Chicago had laid out plans for an extensive network of expressways radiating out from the center of the city,[19] which was defined by a road known as "the Loop," after a nineteenth-century cable car that circled the downtown area.

The city's commitment to road development stemmed from a long history of enjoying the benefits of first-class infrastructure. Chicago's prominence in the Midwest region is derived, in part, from its ports on Lake Michigan, located in the center of the Loop. But other cities, like Milwaukee, Detroit, and Cleveland, were similarly well situated on the lake and roughly as old. The real key to Chicago's dominance was railroads. Compared to other regional hubs, Chicago had a preponderance of rail connections to major cities to the south and west, making it the most productive distribution center for industry. In the 1850s Chicago rapidly expanded its rail lines, leading to an explosion of commerce that helped Chicago bloom into a singular metropolis off the East Coast in the second half of the nineteenth century.[20]

Recognizing early that the automobile would transform the country in much the same way as the railroad, Chicago jumped on the development of roads with the same fervor with which it had coveted railroads in the 1850s. A couple of figures exercised particular influence in initiating the city's prescient road projects, both of whom had backgrounds in railroads. First was the architect and urban planner Daniel Burnham, who contributed the design for the skeleton of Chicago's road system. Known as the Chicago Plan, or the Burnham plan, the design imagined a series of roadways stretching out like sun rays from Chicago's central Loop, leading to its surrounding suburbs and into the American West. Despite Burnham's early death in 1912, over the next forty years the city followed the architect's vision nearly exactly.[21] The execution of Burnham's plan occurred in part thanks to another central figure in road development: the banker and financier William Edens, an all but forgotten character today save for the Chicago expressway that bears his name. Vice president of the Central Trust Company, one of Chicago's principal banks, assistant general superintendent of Chicago's Post Office, and president of the Illinois Highway Improvement Association, Edens championed both the road project and an innovative way to finance it. Edens advocated that the city issue bonds to private investors in order to fund the transition from a railroad capital to an automobile city.[22] The interest on these loans, according to Edens's plan, could be paid with a $12 annual car registration fee.[23] Edens was the perfect example of the early entrepreneurial spirit that built American infrastructure. Born in 1864, three years into the Civil War, in Richmond, Indiana, an early Quaker settlement in the region, he started his career as a telegraph messenger and then joined the railroad business as an assistant station master, soon becoming a passenger train conductor. His obituary describes him as a promoter of good roads: one more figure in the establishment of our infrastructure system.[24]

With one foot planted in the world of private finance and one in the public arena, Edens could promise coordination between the two worlds and guaranteed that private investors, including the Central Trust Company, would purchase the bonds at reasonable interest rates. The city adopted the plan, and in 1918, under Edens's guidance, Chicago sold $60 million in municipal bond issuances, which, in conjunction with funding from both the federal and state governments, allowed the city to build forty-eight hundred miles of road.[25] Edens established the precedent in Chicago for infrastructure to be financed through the issuance of bonds, but as the leader of the Highway Association he also oversaw subsequent road planning. In 1939 he urged the city to develop the wide boulevards designed by Burnham into modern expressways, in what the city termed the Comprehensive Superhighway Program.[26] These expressways still serve as the central arteries in the city today. The first to be completed were the Tri-State Expressway (renamed the Kingery Expressway), which opened in 1950; the Eisenhower Expressway, also in 1950; and the Calumet Expressway (now the Bishop Ford Expressway), in 1951. As a financier and public servant, Edens embodied the cooperation between public and private sectors that Mayor Daley hoped to foster again in the twenty-first century.

Importantly, the Chicago Skyway was not part of the original Chicago Plan. Rather, city officials announced plans for the Chicago Skyway (initially called the Calumet Skyway) in 1954, in large part as a reaction to the construction of a long toll road in neighboring Indiana.[27] Indeed, the Chicago Skyway would likely not exist at all had it not been for the lack of coordination between Illinois and Indiana. The Indiana Toll Road Commission, established in 1951, had originally promised that its new state highway would run East-West, extending the path of the Ohio turnpike to link up with Illinois's Tri-State Expressway, which had just opened. However, in 1953 the Indiana Commission announced the toll road would no longer be simply East-West, but also North-South, turning at Indianapolis to connect to Gary, a newly prosperous industrial city situated immediately on Chicago's southern border with Indiana. Chicago officials panicked. Rather than route vehicles into the southwest of Chicago, where motorists would have a choice of entries into the city, the Indiana toll road would now dump its northbound traffic directly into one of Chicago's most congested areas, just south of the Loop where traffic in and out of the ports was worst.[28] One city alderman called the construction of the Indiana Toll Road an "emergency situation,"[29] and another city councilor lamented, "Transportation planning could become a hopeless task."[30] All agreed a new outlet would be needed to alleviate congestion. This new road would require the construction of a new bridge across the Calumet River, which at the time had only narrow, two-lane crossings.

In the proposal announced by city lawmakers in 1954, the Chicago Skyway would pick up directly where the Indiana Toll Road left off and whisk vehicles through the clogged arteries on a raised highway with few exits, preventing cars from merging into the most heavily congested sections of the city. Despite the city's sense of urgency, however, state officials from the Illinois Toll Road Commission were unmoved and rejected the city's request for a new toll road. Searching for workarounds, the city discovered that no state authorization was required to build a new toll bridge, and so the Chicago Skyway was categorized as a bridge, eschewing the need for state involvement, and was built using solely city funds and municipal bonds. This fact would prove essential to Daley's privatization of the road in the mid-2000s. In 1958, two years after the completion of the Indiana Toll Road, the Chicago Skyway opened to motorists.

From the very beginning, the Skyway underperformed. On its opening day, the toll bridge and connector road saw less than half the anticipated traffic. For the following three decades, the bridge would rarely carry more than half its capacity.[31] The low ridership devastated the financial projections for the bridge, as the city expected to use revenue from tolls to fulfill its obligations on the bonds used to finance it. From its first year the Skyway ran a deficit, and in 1963 the municipal bonds went into default. It was the largest municipal default in US history and carried that unfortunate superlative until 1983.[32] The Skyway remained in default until the late 1980s, just as Mayor Daley came to power.

For decades, scholars, columnists, and the public deemed the Skyway a failure, both for bondholders and for the city. In addition to its poor returns, the Skyway had some obvious drawbacks. For instance, its few on-ramps and exits made it of limited use for local residents and even a nuisance to navigate—"more of an obstacle than a benefit to local traffic," as the urban infrastructure historian Louise Nelson Dyble writes.[33] The Skyway also bifurcated the south side of Chicago, cutting neighborhoods in half and disrupting the local residential and commercial flow.[34] In particular, it isolated the neighborhood of South Chicago, which beginning in the 1920s had become home primarily to working-class African American families.[35]

How did Chicago get it so wrong? Why did this urgent construction end up looking unnecessary? One might assume that the expectation that there would be heavy congestion resulted from inexpert hand-wringing on the part of Chicago officials, but this was not the case. The city's traffic projections had been confirmed by one of the most renowned private consultancies in the country at the time, Coverdale and Calpitts, which calculated annual traffic on the Chicago Skyway would go from fifteen million cars upon opening to over twenty-five million by 1990. In reality, between 1958 and 1990 annual traffic on the Skyway was consistently below ten million vehicles.[36] Both the experts and the politicians misjudged—evidence of the difficulty of predicting urban trends and the risks of infrastructure plans built around such forecasts.

Projecting traffic growth for newly built bridges or roads is notoriously difficult. That is because there is no historical data on which to build projections. The modeler needs therefore to assume a whole economic system, not just for the particular road or bridge but also for the immediate region as a whole, modeling all the roads, economic growth, and alternative means of transport, a near impossible task even today with the use of highly sophisticated data analytics. Though why estimates strayed so completely from reality remains unsolved, Dyble offers a few answers as to what may have happened. As a one-off solution to a hypothetical problem, the Skyway served only one real purpose—to manage Indiana Toll Road runoff—and did not fit into Chicago's larger system of roads. Because of this, Dyble writes, "The Skyway was uniquely positioned to *avoid* traffic because of its relationship with surrounding areas and its lack of integration with emerging regional highway systems" (emphasis added).[37] The hasty, reactive planning of the Skyway likely contributed to this lack of integration with the city's highway plan, making the road difficult to access and of limited use to the residents. But this problem arose as a result of a larger one. The true issue lay in the lack of cooperation between Indiana and Illinois, an "egregious failure of coordination," in Dyble's words.

The Indiana Toll Road catalyzed the construction of the underperforming Skyway, and six years after its opening, another Indiana road would undermine Skyway traffic. In 1964 Indiana cut the ribbon on a new stretch of freeway, known as the Burns-Harbor Interchange, which connected the Indiana Toll Road to the toll-free Tri-State Expressway just east of Gary, in

Illinois[38]—as had been the original plan in 1951. This meant that traffic heading west could avoid the Skyway toll entirely, obviating the original need for the bridge. Revenue sank even further, dashing any hope of bringing Skyway bonds out of default.[39]

The Skyway foundered not only from interstate discoordination but also because of intrastate tensions. The city found itself in conflict not only with Indiana but also with Illinois and the state Highway Authority. Because Chicago had worked around state government to build the bridge and road and had financed it independently, Illinois felt no obligation to alleviate the city's debt or assist with maintenance.[40] In fact, well before Indiana's Burns-Harbor exchange, the state of Illinois, flush with capital after the passage of the 1956 Federal Highway Act, contributed funding for additional freeways through Chicago that also undercut the profitability of the Skyway.[41] Construction on a section of connector road between the Bishop Ford Expressway and the Dan Ryan Expressway began in 1957 and was completed in 1962, creating the first, toll-free alternative to the Skyway.

The story of the Skyway does not end with failure, however. With the election of Mayor Richard M. Daley in 1989, Chicago embraced a new approach to governance. Engaging the private sector for greater investment in city infrastructure and enforcing stricter economic controls on the city's assets, Daley lifted Chicago out of the malaise into which it had fallen since the 1960s.

Privatization of the Chicago Skyway

In the 1970s and 1980s the era of large-scale federal investment in urban infrastructure came to an end. Some give this closure a precise date: Richard Nixon's 1973 declaration that America's "cities crisis" was over,[42] and that the federal government's investment responsibilities to cities had been satisfied. In response, municipalities across the country began shifting from a managerial model of governance to an entrepreneurial one.[43] To this day, scholars of urban planning and public policy debate the concept of the "entrepreneurial city,"[44] but in broad terms it posits that the primary job of city officials is to generate economic growth, often in competition with other municipalities.[45]

Richard M. Daley adopted this new model for Chicago with enthusiasm. His father, the legendary Chicago mayor Richard J. Daley, had governed the city from 1955 to 1976 and overseen the construction of the city's elaborate expressway infrastructure, earning him the sobriquet "Dick the Builder."[46] Richard M. Daley wanted to match his father's legacy, and by most measures, he succeeded. He tied his father for most terms served by a Chicago mayor (six) and left behind a comparably indelible mark on the city's character and image.

An entrepreneurial model suited the city of Chicago well, and Daley's experimentation with the privatization of infrastructure was as likely to win approval there as anywhere in the country. Since the 1950s Chicago had been a hotbed of free market economic theory. The pathbreaking work of economists Milton Friedman and George Stigler, at the University of Chicago, argued that the free market would produce a better quality of life and greater amounts of freedom and equality than any well-intentioned government program. As Friedman famously told the television personality Phil Donahue during an interview: "There is no alternative way, so far discovered, of improving the lot of the ordinary people that can hold a candle to the productive activities that are unleashed by a free enterprise system."[47] Friedman's ideas influenced the city, the country, and the world. Credited with coining the term *neoliberalism* to describe his economic theory, Friedman became an adviser to Nixon and, according to then attorney general Edwin Meese, was an economic "guru" to Ronald Reagan.[48] Friedman's influence extended around the world, particularly impacting Chile, which after the collapse of the socialist government of Salvador Allende instituted austere free market principles under the advisement of Friedman, including the privatization of much of the state's infrastructure. It was reasonable to believe that a city steeped in neoliberal thinking would make a good proving ground for greater private sector involvement in infrastructure delivery.

Daley envisioned his new Chicago as a service economy that would cater to multinational corporations, bringing in jobs, tourism, and investment. This would be a continuation of the city's proud tradition as a center of trade, even if it was no longer a center of industry as well.[49] Chicago's revitalization involved a conscious and costly effort to change perceptions of the city[50]—in short, to rebrand it. (In this respect, too, Chicago set an example for many smaller cities, which in the 2010s attempted to generate growth through branding campaigns.)[51] Through a series of high-profile construction projects the Daley administration threw off the city's old associations with organized crime and political corruption to present a modern image that would attract new residents, boost tourism, and drum up revenue. The most notable of the new Chicago landmarks was Millennium Park, a twenty-five-acre, sculpture-strewn greenway designed by the architect Frank Gehry. Part of the intention in these projects was to attract Fortune 500 companies to relocate their headquarters to Chicago, an effort led by an economic development group, World Business Chicago. The plan succeeded; McDonald's, Boeing, and United Airlines moved their offices to downtown Chicago, delivering a jolt of economic activity to the city.

The political and economic landscape for building such projects had shifted since Daley's father's construction boom, however, and his ambitions for a "New Chicago" could not rely on federal or state help.[52] Instead, Daley's urban rejuvenation would count on private capital, and many investors came forward. The mayor conceived Millennium Park itself as a solely private venture (though in actuality the $200 million raised through private institutions ultimately required additional loans as a result of overruns, including $100 million from the city).[53] The role of private investments in these paradigm-shifting icons of a new Chicago allayed fears in the city about private participation in civil infrastructure, particularly as many private contributions were made in exchange solely for naming rights.[54]

From the beginning of his career, Daley eyed the Chicago Skyway as a potential source of additional revenue. In 1989, the year of his first election, the toll bridge turned a profit for the first time in twenty years.[55] After thirty years of development, congestion on I-94 and I-90 worsened, and the city finally needed the additional lanes offered by the Skyway.[56] Additionally, the Skyway increased its profitability by increasing tolls. Government managers did initiate these sustaining toll hikes themselves, but only after bondholders sued the city for faster progress on repayment.[57] (As with Chicago's parking system privatization, the city was never willing or able to increase rates except through a third party.)

Daley cannot claim credit for the recovery of the Skyway, but he did capitalize on it. In the early 1990s, the Skyway had turned its finances around to such a degree that the city paid off its initial bond obligations of $101 million. By 1994, ten years prior to its privatization, the Skyway was generating $17 million in annual revenue above maintenance and debt payments.[58] According to municipal laws, once the Skyway cleared its debts the city could issue further bonds against future revenue from the bridge. The Daley administration issued an additional $110 million in bonds and in 1996 issued another set totaling $183 million. Chicago's rebrand was underway.

Residents objected to Daley's strategy for the Skyway, however, arguing that improvements to the city should not come from toll revenue, which affected only a small portion of the city, but from universal taxes. To keep tolls low, revenue should only be used to maintain the Skyway, went the argument. In 1998, two toll-payers sued the city of Chicago over the fares, claiming the high toll violated interstate commerce statutes by charging more than was needed to maintain the bridge.[59] A federal judge dismissed the suit, but the debate continues to this day. This debate belies a much more fundamental issue of equitable distribution. Who should pay for these services? Should the user bear the brunt, or should the taxpayer pay? And if the taxpayer bears the cost, which taxpayers? All of them, or those with the highest income level? We will discuss this issue in more detail in the next chapter in the context of the gasoline tax used to maintain roads.

Anyway, Daley had his own complaints about the fund-raising strategy, though they tended in the opposite direction. A long-standing tradition in Chicago dictated that revenue from expressway bond issuances could only be used to invest further in surface infrastructure;[60] it would be illegal to issue a bond for an expressway and use the capital to upgrade the sewer system, for instance. Daley's vision for the city's revitalization required investment in much more than roads, which thus limited the value of the newly profitable Skyway.

Because the city owned the toll bridge independently, the state had no say in its management, and if it chose to, the city could sell it unilaterally. This independence, known as "Home Rule," may be the key reason Chicago managed to be the first major American city to experiment with privatization in the twenty-first century. As Kent Rowey told me:

> The privatizations in Chicago were all a function of having autonomy as a first-class city within Illinois. Illinois has a legal system where you have class-one cities that basically are exempt from state procurement laws and have quite a bit of autonomy. Chicago didn't have to worry about state laws or going back to the Illinois legislature. I think that was a distinguishing feature. If you want to do something at the state level, you do it in a state that has a legal system where first-class cities can basically write their own destiny. When you combine that independence with P3 legislation, you've got a pretty powerful combination to set the right tone to do these P3 investments.

This is precisely what Chicago counted on, and it paid off. And in the aspects that had less clear benefits, Chicago provided invaluable experience for other US cities interested in the same sort of solutions.

In 2004 Daley's administration issued a request for qualifications to entertain offers on the toll bridge from private investors. The city invited five bidders to submit proposals for operations of the toll bridge, including a bid of $700 million from a French and Canadian consortium led by Vinci Concessions, one of the largest private operators of roads, bridges, and airports in the world, which is traded on the French stock exchange, as well as a $500 million offer from Abertis, a Spanish conglomerate that specializes in private highways. The winning proposal came from a group of investors that named itself the Skyway Concessions Company, a consortium of companies led by the Spanish firm Cintra, a private operator of roads and airports, and the Australian Macquarie Infrastructure Company, one of the largest private investors in infrastructure in the world.

The Skyway Concession Company's proposal involved a ninety-nine-year lease, giving the company the right to all toll revenue in exchange for handling all operating expenses, including major maintenance, such as repaving, as well as incidental costs like snow removal. The Skyway Concession Company paid the city $1.83 billion up front for the operation rights, more than twice the second highest bid. Chicago retained the right to reclaim operation of the bridge if Skyway Concessions faced bankruptcy or violated the terms of the agreement. It also established restrictions on when and how the private operator could raise toll rates.[61] I remember bidding on the asset at Morgan Stanley before the Morgan Stanley infrastructure platform had launched. At the time, Morgan Stanley was bidding to make principal investments, and I argued that these infrastructure investments could be attractive opportunities for pension funds and that Morgan Stanley should invest in the asset. If I remember correctly, our bid was below $500 million, so the $1.8 billion the city received was a home run!

The $1.83 billion far exceeded the city's expectations (it anticipated around $650 million for the sale), and the additional revenue led to unanticipated benefits. Immediately, the city used the windfall to pay off substantial portions of its debt, including the entirety of its extant Skyway debt ($463 million), a portion of the city's long-term debt ($134 million), and some of its short-term debt ($258 million).[62] This debt relief freed revenue for other services and bulwarked the city's credit rating, which in 2003 included a number of A– grades.[63] But Chicago did something else innovative with the proceeds from the concession: it established a $500 million long-term reserve fund, a "rainy day" fund that could be invested in infrastructure and other areas in perpetuity as need arose. This fund continued to grow as Daley kept pursuing his plan for an "entrepreneurial city." The remaining capital, $100 million, Daley directed into a "neighborhood, human, and business infrastructure fund,"[64] including Meals on Wheels and other social programs.

It is perhaps surprising, given that privatization has become fairly controversial in the intervening years,[65] that in 2004 the sale of the Chicago Skyway to a private company was met with almost no resistance. There were figures in leadership positions who objected to the terms of the deal, if not the deal itself. Notably, the president of the watchdog group Civic Federation, Laurence Msall, criticized Daley for his decision to spend so much of the city's new capital so quickly, arguing that the city needed to preserve those funds more conservatively for the future.[66] Msall may have had a point; today the city once more suffers from looming debt and has returned to heavy borrowing to pay its bills.[67]

In many ways the confusion about the benefits of privatization of operating assets stems from the controversy around how to use the proceeds. There is greater acceptance of P3s when the infrastructure project is new—a "greenfield" project. That is because the private operator needs to build a facility that does not exist. Monetizing an existing asset is an altogether different matter for many people. Once the funds are collected from a public-private partnership like the Chicago Skyway, what should the city do with them? Establish a fund for a rainy day? Pay down debt? Use it to improve other infrastructure? In many situations, privatization has been used to avoid tax increases that would otherwise have been necessary to fund a deficit. There is no right or wrong answer, but transparency about how proceeds will be used encourages buy-in from taxpayers. When residents understand and approve of the payoffs, they are more likely to consider privatization. While privatization might result in higher tariffs for users, it also produces funding for other services. Most taxpayers recognize the benefits of such trade-offs.[68]

The use of up-front payments to the city is a policy issue independent of the privatization mechanism. Daley decided to repay debt and create a long-term fund. This choice helped secure Chicago's credit rating and freed funds scheduled for debt service to be used for other purposes. That may have been the best choice for the city, though inevitably that will be subject to political debate. We should not confuse the policy question with the separate managerial question of privatization. As the poll shows, residents by and large approved of the management structure, even if they might disagree about how to use the proceeds.

After the success of the public-private partnership to build Millennium Park and the privatization of the Skyway, the mayor advanced his privatization plans further—perhaps too far for the people of Chicago. He next proposed that the city lease a handful of parking garages around the main Loop

Road, then suggested privatization of Midway Airport (which did not go through), and finally the privatization of parking meters. In 2009 Chicago leased thirty-six thousand parking spaces to Morgan Stanley Infrastructure Partners for $1.2 billion on a seventy-five-year lease.[69] In addition to paying down further debt, Chicago used the up-front capital to add $300 million to its reserve trust, which then totaled $800 million.[70]

At the time, I was leading the Morgan Stanley Infrastructure Fund and was proud to have been part of this privatization because of the belief that municipalities, in general, should not be in the business of running nonessential assets like parking systems so long as the terms of a concession to a private operator meet the public policy objectives of the city, and this is not just from a policy objective standpoint, but from a practical investment perspective. If there is no support, sooner or later the private operator will pay the price. We had teamed up with Alan Lazowski, the head of Laz Parking, who was a gregarious person, full of life and always optimistic. At the time of our bid, we had spent quite some time visiting the parking system, and I remember discussing with Alan its massive size—a series of towering parking complexes that dot the main downtown area. We became good friends, and I still remember reading his father's book, *Faith and Destiny*, about surviving the Holocaust. After living through such a horrifying event, Rabbi Laz still had faith in life and this, I thought, helped explain why Alan so consistently looked on the positive side of life.

We spent the first year redesigning the whole system, even improving signage and developing a new logo (the butterfly, which is still in use today). The parking system also constituted something of a risk, as any investment does, and the city benefited enormously from transferring that risk to the private sector. A year after the concession was signed, the 2008 financial crisis hit. As a result, the loop parking system failed financially, despite all our best efforts. But the city had protected itself against this financial downturn and had gotten its proceeds up front. Had the city issued municipal bonds against the system, it certainly would have defaulted on them. No one mentions that benefit when talking about Daley's legacy and the Chicago privatization. Today the parking system still operates privately, and no one thinks twice about who owns it. As Deng Xiaoping said: "Black cat or white cat, as long as it catches the mouse, it's a good cat."

The Chicago Skyway itself drew considerable fire in the media for toll increases. The Skyway Concession Company's contract granted it the right to raise fares between 2 and 7 percent annually, calibrated against the city's GDP, and after a twelve-year grace period during which it could not raise the toll rate at all.[71] In 2004, prior to privatization, the toll bridge charged $2 for passenger vehicles to access the road and $11.80 for trucks with seven axles. By 2022, six years after the end of the grace period, the ride cost $5.90 for cars and $48.60 for commercial trucks.[72] An analytic review of the horizon of these increases found that at this rate, the fare for the bridge will be between $65 and $1,800 by the end of the ninety-nine-year lease.[73] Of course, as we saw regarding the water sector in England, it is more likely this rate of increase will stabilize or fall once the true price of the bridge's upkeep and operation becomes apparent.

Tolls are only one element of the Skyway's financial health, and in a wider view, the effects of privatization are more complicated. Dana Levenson, the city's chief financial officer during the Skyway sale, defended the decision in the face of criticism to the *Chicago Sun Times* in 2022: "We paid off over $800 million in direct Skyway debt and city debt that we haven't had to pay interest on over the past 17 years. We took $500 million, and we put it into a long-term reserve fund which, in and of itself, is making a return. That has actually been beneficial to Chicago's bond ratings."[74] When examining the overall balance sheet of privatization of such megaprojects, it is easy to focus on how they impact average residents' pocketbooks, and this is undoubtedly important. But it can miss the forest for the trees. As Levenson has argued recently, the Chicago deals have paid off in the long run, and Chicago ought to consider participating in new P3 efforts.[75]

There are, as always, more theoretical economic questions involved. On the issue of tolls, Adam Smith advised taking the larger picture into account. Tolls, he believed, were among the most equitable ways to pay for infrastructure. After all, tolls are one of the oldest forms of infrastructure finance. The Old London Bridge, constructed in 1209, paid for its upkeep with a toll.[76] In Book IV of *The Wealth of Nations*, in a section on public works, Smith writes:

> This tax or toll . . . is finally paid by the consumer, to whom it must always be charged in the price of the goods. As the expense of carriage [a bridge, canal, or road], however, is very much reduced by means of such public works, the goods, notwithstanding the toll, come cheaper to the consumer than they could otherwise have done; *their price not being so much raised by the toll, as it is lowered by the cheapness of the carriage* [my emphasis]. The person who finally pays this tax, therefore, gains by the application, more than he loses by the payment of it.[77]

The value of the infrastructure—the ease and efficiency it provides—has such an impact on the overall profits of the users and their ability to conduct commerce that the toll will inevitably be a small price to pay, at least if the alternative is to have no bridge or a road at all. We should, then, gladly pay a premium for the transportation infrastructure we have. If the state cannot or will not finance its infrastructure, then the real price of infrastructure for users involves the conditions established by private operators who can provide the finance to create the modes of "carriage." This is the same argument Ronald Coase made in his famous 1974 article about the economics of the lighthouse.[78]

In some cases, Smith preferred private operators of tolls to public commissioners. "Canals are better in the hands of private persons than of commissioners," he writes. "If [a canal] is not kept in tolerable order, the navigation necessarily ceases altogether, and along with it the whole profit which they can make by the tolls. If those tolls were put under the management of commissioners, who had themselves no interest in them, they might be less attentive to the maintenance of the works."[79] However, Smith also warns that "the tolls for the maintenance of a high road cannot with any safety be made the property of private persons" if there is no incentive to maintain a road. Unlike canals, roads in Smith's time remained passable even in disrepair, so "the proprietors of the tolls upon a high road, therefore, might neglect altogether the repair of the road, and yet continue to levy very nearly the same tolls."[80] The final qualification to his embrace of tolls, and privately managed toll carriages, requires that an operator maintain their infrastructure in good condition. With this in place, Smith is indifferent to who collects the toll, and even how steep the rate is. In our current contracts, the ability to ensure the operator maintains the infrastructure asset occurs through a regulatory framework. The tolls for the Skyway certainly kept the bridge and expressway in good condition, and the city did build in incentives to ensure the private operators would not neglect the Skyway's repairs.

The contract with the Skyway Concession Company not only gave it the right to raise tolls, but also allowed the company, if it desired, to lease the bridge to another firm. In 2015 it exercised this right, selling its interest in the Skyway to a consortium of three Canadian pension funds, which paid $2.8 billion for the toll bridge. The Canadian Pension Plan Investment Board, the Ontario Municipal Employees Retirement System, and the Ontario Teachers' Pension Plan banded together to form an investment group that, in 2015, wielded capital upward of $374 billion.[81] These pension funds then themselves resold the Skyway in 2022, fetching $2 billion for a two-thirds stake in the toll bridge from the Australian firm Atlas Arteria, another major investor in roads around the world (the pension funds retained one-third of their stake).[82] According to these figures, between 2004 and 2022 the value of the Skyway ballooned from $1.8 billion to $4 billion.

Residents worried that the Skyway had been undervalued upon its initial sale, given that only ten years later the Skyway Concession Company sold the same asset for an additional $1 billion, and by 2022 the value had risen even higher. But this objection, again, does not take the whole picture into account. In the first place, due to the real estate transfer tax system in Illinois, the city received an injection of capital each time the asset changed hands—in the most recent trade, the city garnered $22 million. If the city had not privatized in the first place, it would have received nothing. The concern also ignored the fact that the increase in value was in large part due to an increase in operational efficiency and an increase in tolls that allowed the value to go up.

Taking the long view, the more important benefit to the city is the value added through the series of private operators. The tolls generated $114 million in 2021, up $84.9 million from 2020,[83] demonstrating the potential growth remaining in the Skyway project. Dana Levenson put this in perspective in his interview with the *Sun Times*. "What are the implications for the value of the Skyway when it comes back to the city in 2104?" he asked. "Based on the equity value of $3 billion, it's gonna be north of $15 billion in value."[84] In other words, despite criticisms that the city sacrificed long-term earning for a one-time, short-term windfall, Chicago will nevertheless reap long-term benefits from the sale. By allowing private operators to grow the value of the asset outside the limiting conditions of electoral politics, which discourage the toll hikes that make growth possible, it has set itself up to re-claim control over a much more valuable asset when the lease expires. One might argue the length of the lease is too long, or the terms of the contract were flawed, or the proceeds were misdirected, or the city should have kept a residual interest. But in broad strokes the deal planned both short-term and long-term benefits for the city. Several mechanisms can be introduced to ensure that future sales provide lasting upsides to the city, also called "shmuck insurance." For example, one can specify that for any future sales above a certain return, the city would be entitled to receive a certain percentage of the profits. The point is that there are many mechanisms to allow both partners in a P3 to share in the upside if that is a clear objective. Chicago's choices about how to structure their Skyway lease illustrate just one set of possibilities. Other cities and states have made different decisions based on what worked, and what didn't, in Chicago.

Chicago Privatization Today

The public seems to agree with Deng Xiao Ping—at least on this point. Over fifteen years have passed since the privatization of the Skyway, Millennium Park, and Chicago's parking meters, changes that caused much grief and uproar at the time and unfortunately led to negative views of the privatization of operating assets. I was curious to know how Chicagoans felt about these privatizations after the passage of time, so in 2023 I conducted a survey of 1,025 Chicago residents aged eighteen and older to find out.[85]

The first thing to note about the subsequent findings is that 75 percent of those interviewed or surveyed felt that their infrastructure was at least very important or extremely important for their community. While infrastructure may be the most "unsexy" word in the English language, it still is of critical importance to people. Baby Boomers felt that infrastructure was very important for them (77 percent) and, interestingly, Generation X had the same view (77 percent). Millennials' responses were nearly identical, too, with 76 percent responding that infrastructure is "very important."

I also asked whether people trusted city politicians to plan large-scale infrastructure projects efficiently. The majority of those who expressed a definite view did not trust politicians. And interestingly, across income levels, the majority of those who earn less than $50,000 a year, along with those who earn more than $100,000 annually, simply do not trust city politicians to plan large-scale infrastructure projects.

I was especially curious to know if attitudes about privatization had changed over the last fifteen years. Figure 4.1 shows the summary answers when people were asked if they believed that private companies should be allowed to manage infrastructure assets. As the figure shows, 40 percent indicated they would probably approve or definitely approve private companies managing bridges, compared to 32 percent who expressed a negative view. Even when it came to the infamous on-street parking, those who expressed a view were split between supporting and not supporting, with greater support for private operators (39 percent) than against private operators (34 percent). I also looked at any differences among generations; only 34 percent of Baby Boomers said "yes," while 78 percent of Gen Z and 67 percent of Millennials said "yes." The same results were revealed when

Do you believe that private companies should be allowed to manage these various types of infrastructure?

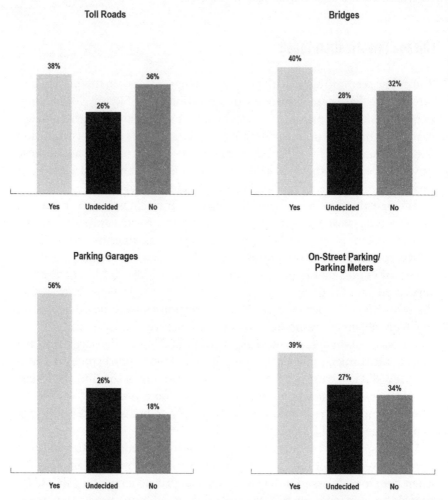

Note: For "Yes," survey respondents indicated "definitely yes" or "probably yes"; for "Undecided," they indicated "might or might not"; for "No," they indicated "definitely not" or "probably not." See Chicagoans and Infrastructure 2023 on the Development Research Institute at NYU's website for the survey methodology and more findings. https://static1.squarespace.com/static/5605cc76e4b0829832a5b0a4/t/64d352e50dddd-8603dad9eb8/1691570917882/Chicagoans+and+Infrastructure+2023.pdf

Figure 4.1. Chicago residents' attitudes toward private management of infrastructure. *Source:* Sadek Wahba, "Chicagoans and Infrastructure Survey, 2023," New York University Development Research Institute, https://static1.squarespace.com/static/5605cc76e4b0829832a5b0a4/t/64d352e50dddd8603dad9eb8/1691570917882/Chicagoans+and+Infrastructure+2023.pdf.

asked about on-street parking: 42 percent of Baby Boomers who expressed an opinion in the survey said "yes" to private operators (with 58 percent saying probably or definitely not), whereas 66 percent of Gen Z and 64 percent of Millennials said "yes." The same trend was also confirmed for toll roads. This generational shift has been completely ignored by the ideological critics of privatization—at their peril.

For me, the question of how proceeds should be used has always been an important indicator of whether a P3 scheme can get public support, so we asked if respondents would be willing to pay more to drive on a toll road if the money was to be used in any of the following ways, as shown in figure 4.2. Some 44 percent of all respondents said "yes," they would pay more if the proceeds would go toward improving social services. The next most popular uses of privatization proceeds were improvements to public transportation and reduction of city debt, followed by reduction of carbon emissions.

As the first toll bridge, and toll highway, to be privatized in the United States, the Chicago Skyway deal inspired others. With an irony we can now better appreciate after understanding the history of the Skyway, the most immediate follower was the Indiana Toll Road, which the state privatized in 2006 in a deal with the same investors who purchased the Skyway, the US division of the Australia giant Macquarie and the Spanish conglomerate Ferrovial, of which Cintra is a subsidiary.

With a few exceptions, efforts to privatize roads in the United States have largely failed (see chapter 5), but when it comes to bridges, the absence of private ownership or operation is even more stark. Of the 230,000 spans in the United States, only one major bridge is entirely privately owned, but the number of toll bridges following the P3 model is growing.[86] There are, in addition, a number of privately owned bridges serving small communities, making short crossings, mostly holdovers from a bygone age when almost all bridges were owned privately.[87]

The only bridge constructed with private funds in the last fifty years, the Fargo-Moorehead Bridge, was designed and built over the Red River, on the border of North Dakota and Minnesota, in 1988 by Bridge Co. The private company was granted a twenty-five-year charter by the state using a BOT, allowing it to construct and operate the bridge for twenty-five years, at which point the company would transfer ownership over to the state. In 2013 state courts granted a five-year extension to the charter, which prompted the cities of Fargo and Moorehead to sue the bridge's owner. The cities won their suit, and in 2018, after the extension expired, the bridge came under public ownership.

Would you be willing to pay more to drive on a toll road if the money was to be used in any of the following ways?

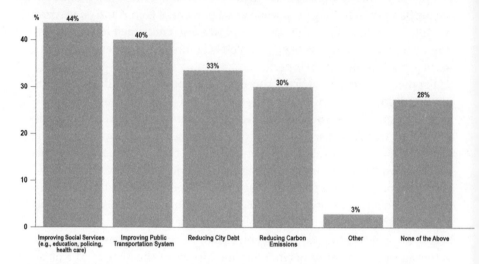

See Chicagoans and Infrastructure 2023 on the Development Research Institute at NYU's website for the survey methodology and more findings. https://static1.squarespace.com/static/5605cc76e4b0829832a5b0a4/t/64d352e50dddd8603dad9eb8/1691570917882/Chicagoans +and+Infrastructure+2023.pdf

Figure 4.2. Chicago residents' priorities for toll revenue. *Source:* Sadek Wahba, "Chicagoans and Infrastructure Survey, 2023," New York University Development Research Institute, https://static1.squarespace.com/static/5605cc76e4b0829832a5b0a4 /t/64d352e50dddd8603dad9eb8/1691570917882/Chicagoans+and+Infrastructure+2023 .pdf.

The Ambassador Bridge, by far the most significant example of a truly privately owned span and still the largest international suspension bridge in the world, also ignited controversy. Designed, built, and operated by a single investor, Joseph A. Bower, the bridge connects Detroit, Michigan, with Windsor, Ontario, on the other side of the Detroit River. To build the bridge, Bower, an eccentric financier,[88] created two companies, one in the United States and one in Canada, and raised $23.5 million in start-up capital ($400 million in 2023 dollars).[89] City leaders had been unwilling to countenance the costs of the bridge, but once it was built, it yielded great profits for its owner. Warren Buffet famously once compared market-dominant or monopoly ownership to ownership of an unregulated toll bridge, because the owner can raise rates at their pleasure.[90] (And indeed, Buffett had a small ownership of the Ambassador Bridge in the 1970s;[91] when Bower sold the bridge in 1979, he attempted to buy the entire asset.)[92]

As construction began on the Ambassador, however, city leaders in Detroit made a final effort to stop Bower's plan, despite its having been cleared by a wide array of governmental bodies in both countries, from the US Congress and the state of Michigan to Canada's Dominion Marine Association, a shipbuilders' association. Detroit's mayor, John W. Smith, called for a city referendum in an attempt to annul the project. Smith argued the private bridge would put too high a financial burden on motorists. The referendum failed, and the bridge project went forward, but that was not the end of controversy. In the twenty-first century, the bridge's private ownership returned to newspapers, but this time for lack of cooperation from the private sector. The longtime owner, Manuel Moroun, who took over the bridge's ownership from Bower (and won the bidding against Buffet), resisted the state of Michigan's order to increase the number of on-ramps. His obstinance landed him briefly in jail before he finally relented. How can such antipathy between private and public sectors be overcome?

Recent developments provide reason to believe the inveterate US allergy to privatized bridges, imbued through the philosophy of the New Deal, may be waning. In 2018 the new Goethals Bridge replacement opened. The new bridge, which spans the Gulfport Reach between New York's Staten Island and Elizabeth, New Jersey, outside Newark, was financed through a partnership between the Port Authority of New York and New Jersey and the NYNJ Link Partnership, a consortium that includes Kiewit, a design, engineering, and construction company, and Macquarie Group, which originally bought the Chicago Skyway.

The first new bridge construction project undertaken by the Port Authority since 1931, when it completed the George Washington Bridge, the Goethals replacement is also the first major bridge project in the Northeast to be financed through a long-term public-private partnership. In the late 1980s, in the same era as Richard M. Daley's first mayoral victory, New York began discussing how to involve private capital to rebuild the bridge.[93] After the 2008 crisis, the plans for privatization looked prescient. With construction costs to rebuild the 1928 bridge reaching $1.5 billion, the NYNJ Link Partnership furnished $106 million up front and was instrumental in securing two loans totaling $927 million. The Port Authority put up the additional $425 million.[94] The value of the private partnership came not just from private capital and management expertise, but also from the NYNJ Link Partnership's ability to raise funds from other sources in the business community.

From the start, the project enjoyed public support, and today the new bridge has provided lane expansions as well as shared-use lanes for pedestrians and cyclists. Unlike in the case of the Skyway, for the Goethals Bridge replacement, the Port Authority maintained control over toll rates. In this sense, the project is more straightforwardly a public-private partnership than the lease model employed by the Chicago Skyway or the Indiana Toll Road. This approach has its benefits and its drawbacks.

In the wake of the successful replacement of the Goethals, other states followed suit. In 2020 the state of Pennsylvania started planning a series of major bridge replacements that would use a similar structure to the one employed by New York, although the state legislature prohibited the use of tolls entirely.[95] The state has slated six major bridges in Pennsylvania for replacement using public-private partnerships.[96] Detroit, too, used a P3 to construct a new bridge—in fact, it built a second bridge to Windsor, Ontario, the Gordie Howe Bridge, a $4.4 billion endeavor by the Windsor-Detroit Port Authority and a conglomerate of construction and infrastructure management firms. It hopes to draw customers from the Ambassador Bridge, creating exactly the sort of competition healthy private sector involvement is meant to yield.

Lessons from Abroad

Databases rarely separate bridges from roads, despite the apparent and important distinctions, which makes it difficult to track the exact number of bridges under private management in the United States or globally. However, the growing number of bridges built and operated through public-private partnerships in the United States reflects an international trend. It's possible to grasp the widespread nature of privatized bridges by reviewing a few examples. The following bridges represent only a portion of all such public-private projects in the world, but they convey the flavor of the overarching trend, in terms of where they are situated and the scale of their construction. A $2 billion, four-lane suspension bridge between Bergen and the island of Sotra, in the fjords on the west coast of Norway, was designed, was built, and is now operated by Macquarie, the concessionaire that first acquired the Chicago Skyway and the Indiana Toll Road, and participated in the Goethals project also.[97] The A-6 suspension bridge in Madrid, a strikingly designed four-lane overpass that opened in 2007, is managed by Ferrovial, also a partner in the Skyway and Indiana Toll Road projects.[98] A private consortium of construction companies owns the €2 billion Øresund Bridge, a nearly five-mile-long bridge that crosses the Øresund Strait between Denmark and Sweden, which opened in 1999.[99] The Vasco de Gama Bridge in Lisbon, Portugal, an enormous construction spanning the mouth of the Tagus River, which cost $1 billion to build and opened in 1998, is operated on concession by Lusoponte, a subsidiary of the French company Vinci.[100] The Confederation Bridge in Canada, an eight-mile stretch between Prince Edward Island and New Brunswick, is operated by the Strait Crossing Bridge Limited, a private consortium that includes Vinci and OMERS, the Ontario public servant pension fund.[101]

In 2007 I visited Kolkata and the Second Vivekananda Bridge,[102] an enormous, privately managed, multispan bridge that crosses the Hooghly River, an offshoot of the Ganges that is also held sacred in Hinduism. It was somewhat surprising, upon arriving at the bridge, to see so few cars using the crossing. Apparently, on certain days commercial traffic was prohibited from entering Kolkata between 3:00 p.m. and midnight. I asked to return after the bridge opened to commercial vehicles, and sure enough, as promised, half an hour after midnight, the bridge was packed with trucks. It was quite a sight and made sense: the first Vivekananda Bridge was built by the British in 1931 and by the 1980s was permanently congested.

Outside India, megaproject bridges operated by private firms also freckle the European landscape and have increased in frequency since the late 1980s. The slow US adoption of a method of financing infrastructure that is now common in Europe and other parts of the world stems from many factors. Wariness of higher tolls or poorer services explains some cases, but in other cases the obstinacy is more ideological, based in fear of corporate overreach into government services. Services and toll rates depend on specific contracts negotiated between partners, but the worry about private overreach ignores the reality of privatization. After all, the European countries listed here enjoy robust government programs and have received excellent service from the bridges built with their private partners.

Similar to the concern about "selling the family jewels," in a well-structured P3 there is little reason to fear private sector overreach. There is a perception that privatization of infrastructure means handing over control completely to an independent body with no accountability to the taxpayers. This is patently false if the P3 is properly structured. In every P3 arrangement, the private firm responds first to the regulatory and financial needs of the state, then as a private corporation. As concessionaires, operators always work under the regulatory framework either in existence or developed as part of a P3.

Canada offers perhaps the clearest example of the compatibility of private infrastructure with strong government. Indeed, Canada illustrates that privatization can simultaneously relieve municipal debt and boost social services. Canada leads the United States in privately managed infrastructure, with 220 assets under private operation.[103] The majority of these new infrastructure assets grew out of Canada's ambitious 2006 federal infrastructure investment plan, known as Building Canada, which committed C$33 billion to infrastructure development.[104] One of the keys to Canada's success is that in the late 1990s Canada's pension funds managers began heavily investing in infrastructure.[105] Today, Canada leads the world in pension fund investments in infrastructure, allocating more than eight times the resources toward infrastructure that US pension funds invest. Pension funds in the United States still invest primarily in public equity or government bonds but typically eschew infrastructure private equity (often categorized as "alternative" private equity funds). Only 1.1 percent of total pension investment in the United States is directed toward infrastructure. By contrast, Canadian pension funds allocated 8.4 percent of their assets under management to infrastructure, the highest portion in the world, with Australia just behind at 7 percent.[106] The partnership between pension managers and infrastructure managers also drove privatization in the United Kingdom; it has also been adopted by Australian pension funds as part of the country's own large-scale infrastructure investment push.

Macky Tall explains the motives of concessionaires well:

What made CDPQ's partnerships successful as illustrated well with the REM project (a $6.7 billion automated light rail system that runs throughout Montréal) was that we defined the roles of the government and private operator very clearly and had a very transparent, collaborative partnership. The government's role is to protect the public interest by determining the objectives, the required performance, and making sure that the cost for users would be competitive compared to other alternatives in the public domain. The role and responsibility of CDPQ Infrastructure as a partner was to lead every phase of development, take the government specifications and requirements and come up with the best solutions. We put in meaningful resources and brought in the best experts in the world to find solutions.

While the private company in a P3 may pay the government for the privilege of running an infrastructure asset, the company nevertheless works for the government to achieve the state's goals. This collaborative aspect, which critics of P3s like to ignore, is all about the third 'P', partnership.

As I argued in *Pensions & Investments* in the lead-up to the IIJA, tapping into greater investment from pension funds could usher in a new golden age of American infrastructure.[107] American pensions collectively hold $5.6 trillion in assets,[108] enough to kick our infrastructure decade into high gear. Not only would this benefit infrastructure, but it could also strengthen pension funds themselves. Pension investments carry many interested parties by nature (including everyone who pays into the pension system), so shifts in investment portfolios can be complex affairs. But the economic analysis points to the conclusion that increased pension investment, if it can be achieved, offers universal benefits. According to some scholars, the pressing question is not if funds should invest, but rather how the United States can incentivize them to do so.[109] Potential solutions to this problem might involve tax easements or subsidies. Whatever the answer, increased participation from US pension funds, following the Canadian example, ought to be an easy choice.

The Chicago Skyway and the Goethals Bridge show that the private sector can be an invaluable partner in civil infrastructure, and when governments work out smart contracts with private operators, everyone can win. In the next chapter, however, even more obstacles to this success will come into focus.

five

SURFACE TENSION

Roads, Highways, and the Pennsylvania Turnpike

GEORGE: "You know, this used to be a helluva good country. I can't understand what's gone wrong with it."
BILLY: "Man, everybody got chicken, that's what happened."
—*Easy Rider* (1969)

Whether one drives the pothole-riddled highways leaving New York City or the disintegrating country roads of Louisiana, it's obvious that America's roads are in desperate need of attention. What may not be immediately obvious, however, is the daunting scale of the problem. According to the American Society of Civil Engineers (ASCE), only 41 percent of US roads are in good condition, while 43 percent are in poor condition, and in one of the largest investment gaps of any infrastructure sector, repairing US roadways will require a staggering $786 billion.[1] Because roads play a particularly critical role in increasing national productivity, it is especially important to get the solution right.[2] Yet as in other sectors, lawmakers have often eschewed pragmatic solutions to the road crisis. In this chapter we will look at a glaring example of how attempts to address the crisis in surface transportation have failed: the effort to privatize the Pennsylvania Turnpike.

In the early days of the United States, private entities constructed the vast majority of the nation's roads, often funding them by tolling users. This began to change in the 1920s, as automobiles grew more common, and during the New Deal era publicly funded roads became the norm. Under the influence of President Roosevelt's New Deal economics, when President Eisenhower proposed the creation of the National Interstate Highway System, he envisioned it as a federally funded initiative. That vision has been difficult to maintain. Today, the federal government continues to fund the vast majority of roadways, with private investment representing a tiny fraction of all road spending, and the outcome has been well below expectations. The situation did not need to be this way. Indeed, when Eisenhower explained his plan to finance the interstate highways in the 1950s, many argued that privately managed toll roads would be more economically realistic than federally funded roads.

To get a glimpse of how US surface infrastructure might have developed had Eisenhower's critics won out, we can look to India, which for more than twenty-five years has been constructing an enormous network of new toll roads managed by private companies. The United States may be unlikely to look to a developing country as a model, but India's story gives us a peek at a path America might have chosen—a road not taken. It still could be the US model in the future.

Before turning to the situation in the United States, then, it will be useful to review what India has done. Over the last fifteen years I have participated in a number of roadworks initiatives in India and have a deep appreciation of the challenges the country has overcome in its pursuit of a comprehensive system of highways. In 2013 I arrived in the state of Rajasthan, the largest state of India, to survey a toll road connecting the city of Jaipur to the city of Agra. Home to the Taj Mahal and India's largest tourist economy, Agra welcomes more than four million tourists each year,[3] and Jaipur, sometimes called the "Paris of India," also enjoys a steady stream of visitors to its sites. Jaipur is one of my favorite cities in the world, bustling with people, activity, and incredible architecture. As many as fifteen million vehicles travel the highway between Agra and Jaipur annually,[4] each paying a toll of 43¢ (45 rupees). The road is privately operated, originally leased by a Malaysian company on a twenty-five-year concession, as are many of India's roads. Cube Highways, an infrastructure management firm in which I Squared Capital holds a controlling stake, had just tendered a bid to take over operations of the road. India is a country of conflicting superlatives, at once majestic and chaotic, at once a vibrant, brimming culture situated in an incomparably beautiful and variegated landscape and a society marked by pollution, poverty, and disorder, especially in cities like Delhi, with a population of 18 million, or Mumbai with 20 million. It must be noted, though, that India has made enormous strides, managing to lift over 271 million people out of poverty in the last decade[5]—a remarkable feat surpassed only by China. Roughly once a year I travel to India to visit as many places where we have invested as possible, and in the last twenty years I have surveyed many of the roads crisscrossing the country, spending time in Delhi, Calcutta, and Sikkim, a small state in the foothills of the Himalayas.

In more ways than one, investing in Indian infrastructure can entail extra demands and extra rewards. Some time ago, my partner Gautam Bhandari and I experienced this in a concrete way when we went to survey a hydro-electric power plant under construction on the Teesta River. I have known and worked with Gautam for over twenty years, and he is an invaluable part-ner when navigating both the boardroom and in this case the backroads of India. To get to the plant we landed at Pakyong Airport in Sikkim and from there took a military helicopter (it had to be a military chopper, being on the border with China and in an area of historic conflict) over a string of small villages into the mountains. After a forty-five-minute flight, we landed at a key engineering workstation. The day was beautiful, and we were staring up at the tallest mountain ranges in the world. What more can one ask? After a long presentation, we enjoyed our surroundings outside on a long bench, eating a most delicious meal—Sikkim aloo dum, a spicy potato-based dish associated with nearby Nepal that includes stewed tomatoes, onion, garlic, mustard seed, coriander, cumin, and a lot of red chilies. A must-try! At that point the weather changed, and we had to decide whether to drive down to the headrace (the channel that delivers water into the turbine) or spend the night where we were and lose a day. "Are the roads okay to drive?" I asked. I was given an emphatic "yes" but was told dissuasively it would take around six hours to get where we were going. "We should definitely do it," I said. Why not? I was imagining an unparalleled scenic drive. I noticed, though, for a split second, a furtive glance between the chief engineer and his col-leagues. The drive through those sheer, skyscraping cliffs was indeed spec-tacularly beautiful—but also the most terrifying, hair-raising infrastructure experience of my life. The one-lane road, at a height of over six thousand feet along the mountainside, was a vertical drop, which had turned to mud in the rain, and every few hundred yards a waterfall gushed across the mud—and could easily have washed away our SUV, too. My nerves were not helped by the fact that behind the wheel our driver looked unsettlingly young, perhaps even a teenager. By the end of it, one could safely con-clude that he was probably one of the most skilled drivers in the country. After six hours driving those roads, we made it in time for sunset. The prize was waking up the next day with a perfect view of Kanchenjunga, the world's third highest mountain at slightly over twenty-eight thousand feet.

Roads in India are definitely interesting. And they are dangerous every-where, not just in the Himalayas. India leads the world in traffic fatalities, with 450,000 accidents each year that result in 150,000 deaths.[6] Although India only owns 10 percent of the world's cars, it experiences 22 percent of all the world's traffic fatalities.[7] There is much room for improvement in Indian surface transportation—one of the reasons I was interested in investing. But it is also a leader in highway construction. India realized that to pursue more aggressive development, it needed better surface infrastructure. Roads bring employment, economic activity, and commerce and provide a livelihood for everyone along the road. They also alleviate congestion, and better roads can help decrease carbon emissions. For example, India has planted twenty-two million trees along its highways,[8] including those that Cube Highways planted to line its twenty-eight toll roads in the country. For comparison, Central Park in New York is home to eighteen thousand trees![9]

To accomplish the construction of its road network, over the last two and a half decades India has become a world leader in public-private partnerships. Beginning in 1996, India initiated its equivalent to President Eisenhower's National Highway and Defense Act, which established the Interstate Highway System. India's program, however, took a different route than that of the United States. Rather than financing its highway development entirely with federal spending, state funds, and bond issuances, which it could not afford, India, from the beginning, invited private investors to participate, allowing for greater efficiency. The National Highway Development Program adopted tax incentives to attract the private sector and established legal standards, known as "enabling legislation," to secure expectations for public-private partnerships. These conditions succeeded in drawing in private finance from around the world, and after penning a series of public-private partnership contracts, the country set about upgrading and replacing 8,000 miles of roadway between 1996 and 2006,[10] partially funding the $12 billion project with investment from companies based in Canada, Spain, the United States, Malaysia, China, Russia, and South Africa—a truly international group.[11] Today, India boasts the third largest network of roads in the world (after the United States and China). National highways account for 2.4 million miles of road,[12] which carry 40 percent of the country's traffic.[13] By comparison, US roads encompass 4.1 million miles,[14] and in China there are over 3.2 million miles.[15] Since the 1990s, India's Highway Development Project has constructed 31,000 miles of new road,[16] and 32 percent of these new projects used P3 models.[17]

Dr. Harikishan Reddy, the CEO of Cube Highways, the largest private manager of toll roads in India, has a deep knowledge of the history of India's P3 projects and understands the structure of the country's P3 contracts as well as anyone. Dr. Reddy grew up in the state of Telangana, a forested region in south-central India situated on the Deccan plateau. The Deccan plateau is famous for many things, including Deccani architecture, developed during the medieval period in the Indo-Islamic style and later influenced by Mughal architecture. Every day between eighth and tenth grades he walked four kilometers (2.5 miles) each way from home to school. Reddy's long commute followed a dirt road—"really just car tracks," he said.[18] There was no public transit, and the road was mostly mud. When he told me this story, my experience in Côte d'Ivoire immediately sprang to mind, one that inspired me to begin exploring infrastructure investment as part of economic development. Reddy did not imagine his commute, or the lack of roads, was in any way related to his future career in transportation. As a young student, he planned to be a teacher and was accepted into an honors program in a city away from his parents to pursue his education. The idea of studying infrastructure arose only when he began a master's degree at McCarthy University and an "amazing professor," Dr. Rav Atari, inspired him to study transportation engineering. Abandoning earlier plans of becoming a teacher, Reddy enrolled in a PhD program at the Indian Institute of Technology in Kharagpur to study engineering with a specialization in surface transportation. While studying, he struck up an apprenticeship with Desendra Halthea, who, as it turned out, was in the midst of writing a book detailing the regulations that would guide India's embrace of P3s in the mid-1990s. "He would dictate and I would write, and that's how most of the chapters of the book were completed." Reddy began a career working with government and the private sector to engineer roads during India's transportation boom.

For India, Reddy explained, there was only one logical choice when it came to funding the massive road project that began in the 1990s. The amount of work that was required and the costs that would be involved essentially ruled out the possibility that the state would tackle the project on its own: "Given the massive network to be built in a short period of time and the finite resources that the government had, and also the fact that somebody would then have to operate and maintain this network, the government thought involving private sector would be a good idea." In the early 1990s, he explained, "We had about 40,000 kilometers of national network at that time. About 20,000 kilometers of that road network was usable. The other 20,000 was largely unserviceable because, even though they were national highways, they only had very narrow, single carriageways and were not well maintained." The rapid expansion the state planned has been a success. "Now the network has about 150,000 kilometers of road and it's continuing to grow."

Perhaps most surprisingly, there was hardly any pushback from the public, according to Reddy. Although including the private sector would mean that the roads would be tolled, users were happy to pay a fee. "The road conditions were extremely poor. When I started doing traffic service in 1998, I asked road users: Will you pay X amount extra in tolls for better roads? And people said yes. I asked if they would pay double the current toll rate, and even then, people still said yes. They were not happy with the baseline situation and for want of good roads, people were willing to pay significantly higher tolls." This is a telling case. Would Americans make the same decision, to pay a toll to improve road service? The answer is a resounding "yes," as the survey I conducted indicates.[19] Within the first decade, Reddy and the private operators proved that P3s could fit the needs of many Indian states. "By 2005," he said, "the ministry reached a conclusion that P3s are the way to develop roads and they put 100% of the projects into P3s."

The key to selling the private role in road development was the regulatory framework written by Desendra Halthea, which created a system of checks and balances and guaranteed no party in a P3 would accrue undue benefits. "In the standard concession there's the private sector which is actually executing the contract. There is a regulator who is assigned and obviously regulating or monitoring the contract, and there's an independent engineer to provide unbiased assessment. We basically ensure that both parties are necessarily playing their role and one party is not getting into the other's domain," Reddy explained. Halthea's system, novel as it was, laid out a comprehensive plan—"it literally covers every aspect for a participatory framework between the private sector and government," he told me. "In 1998, the first concession was awarded, and Congress said, 'after ten years we will examine the progress and, in 2008, revise if necessary.' If you look at the 2008 contracts vis-à-vis the first one in 1998, there were not many changes." Given the success of the P3 model employed in India, the state does not have plans to take over operations of the toll roads, but according to Reddy, it plans to continue leasing operations to the private sector even after the current concession period is over. "They have no intention to take over those roads," he said.

Throughout its explosive road development, India continued to pursue successful partnerships with the private sector by expanding legislation that incentivized and standardized public-private collaborations. The concessions included novel features. For instance, if traffic was better than forecasted, the concession's life would shorten, and conversely, if traffic was lower than expected, the concession would be prolonged. In 2016 India's

Ministry of Road and Transport Highways elaborated its original incentives by introducing a hybrid annuity model for private sector participation in infrastructure, which allowed for greater risk-sharing between public and private partners. The government could garner a larger share of profits, and investors could reduce their risks. Development continued to expand. At least one lesson the United States should draw from India's experience is that enabling legislation opens many doors and helps to streamline private investment. The intentionality of India's approach to private investment created perfect conditions for its infrastructural growth spurt.

Given the size of the US investment gap, even after the IIJA, the country should take the success of India's strategy to heart. This does not mean all toll roads should be privatized, but every state should carefully analyze its long-term capital investment program, the amount it receives from the federal government, and the additional investment it will be undertaking to account for carbon reduction strategies and ask how the private sector can help in that long-term plan. This is not just a question of building or maintaining roads; it is also about investing in the technology that is needed today to ensure the infrastructure is integrated into the country's digital network. The other issue with the management of US highways is efficiency within public procurement processes, which needs to be addressed whether one supports privatization or not.

An article entitled "Can America Reduce Highway Spending" highlights that the cost of building roads between 1956 to 1969 was $8.7 million in 2016 dollars, but by the 1980s, US states were spending roughly $25 million (in 2016 dollars) to build one new mile of interstate, roughly three times more than in the past.[20] The authors note that because labor or material prices did not increase significantly, there must be other reasons for the spending increase. Running through their model, they indicate that this increase in inefficiency, which by all accounts everyone has observed, could be attributed to poor procurement and implementation. Other economists have pointed out that increased efficiency in the US transport system should not come just by means of improving the cost of building the roads or increasing the road network itself, but also by appropriate efficient pricing through user charges for road utilization.[21]

To compare the complexity and inefficiency of the US system to the Indian system, we can look at Pennsylvania's failed effort in 2008 to privatize the Pennsylvania Turnpike. The story of the Pennsylvania Turnpike exposes the impact of political machinations on infrastructure and how catastrophic dependence on federal spending can be. In addition, the story reveals the need for enabling legislation that would standardize and de-mystify public-private partnerships, the same kind that India put in place back in the 1990s. The story of the turnpike, like many of the stories in this book, is one of missed opportunities and roads not taken, about how out-moded and ill-conceived conventions for funding infrastructure have put the United States on a shaky footing for the economic competition of the twenty-first century.

The governor of Pennsylvania during the privatization effort, Ed Rendell, furnishes an exemplary model of the sort of pragmatic approach US infra-structure requires. I met Governor Rendell many times in the context of infrastructure investment and have always been impressed with his com-mitment to infrastructure. I was not directly involved in the turnpike privat-ization efforts but kept a close eye on them as they unfolded. "Voters should know that infrastructure is something we can do something about," he said about the project when I recently spoke to him. "We can improve our own infrastructure. In fact, if we want to continue to be the world's greatest eco-nomic power, we've got to have a better infrastructure."[22]

When he first came to office, Rendell knew his state needed a long-term solution to the turnpike's debt and was willing to use whatever means were available. Yet after navigating a combative state legislature and a host of un-certainties concerning the range of possible funding sources, the attempt to save Pennsylvania's infrastructure concluded with the state accruing a new level of suffocating debt. In Rendell's characteristically pugilistic auto-biography, A Nation of Wusses, the former governor does not mince words: "There is no greater example of the wussification of America than the grow-ing neglect of our nation's infrastructure."[23] Lawmakers worry they will be voted out of office if they make bold maneuvers, he warns us. Worrying they might get it wrong, or hoping someone else will fix the problem, officials ignore what needs to be done. As Rendell writes: "We need leaders with the courage to risk the thing that matters most to them: their own jobs!"[24]

What holds US politicians back from bold action is not just the political risk that comes from introducing any major spending initiative or the risk that a new project might not go off as planned. The larger risk is the depar-ture from political tradition, a jump to a new set of ideas about infrastruc-ture provision and operations. To introduce alternative methods of fund-ing infrastructure means shifting the way US voters think about the public and private sectors; it means breaking difficult assumptions about the true cost of services and the virtue of current systems and means higher user fees. Democrats believe increasing user fees is regressive (which is not so simple—subsidizing high-income earners for parking spaces is regressive), and Republicans assume user fees mean higher taxes, which is anathema for them—and this is before any discussion of P3s. In the case of Pennsylvania, the lack of confident action in this regard sabotaged the state's best hope of salvaging its infrastructure.

Pennsylvania's Turnpike: A Hope for State Infrastructure

Just as it was with water, so it was with roads. The earliest roadways, like the earliest water delivery systems, were owned by private operators who charged a toll to users. More than two thousand private companies financed, built, and operated toll roads in the nineteenth century throughout the country. The oldest road in Pennsylvania was built in 1792, when the state contracted with a private company to build a gravel carriage road from Philadelphia to Lancaster.[25] William Bingham, a wealthy saddler, future politician, and weapons trader in Philadelphia who had helped arm the American army during the Revolution,[26] organized a group of merchants to lobby the state to award a charter for a new road. The charter was granted, and Bingham became the first president of the Philadelphia and Lancaster Turnpike Corporation. The turnpike would be an upgrade from the dirt and gravel roads that ran through the countryside in Pennsylvania and the rest of New England; it would be paved with stone—the first hard-surfaced road in the United States. Financing for the project came not only from the immediate owners of the corporations, but also from the general public. Residents in Lancaster, Pennsylvania, bought a thousand shares of the new company at $300 apiece.[27]

During the 1920s and 1930s, while undergoing the automobile boom and still operating with a Progressive Era mentality, the United States began nationalizing private roads, including the Philadelphia-Lancaster Turnpike. The Lancaster Turnpike, first purchased by the Pennsylvania Railroad Company in 1876, was taken over by the state in 1913, which removed its tollhouses in 1917.[28] These nationalizations foreshadowed the more wholesale government appropriation of infrastructure during the New Deal and World War II.

The Pennsylvania Turnpike was something different, however. It was not a repurposed private road, burgeoning from with state funds, but a new vision for transportation: the first "superhighway."[29] Without stop signs or intersections, the four-lane highway offered a scenic, undisturbed, and speedy

Figure 5.1. Cover of 1950s brochure from the Pennsylvania Turnpike Commission. The brochure includes maps, mileage tables, driving rules and regulations, and a fare schedule. *Source:* Pennsylvania Turnpike Commission, "Pennsylvania Turnpike System–The World's Greatest Highway," circa 1952, brochure, The Henry Ford, https://www .thehenryford.org/collections -and-research/digital -collections/artifact/365720.

trip from one end of the state to the other.[30] Figure 5.1 shows a brochure from the 1950s advertising the turnpike, which today would feel strange to many, but in the middle of the previous century, the turnpike was a big deal!

Unlike the expressways of New York and Chicago, the road traversed open country and created easy access to the cities for those in rural towns along the turnpike, drumming up business along the way. The road provided a model for the stream of interstate highways that would follow a decade and a half later. From its opening day, the road drew steady traffic and strong tolling revenue—it was an immediate success. This success came as a surprise to many and demonstrated again the uncertainty of infrastructure development.

In 1935 Cliff Patterson, a state legislator, was approached by a representative of the Pennsylvania Motor Truck Association and a member of the Pennsylvania State Planning Commission with a plan to build a road on the abandoned railroad ties of one of J. P. Morgan's trains, which had been run out of business by a competitor.[31] Patterson adopted the plan and introduced it to the state legislature, estimating a cost of $60–70 million for the construction ($1.2 billion in 2023). After winning a grant for $35,000 from the federal Works Progress Administration, Patterson argued that the remaining funds could be raised through bond issuances. The WPA and the Public Works Administration (PWA) were central institutions in the New Deal, created by Roosevelt to distribute capital to states for infrastructure projects. These bodies had enormous influence over state infrastructure and succeeded in creating jobs and constructing some of the nation's most iconic infrastructure. But the system also established the conditions that led to government overreach and municipal insolvency. As the effects of the Great Depression waned, partly due to a wartime boom in production, these huge distributive projects began to seem a vestige of the past—the Pennsylvania Turnpike was one of the WPA's final projects.

The bill to construct the turnpike passed in 1937,[32] but quickly Patterson's plan hit a wall: bond buyers did not believe the road would be profitable. No one would use a highway through the middle of nowhere, and without traffic to generate tolls the road would go bankrupt, they cautioned. Pennsylvania withdrew its bond offering, and the turnpike, for the time being, looked dead. In a foreshadowing of challenges to come, turnpike advocates made a final appeal to the federal government for salvation. A state lawmaker named Walter A. Jones leaned on his ties to the White House to bring the languishing road project to Roosevelt's personal attention.[33] Seeing the road as both an opportunity for growth in Pennsylvania and a strategic military route—from the east coast to Pittsburgh and on to Cleveland, on the border of Lake Erie and Canada—Roosevelt agreed to purchase $35 million worth of turnpike bonds through the PWA and also to directly fund nearly half the construction. Perhaps this origin, bailed out by an expansive federal government, sheds light on the faith the Pennsylvania Turnpike Commission had in federal benefactors. But it also sheds light on another key point: not all infrastructure projects must or can be financed by the private sector. In this case, the nation's strategic needs diverged from the incentives that motivate private investors, and state funding presented the only course for infrastructure development. There is no doubt government investment in infrastructure is necessary. This does not mean, however, that government should always and forever be the funder and operator of civil infrastructure.

Once funding had been secured, construction began with a bonanza of contracts. The PWA planned to disband after 1940, so in order to receive its funding, the Pennsylvania Turnpike—the longest road ever to be built up to that point—would need to be completed in just three years. To maximize productivity, the state employed 155 companies from eighteen states and a total of fifteen thousand workers to clear the path and lay the pavement.[34] In an effort that might have impressed even the builders of the transcontinental railroad, construction ended on time and before the closing of the PWA. The nation's first superhighway opened to motorists as Roosevelt campaigned for his third term in the oval office. In a reversal of the planning issues experienced by the Chicago Skyway, the expectations for low traffic volume didn't materialize. In the first four days of its operation, the turnpike was used by 240,000 vehicles—far exceeding expectations.[35] The turnpike was an immediate success, and Walter A. Jones, who had saved the project with his connection to the White House, was named the first commissioner of the Pennsylvania Turnpike Commission.

Traffic on the turnpike has only increased since the 1940s. Today, more than 500,000 vehicles pass through its toll booths on a daily basis.[36] By and large, the project served the state well; between 1940 and 2004, the Pennsylvania Turnpike Commission raised tolls only six times but managed to cover the cost of upkeep and its bond service. The turnpike expanded in the 1950s, added lanes to sections in the 1970s, expanded again in the 1980s, and then underwent a major overhaul in the 1990s. Originally only 160 miles long, by 2000 the road stretched for 360 miles.[37] Despite the debt accumulated through these additions, the highway continued to be solvent.

Surrounding the turnpike, though, Pennsylvania's infrastructure rapidly declined. By 2006 Pennsylvania faced an annual infrastructure budget shortfall of $1.7 billion.[38] Roads in Philadelphia and Pittsburgh crumbled, and bridges threatened to and sometimes did collapse.[39] Not only did the state lack the capital to repair its infrastructure but, just as great an obstacle, many of Pennsylvania's most affected areas suffered from poor credit ratings, scaring away investors from buying their municipal bonds and thereby closing the only other traditional avenue for funding.

Enter Ed Rendell. Rendell won election to the governor's office in 2003, running on his reputation as the no-nonsense, tough-love mayor of Philadelphia, who brought about what many felt was a miraculous economic turnaround in the city. During Rendell's governorship, Pennsylvania simultaneously incentivized business in the state, lowered the sales tax, balanced the budget,[40] diversified the state's revenue streams, and improved its infrastructure. Most impressively, compared to similar states, Pennsylvania weathered the financial crisis of 2008 in good form. Though it experienced a sharp contraction and a slow climb back to pre-recession job numbers, the rate of unemployment was below the national average, and it rebounded more quickly. According to a study by Penn State, employment declined by only 4 percent overall from 2008 to 2009,[41] and unemployment rose to only 8.7 percent, while the national average hit 10 percent.[42] This is especially significant when contrasted with a comparable state such as Illinois, whose economy shrank by 5 percent and which saw unemployment rates rise to 11 percent,[43] with the number of unemployed Illinoisans jumping from approximately 340,000 in January 2007 to 700,000 in January 2010.[44]

As Governor Rendell's national profile surged, he became embroiled in a series of combustible legislative debates. Even before becoming governor, he had built a national profile campaigning for Al Gore's presidential bid in 2000. As Rendell crisscrossed the country for John Kerry and Barack Obama in the 2004 and 2008 campaigns, he came ever more to embody the success of a new brand of municipal leader and a new brand of Democrat, who would not let partisan pieties stand in the way of getting results. To understand how powerfully Rendell projected his new vision for government finance, it's worth spending a moment to review his tenure as mayor of Philadelphia, because in the city he implemented his plans more fully, and more successfully, than he could statewide. One of the frustrations of the failure to privatize the Pennsylvania Turnpike arises from the fact that Rendell had already demonstrated the success of his approach so soundly as mayor.

Philadelphia Is Reborn

When Rendell took the reins in Philadelphia, the city had fallen to one of the lowest points in its history. Over the previous thirty years, the city had contracted as its industrial jobs moved overseas and its people moved elsewhere, too: 200,000 jobs disappeared from Philadelphia between the 1960s and 1990s, and the population dwindled by 400,000.[45] By 1992 the city's deficit had ballooned to $200 million (within a $2.4 billion budget), and its credit rating had depreciated to "junk"[46]—the lowest rated bonds of any large city in the United States.[47] The city feared bankruptcy. "Make no mistake," the mayor advised in his inaugural speech, which centered on his plans to address the city's financial crisis, "our situation is worse than we thought it could ever be."[48] That May, as if to confirm the precarity of the city's situation and perhaps its very autonomy, the US Department of Housing and Urban Development seized the Philadelphia Housing Authority and its thirteen thousand units, citing corruption, mismanagement of federal funds, and substandard, sometimes squalid conditions in the city's public housing.

The mismanagement at the Housing Authority reflected the world of many city officials and the leaders of the utility unions in Philadelphia. In the federal investigation into the Housing Authority, auditors discovered when surveying grant outcomes that on several occasions the city had received federal grants for housing repairs it had reported as completed but that had in fact never been started. Where did the money go? In one case, the authority applied for a grant to undertake the renovation of a public housing complex named Southwark, in West Philadelphia, and reported spending $5.8 million over four years on the project. On a survey of the site, inspectors found that construction on the renovation had not even begun. Additionally, it found that the authority had collected federal subsidies for five hundred units that no longer existed, having been demolished by the Housing Authority itself as uninhabitable.[49]

Rendell knew the city had lost large sums like this in myriad ways and staked his political career on eliminating such excessive waste. It was all in his five-year plan, as he promised on the campaign trail in 1991. The mayor would submit city budgets to a rigorous housecleaning by trimming fat and transferring services to the private sector. Rendell wanted to avoid as many job terminations as possible and, demonstrating the courage to tell difficult truths, proposed that city employees would all keep their jobs if they agreed to some short-term sacrifices—including a temporary freeze on raises, reduction in hours, and decreased benefits programs—and guaranteed that municipal workers in any programs that faced the chopping block would be offered replacement jobs.[50] The administration identified a number of wasteful projects for elimination.[51] In one of his first symbolic efforts to bypass wasteful city programs, Rendell organized a volunteer team to clean up City Hall, attracting some of his first national headlines.[52]

Rendell also implemented a series of privatizations, opening what had traditionally been city contracts to bids from private companies. In the course of his three years as mayor, Rendell transitioned twenty-six contracts to private entities,[53] including contracts to guard and maintain the famous Philadelphia Museum of Art and other publicly managed institutions.[54] In the administration's largest privatization, it contracted the city-run Philadelphia Nursing Home to the nonprofit organization Episcopal Long-Term Care. The privatization caused a commotion, including accusations that the quality of care decreased, although no evidence supported the claim, given that the quality of care was already poor, and poorly monitored, prior to privatization.[55] What was certain was that the deal resulted in $4 million in savings for the city annually.[56] All told, Rendell's privatizations in Philadelphia between 1992 and 1995 captured $36 million in wasteful spending.

In the years since they were implemented, these privatizations have had mixed results and caused some controversy. Like Chicago, Philadelphia led the way on the issue, and inevitably contracts were written without the benefit of experience. In 2009 guards at the Philadelphia Art Museum unionized for higher pay and better training, and in 2022 they went on strike for raises, paid family leave, and other benefits. After a nineteen-day work stoppage, the union won its contract demands.[57] In particular, the privatization of nursing homes has come under scrutiny, with some findings pointing to a reduction in services and quality under private management.[58] In 2022 one of the homes privatized by Rendell, the Philadelphia Nursing Home, which was run by the private nonprofit Fairmount Long Term Care, closed its doors, citing financial shortfalls and underperformance compared to other private facilities.[59] Poor operators can undermine privatization deals, certainly, but that residents are moving from one private residence to another is not evidence that privatization doesn't work. The lesson is that privatization works best if the city develops a strong, well-funded regulator, which could oversee shortfalls like those in the Philadelphia Nursing Home.

The most controversial and difficult fights Rendell entered into as mayor concerned his criticism of the Philadelphia unions. In the spring of 1992, in his first months in office, Rendell aimed to renegotiate the city's union contracts. The two largest unions representing municipal workers exercised considerable power in the city and, in Rendell's view, their wasteful spending contributed significantly to the city's budget shortfalls. The task was not one for a "wuss"—that much was clear. Governing as a Democrat, being seen as anti-union could anger Rendell's base of support; in a blue-collar town like Philly, residents historically sided with the union bosses. Moreover, contract disputes with unions had a way of devolving into acrimonious threats and grandstanding, almost always attracting the media. But the inefficiencies had become so glaring that Rendell had no choice; all he could do was hope his city council, and the voters, would see things his way. Rendell liked to quote the statistics concerning public employee raises to make his case. During the 1980s, pay increases for employees in the private sector averaged 3.4 percent, or $960, each year. Public employees, by contrast, had seen raises of 14.6 percent on average, or an increase of $4,031 per year.[60] Rendell's proposed wage freezes would save the city $110 million annually on labor costs, which had already doubled over the last decade.[61]

At the start of negotiations in spring 1992, the major unions—led by Jim Sutton of District Council 33, representing municipal workers, and Tom Cronin, head of District Council 47, for white-collar workers—demanded an 18 percent pay increase.[62] When the city alerted the union bosses that the city had no money and counteroffered with no raises at all, the unions began plotting a city-wide strike. The city's new contract for union workers offered no pay raises for the first two years, followed by a maximum of 3 percent raises afterward, but more important to the union bosses—and the city budget—it gave the city executive control over municipal employees' health-care benefits and vacation time. (In 1992, union members enjoyed seven weeks of paid vacation, an unthinkable luxury to most workers in the private sector.) The deadline for the unions to sign arrived that June, but negotiations grew hostile as the summer warmed up, dragging on into the following fall.[63] Rendell's tactics changed the calculus of typical union contract negotiations, above all because he credibly threatened to privatize some of the key functions fulfilled by union workers, including trash collection and water delivery. The fact that he had turned other city contracts over to the private sector gave him a new kind of power over the unions. The combination of these tactics and the dire financial predicament the city faced enabled Rendell to come out on top—"breaking" the unions, as the media put it. The strike the union leaders initiated on October 6 lasted only fourteen hours before they agreed to a deal. The city would not budge on the central clauses of its contract, though the mayor backed off on the city's demand for control over municipal workers' health-care benefits. When the strike concluded, "the mayor got 90% of what he wanted," said John Street, City Council president at the time and future successor to Rendell as Philadelphia mayor.[64] Acknowledging the desperate financial straits in Philadelphia and the mayor's determination to curb union expenditures, union leader Jim Sutton conceded the weakness of the union position, lamenting that it was "the best deal we could get."[65]

In 1994 Philadelphia ran a surplus for the first time in over thirty years, and by 1999, Rendell's last year in office, the city boasted a $205 million surplus. Though his methods scandalized some, Rendell's success could not be denied. At the end of his term the national press had begun referring to him as "America's mayor." On the whole, his vision aligned with the philosophy of the "entrepreneurial city," especially as described by the influential book *Reinventing Government: How the Entrepreneurial Spirit Is Transforming the Public Sector*,[66] which according to one profile, Rendell read during his early days in the mayor's office.

Debate persists about the long-term legacy of Rendell's strategy for Philadelphia, among those who believe his privatizations hurt key elements of the city,[67] as well as among those who believe he should have gone further to make

Philadelphia more independent of federal funding.[68] It is true that Philadelphia has not overcome all its problems, but it is difficult to deny that Rendell's methods lifted Philadelphia out of what might have been a death spiral.

The Rocky-like underdog story of Philadelphia's miraculous revival distinguished Rendell from other mayors pursuing similar goals. In the mid-1990s Rendell became a close ally of then president Clinton, the leader of these "new Democrats." When he left the mayor's office, he rose to head the Democratic National Committee, where he served for three years. By 2003 it was time to pursue a larger goal: the governorship of Pennsylvania. The political dynamics in Harrisburg, though, would prove significantly more averse to innovation than those in the chambers of City Hall.

Rendell Takes the State House

Just as he had taken over Philadelphia in the midst of financial collapse, Ed Rendell moved into the Pennsylvania Governor's House staring down a state deficit of $2.4 billion,[69] distressed infrastructure, underperforming schools, and a nation on the brink of war in Iraq. In neighboring New York and New Jersey, which also faced deficits in the billions, the governors planned deep cuts in education spending, but Pennsylvania could not afford to do the same given the condition of the state's education system. Rendell returned to the same playbook that had worked so well in Philly: increase budgetary efficiency, reduce costs and waste, and privatize contracts wherever a private company can do a better job—and do it all with the least impact on voters. In his first months as governor, Rendell proposed a $21 billion budget that included $1.6 billion in spending cuts.[70] Unlike New York and New Jersey, Rendell not only spared schools from reduced funding but promised to increase the education budget. This, he calculated, would be paid for with a modest hike in income tax, in addition to some more innovative measures: Rendell proposed legalizing slot machines at racetracks. The Republican leaders at the state house approved the bill without debate, while his own party showed more reluctance.[71]

The infrastructure problem presented another difficulty, however, one that could not be solved by digging up a spare million or two through budget overhaul. Where could this kind of capital be found? In 2006 Rendell established the Transportation Funding and Reform Commission to evaluate the options Pennsylvania had to solve its infrastructure shortfalls. The commission concluded that Pennsylvania needed $1.7 billion in additional annual funding to maintain current systems and another $14 billion for repairs ($2.5 billion and $20.6 billion in 2023 dollars).[72] A year later Rendell settled on a plan to raise these extraordinary additional funds. He sent a letter to the state legislature laying out a lease of the Pennsylvania Turnpike, suggesting a deal could potentially bring the city as much as $20 billion.[73] Privatization could produce the up-front capital needed to repair and upgrade the state's infrastructure as a whole. And the up-front capital would not only provide a one-time injection; if invested it could supply an ongoing source of funds that could be apportioned regularly.

When news of the governor's plan reached the leaders at the Pennsylvania Turnpike Commission, they sprang into action to field an alternative proposal. Their counteroffer suggested instituting a new toll on the other East-West artery in Pennsylvania, I-80. This would increase revenue and also conveniently expand the commission's tolling authority.

The road the commission proposed tolling, I-80, traverses the north of the state. A federal highway built primarily to connect New York to Cleveland, it skips all the major Pennsylvania hubs. The commission argued that if it tolled vehicles driving I-80, it could provide the state with the funds needed to finance Rendell's infrastructure overhaul. Because the Federal Highway Administration (FHWA) managed the road, however, the state would need authorization. One of the key questions is why the commission did not make that proposal earlier. Why did it take the possibility of privatization to spur the commission to action? Why would such a body, responsible for managing our infrastructure, not make such a basic change as increasing tariffs to offer better services, or at least to maintain consistent real rates?

Ever the pragmatist, Rendell assented to the Turnpike Commission's lobbying and withdrew his proposal for privatization, and the alternative solution moved forward in the Pennsylvania legislature. Under the official name Act 44, the commission's proposal guaranteed the Turnpike Commission would pay the state $22.5 billion over fifty years, generated from tolls on both the turnpike and I-80, enough to cover the state's transportation infrastructure needs from mass transit to bridges and roads.[74] There was one major gamble written into the bill, however. The possibility of the Turnpike Commission's providing such a large sum to the state hinged on its ability to add tolls to I-80, but at the time of the bill's passage, the state's application had not been approved. The FHWA maintained managerial control over the federal roads, including whether a state could install a toll. In 2006 the FHWA announced a program to allow three states to adopt tolling on nationally managed freeways. Two slots had already been filled by Virginia and Missouri,[75] and Pennsylvania assured itself that it could secure the third slot. As it had depended on federal intervention when its first sections were built in 1940, now the turnpike again hoped for salvation through federal relief.

Regardless of the tolling gamble, immediately after the passage of Act 44, Rendell was worried. The toll increase over fifty years would provide additional revenue, certainly, but it would not deliver an up-front injection of capital that would permit the urgent repairs that the state needed. Moreover, the actual ability of the state to raise revenue from tolls assumed all the risk associated with transportation infrastructure profits, risks that are not always apparent, as the story of the Chicago Skyway makes clear. Act 44 could not furnish the funds that Rendell desired and that the state needed. It would simply not be enough. So he returned to the idea of privatization.

Rendell brought in Morgan Stanley to advise the state on the best methods of privatizing the toll road, and together they agreed on a long-term lease that would allow a private firm to control tolling, within limits established by the state.[76] Morgan Stanley estimated the deal could bring in between $12 and $16 billion. Just months after the passage of Act 44, Pennsylvania submitted a request for qualifications, and fourteen companies tendered bids.[77]

After ten months of negotiations, the state selected the winning bid, which came from a partnership between Citi Bank and Abertis, a Spanish company specializing in the management of toll roads. In the final months of negotiations, Citi and Abertis merged their individual bids to compete against a partnership between Macquarie and Goldman Sachs. Just as the Indiana Toll Road had managed to drive up offers by pitting investors against one another, Pennsylvania orchestrated the deal to maximize the state's profit. In the final lease agreement, the Citi-Abertis group would pay $12.8 billion up front for a seventy-five-year lease on the turnpike. It would have been the largest privatization deal in the history of the country.

When Rendell reanimated his privatization plan, after the passage of Act 44, it struck many in the Pennsylvania legislature as a betrayal, even though Rendell had done what he could to make the Turnpike Commission's proposal viable. Rumors and misinformation circulated through the state house. Some accused Rendell of striking a bad deal, believing the turnpike could have fetched as much as $30 billion.[78] Somewhat ironically, the state assembly's Democratic caucus, Rendell's own party, released a study titled "For Whom the Road Tolls: Corporate Asset or Public Good; An

Analysis of Financial and Strategic Alternatives for the Pennsylvania Turnpike,"[79] which argued that privatization was undesirable because, among
other things, lawmakers would misspend the revenue—not much of a vote
of confidence.[80] Misallocation of proceeds certainly can be a consequence
of privatization, but it is not related to the operation of an infrastructure
asset by a private company per se. Before any P3 agreement is finalized, the
state must clearly identify the use of proceeds in order to garner support
from legislative councils and voters. Otherwise, privatization can lose some
of its benefits. But ultimately, if politicians cannot be trusted to manage a
large capital windfall, how can they be trusted to manage infrastructure of
the same value?

More pernicious was the manufactured panic about foreign investment,
with lawmakers drumming up nationalistic fear by suggesting that Abertis,
the prospective Spanish operator of the turnpike, would somehow be disastrous for Pennsylvania. (I have heard this argument many times before.)
The panic over foreign entities, to the extent it was genuine, stemmed from
confused xenophobia, or else from a disingenuous attempt to scuttle the
deal. It is understandable that we might reject ownership from unfriendly
foreign actors of critical assets such as telecom networks, since they could
be used for all sorts of nefarious activities including facilitating cyberat-
tacks. But a road? In Pennsylvania, many were just as doubtful about the
arguments. "There was fuzzy math; there was misinformation; and there
was pure spin," recalled Rick Geist, the co-chair of the House Transportation Committee who was an advocate of the privatization deal. "The misinformation was almost to the point that people thought the Spaniards were
going to take the highway and move it back to Spain," he lamented.[81] Legislators knew foreign investment posed no risk to the state—foreign investors already had a stake in many infrastructure projects around the country
(including the Indiana Toll Road and the Chicago Skyway) with no unexpected negative consequences. Moreover, foreign companies provided
much of the energy infrastructure that Pennsylvania relied on, through both
gas and electric. Ironically, during that period Spanish companies heavily
invested in Pennsylvania infrastructure in other sectors. Between 2003 and
2017, Pennsylvania had the third greatest amount of foreign direct investment among northeastern states, with plenty of Spanish participation specifically.[82] The worry over foreign investment clashed with the state's overall embrace of foreign investment elsewhere, suggesting the hype may have
been manufactured rather than genuine. To be clear, the Indiana Toll Road
and other P3s also faced major opposition at the federal level. For example,

two Democratic members of Congress, James Obestar (D-MN) and Peter Defazio (D-OR), sent a letter to every governor in the country "to discourage [them] from entering into PPP agreements that are not in the long-term public interest in a safe integrated national transport system."[83] The head of the American Trucking Association joined the chorus, too, as did several right-wing populist shows.

Governor Jeb Bush, who spoke highly of Rendell's effort, pointed out that lawmakers often pose the largest obstacle to accomplishing major change. About the Pennsylvania Turnpike, he told me, "From a business perspective it made all the sense in the world. The problem became pretty apparent when members of the legislature began thinking, 'well, what's in it for me'?" Bush drew two lessons from this privatization attempt. "The first lesson in privatizing existing infrastructure is that there has to be a broad benefit to the larger community. The second lesson is that it has to be sold aggressively and continually. You can't even stop after the transaction has taken place." Lawmakers aren't always incentivized to do what makes sense for the state, or the country, unless it also has a benefit for their own reelection. The only hope is a hard and unrelenting pitch.

The true opponents of the turnpike privatization bill came from three groups: those who wanted to maintain the status quo because it would protect the system of patronage traditionally associated with these infrastructure assets, those who had a strong public policy view that privatization would lead to higher tolls on the turnpike and was therefore a regressive tax, and those who believed that infrastructure should remain in the hands of state operators. Of the three, only the second group brings up a debatable point, because there are many ways to address the issue of a regressive tax, if indeed that was applicable.

On the other side, proponents of the Citi-Abertis deal believed privatization offered the best solution to the budget crisis—joined by those who lived along I-80 and opposed Act 44 because it would install tolls on their road. The crux of the dispute boiled down to tolls: who would be tolled and how much. Rendell's deputy chief of staff, Roy Kienitz, tried to cut through the heated debates by pointing out that, given Pennsylvania's dire infrastructure shortfalls, tolls on the turnpike would be raised regardless of who operated it.[84] Since 2009 tolls have indeed increased every year under government management, by 5–6 percent, in order to address the new debt crisis.

Within this local debate, a wider debate also played out about the nature of tolling. Is tolling a regressive tax or a progressive tax? The debate continues today, still framed through James Poterba's seminal 1991 paper "Is the

Gasoline Tax Regressive?"[85] Many in the infrastructure world judge that tolls represent a regressive way to pay for infrastructure. This means that the impact of the tax recedes as it is applied to wealthier taxpayers. A progressive tax has the opposite effect, impacting wealthier payers more than poorer ones. Typically, tolls do not discriminate between income levels, so it is simply a matter of how significant the flat tariff rate is to a particular user, rather than a calculated change of rate based on income. Whether one considers tolls regressive or not is only part of the question. Another question to ask is: Who has the responsibility to pay for infrastructure? Adam Smith suggests that it is the user who has the most immediate responsibility to pay, and because the service is the same for all users, it makes sense to have a flat toll for all users, too. Alternative means of paying for infrastructure would separate payment from use, for instance by raising sales taxes, as some have suggested. These debates do not have a simple answer, but careful analysis can provide a viable framework.

The fearmongering and misinformation in Pennsylvania helped to tip the balance in favor of the nays. In 2008 the state legislature voted down Rendell's deal with Citi-Abertis.[86] It was a stinging defeat for Rendell—but the pain it would cause in Pennsylvania could only be guessed.

Only weeks later, the FHWA reached a decision on Pennsylvania's application to toll I-80, the essential piece of the puzzle to make Act 44 viable. It was no. According to the federal government, the plan did not meet technical and statutory requirements.[87] When the federal government barred the state from collecting revenue from traffic using I-80, it effectively killed any chance the Pennsylvania Turnpike Commission had of fulfilling the responsibilities it had taken on as part of Act 44. But Act 44 had already been enshrined as law, and the Turnpike Commission was thus legally obligated to pay the state the $22.5 billion it had promised.

Without tolling on I-80, the Pennsylvania Turnpike Commission quickly sank into staggering debt. Since the enactment of Act 44, the commission has been forced to pay $450 million annually to the state of Pennsylvania, raised entirely from turnpike tolls. As of 2021, it had accumulated $13.2 billion in debt.[88] The state legislature's commitment to retaining control over infrastructure killed a deal that could have impacted Pennsylvania's economy in profoundly positive ways. And relying on federal intervention, even in modest regulatory matters, again proved a failing strategy.

The turnpike privatization aimed not to fix one road, but to fix all of the roads and bridges in the state and to fund their maintenance in perpetuity. The cost to motorists, which had been one of the only real arguments against privatization, ended up a moot point, because tolls on the turnpike increased anyway—and more precipitously than if Abertis-Citi were operating it at 3 percent annual increases.

After a decade of heavy tolling and under a revised agreement, the turnpike paid its last installment of $450 million to the Pennsylvania DOT, bringing total turnpike payments to the state to $7.9 billion following a state vote in 2013 to provide a modicum of debt relief to the commission, resulting in a lower total required payment to PennDOT.[89] All the original problems that privatization hoped to solve, however, remain, and the commission is still buried in an additional $14 billion in debt.[90] The IIJA will deliver some relief, but not enough. The bill allocated only $2 billion to Pennsylvania to repair and develop its roads, while the ASCE estimated the state needed $7.2 billion in 2018.

Why didn't privatization efforts pay off in Harrisburg? There were many factors, from uncertainty about the nature of privatized infrastructure, to ideological stubbornness, to political worries about voter opinions. In Rendell's terms, what happened constituted "wussing out," a lack of courage to take a risk that might produce a transformative payoff. To get a better sense of why the state rejected the privatization deal and how the turnpike's fortunes took such a disastrous turn, I asked the man himself, Ed Rendell.

When I spoke with Governor Rendell, he struck an upbeat tone on the future of US infrastructure. "People have become aware that we must continue to spend money, because a superior infrastructure helps save money in the end," he said. Moreover, he thinks the benefits of P3s and private participation are starting to become clearer to the public. Americans have begun to come around, and so have politicians, Rendell believes. "Politicians are emboldened by the success of P3s. And they've finally gotten the idea across to citizens that putting money into infrastructure is an economic plus, not a minus. In the years between 2012 and 2016, 70% of ballot referendums on privatization received the 'yes' vote from citizens." In these referenda, "citizens agreed to pay more to create better infrastructure," he said. Americans are willing to pay more for infrastructure if the benefits are clearly articulated. What has changed, according to Rendell, is not a decrease in federal or state spending but rather attitudes and understanding about the topic. "It's not about less money being available," Rendell said. "Because, in fact, states have begun to step up and put their money where their mouth is on infrastructure projects. Almost thirty states have recently raised taxes or tolls for increased infrastructure." The difference is that "people are beginning to realize—good infrastructure, if you pay up front, in the long run you generate more income, and cut costs, and it's a good investment." About his own abortive attempt to privatize the Pennsylvania Turnpike, Rendell commented tersely, "I think it's easier now to get infrastructure projects adopted than it was." This is not a rueful but rather a satisfied sentiment.

Rendell believes that P3s in particular will grow in popularity and continue to be used more frequently. "Private-public partnerships are an even cheaper way for the public to finance infrastructure," he said, "and can be successful if they're done right." He added something we have already learned well: "That's a big if." But the chances of working out strong P3 structures have increased. "The public has become aware of the value of them, so it makes politicians more likely to do those deals." Working out the proper terms of P3s has been a long road in the United States, but experiences like those of Pennsylvania and Indiana have helped clarify the situation. "Private-public partnerships got off to a bad start in this country. When I was governor, I wanted to privatize the Pennsylvania Turnpike, have a private company take it over. Now, that private company would have had to agree to a set of conditions and those conditions would be tightly drawn to make sure the public interest was protected. You have got to have tightly drawn public-private partnerships." Having worked out this basic approach to private participation, Rendell believes that "public-private partnerships will be increasingly used."

Roads to Nowhere

Roads play a profound role in the American imagination. From the early days of hot rods drag racing on the backstreets of smalltown America, to the frenetic transcontinental zigzagging of Jack Kerouac and Alan Ginsburg, to the *Fast and Furious* franchise, roads and highways tap into essential American values: freedom, individual autonomy, the exploration of a vast territory. Yet the United States by and large fails its roadways. American roads also suffer from worse congestion than those in many parts of the world and are more dangerous than those in comparable economies.[91] The wear on roads and the need for expansion have increased dramatically since the 1980s, when the number of vehicles on the road and the number of vehicle miles traveled began to sharply increase, even while the number of roads remained steady.

The current system of financing roads offers no obvious way to close this gap. The states receive funding for federal roads through the FHWA and the Highway Trust Fund. Both were created in 1956 as part of Eisenhower's National and Defense Highways Act; the FHWA distributes allocations to the states from capital supplied by the Highway Trust Fund. The Highway Trust draws most of its revenue from the federal fuel tax, which dates back to Herbert Hoover and the Great Depression.[92] Politicians go to extreme lengths to avoid increasing the famously unpopular "gas tax," and since Bill Clinton raised the tax in 1993 by 4 cents, every subsequent president has managed to dodge the issue.[93] (Although many states have independently raised fuel taxes on their own.)[94] In fact, in real terms the value of the tax has gone down by 45 percent.[95] As a result, however, the Highway Trust requires supplemental funding, which means that roughly every five years Congress must approve additional funds for the Highway Trust Fund. In 2012, 2016, and again in 2021, Congress had to navigate a negotiation about federal funding—a subject that has always divided the United States and has animated it since the rivalry between Jefferson and Hamilton. It's not going away anytime soon. In the reality of US politics today, not only can federal funding be controversial, but even a vote for a bipartisan agreement might provoke accusations of capitulation to the other side. As long as highway maintenance hangs in the balance of political battles, even routine funding can be derailed. With the advent of electric vehicles, the tax receipts will come down, and the gasoline tax will truly become regressive. Discussions of a vehicle miles traveled (VMT) tax has been going on for some time.[96] The IIJA included some funds to develop a pilot study on VMT tax, but as Clifford Winston describes in an essay in the *New York Times*, politics and special interests will probably slow down the process.[97]

Eisenhower's decision to finance the construction of roadways with taxpayer dollars had its opponents, of course. In the lead-up to the National and Defense Highways Act, the nation debated whether federal funding could in fact keep up with road maintenance in the long term. In the early 1950s, Texas had granted concessions to corporate investors to construct tolled expressways through the state, and some economists urged the president to consider following Texas's lead rather than burden the state with upkeep costs in perpetuity. An article in *Time* magazine, published in March 1955 in response to Eisenhower's recent proposal for a federal highway system, warned that existing municipal and state-funded expressways at the time had seen mixed results, experienced unexpectedly low traffic, and flagged on bond payments. More worrying, the article forecasted that these state-funded roads would not be able to afford the necessary maintenance costs as they aged. Describing exactly the predicament the country faces today, the magazine wrote: "For the most part, the nation's roads are still being built or repaired with revenue from gasoline taxes, license-plate fees and other taxes on motorists and truckers. But in most states the immediate need for roads is greater than the immediate income, and the double-edged question of taxing motorists and building highways regularly touches off pitched battles in state capitals."[98] How can it be that the United States has yet to resolve such an important dilemma? The magazine advised Eisenhower instead to consider a network of roads built with private concessions, as Texas had done. "Allowing private investors to put up the necessary cash to build roads would get roads built without either federal or state governments going further into debt," the author concluded.[99] The predictions about state and municipal debt have decisively come true, but it is not too late to adopt this alternative model.

The reasons to include P3s are many. Given how difficult it is to secure the funding for roads, we might expect the state to be meticulous with how it is spent. But this is often not the case. State governments can mismanage funds and, in the worst cases, channel exorbitant payments to their preferred contractors. The most famous example of spectacular government inefficiency may be Alaska's "bridge to nowhere," otherwise known as the Gravina Bridge project, which would have connected Ketchikan, Alaska, with Gravina Island, replacing a ferry. The federal government earmarked $325 million in funds for the bridge (at a projected cost of $398 million),[100] which had been proposed by Governor Frank Murkowski and backed by his successor, Sarah Palin. Then, in 2007, the political winds changed in Alaska. Palin accepted the Republican Party's nomination for vice president alongside John McCain, and the media turned its attention to her record. With a higher profile, the federal allocation came under fire in the national media as an example of wasteful "pork barrel" spending. Palin backtracked on her initial support and announced that Alaska would no longer build the bridge. However, the state had already begun construction on the road leading to the would-be bridge—using funding that legally could not be used for other purposes. Even after the governor canceled the project, the state nevertheless built a road to a bridge that would not exist. As so many roads across the country require urgent investment, such useless spending shocks us, but smaller versions of this sort of waste happen on a regular basis in road construction. Public Interest Research Group (PIRG) reports annually on wasteful government spending projects, from poorly planned road expansions to unnecessary road constructions, running to costs in the billions,[101] and there are regular reports of corruption in state contracts with construction firms and simple embezzlement, as occurred in Philadelphia's Housing Authority.

Sometimes roads and bridges are put on indefinite pause, with promises of completion when the needed capital materializes. The Birmingham Northern Beltway in Alabama, a proposed loop road circling one of the state's largest cities, has been in development for sixty years. After several rounds of funding and a series of construction stoppages, only a mile of the proposed fifty-two-mile road has been built. A work stoppage due to funding shortfalls in 2016 stalled the road construction for five years, during which time the road became known in Alabama as the "phantom highway."[102] Construction has started again, thanks to investment from the IIJA, but the road will not be completed, even if everything goes according to plan, until 2047. The United States should encourage Chinese construction companies to invest in its toll roads and finish the Birmingham Northern Beltway. In a 2023 talk at the Wahba Institute for Strategic Competition at the Wilson Center in Washington, DC, Secretary of Commerce Gina Raimondo stated that "we need to do business with China wherever we can; we need to promote wherever we can. . . . [T]here is no national security risk to the United States selling coffee and health and beauty aids in China—it creates jobs in America and there's a lot of benefit to doing business where we can."[103] The inverse is also true. The United States should acknowledge China's comparative advantage in civil engineering when it comes to infrastructure development and allow Chinese enterprises to invest in its toll road development. Needless to say, it should not take nearly a hundred years to build a road around a major American city. With rising construction costs and anticipated overruns, even states that have secured initial investment for a road project sometimes cancel their projects for fear of runaway spending. In 2019, for instance, Maine cut $59 million in proposed road projects from its transportation budget over worries that rising construction costs would sink the state into debt.[104]

In the midst of this inability to advance, states should be more open to alternative modes of funding, including VMT taxes, congestion charges, independent regional authority with strong management such as DC Water, and the sort of P3s that Ed Rendell sought for the Pennsylvania Turnpike. In addition to the Chicago Skyway and the Indiana Toll Road, there are privately operated toll roads across the country, including the Dulles Greenway in Virginia, near D.C.; the Orchard Pond Parkway outside Tallahassee, Florida; the Dalton Highway in Alaska; the LBJ Expressway, near Dallas, Texas;

and roads in Colorado, Alabama, and elsewhere. But given the degraded state of American roadways and the financial straits many cities and states have to navigate, it is still surprising P3s are not more common. Moreover, only a small percentage of P3s include long-term concessions on roads. In 2009, after the peak of private concession offers in the United States, only 11 percent of P3 projects in roads and highways offered extended operational rights to private companies.[105] In 2021 the number of public-private partnerships in the country continued to rise, but new P3 contracts included few road or highway projects.[106]

Why does hesitancy about P3s in road projects persist? Highway and road privatization does not always result in success, but even properly structured P3 can shield the taxpayers from any bankruptcy risk. Take the Indiana Toll Road. After its initial privatization in 2007 (which brought in $3.8 billion for the state), the road generated less revenue than its concessionaire expected—again, overestimation of traffic. The flagging motorists and decreased tolling brought the private operator to bankruptcy in 2011, and the creditors sold the asset in 2015 to IFM, another infrastructure firm from Australia (unfortunately for IFM, it could not take the road back to Australia).[107] Although Rendell is correct that the Indiana Toll Road faced stiff criticism from the public, the deal Indiana wrote also protected the state (and taxpayers) from the financial risk of running the road. By allowing the operator to transfer operational rights to the private sector, Indiana also transferred the risk of bankruptcy. This is precisely the value of involving the private sector, which manages risk professionally and accepts such risks as part of its business model. When the company went bankrupt, it was still required to pay its debts and restructured itself to do so. More important, the road continued to function, and the state did not need to assume the bankrupted company's debt—all thanks to the terms of the original lease, as lawmakers reminded voters at the time.[108] The state itself lost *nothing* in the bankruptcy process: it kept its $3.8 billion and, under certain circumstances, could take the road back and sell it again for a new price. Not bad!

Learning from Other Countries

Across the world, countries have increasingly embraced public-private partnerships as a way to generate the necessary capital to develop their infrastructure. In both developing and developed nations, the private sector has increased its participation in funding infrastructure. India, Australia, France, Spain, Chile, Italy—these countries and many others have all invited the private sector to invest in and operate highways.

In addition to India, Australia is one of the world's leaders in P3s and privatized roads. In the early 2010s, Australia embarked on an ambitious effort to upgrade its infrastructure. Despite the fact that over the last decade the country has spent twice as large a percentage of its GDP on infrastructure as the United States, Australia nevertheless saw the necessity of private investment, too. The groundwork for this push began back in the 1980s, with a series of small privatizations and, more importantly, the establishment of enabling laws.[109]

The state of New South Wales, situated on the southwest side of the continent and home to Sydney, leads the country in privatized infrastructure assets, especially roads. In 2016 Sydney announced plans for a system of underground motorways stretching throughout the city, a project known as WestConnex, which is slated for completion in the mid-2020s. Two years later, in 2018, under the administration of Gladys Berejiklian, the city sold a majority stake in the project, 51 percent, to Sydney Transport Partners, comprised of AustralianSuper, Abu Dhabi Investment Authority (it, too, did not take the roads back to Abu Dhabi), and the Canada Pension Plan Investment Board, for $9.3 billion.[110] In 2021 the state sold the company its remaining shares for $11.1 billion,[111] collecting over $20 billion all told for the city. Critics point out that, according to its own estimates, New South Wales may spend more in contributions to financing WestConnex than it received from the private consortium for the lease.[112] But the true benefit of the WestConnex deal derives from the capital investment in a growth fund that will provide long-term debt management.[113]

Today, only four out of all New South Wales's twenty-one major roadways are not owned by Sydney Transportation Partners. With the proceeds from its first road privatizations, New South Wales created the Generations Fund, an investment management entity that will grow the original capital for the state. Its explicit purpose is to eliminate municipal debt for future generations. In 2021 the fund had reached $28 billion.[114] The critical element of that plan was that the state government was able to identify the *use of proceeds* for the taxpayers. Using the proceeds of privatizing basic infrastructure to create a generation fund is a clear, understandable objective that voters can support or not. Between 1988 and 2021 New South Wales privatized much more, too, including its electricity grid, its ports, gas pipelines, a railroad, and many smaller municipal services.[115] It may be too early to confidently judge the outcomes of privatization in Sydney and New South Wales, but the series of bold partnerships with private investors will change the calculus for the city's finances in powerful ways.[116]

Australia stands out as an example of a developed country that has aggressively pursued privatization of its major infrastructure assets, but private roads are growing more common around the world. In 2005 France licensed half of its autoroutes to Vinci, a publicly traded company on the French stock exchange, fetching €15 billion and, more significantly, transferring €19.5 billion of debt to the firm.[117] While privatization did go through, it generated the same type of negative press seen in the United States, mainly driven by increased tolls.

In Spain the story is somewhat different. Spanish infrastructure has been funded with public-private partnerships for much longer than many other countries, since 1967, when the government offered thirty-two eight-year highway concessions. These short-term leases ended in 1975, however, and for twenty years Spain managed its roads directly. Then, between 1998 and 2004, the Spanish state commissioned ten new toll roads to be built around Madrid and the southeast, which were procured using a model in which the concessionaires would build, finance, maintain, and operate the roads. The ten toll roads were developed as nine concession contracts with private firms and became operational just before the start of the financial crisis.

From 2009 forward, the toll roads experienced a sharp drop in traffic levels on the back of reduced economic activity, which significantly impacted the financial performance of the concession companies. Reduced traffic levels, coupled with very optimistic traffic and cost forecasts, resulted in eight of the nine concessions defaulting.[118] The government put in place some measures to try to save concession companies from this fate, including subsidies, loans compensating concessionaires for higher costs, and clearing accounts, but it became apparent that the probability of default was still very high. The state stopped providing financial help to concession companies in 2012 and 2013, which resulted in concessionaires filing for insolvency. In 2018 the toll roads were finally transferred to the state, which has been operating them since then through the state-owned company SEITTSA. Disputes are ongoing between concessionaires, distressed funds, and the government about the compensation amount owed to companies by the state due to the early termination of the concessions.[119] Currently, at least twenty private companies still operate under concessions by the Spanish state and regional governments, running through Léon, Malaga, Cartagena, and many other cities.

In Italy, privatization is even more widespread. The majority of highways in Italy (60 percent) are operated by Autostrade, a company that formed as a state-owned entity in the 1950s and built the majority of the country's highways. In 1999 Italy privatized Autostrade in a €6.6 billion deal, offering the newly private entity a concession until 2038, after which point the network of roads will be handed back to the state. This would be equivalent to the United States privatizing the federal highway system.[120] Chile, another leader in private roads, has a similar story. After it embarked on a large-scale privatization of its roads, which required substantial capital expenditure, the Chilean government updated its concession model, drawing from its early experience to further strengthen the P3 model.[121]

As Rendell proved in Philadelphia, innovative and novel solutions can produce tremendous changes. Too often, even after a detailed analysis of the unique conditions of the financial health of an infrastructure asset, political leaders shy away from doing what is necessary.

The next chapter examines one of the most overlooked opportunities for municipal wealth creation in the country: airports. Once the United States begins considering alternative methods of funding, avenues for recovering its financial health should proliferate.

SİX

TAKING FLIGHT

Bringing US Airports Up to Speed from Missouri to Puerto Rico

RICK: "Louis, I think this is the beginning of a beautiful friendship."
—*Casablanca* (1942)

On July 17, 1996, TWA Flight 800 exploded in the sky minutes after taking off from JFK International Airport in New York. All 230 people on board perished. After a years-long investigation, officials from the National Transportation Safety Board determined the explosion had not been an act of terrorism but was most likely caused by a short circuit near the fuel chamber.[1] Whatever the cause, it was clear to Congress that the catastrophe demanded a review of airport and flight safety, and that fall it introduced the Federal Aviation Reauthorization Act. Reauthorizations of the Federal Aviation Administration (FAA), which is responsible for regulating US airspace and managing air traffic, are not uncommon, but in the 1990s air safety had become more complex, and air traffic had increased heavily. It was time to try something new.

The 1996 reauthorization bill contained updates for safety protocols, as well as accessibility and environmental requirements.[2] But it also established broader ambitions for airports. President Clinton, who signed the bill into law, promised the legislation would form a committee to "create the foundation for a careful analysis of what funding mechanisms will best address the needs of our air transportation system."[3] One of the funding mechanisms lawmakers wanted to explore was privatization, and the Reauthorization Act included a provision for the Airport Privatization Pilot Program, which offered to consider privatization applications from up to five cities and established some incentives for cities to privatize airports, including federal tax breaks.[4]

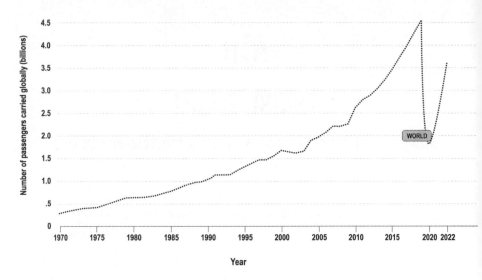

Figure 6.1. Growth of air passengers carried globally, 1970–2022. *Source:* "Air Transport, Passengers Carried—United States," World Bank, accessed July 24, 2023, https://data.worldbank.org/indicator/IS.AIR.PSGR?locations=US; and "Number of Scheduled Passengers Boarded by the Global Airline Industry from 2004 to 2022," Statista, accessed April 25, 2023, https://www.statista.com/statistics/564717/airline-industry -passenger-traffic-globally.

The Airport Privatization Pilot Program aimed to address a number of issues. Air travel has risen sharply and steadily since the 1970s, both in the United States and around the world,[5] and airport capacity has struggled to keep pace. Between 1991 and 2001, US airport capacity increased by only 1 percent, while total air traffic in the United States went up 37 percent.[6] The capacity crunch not only created delays but also affected safety, as congestion can increase the risk of runway accidents.[7] This explosive growth was not limited to the United States, as figure 6.1 shows. Globally, passenger volumes increased in particular during the second decade of the twenty-first century, with an unexpected collapse due to the COVID-19 pandemic followed by a rebound.

At the same time that airports grappled with congestion, they also had to contend with increasing security concerns.[8] Hijackings throughout the 1960s and 1970s ushered in a battery of new safety measures, beginning with anti-hijacking screening and profiling programs, which were first introduced to New Orleans's Moisant Airport in 1970 (now Louis Armstrong

International Airport) but were soon implemented nationally by President Nixon.[9] In 1988 the FAA mandated baggage screening at all US airports, and after al-Qaeda hijacked and turned four planes into weapons on September 11, 2001, airports embraced an even more stringent set of security requirements.[10] In 2022 I joined the National Infrastructure Advisory Council, originally created by President George W. Bush in the aftermath of 9/11 to address these concerns,[11] and I can attest to the rigorous security requirements it set in place and to the challenges airports continually face in terms of physical threats as well as cybersecurity attacks.

In addition to the costs associated with these security measures, throughout the 1980s, 1990s, and 2000s, the FAA also began to require airports to install new radar, meteorological, and GPS technology.[12] As the cost of running airports increased with new security and technology requirements, the government devoted little capital to airport expansion that would address the original capacity problem.[13] Overcrowding ballooned, and nationwide the investment gap grew. In 1998 the ASCE Infrastructure Report Card gave US aviation a C–,[14] which by 2001 had fallen to a D.[15]

It made sense, then, for Congress to want to transfer operations of airports back to the private sector. As with roads, water systems, and the electric grid, US airports were originally owned and operated by private entities. In the first half of the twentieth century, Ford Motor Company built and owned one of the world's first modern airports, located in Dearborn, Michigan, and Pan American Airlines owned its own airport in Miami. At the start of the 1930s, roughly half of the country's 1,100 airports were owned by private operators.[16] Over the course of the 1930s, things changed dramatically. With the 1926 Air Commerce Act, Congress rejected the notion that the federal government should be involved in funding or managing airports and ruled instead that aerodromes and airfields should be regulated much the same way as ports, giving rise to the neologism "airport."[17] With the growing risks of a global war, however, the government switched its posture, arguing that airports had become vital to national security. In the Civil Aeronautics Act of 1938, Congress appropriated $40 million ($848 million in 2023 dollars) for the construction and improvement of 250 airports, and at the end of World War II the Surplus Property Act of 1944 transferred many military airbases to civilian management for commercial use. By 1958 the government had so completely reversed its initial position that the newly created FAA even prohibited private entities from controlling airports with commercial traffic,[18] spelling the final end of the privately owned American airport.[19] In the 1990s the stringency of US policy with respect to private operators began to ease. Yet as the Airport Privatization Pilot Program got off the ground, it did not have the effect policymakers had hoped. There may be renewed interest in public-private partnerships, as Ed Rendell surmised, but today there is still only one large airport in the entire country under private operation—Luis Muñoz Marín International Airport in Puerto Rico—even as capacity and funding shortages persist. Though it is the only example, Luis Muñoz Marín International provides a strong anecdotal case for privatization of US airports. The public-private partnership created to reconstruct Puerto Rico's primary airport has been an enormous success for all parties. Going to an airport today feels more like a bureaucratic ordeal than a trip to a vaunted hub of cultural transmission. The experiential and customer service shortcomings of airports ought to be addressed, but more importantly, airports must be expanded and developed to ensure the global community continues to grow and interact.

This chapter takes a closer look at the causes of the infrastructure investment gap and explores why the Airport Privatization Pilot Program has failed to spur change. As we will see, despite the near total absence of private airports in the United States, airport privatization has become resoundingly popular around the world, and in many instances it has provided positive outcomes. As in the water sector, it is certainly not the case that privatization would work for every US airport, but there is no doubt it can produce positive change at many of them. Once again, privatization means many things: from an outright sale of the airport, as the UK government did in the 1980s, to P3s along the lines of the deals that are transforming JFK and LaGuardia airports in New York City or Puerto Rico's successful P3.

Flying Domestic: The Failed Attempt to Privatize Lambert International Airport

The Airport Privatization Pilot Program, known since 2018 as the Airport Investment Partnership Program (AIPP), did not succeed in creating a truly diversified airport sector. In the years since the program began, only two applications have been successful, and there have been several high-profile failures. One of the most recent examples of a failed attempt was in St. Louis, and the story of what happened to the city's Lambert International Airport illustrates important points about how airport privatization—and privatization more generally—can go wrong. In fact, Lambert International provides a useful case study of how *not* to privatize an airport.

In 2017 St. Louis's longest-serving mayor, Francis Slay, submitted Lambert Airport for consideration by the Airport Privatization Pilot Program. Slay had won a record four terms in the mayor's office. First elected mayor in 2001, Slay had been president of the St. Louis Board of Aldermen and belonged to the generation of New Democrats spearheaded by Bill Clinton, Richard M. Daley, and Ed Rendell. Under Slay's governance, St. Louis constructed major new infrastructure, including Busch Stadium, a new home for the St. Louis Cardinals, and undertook an enormous revitalization of its downtown area. Over two decades, the Washington Avenue Historic District received $6 billion in investments to transform the city's traditional garment district into an arts- and fashion-oriented commercial center, now bustling with upscale restaurants, galleries, and loft apartments.[20] In seven years the city built sixty-six hundred new downtown residences. The effort won the Preserve America Presidential Award in 2007. In addition to the main downtown area, during Slay's tenure St. Louis also revitalized Ballpark Village, around the new stadium, the Kiener Plaza, home to the famous Gateway Arch, as well as the sculpture park Citygarden, the mercantile district, the Central Library, the historic opera house Stifel Theater, and the public aquarium.[21] St. Louis accomplished all this using a combination of public and private investment. Much of the funding came through the St. Louis Development Corporation, a state-run corporation, but additional funds came from the private sector. The St. Louis City Council had passed a law in 1998 offering a 25 percent tax credit to private businesses developing the downtown area, and a public-private partnership, Downtown Now!, offered funding for private enterprises through grants.[22]

Considering the role given to the private sector in St. Louis's new development, privatizing Lambert Airport made sense as an extension of the city's efforts to refurbish its infrastructure. After a discussion in 2015 with David Agnew, a managing director with the Australian infrastructure firm Macquarie Group and former deputy assistant to President Obama, Mayor Slay began considering the idea of privatization. At the time the airport needed $900 million in capital improvements over a decade,[23] and it had $630 million in debt.[24] More unusually, the airport also suffered from *low* traffic, having more runways and terminals than it needed for its flights. Overall, the airport's finances were stable, and its credit rating was in fact improving. (In 2016, the airport had a BBB+ rating, which by 2017 had risen to A– and in 2018 became an A.)[25] St. Louis itself was also experiencing financial growth, operating at a surplus, and paying down its debts.[26] The problem was not that the airport could not cover its debt obligations, or that the city could not afford to operate it, but rather that the airport was run inefficiently.[27]

To consider the possibility of privatizing the airport, the city needed to fund a formal exploration, but after two decades of large investments this would cost money that the city did not have. Instead, Mayor Slay approached the businessman and political donor Rex Sinquefield. Sinquefield made his name at the National Bank of Chicago as one of the pioneers of passively managed index funds and, after Missouri abolished its campaign contribution limits in 2009, became a political force in his home city of St. Louis through generous contributions to both parties and the creation of a think tank, the Show-Me Institute, which researches public policy issues. Often described as a libertarian, he has advocated for replacing the Missouri income tax with a sales tax and has championed the expansion of charter schools.[28] Sinquefield is also a chess master and dedicated proponent of the game of chess.[29] He built the largest chess club in the world; boasts the most extensive collection of chess memorabilia; and brought the US Chess Hall of Fame to St. Louis in 2011,[30] making the city a "chess mecca," according to a segment on Sinquefield produced by HBO's *Real Sports*.[31]

Sinquefield agreed to fund Slay's exploratory committee and founded a nonprofit organization to conduct the research, which he named Grow Missouri. For president of the organization, Sinquefield chose one of his closest political consultants and lobbyists, Travis Brown. Though he was instrumental in pushing the privatization effort forward, Sinquefield's participation also spelled trouble. With a large private investor taking charge of the exploratory committee, the privatization discussions appeared to exclude public participation, which would later give fodder to activists organizing against a potential deal. It would be one of several accusations that city officials were colluding behind closed doors with business leaders in order to privatize Lambert Airport. In hindsight, the city should have explored a broader set of alternatives, including an independently managed city entity with an independent management reporting to a board free from political influence, as David Gadis, CEO of DC Water, explained.

Slay demurred on privatization until the final months of his last term. In 2018 he submitted the application to the Airport Privatization Pilot Program, then left office. The primary mechanisms supporting the privatization effort belonged to Sinquefield, not the state, and so when a new mayor came into office, she had little commitment to the project. Why did Slay not establish a better framework or legal guardrails to ensure transparent and democratic debate? Why did he wait until he was already out the door to begin such a significant process?

In an op-ed for the *St. Louis Dispatch* in 2018, Slay explained that he had only firmly decided to explore privatization during his last months in office, "after many years of listening to airport stakeholders and the business community talk about the airport's massive debt, limited connectivity, significant excess capacity, and how Lambert does not stack up to airports in other cities." What pushed him over the line toward privatization was a frank accounting of the city's finances. "The long-term outlook for the city budget, even with a strong economy, remains troublesome," he wrote. The rationale behind his decision was reasonable, even if it did not set the city up well for success. "I wanted to leave my successor with the best possible options to move our city forward," he explained, by creating an opportunity to explore privatization more seriously.

> Getting into the FAA program commits the city to nothing. I expect that, unless the city gets a proposal that would keep the airport under city ownership, improve our airport, increase airport revenues without an increased burden on passengers and airlines, protect the jobs of airport employees, and provide a much-needed infusion of cash to stabilize the city's finances and make investments in our people and neighborhoods, the Board of Estimate and Apportionment and Board of Aldermen would choose the status quo. But, given the untapped potential of our airport and the precarious state of city finances, I believe we owe it to ourselves to *explore the possibilities* [emphasis added].[32]

Mayor Slay was absolutely right to want to explore the possibilities, but his explanation is not the sort of pitch that is likely to win over a city council, which historically has been loath to give up control of important infrastructure assets. Slay concluded the op-ed by commenting that "sometimes the best deal is the one you don't make. But we owe it to ourselves to find out what is possible." Though Slay went further than most in pushing for an airport P3, he gave a strong nod to the prevailing attitude of hesitancy. According to former congressman Mark Kennedy of Minnesota, standing behind the value proposition of privatization is essential to convincing voters and politicians alike. "You need governors and mayors that will champion getting the cost benefit analysis, and why it's a good value for them, in some cases, to pay for private operations."

Many additional factors turned opinion against Slay's proposition, however. When Grow Missouri began canvassing the city to poll residents' views on airport privatization, critics accused the nonprofit of bias toward privatization.[33] A group called St. Louis Not for Sale mounted opposition. The group originally organized to protest the long-term lease of St. Louis's water infrastructure to Veolia in 2010[34]—an initiative also advocated by Sinquefield's Show-Me Institute[35]—and reassembled to fight the airport project.[36] St. Louis Not for Sale worked to paint the privatization effort as a plot by the city's political donor class to "sell the family jewels." The group gained support from a number of city leaders, including Alderwoman Megan Green, who argued that "the canvassing at the doors needs to be a transparent, unbiased process, and that's not what's happening right now."[37]

The question of what voters ultimately want is a tricky one. As discussed in the previous chapter, the survey I conducted years after the privatizations in Chicago shows that users want better service *irrespective of who delivers it*, and the majority of them do not view infrastructure management as a question of principle. In the survey conducted in the summer of 2022, 59 percent of those who expressed a view were content to allow private companies to manage assets. Interestingly, those with higher household income, $100,000 or above (who presumably are more frequent users of airports than lower income households), were very much in favor of privatization: 50 percent said "yes" or "probably yes" when asked if the private sector should be allowed to manage infrastructure, compared to 34 percent who said no or probably not. Republicans were slightly more inclined to say yes than Democrats, but not by much (46 v. 42 percent). African American households also felt more strongly than white households that the private sector should be allowed to operate airports (50 percent compared to 40 percent).[38] My point is that ultimately these statistics indicate that no one has a fundamental objection to infrastructure privatization, despite what some politicians argue. What people want is good, efficient, and fair service. And yes, they would even be willing to pay more if they felt they would get better service.

In 2017 Slay retired, declining another run for the mayorship, and left a crowded field of candidates vying to replace him in the Democratic primary. The ultimate winner of the primary, and then the general election, was Lyda Krewson, who resembled Slay in many ways: a former alderwoman, a mainstream Democrat, and friendly to business and the private sector. Born in Iowa, Krewson relocated to St. Louis after college; horrifyingly, early in her time in the city, her husband was murdered in front of her by a paroled convict. During her time in office, Krewson spent much of her energy addressing crime and homelessness in the city.[39]

When she took office, Krewson endorsed the privatization exploration plan, if somewhat tentatively. In a statement to the press she said, "This is a great opportunity to explore a public-private partnership for the airport. I appreciate their consideration of our application and look forward to working with the FAA throughout the process, but as always, the key is in the details."[40] As the privatization program continued, however, the public outcry increased.

Opponents of privatization made the case that city officials had been self-dealing or preparing sweetheart deals for friends. After leaving office, Francis Slay took a position as a lobbyist at Ferrovial, the Spanish infrastructure investor, which made a bid on Lambert Airport. Slay's chief of staff, Jeff Rainford, took a lobbying job with STL Aviation Group, a firm that would also later bid on Lambert. Although such transitions from one position to another are common and legal, activists used them as evidence of conflict of interest.[41] In what became the most hot button point in the debate, Sinquefield's longtime colleague Travis Brown, who headed up Grow Missouri, led the team pursuing unbiased exploration into privatization at the same time that he was also leading another city initiative, known as Better Together, which hoped to unify St. Louis with the surrounding county and believed privatization of the airport would aid that effort.[42]

With these crossovers between public and private enterprises and potential conflicts of interest, it was imperative for city officials to offer as much transparency to voters and airport users as possible. But this is not how the city proceeded. In 2018 Krewson formed the Airport Advisory Working Group to facilitate the privatization and generate more political buy-in; several members of the board of aldermen belonged to the group, including privatization critic Cara Green, as well as the city budget director, Paul Payne.[43] The effort backfired, however, when the working group held many of its meetings behind closed doors; forty-seven meetings between 2018 and 2019 were closed to the public.[44] The apparent secrecy of the meetings spurred a lawsuit by the Sunshine and Government Accountability Project, spearheaded by lawyer Mark Pedroli.[45] Missouri's so-called Sunshine Law, officially known as Chapter 610 of the Revised Statutes of Missouri, ensures public access to government proceedings and documents.[46] In 2019 Pedroli sued to invalidate any decisions the group might make, arguing the meetings were illegal. (The lawsuit was ongoing as of 2023.)

The argument that the city's plan catered to private investors rather than the public was strengthened when Grow Missouri, the Sinquefield research group that issued the request for bids on the airport, also submitted a bid to manage the airport itself—and then won the bidding. It appeared Sinquefield's group had established circumstances in which it would itself be given operational control of Lambert. Losing bidders fed the public outcry, accusing the advisory group of "significant conflicts of interest" and establishing "perverse incentives for advisors."[47] It appeared to opponents that Sinquefield had bought himself the airport and that city officials had helped by excluding the public from participation. Once again, it is not unusual for a bidder on an asset to lead a privatization exploration, but what allowed criticism to flourish was the lack of transparency around the organization.

At first Krewson insisted the only approval needed for the deal would come from the working group, the FAA, and the airlines flying into Lambert. Under pressure from critics, however, Krewson eventually acknowledged it might be necessary to put privatization to a vote. Then the meeting minutes of a discussion among the working group about Rainford's apparent conflict of interest were leaked to the press, causing fresh uproar. In the wake of Pedroli's lawsuit and mounting criticisms, Krewson abruptly called a halt to the privatization exploration, citing lack of public support. "When I inherited this idea in April 2017, I agreed to explore the concept to determine if we could get a better airport. As we have worked, I have also been listening closely to residents, business leaders, and other elected officials. They have expressed serious concerns and trepidation about the process, and about the possibility that a private entity might operate the airport."[48] The effort had been killed. Krewson's decision to end the privatization process frustrated advocates of the plan but didn't win her support from its opponents. In 2021 Krewson announced she would not seek another term.

In many ways it is unfortunate for the city that the Lambert privatization failed. The lease of the airport could have paid off the entire $600 million in airport debt and produced an additional $2 billion for the city.[49] What's more, by privatizing the airport the city would have unlocked twelve hundred acres of undeveloped land surrounding the airport, which the city did not control but could have been developed under private ownership, creating more jobs and more commerce surrounding the airport. Moreover, the airport itself might have expanded its traffic, creating more travel to St. Louis and making better use of the airport's capacity.

The city of St. Louis remains in good economic standing, generating a surplus of $32 million in 2021 and $49 million in 2022.[50] Lambert Airport also improved performance over this period; it recorded passenger growth for forty-nine consecutive months and has paid down more than $30 million of its $630 million in debt.[51] Lambert Airport remains an attractive option for privatization in part because it is a healthy asset with room for growth. The airport ultimately produces little capital for the city and has not reached its economic potential.

The privatization effort failed for a number of reasons. The apparent conflicts of interest gave fodder to critics, but ultimately what upset lawmakers was the secrecy with which the process was conducted. Ensuring public buy-in is one of the most important requisites for privatization: without public support, politicians will have a difficult time following through—just as Krewson did.

There is no guarantee that the privatization of Lambert Airport would have gone ahead if meetings had been held in the open. But if Mayor Slay had started the process with an outreach campaign funded through the city itself, rather than a private nonprofit, and had introduced a ballot measure about privatization, there is reason to think it might have gone better. Different mechanisms could also have been explored, such as P3 programs of the kind the Port Authority of New York and New Jersey (PANYNJ) adopted.

St. Louis also faced a steep climb, however. As the first city to consider privatizing a major airport, it was navigating uncharted territory. After shutting down the airport privatization working group, Krewson commented: "We would have been the first, the first in the US. When you're the first at something, there's a lot of risk, there's a lot of trepidation and a lot of concern. And I just think there's too much of that to move forward with this."[52] There was reason to believe St. Louis would serve as a model test case for airport privatization. Missouri has long been a proving ground for the country's future—from its early days as a trading outpost on the edge of the Louisiana Purchase, to its special status in the Missouri Compromise, to its unique position as an independent city. It is to the city's credit that the privatization process went as far as it did, even if it eventually failed. The willingness of political leaders to explore the option at least opened the possibility, and in the future, it may be easier to execute. Merely entertaining the idea is a step in the right direction.

I asked Emilio Gonzalez to explain some of the thinking behind airport privatization and resistance in the United States. Formerly aviation director and CEO of Miami International Airport (MIA), Gonzalez was born in

Havana, Cuba, and moved to Florida in his youth to study international relations. After serving in the Department of Homeland Security as director of US Citizenship and Immigration, he later became the city administrator of Miami before transitioning into a leadership role at the Miami Airport. MIA is ranked among the nation's largest and busiest airports; more travelers passed through Miami's terminals than any other US airport in 2022.[53] It serves roughly fifty million passengers annually, eighty airlines, and 150 destinations. As one of the country's largest cargo airports, it generates $65–70 billion in economic activity annually.[54] "Running an airport is not something you go to school for," Gonzalez told me, noting it was unusual for an airport to hire an outsider like himself. "Essentially, you have professionals that will rise through the ranks in their own airport, or they're recruited from other airports. It is a very incestuous population."

If a hire from federal or municipal government is unusual, it is even rarer for politicians to seek private sector management or to consider a P3 to run an airport. This is not because the private sector would be unable to manage an airport but rather, according to Gonzalez, because of the value of managing local airports to municipal leaders and state politicians. "Airports that are owned and operated by municipalities tend to get stuck in political issues," he said. "Everybody wants to have reach into the airport: the airport generates jobs, brings in money—Miami International is by far the largest economic engine in the state of Florida—and politicians don't want to let go of that. They want to be able to opine on who should get a contract with the airport; they want to review the budget, even though they don't necessarily understand it. They do not want to let that go. It's an economic power that they genuinely don't want to let go."

These are almost the same words David Gadis at DC Water used when I asked him why municipalities do not bring in private operators to improve the state of affairs in their municipal water and waste systems. "They lose control," Gadis said.

> When you think about running a city, as a mayor or a city administrator or whatever it may be, you have different segments to manage, from tax structure to police officers and fire fighters. And most of these structures that you're running as a mayor, they are structures that only spend money. The police department doesn't make money, the fire department doesn't make money. When you think about all of the other things that fall under a mayoralty, the water utility is the one that's bringing cash in the door. And no one wants to lose control of a cash cow.

The reticence is not based solely on city or state economics, though, because in the case of Miami International, like nearly all airports, revenue goes directly back into the airport and cannot be used for other purposes in the municipal budget. The fear of losing control itself—influence over decision-making around operations and development—seems to be a primary motivation.

It is, then, laudable of Mayor Slay to have even broached the possibility. But St. Louis is not the only city to have attempted to escape the governmental model of airport management. Twelve other municipalities have submitted applications to the Airport Privatization Pilot Program: nine were withdrawn by the applying airport, one was terminated, and only two have been approved. When cities do try to change operational approaches, they confront a variety of challenges from myriad sources.

What's Wrong with US Airports?

Today, US airports face a host of issues. Unlike St. Louis, most American airports suffer from terrible congestion. In 2019 alone, the year before the COVID-19 pandemic profoundly disrupted the aviation industry, US airports ran with ninety-five million minutes of delays. Between 2017 and 2019 the percentage of flights that provided on-time service fell further from 80 to 79 percent. Travelers also rate US airports below foreign facilities when it comes to service; of the most popular airports in the world, only George Bush Intercontinental, in Houston, Texas, breaks into the top twenty-five, coming in at twenty-fifth in the world.[55] What's more, US airports are accused of running inefficiently, wasting government grant money and allocating funds to projects determined by political calculation rather than market need.[56] Funding often goes to low-growth airports rather than major airports, as well. The FAA's Airport Improvement Fund disproportionately issues grants to smaller airports, leaving larger facilities to invest in their own development.[57] (The Airport Improvement Program covers 75 percent of costs for improvements to large and medium airports, but 90–95 percent of costs for small airports.)[58] The question is, why should taxpayers foot the bill?

When considering what ought to be done about US airports, one must also factor them into the larger picture of state and local economies. The allocations from the federal government through the FAA, as well as the debt incurred by states and cities for airport expansions and new construction, could all be diverted to sectors better suited to state management, such as education and policing. Airports are among the most valuable assets owned by government agencies, and their sale or lease would generate transformative injections of capital into local budgets, which could in turn help invest in infrastructure and other services more broadly. Despite airports' great value, operation of an airport typically provides relatively modest reserve capital for local governments. Moreover, airports benefit communities through more than just operational profits; airports are themselves centers of commerce that generate significant sales tax for cities and states, and they also directly generate economic and population growth, as several studies have confirmed.[59]

It is understandable that states want to protect these assets (even if sometimes for the wrong reasons), and any privatization effort must be done carefully. But the true potential of airports to generate revenue has not been realized. Without the needed investment to expand airports, there is no ability to create more jobs and generate more tax revenue through expanded flights and the increased commerce that flights yield.

Why has the absence of privatization been so complete among US airports? According to opponents of privatization, it is simply that there is no need for it. It is "a solution to a non-existent problem," as one airline official put it.[60] This might be unexpected, given the clear need for expansion and the outcry over underfunding from aviation groups like the Airport Council International.[61] The reason privatization may not seem a useful solution is that airports maintain diverse streams of revenue, and therefore airports have other ways of increasing revenue to address capacity issues. Though airports do issue bonds to finance major projects, they do not rely on taxation to service their bond obligations. In fact, large airports typically do not rely on tax revenue at all. Airport funding comes primarily from three sources: (1) the FAA's Airport Improvement Program, which draws funds from taxes on airplane fuel and ticket sales (a user fee); (2) the passenger facility charge, a user fee added to ticket prices; and (3) terminal and concession rents and fees paid by airlines for runway use and tenants who operate duty-free shops, concessions in food courts, or other airport businesses.[62]

To see this more concretely, let's look at Los Angeles International Airport's budget summarized in figure 6.2. In the proposed budget for 2023, 74 percent of LAX's revenue came from rents and fees charged to airlines, of which 47 percent came from terminal rents and another 26 percent from concession revenues including parking revenues as well as fees generated from lease rentals of shops and other facilities. LAX projected a total

FY2023 vs FY2022 LAWA Operating Budget

($ Millions)	FY2022 Adopted Budget	FY2023 Proposed Budget	Increase/(Decrease) $	%
Revenues	$1,313	$1,731	$418	32%
Expenses	(910)	(988)	78	9%
Operating Income	$403	$743	$340	84%
Net Debt Service	(254)	(345)	91	36%
Remaining for Capital and Reserves	$149	$398	$249	167%
LAX Debt Service Coverage	1.8x	2.3x	0.5x	28%

Figure 6.2. LAX 2023 projected budget. *Source:* "Fiscal Year 2022–2023 Proposed Budget," Los Angeles World Airports, June 2, 2022, https://www.lawa.org/lawa -investor-relations.

revenue of $1.7 billion; after meeting its debt obligations, totaling $345 million, and accounting for operating expenses of $988 million, the airport expected $398 million remaining for capital and reserves.[63]

For major development projects, too, airports enjoy more diverse sources of capital than other forms of infrastructure do, largely because airports already work closely with the private sector. Airlines, which are almost entirely privately owned, contribute significant amounts to airport development, on top of what cities, states, and the federal government contribute with bond issuances and grants. The expansion of LaGuardia airport in New York, for instance, saw billions in investment from Delta Airlines.[64] One could argue that the private sector, through airline companies, is already very much invested in airports. But that is like inviting the fox to invest in the henhouse.

Although airports receive adequate funding for operations, what they lack is capital for growth, which is badly needed both for systems upgrades and to expand with demand. According to the ASCE, 50 percent of airports' financial need is in construction of new terminals and runways. Need for terminal repair grew by 60 percent between 2017 and 2019, and runway repair needs increased by 28 percent. In total, the aviation sector needs investment of $27.6 billion to bring its systems up to par.[65] The lobbying group Airports Council International offered a much larger number, estimating the total need for airports through 2023 was $128 billion.[66] The capital needed for these expansions cannot be generated through the means at the disposal of airport operators. The FAA's Airport Improvement Program provides grants to states, but they are not sufficient to match the increases in air traffic. Even the Biden administration's allocation of $1 billion to ninety-nine airports through the IIJA in 2023 will only scratch the surface.[67] As shown in figure 6.1, between 2017 and 2019 (again excluding the sharp drop in traffic due to the COVID-19 pandemic), the number of airport users rose from 964 million to 1.2 billion. Total US delays increased during this period from sixty-five million minutes to ninety-five million minutes.[68]

The need for airports to grow extends beyond the capacity crunch as well. There is enormous pressure on airports to increase revenue because, as Emilio Gonzalez put it, "if you're not growing as an airport, you become a very, very expensive real estate property." The imperative for growth means that airport administrations need constantly to innovate new streams of revenue, not only for large capital projects but merely to justify occupying real estate that could otherwise be growing the economy. "You've always got to find a way to monetize the airport, whether it is with additional flights from existing carriers or it is additional flights from new carriers," Gonzalez said.

Besides the St. Louis case, there has been one other infamous failure since the inception of the 1996 Airport Privatization Pilot Program. The airport perhaps most discussed for privatization is Chicago's Midway International Airport, the Second City's second, smaller airport after O'Hare. In 2007 Mayor Richard M. Daley applied to privatize the airport. Chicago advanced to the final stage of the privatization process and secured a deal with the Midway Investment and Development Corporation, a consortium that included Citi Infrastructure Investors, Vancouver Airport Services, and John Hancock Life Insurance Company. In 2009, just as the deal was nearing completion, private investors were unable to raise the capital to meet the $2.5 billion the city had negotiated for a ninety-nine-year lease of the airport.[69] Four years later, in 2013, Mayor Rahm Emanuel tried again. The Great Lakes Airport Alliance, a group comprised of Macquarie Infrastructure and Real Assets and Ferrovial, as well as a partnership between Industry Funds Management and Manchester Airports Group (the airport management team controlled by borough councils of Greater Manchester in the United Kingdom), initially both bid on the airport. But when the latter withdrew itself from consideration, and only the Great Lakes Airport

Alliance was left in the bidding, Emanuel canceled the privatization plans, arguing the city needed a bidding war to obtain the best deal for Chicago, and with only one bidder, the city had lost leverage.[70]

There have been several similar failed attempts. In 2003 New Orleans began a five-year process of applying to privatize a small, reliever facility outside New Orleans called Lakefront Airport, and then in 2009 tried to privatize its largest airport, Louis Armstrong International Airport. In both cases the city withdrew its application after aviation experts, and groups like the Aircraft Owners and Pilots Association,[71] opposed the city's plan due to uncertainty over the relatively untested Privatization Pilot Program and the FAA requirements for private investors, which asked applicants to overcome significant hurdles and stipulated unfavorable operating conditions, according to critics.[72]

The first, and for nearly twenty years the only, commercial airport to apply successfully for the FAA's Investment Partnership Program was Stewart International Airport in Newburgh, New York, which the state licensed in 2000 to National Express, a British transportation company, on a ninety-nine-year lease, for $35 million. But in 2007 National Express announced it would focus its US investments on school bus services and opted to re-license Stewart to another infrastructure management firm. Instead, the PANYNJ voted to buy the lease from National Express for $78 million, bringing the airport back under state control.[73] The privatization lasted only seven years, and after it ended there were once again no privately operated airports in the country.

The process could be improved, however. One of the persistent criticisms of the Airport Privatization Pilot Program (before it became the AIPP) concerned the cap it placed on the number of airports that may apply. Beginning in 1997, Congress limited the number of privatized airports in the country to five. The federal government raised the cap from five to ten in the 2012 reauthorization of the FAA, and a year later Puerto Rico submitted its application to privatize Luis Muñoz Marín International Airport, the most successful of any infrastructure privatization. In 2018 Congress removed the cap entirely, and the following year, Hendry County Airglade Airport finalized an application it had begun in 2010, in what would be the second successful application after the Stewart Airport debacle. (As of 2023, the airport's application remained in limbo, awaiting financial documents from investors and environmental assessments.)[74] The new applications that followed the loosening of the applicant cap do not imply directly that more airports would privatize in the absence of limits; since the cap was removed in 2018, applications have not dramatically increased. But critics argue on several fronts that a less restrictive attitude toward privatization would create greater interest among both local governments and private investors. Even since the 2018 change, the process still poses considerable obstacles to applicants, and the same problems persist, as the example of Lambert Airport demonstrates.

The AIPP still offers too few incentives for local officials to apply. A report on how to improve the program, which Congress commissioned from the RAND Corporation as part of the 2018 Reauthorization Act, recommends a number of measures. It suggests, for instance, allowing the public sector to direct privatization revenue toward non-airport spending and argues that the United States should offer tax exempt bond issuances not only to state operators but also to private operators.[75]

Given the set of challenges, it would seem that private sector involvement could provide an alternative for airport management; after all, if state-run entities have to date not done a satisfactory job pursuing economic growth, generating innovative revenue streams, or maximizing efficiency and production, then alternative solutions should be examined. The aviation industry has already tacitly acknowledged this. In part, airport authorities were created to function like private sector entities within the public sector. "Airports that are owned and operated by independent authorities run much more like a business, much smoother than those that are run directly by municipal government," Gonzalez argued. But efficiency still lags, as does profit. When asked about the ideal model for airport management, Gonzalez did not hesitate:

> A totally private model. A municipality or an authority selling its asset. You create a strategic plan so that the buying entity lays out what its plan is for the airport, what the minimum guarantees would be for the community up front, what costs there would be for the community, and what benefits there would be for the community. And then you move out of the way, create a nominal oversight structure, maybe for reporting purposes, but not one that has administrative responsibilities, and then you just unleash the power of the private entity.

Of course, which economic framework is best suited for a given project, including regulatory oversight and governance, can depend on the objectives of the community.

Not everyone agrees with Gonzalez. In the absence of privatization, there are other steps that can and should be taken to increase airport revenue and capacity. One thing all who advocate for airports agree on is that the passenger facility charge—the airport user fee—is too low. Congress sets the rates airports can charge customers who land or depart, and this fee has remained flat for over twenty years.[76] It is a reasonable question to ask why Congress should have the power to regulate airport rates. Does it regulate parking rates? Should the state determine that pricing?

The passenger facility charge originated in Evansville, Indiana (the crossroads of America again at the center of infrastructure development) in 1967, when the city began charging a "head tax," a $1 enplaning fee that would go toward funding airport operations. Airlines disliked the policy, as did many lawmakers, but the strategy caught on at airports around the country. In 1972, in a decision on a lawsuit filed by Delta Airlines that argued the charge amounted to an illegal tax rather than a user fee, the Supreme Court ruled in favor of the airports and deemed the head tax constitutional.[77] But this was not the end of the issue; that same year Congress, more sympathetic to the airlines' argument, banned such airport fees. They remained outlawed until 1990, when the financial situation of airports became more acute.

In 1990 Congress struck the law banning the passenger facility charge and instituted a national limit on such fees instead. The passenger fee was initially capped at $3.00. In 2000, as the airport credit crunch came into clearer view, Congress increased the cap to $4.50, where it has stayed ever since; in real terms that fee is equivalent to $2.72 in 2023 dollars, according to the RAND Corporation's study,[78] less than the original cap. Like the fuel tax, the controversy surrounding the passenger charge scares politicians away from attempting to raise it, despite the clear need.

Some argue that raising the passenger facility charge alone could satisfy the development needs of US airports.[79] Depending on the rate hike, this may be correct. But this focuses on revenue issues when we need to account for passenger experience as well as the opportunity to increase economic development around economic agents like airports. It does not address inefficiencies in management, either, or the vulnerability of state governments and budgets to shortfalls in airport revenue. And we should remember again the rest of the economy: cash-strapped municipalities are sitting on enormous, untapped potential capital they could unlock by leasing airports.

Even understanding the obstacles, the lack of success in privatizing US airports is still puzzling, especially given how common private management of airports is outside of the United States and how successful privatized airports have been relative to nonprivatized airports.

Flying International: How Privatization Swept European Airports

Before 1987 the government of the United Kingdom owned and operated all of the country's airports, much as states and cities hold virtual monopoly ownership of airports in the United States today. When Margaret Thatcher turned her privatization program to the aviation sector, however, that quickly changed. In July 1987, having passed through Parliament the previous year a law authorizing airport privatization, the United Kingdom floated the British Airports Authority (BAA) on the London stock exchange. I was in England studying at the London School of Economics and managed to save £500 to invest in the BAA privatization. The authority, along with the seven major airports under its management, had an estimated worth of £1.2 billion (£4 billion in 2023 pounds, or $4.9 billion).[80] That year, Heathrow, Gatwick, Stansted, Southampton, Glasgow, Edinburgh, and Luton airports were sold in 1.4 billion shares to 2.2 million shareholders.[81]

The privatization of British airports kicked up a wave of privatizations that swept across Europe throughout the 1990s and continues today.[82] Vienna privatized its airport in 1992 through floatation.[83] Copenhagen followed suit in 1994, and then Rome in 1997. By 2000 Rome had sold over 99 percent of Aeroporti di Roma, the Roman aviation authority, along with both its major airports, to a single operator. Frankfurt and Athens privatized their airports in 2001, and Brussels and Budapest did so in 2005. Paris's Charles de Gaulle Airport was floated on the Paris stock exchange in 2006, with the French government maintaining a majority share (another interesting variation on the privatization model). Privatizations continued into the 2010s as well. In 2011 Spain privatized the authority that manages all of the country's major airports. In 2017 Greece sold its entire regional airport system, and that same year France expanded its privatizations to the south, in Toulouse, Nice, and Lyon.[84]

The percent of airports with private participation in the United States is under 1 percent, while in Europe 43 percent of airports have some private sector participation. More tellingly, privatized hubs in Europe handle 75 percent of the continent's passenger volume. The number of privatized airports in Asia (26 percent) also far exceeds that of the United States, as does the number in Latin America and the Caribbean (25 percent).[85] Not only did privatization pass through European governments, but it has also been successful on several measures. Privatized airports are well represented among the highest rated airports in the world. Of the top twenty highest ranked airports, as determined by the World Bank, five are privately owned, eight are managed through public-private partnerships, and the remaining seven are under state ownership.[86] The airport growth crunch is a global phenomenon, and it can seem that the United States is the only country that is not doing everything it can to address the problem.

The example of Paris illustrates a successful privatization, or partial privatization. Paris's airports—Charles de Gaulle, Orly, and Le Bourget—belong to Aéroports de Paris (ADP), which was established in 1945 as a public corporation. Under the administration of President Jacques Chirac, France enacted a law in 2005 to transform the institution into an LLC, and the following year the French government sold 30 percent of the authority's shares on the stock exchange, reaping about €600 million in revenue (€847 million 2023 euros, or $896 million).[87] The government poured this capital into terminal facilities at Charles de Gaulle, greatly expanding capacity and updating its systems.[88] It also used the influx to pay down airport debt obligations.[89]

In France the government promised to maintain a majority share of the authority, in recognition of the opposition mounted against the privatization by the French Airports Union. In 2023 the government still controlled 50.6 percent of the corporate shares. Foreign institutional investors owned 17 percent (a telling number in comparison to the 4 percent owned by French institutions), and the French VINCI and the Dutch Schiphol Group, both private infrastructure investors, each own 8 percent, with the rest owned by a variety of smaller entities.[90] In 2023, after President Emmanuel Macron had passed a law in 2019 annulling the earlier requirement of government majority control, efforts were underway to privatize ADP entirely by selling a majority share to a nongovernment entity.

When it first partially privatized, Charles de Gaulle was the second largest airport in Europe. Today it is the largest. It has managed to expand to meet demand and to increase profitability in part by diversifying into other countries. The firm operates, directly or indirectly, 29 airports around the world and participates in the management of 125 airports in fifty countries. Airports aren't the only beneficiaries of this growth. The French government has itself benefited from the private management of the group: the state's share of ADP is now valued at $9.7 billion, which it plans to invest in new technologies for the airport.[91] This is an example of a partial privatization in which the state continues to hold a share of the company, yet the business is run as an independent, publicly traded company, similar to many infrastructure companies in China. ADP is now a global player in the airport management business. To date, there isn't a single US airport manager that operates internationally in any significant way, even though the United States has thirteen out of the thirty largest airports in the world. The United States does not need to be the best in every domain, but when policymakers are surprised that US airports, the largest in the world, have no presence outside the country, they have only themselves to blame.

Not all privatizations are created equal, and not all work out smoothly. In England, privatization achieved many of the goals it set out to, including bringing down debt and eliminating the deficit. It did not, however, result in uniformly successful outcomes. The story of Heathrow Airport, for instance, is something of a mixed bag. Some analysts argue the airport privatization has been a success, but the airport still faces a number of shortcomings. In the immediate aftermath of privatization, Heathrow Airport's performance improved; between 1989 and 1997, the airport operated with an efficiency rating above 95 percent, and for five of those eight years, it operated at 100 percent efficiency.[92] In 2006 the Spanish transportation management firm Ferrovial bought a majority stake (55 percent) of Heathrow for £10 billion (£17.1 billion in 2023 pounds, or $21 billion). The deal afforded a 42 percent profit margin for the company, in anticipation of capital investments, but during the firm's operations, passengers complained of poor service, delays, and overcrowding. By 2013 Ferrovial had reduced its share in Heathrow to 25 percent, and in late 2023 it announced it was selling its remaining stake to a private equity firm and the Saudi sovereign fund. No one in the United Kingdom objected to the nationality of the buyer, nor did they express concern the Saudis would run off with Heathrow.[93] Looking back, the privatization did not expand Heathrow's capacity, largely due to regulatory hold-ups in Parliament, and the airport remains among the most congested in the world. For years Heathrow has been in negotiations with British regulators to build an additional terminal to address congestion,[94] but so far no progress has been made toward the goal. Delays mounted as ticket prices climbed, and Heathrow became one of the least popular major airports among customers in the world.[95] In 2022 the airport began cutting flights, even in the reduced air traffic conditions in the wake of the COVID-19 pandemic, and issued an apology to customers for poor service.[96] It is important to note the role of Parliament and regulators in the continued congestion at Heathrow, but the fact remains that privatization did not solve some of the airport's most pressing problems. Nevertheless, Heathrow in many respects has improved dramatically, especially since Ferrovial became involved. Its Air Service Quality score, a key indicator of airport success handed out by Airports Council International, rose after 2006, and two of its terminals, if not the airport as a whole, are still among the highest rated by customers.

Despite some instances of failure, the overwhelming privatization of airports in Europe indicates that the United States ought at least to expand its efforts. And in fact we are beginning to see some signs that the wave that swept across Europe may finally be reaching American shores. Specifically, it has come to Puerto Rico.

The Beginning of a Beautiful Friendship?

One promising sign for the future of US airports is the success of the privatization of Luis Muñoz Marín International Airport in Puerto Rico. For twenty years the island struggled to maintain its airports and attempted multiple times to bring in the private sector to help. The complexity of entering into public-private partnerships, however, stymied the territory's effort for years. On its second attempt, though, Puerto Rico managed to create the conditions for a public-private partnership that would bring its airport up to speed, alleviate the island's debt responsibilities, and supply its government with much-needed capital. Given the island's dire economic situation going back to the early 2000s, it might not be surprising that Puerto Rico pushed to transfer responsibility for airport management to the private sector. Nevertheless, the agreement Puerto Rico reached to lease the San Juan airport provides a useful map for partnerships that might appeal to both investors and policymakers.

Puerto Rico finalized its public-private partnerships for Marín International in 2013. The event marked the culmination of an effort that began in the 1990s. Puerto Rico was in fact one of the first to apply to privatize an airport after the creation of the Privatization Pilot Program. Initially the privatization target was not Luis Marín, but a smaller regional airport, which may have looked like a simpler project. All the way back in 1998, the Puerto Rico Port Authority and the Government Development Bank, which issues bonds for the island and manages its interstate banking needs, had set their sights on the privatization of Rafael Hernandez Airport in Aguadilla, on the island's far west coast.[97] The FAA accepted the airport's application for review in 2000 but ultimately determined it was not well suited for privatization, and the Port Authority withdrew the application a year later. But the island had few options for funding major infrastructure improvements, and it decided to try again—on a larger scale.

A colony of Spain from 1493 to 1898, today Puerto Rico is a territory of the United States. Its 3.2 million people cannot participate in federal elections and do not pay federal income taxes, but Puerto Ricans are full US citizens. This citizenship deal was orchestrated in 1948 by Luis Muños Marín, namesake of the San Juan airport and the first popularly elected governor of Puerto Rico. Marín initiated the great economic boom on the island between the 1950s and the 2000s. During this period, the island's economy performed impressively well, not only keeping up with employment growth in the United States as a whole, but in some periods outpacing it.[98] Beginning in the mid-2000s, though, Puerto Rico fell on severe financial hardship, mostly as a result of its debt. For most of its history as part of the United States, Puerto Rico enjoyed broad tax exemptions to spur its development. In the 1980s, however, Congress began eliminating some of these tax exemptions, specifically for the manufacturing sector, which had exploded in Puerto Rico with the arrival of pharmaceutical companies on the island. Johnson and Johnson, Pfizer, AstraZeneca, and other large pharmaceutical companies have extensive manufacturing operations on the island. (Initially drawn by tax exemptions, many companies, most notably Johnson and Johnson, have expanded their footprint on the island even since the end of manufacturing tax exemptions.)[99] Though municipal bonds remained tax exempt, the end of these manufacturing exemptions caused Puerto Rico's economy to sharply contract. The territory raised sales taxes and tried other means of raising revenue to keep up with its bond obligations, but the revenue was not sufficient.[100] When the island's debt ballooned to $71 billion, or 68 percent of its GDP, bond credit ratings agencies downgraded its bonds to "junk," and Puerto Rico had no clear way to service its debts. In 2022, after years of failure to remunerate bondholders, Puerto Rico underwent the largest debt restructuring in American history.[101]

In the midst of the crisis (prior to restructuring), the island continued its attempts at airport privatization. In 2011 it returned with a different proposal: instead of the smaller airport in Aguadilla, it would apply to privatize the island's largest airport, in San Juan. The concern was not simply that the island needed capital and could no longer sustain debt payments. Luis Muñoz Marín Airport also had significant difficulties itself, and according to its own operator, the Puerto Rico Port Authority, the airport did not satisfactorily serve its customers and was in need of reform if it were to become financially stable.[102] The airport suffered from deficiencies in pavement, lighting, and signage (all safety concerns) and, more pressingly, had seen little growth in passenger traffic over the previous two decades.[103]

Unlike its effort for Aguadilla, Puerto Rico went all in on its bid to privatize Marín International. Perhaps most importantly, officials laid the groundwork for the privatization application by passing a law in 2009 known as the Puerto Rico P3 Act, an enabling law that created rules to govern public-private partnerships on the island. The following year, Puerto Rico also released a study on the effects of privatizing Luis Muñoz Marín. This "desirability report" outlined what the island would gain from privatization, offering a transparent accounting of its reasons for courting private investors to reassure the public, and also why private operators should be interested in managing the airport. Simultaneously selling the deal to the public and investors established exactly the conditions that were absent from the St. Louis effort. Among other key findings, the report concluded that lease payments from a private partner, and the value of private investment, would surpass the potential revenue of the airport if it remained in government hands. With these new weapons in hand, Puerto Rico went back to the FAA, and this time the FAA accepted the proposal.

The governor of Puerto Rico at the time, Luis Fortuño, who was instrumental in the effort, said the deal exceeded expectations. In an interesting symmetry with St. Louis, Fortuño exited the governor's office in 2013, just before the deal was finalized, leaving an opening for his successor, Alejandro Garcia Padilla, to cancel it if he desired. But Garcia Padilla vowed not to disrupt the transfer of the airport to private operators. Had such extensive planning not been executed prior to the contract, including the creation of new legislation, things might have gone differently—as they did in St. Louis. As it stands, however, the enabling legislation continues to have a profound effect on the economy of Puerto Rico. In 2022 the island began requesting bids from private operators for public-private partnerships to build toll roads on the island.[104]

In 2012 Puerto Rico announced that two firms had tendered bids for the airport: Grupo Aeropuerto Avance and Aerostar Airport Holdings (a partnership between a Mexican airport operator, Grupo Aeroportuario del Sureste, and an American one, Highstar Capital, later acquired by Oaktree Capital). After bidding completed, the island awarded the contract to Aerostar. The terms of the forty-year lease (not ninety-nine years) the island offered Aerostar served the island well, especially as it navigated a new phase of its debt crisis in 2014.[105] Puerto Rico received $615 million up front and would also receive $2.5 million every year for the first five years of the lease. After that, it would receive 5 percent of the airport's total profits annually for the following twenty-five years, and in the last ten years of the lease the island would reap 10 percent of the airport's profits, after the privatization had achieved optimal efficiency. In addition, the private operators agreed to invest a minimum of $1.4 billion in the airport, guaranteeing improved service for customers.[106] It was a home run for the island, which secured itself up-front capital and continued revenue from lease payments and a guaranteed source of capital for the following four decades. By pegging its own portion of revenue to the success of the private operator, the contract created a genuine partnership of mutual benefit, in which both the government and the private operator had a vested interest in the success of the airport. So far the privatization has been successful, despite Puerto Rico's ongoing financial straits.

Brent Tasugi, who was a principal at Highstar Capital at the time it acquired the airport as part of the Aerostar consortium, told me that "the desire to explore privatization was motivated by enhancing the financial position of Puerto Rico and allowing the use of airport proceeds for other purposes." When the deal had been completed, the existing conditions at the airport turned out to be worse than expected. Critical maintenance investment had been delayed, leaving broken escalators and serious leaks. Many of the concession stands in the airport, which might have generated significant revenue, were closed. Brent was part of the team that transitioned the airport from municipal hands to private operations. "We needed to think in a transformative way about running of the airport and that meant consolidating the footprint of the airport in a more efficient way" he told me. "Part of the endeavor was to develop extensive outreach to the community, including to unions and neighborhoods around the airport, and beyond, to discuss our plan and how it could help everyone around the airport."[107]

Puerto Rico used the initial up-front payment of $615 million to defray the territory's debt obligations, which exceeded $800 million at the time. In addition to the annual $2.5 million it would receive, the potential revenue it could hope to garner by the end of the lease, when profit sharing would increase, began to grow. At the time of the deal, the airport generated approximately $30 million of net revenues. Within three years, revenue increased to $70 million, and the airport began receiving international flights from Europe. It is estimated that Puerto Rico will reap $2.6 billion over the life of the concession. In 2017 the airport was partially sold by the original owners to PSP, a Canadian pension fund. (US pension funds must play a greater role in the ownership and management of infrastructure assets, too.)

Signs that privatization may finally arrive on this side of the Atlantic are increasing, and Puerto Rico's public-private partnership offers a model for other cities and states. Since the reauthorization of the FAA in 2012, more projects across the country have experimented with P3s. In New York, expansions and upgrades to JFK and LaGuardia both leaned on the private sector to provide up-front capital in exchange for a share of profits. LaGuardia added two new terminals: Terminal B, which opened in 2020, and Terminal C, unveiled in 2022. These expansions represented the largest public-private partnership in the country's history and the first new major construction of airport infrastructure in twenty-five years. In the agreement, the PANYNJ granted leases up until 2050 to an investor-led consortium for Terminal B and Delta Air Lines for Terminal C. The Terminal B consortium, LaGuardia Gateway Partners, included the Canadian Vantage Airport Group, Swedish infrastructure investor Skanska Infrastructure Development, and the French private equity firm Meridiam. Meridiam also manages Sofia airport in Bulgaria, as well as airports in Madagascar. Costs ran to $8 billion, roughly $4 billion for each terminal, with two-thirds of funding coming from private sources.[108] Additional construction capital came through bond issuances by the PANYNJ.

I spoke with Derek Utter, the chief development officer at the PANYNJ, which oversees and operates both LaGuardia and JFK, as well as Newark airport, the container ports, bus terminals, and a variety of other transportation assets in the region, about the logic behind the airport P3s. Before arriving at PANYNJ, Utter worked for the governor's office in Andrew Cuomo's administration, and he intimately understands the political dynamics of infrastructure management. Utter explained that airports are of particular importance to New York and New Jersey because they are major gateways to the United States—with consistent and strong traffic—but for years have been among the lowest rated in the country. Therein lay a major opportunity. The P3 deals on LaGuardia have already demonstrated that a shift is underway. In March 2023 Terminal B was named the best new airport terminal in the world and received the first five-star rating for an airport terminal in North America from Skytrax, the leading airport rating authority. In addition, airports are key to the Port Authority because, unlike most port authorities, the FAA allows the PANYNJ to distribute airport revenue to other infrastructure assets managed by the authority, making it more akin to an infrastructure company with multiple assets. Maintaining control of airport revenue, then, is of more concern than it is to Miami or St. Louis, for instance, where it is illegal to use airport revenue outside the airport.

The Port Authority has a long history of working with private companies and seeking ways to leverage outside expertise and capital to accomplish its mission. Utter said, "We look at each situation uniquely and ask what value the private sector can bring. We have no preconceived ideas and we're always very open-minded."[109] As a result, the Port Authority has partners who have provided capital and expertise to rebuild the World Trade Center site (including Silverstein Properties, the Durst Organization, and Westfield, the retail operator), build and operate the Newark and JFK AirTrains, rebuild the Goethals Bridge, rebuild the George Washington Bridge Bus Station, and expand and operate the container ports—in addition to redeveloping the airports.

The authority always seeks creative means of funding, whether through its own means or the private sector. For example, PANYNJ looks at real estate development rights and PILOTs, or "payment in lieu of taxes." This involves reaching an agreement with New York City and ultimately with private developers interested in building one or more commercial buildings on the site. "Instead of paying property taxes to the city, for a defined period, those payments would be captured as a source of revenue to help fund the project," Utter explained.

The IIJA's airport allocations, for instance, can be of only minimal assistance, he believes, because of the many restrictions and requirements such grants come with.

> One of the challenges with the infrastructure bill is that despite the huge amount of money and our capital plan, we find it very hard to match up our needs with the sources of funds. Either they tend to be doled out in small pieces or they come with a lot of red tape. The funds that are made available for the airports oftentimes have a lot of strings attached, and so we have to sift through everything in our capital plan to find those unique situations that might work for those funds. When we do apply, in the area of sustainability, for example, we find that there are complex rules, and at the end of the day, we spend a lot of time on paperwork to get relatively little money.

As a result, the authority ends up working with third parties.

Kennedy International Airport is also in the early stages of a major, $19 billion redevelopment using a public-private partnership to build two new world-class terminals; expand two existing terminals; and modernize the roads, utilities, and other supporting infrastructure. The program includes over $15 billion of private capital, including $9.5 billion for a new Terminal One, $4.2 billion for a new Terminal Six, $1.5 billion to expand the existing Terminal Four, and $400 million to expand the existing Terminal Eight.[110] Both new terminals are P3 transactions whereby the private consortiums finance, construct, and operate the terminals under a lease agreement that will last until 2060. The new Terminal One team includes the Spanish infrastructure firm Ferrovial, JLC Infrastructure, a minority-owned infrastructure developer, and Ullico, the Union Labor Life Insurance Company. The new Terminal Six team includes the Vantage Airport Group, American Triple I, a minority-owned infrastructure developer, RXR Realty, and JetBlue.

Unlike most airports in the United States, JFK has a history of leveraging private capital. Starting in the 1960s, airlines built and operated their own flagship terminals at JFK under long-term lease agreements. The PanAm Worldport opened in 1960, the TWA Flight Center opened in 1962, and the National Airlines Sundrome (designed by IM Pei) opened in 1969. There has been little private participation since then, however, and JFK has been operating over capacity for decades. Starting in 2022, the airport brought the private sector into its development plans once again to address its congestion issues. The planned expansion of Terminal One, which currently has ten gates, will add an additional four gates in its first phase A of construction and eventually add another nine gates (phase B), for a total of twenty-three gates at the new Terminal One.[111] The entire terminal will be rebuilt, including the existing gates—a massive, 2.4-million-square-foot undertaking, which upon completion will be more than twice the size of the old Terminal One. The plan relies on a design-build-operate (DBO) model in which separate entities are contracted for the design and construction phase and for the operational phase. Private entities are providing the bulk of the funding for reconstruction, and the Port Authority is providing $3.9 billion for roads, utilities, and other infrastructure improvements—resulting in a 4 to 1 leveraging of public to private capital. The rebuild was projected to create ten thousand new jobs, and importantly, the Port Authority required at least 30 percent of each team's equity to be provided by a minority-owned investment group. In addition, the construction will follow the Port Authority's commitment to net zero greenhouse gas emissions, using sustainable design techniques and energy systems.

In the wake of COVID-19, the PANYNJ agreed to modify the plan and extend the lease of Terminal One by ten years in order to compensate for the loss of business during the pandemic and account for the recovery period (traffic was not expected to fully recover until 2024).[112] Here is an example of a smart renegotiation of a P3.

Compared to the planning in St. Louis and other attempted privatizations, the effort at JFK was highly organized. The P3 included provisions for addressing potential cost overruns, which might scare off private investors, as well as guarantees from airlines that committed to anchoring at the new Terminal One and oversight from a governing entity, New Terminal One, to ensure streamlining of construction and operational phases. In addition, the project made commitments to renewable energy technology as well as to community development, including a guarantee that 30 percent of the new terminal's concessions will go to minority and women-owned businesses. Overall, the project is expected to create five thousand construction jobs and an additional ten thousand permanent jobs.[113] The winning elements of the authority are clear: management independence, strong community involvement, a keen eye on efficiency, and agnosticism as to whom it works with. In this case, there is an argument to be made that there is no need to privatize PANYNJ, as it is doing its job as an independent authority given its flexibility to allocate profits across the different infrastructure assets it owns.

Regardless of whether airport profitability or efficiency rises with private operators, it is still the case that state ownership of airports passes up an opportunity for large capital investment in other state services. Privatization would disentangle airport management from political motivations and election cycles. As with other infrastructure sectors, US airports are not owned by the government according to ancient tradition—they began in private hands—and there is no obvious reason why the state can operate them more successfully than private firms. Or why it *should* operate them, if transferring management to a private company would benefit the municipality.

As both a former CEO of MIA and a former city manager of Miami, Emilio Gonzalez believes privatization would be a logical decision for the airport. "The only benefit the city gets from the airport is the political benefit of overseeing the airport," he told me. "Miami International generates about $65 billion a year in economic activity and that includes internal plus external, but not one penny goes directly to the municipal government."

The county gets no dividends and no distributions, and all airport revenue must legally be reinvested in the airport. "Imagine if you could guarantee Miami-Dade County $200 million a year for 50 years? It comes down to the value proposition to a municipality." And this could well be extended to other airports, he believes, especially midsize hubs in the Midwest, where $50 million a year could make a significant impact on a municipal budget. Gonzalez says the prospect has simply not been pitched well enough.

> I think that there is a case to be made, particularly among midsize airports, that they can be better run, they can be more profitable, and that the community will reap greater dividends if they were to privatize the airport. I don't think anybody has ever made the value proposition to a municipality that says, "Hey, look, this is how you're running it now. These are your expenses. If you privatize this, if you let a private firm run this, this is what we can do for you."

Once again, the pitch to lawmakers and constituents can make all the difference.

Not everyone is as sure privatization will happen or be so easy. Derek Utter, for instance, has his doubts. "I think it's hard to envision wholesale privatizations of airports," he told me. "In some places, in other countries, there may be a handful of airports and only one decision-maker, and that decision-maker decides in one fell swoop to privatize the airports. Here, the airports are run by municipalities and so it would be a much more complicated thing. They would have to diverge from everybody else and do something different, make a proactive decision to do something different at a local level. It's hard to envision people taking that kind of risk." Utter has correctly identified one of the primary obstacles to privatization in the US system, which played a significant role in the case of St. Louis: political risk. It is difficult to be the first, as Mayor Lyda Krewson acknowledged, and much easier to let someone else take the risk. It is this kind of thinking that Ed Rendell had in mind when he titled his book *A Nation of Wusses*: no one will be the first to put their own careers on the line. Eventually, however, someone will have to confront the challenge.

In thinking through the future of airports, it may be helpful to put them in juxtaposition with a similar sort of infrastructure, one that has always been negotiated through partnerships between public and private entities: the nation's ports.

seven

PORT OF ORIGIN

PANYNJ and the History and Methods of US Seaports

LINUS: "A new product has been found, something of use to the world, so a new industry moves into an undeveloped area. Factories go up, machines are brought in, a harbor is dug, and you're in business."

—*Sabrina* (1954)

There may be no better symbol of the interconnectedness of the planet than the intermodal twenty-foot equivalent unit: the shipping container. In 2021 there were over 850 million TEUs circulating the globe,[1] crossing the oceans stacked on cargo ships, traversing the deserts and plains on railroads and trucks, scattered throughout the largest and smallest communities in the world, from the National Science Foundation's McMurdo Station in Antarctica to the jungle town of Isiro in the Democratic Republic of the Congo. First introduced in 1956 by the businessman Malcolm McLean, "containerization" revolutionized the shipping industry. The standardized shipping container has become the lingua franca that facilitates trade between the most disparate regions of the world.

The global ubiquity of the twenty-foot equivalent unit (TEU) also testifies to the essential role that seaports play in the global economy. Seaports and maritime trade routes are the heart of world trade: across the globe, 90 percent of goods move by ocean liner.[2] In contrast to other forms of infrastructure, the private sector participates heavily in the management and operation of US seaports, and many of the operators belong to foreign entities. This might come as a surprise, given the sometimes vigorous opposition to privatization in other transportation sectors—especially because that opposition, in some cases, has been justified on grounds of national security and geopolitical strategy. Nevertheless, not only have US seaports experimented with privatization, but ports have been primarily under private management for centuries.

Many of the largest shipping companies, in fact, are privately held, family-run businesses, vigilantly managed by experts who have dedicated their lives to the shipping industry. I remember having dinner one evening in Geneva with Diego Aponte, now president of Mediterranean Shipping Company, known as MSC, which competes with Maersk to be the largest shipping company in the world.[3] During the meal, Aponte took a call regarding a container ship in the mid-Atlantic and then set about examining his iPhone. I was curious to know what he was looking at, and he showed me an app the company had developed to track its entire fleet around the world in real time. The Aponte family started their business with a small vessel, sailing between the port of Naples and the island of Capri, in Italy, eventually growing the business to expand to Africa and then the globe. A brilliant family with an incredible work ethic, who command extraordinary loyalty among their employees, the Apontes have maintained family control of MSC since its founding in 1970, the dawn of global containerization.

A. P. Møller-Maersk, often counted as the largest shipping company in the world, is also a family business, and its majority share is still controlled by the relatives of the company's founder, Arnold Peter Møller. CMA-CGM, currently the third largest shipping company,[4] is privately held, too, and controlled by the Saadé family, who started their shipping business in the port of Lebanon in 1978. I met the company's founder, Jacques Saadé, an elegant patriarch, fluent in French, English, and Arabic, many times. I visited him in his headquarters before the company built and moved to the elegant tower in Marseille designed by the architect Zaha Hadid. Saadé's boardroom looked like something out of a James Bond movie, and over the course of that meeting he called in a variety of managers to ask them pointed questions, such as, "How long is the quay in the container port of Pipavav?" The poor managers, obviously terrified, would venture a reply—"about 700 meters in total?"—but Jacques Saadé would immediately cut them off to correct them: "You mean 735 meters!" I imagined Saadé stroking a Siamese cat as he pressed a button and the unfortunate manager was eliminated, like Ernst Stavro Blofeld in *Thunderball*. No cat appeared, however, and as intimidating as Saadé could be, one had to be impressed by his knowledge of the minutiae of his business.

These three companies alone control 46.8 percent of the global liner fleet,[5] all of them highly entrepreneurial, daring, and great believers, as one would expect, in international trade. All of them are also major owners of port concessions across the United States.

Among large ports in the United States, the majority are "landlord" ports, or ports at which private companies lease seaport terminals from a state-run port authority, in distinction from "operator" ports, which are managed directly by the port authority or municipality. In the United States, landlord ports outnumber state-operated ports more than 2 to 1,[6] and the largest and busiest seaports are all landlord ports, including the Port of Los Angeles, the Port of Long Beach, and the Port of New York and New Jersey. Interestingly, one rarely hears complaints that US ports are operated by private entities. Why are certain forms of infrastructure deemed the sacrosanct property of the state, while others can be licensed to the highest bidder almost without comment?

Figure 7.1 shows the US import and export volumes by mode of transportation for 2022. Water transportation is the largest mode for both imports and exports. By and large, American ports are well run, well funded, well regulated, and often in the vanguard of technological innovation. Investment has been steadily increasing since 2012, and that trend is projected to continue. Between 2012 and 2016, the private sector directed $27 billion

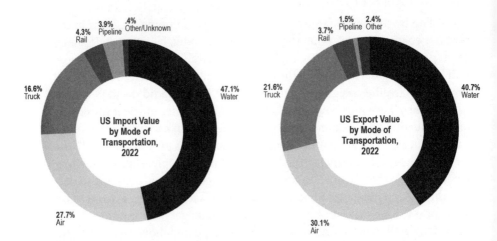

Figure 7.1. US import and export value by mode of transportation. *Source:* "U.S.-International Freight Trade by Transportation Mode," US Bureau of Transportation Statistics, accessed November 1, 2023, https://www.bts.gov/browse-statistical-products-and-data/freight-facts-and-figures/us-international-freight-trade.

to seaports around the country, and during the following five-year period, 2016 to 2021, private investment skyrocketed to $132 billion, a 388 percent increase.[7] Investors expect these spending levels will continue. In a survey asking about plans for the years 2021–2025, private sector participants said they plan for $140 billion in seaport capital expenditures.[8] Others report projections of $163 billion in spending overall between 2020 and 2025.[9] The federal government boosted its investment as well. The Infrastructure Investment and Jobs Act allocated $14 billion to strengthen supply chains and bolster climate resilience,[10] and in 2022 the first installment arrived as a $703 million investment in forty-one ports across twenty-two states, funding projects to modernize facilities and increase capacity and efficiency.[11] The investment is necessary to keep pace with the growth, and growing costs, of maritime shipping. American ports broke records in 2021 both for volume of freight imported and exported and for cost of shipping. The global spike was reflected at the Port of Los Angeles and Port of Long Beach,[12] which registered 13 percent and 14 percent increases in shipping costs in 2021 respectively.[13]

Overall, the ASCE gave a B– to America's ports—an improvement, at least, over the C– for roads and D+ for airports. The group estimated a $12 billion investment gap in the sector and pointed to delays and congestion in the nation's ports. As the report acknowledged, however, these delays and the vast majority of investment needs are not directly but indirectly related to the management of ports themselves. The most investment is needed in "waterside" infrastructure, particularly in dredging waterways to create more shipping capacity. In other words, much of the inefficiency in ports is not a result of the management of seaport terminals but of the surrounding infrastructure, which is typically controlled not by private entities but by the port authority, state government, or federal regulation.[14]

So why don't privately managed seaports cause much controversy compared to other infrastructure sectors? One reason may be that they are comparatively well run and profitable. Another is that port users are primarily private companies, and average citizens have little direct interaction with ports, despite relying on them on a daily basis. When I spoke to Derek Utter, the chief development officer of PANYNJ, he acknowledged part of the reason privatized ports do not draw criticism is the lack of public-facing operations. "Most people have very little interaction with the seaport's operations, which are different from the airports. As a result, they are a little below the radar screen from the public's perspective. We don't have a lot of discussion about our port operations because it doesn't touch consumers directly," he told me. Perhaps the most significant reason, though, is the legacy of privatized ports and the rich history of the private docks. "The innovations of containerization and intermodal shipping over fifty years ago created private entities with expertise in the full value chain of shipping, transportation, and logistics. I think oftentimes things are dictated by quirks of history. So, it's really important to understand how things got to where they are because a lot of things in government just continue," Utter told me. In this case, the history is long: US ports have been private endeavors since the country's infancy and, in world history, ports and the private sector are nearly inseparable. That said, PANYNJ has made strategic investments that complement investments made by the private sector and enhance the port operations, including investments in rail links, raising of the Bayonne Bridge, and dredging to allow for super large container ships. But ports have always primarily been ecosystems of competing merchants and their infrastructure assets; they were not only built by the private sector but, more than any other infrastructure, are the home of the private sector.

The revolution in shipping ushered in by Malcolm McLean's intermodal container offers a perfect example of how private companies can drive infrastructure innovation. The idea of shipping freight in standardized boxes first hit McLean as a young man, while watching longshoremen loading and unloading vessels with no regularized system of storage.[15] Prior to containerization, the process of transferring cargo from one mode of transport to another—from a ship to a truck or train—involved arduous, inefficient, and costly work; the crates were different shapes and sizes and sometimes even needed to be opened and repacked into another container.[16] The intermodal container facilitated a streamlined system for transferring a single container box from cargo ships to railcars and 18-wheelers.[17] During World War II the US military had developed intermodal crates to address this problem, but McLean introduced the system to the private sector.[18] On the promise of this product, McLean founded the shipping company Sea-Land, which quickly rose to lead the industry (eventually becoming a subsidiary of Maersk).

With the intermodal container, the efficiency of ports improved dramatically, though not without some growing pains. "That simple metal box," writes the economist and containerization expert Marc Levinson, "was what we today label disruptive technology."[19] The new container system transformed ports, trucking, and freight railroads. Because the containers could be removed quickly and new freight stacked easily, boats that used the intermodal TEU no longer idled for packing of irregular cargo, and trucks and trains no longer waited to be unpacked or repacked at all. The container transformed the work of the dockhands in charge of loading and unloading cargo, known as stevedores, as well as the ports themselves. The equipment ports needed to manage container ships and cargo required the construction of new terminals, or the overhaul of existing ones, along with new crane technology, known as derricks, to load and unload containers, and new trucking equipment. But containerization was worth these overhauls because it opened the door to a vast increase in storage capacity and thus enormous savings. When the first container ship left the Port of Newark it carried fifty-eight shipping containers. By comparison, modern cargo vessels on the seas today can haul 24,000 TEU.[20] Between 1980, when containerization began to take off globally, and 2021, world container-terminal throughput rose from 0.5 million TEU to 25.8 million TEU.[21] As Levinson writes, "Even as it helped destroy the old economy, the container helped build a new one."[22]

Raised on a farm in North Carolina, McLean founded his first company at the age of twenty-one. In 1934, when his family purchased a discounted, used truck from a friend, McLean, along with his brother and sister, incorporated McLean Trucking.[23] (Malcolm, who had the business drive, took the CEO position, while his siblings took on administrative roles.) Three years into building his company, McLean was struck by a vision of intermodal palletized shipping containers while watching the stevedores unload on the docks. Over the following fifteen years he built McLean Trucking into an empire, with the goal of using the company as a foundation for his shipping innovation, and this is precisely what he did. In 1952 McLean began experimenting with models for his container system and spent three years perfecting his design. He and his siblings put the family trucking business in a blind trust in 1955 and founded a new company, McLean Industries, which would focus on maritime transport. After a year devoted to building the infrastructure surrounding the container system, including new cargo ships and derricks, in 1956 McLean Industries launched the first intermodal containers from the Port of Newark, bound for the Port of Houston.[24]

McLean's invention may have revolutionized maritime shipping, but it was the market itself—responding to innovation, guided by government-run port authorities—that gave us the modern seaport. This is an important fact to consider when evaluating other infrastructure sectors. But what was the larger history and structure of ports that made this revolution possible?

Who Built the Port of New York and New Jersey?

The Port of New York and New Jersey was, in 2022, the largest port in the country, and it is also one of the oldest. The long, protected coastline of New York Bay provides ample room for many ships to find safe harbor, and the bay has served as a site of exchange and cohabitation since before the arrival of European settlers. With development, anchorages in a safe harbor become berths on a pier, a pier becomes a terminal, and multiple terminals are organized into a port. The many terminals built on New York Bay have been funded for centuries by a myriad of tenants, but the great majority have been private entities.

New York State did not officially organize its Port Authority until 1921, when increased traffic (largely as a result of US Navy vessels departing the Port of Embarkation during World War I) caused congestion and squabbling about jurisdiction between operators in New Jersey and New York.[25] After years of deliberation, the two states negotiated a plan to join forces in regulating maritime activities and form the Port Authority of New York and New Jersey, the first interstate agency in the country.[26]

There was a predecessor to PANYNJ that served as a cautionary tale for these negotiations. The first sector-specific regulator of New York Bay infrastructure, the Commissioner of Docks, was created in 1870 and consisted of five prominent New York businessmen, lawyers, and political operators, appointed by City Hall.[27] From its inception, the commission was dogged by criticism for its close association with Tammany Hall, the most influential political machine in New York during the nineteenth century.[28] In 1871 Tammany was engulfed in scandal after one of its most illustrious figures, the New York State senator and former congressman William "Boss" Tweed, was arrested for embezzling between $30 million and $200 million (in 2023 dollars) from the city of New York.[29] The *New York Times* wrote about the Dock Commission in 1871: "In the meeting of commissioners for the election of officers, they first proceeded to reward Tammany for their appointment by obeying its wishes," and charged that Tammany controlled the Dock Commission in order to give preferential treatment to its benefactors.[30] In 1873 the city reduced the commission to three officials, and by 1901 the bureau was reauthorized as the Docks and Ferry Commission, with only one commissioner overseeing traffic. Yet as ports grew and congestion worsened, the need for a more robust regulatory body, one that could also develop the infrastructure surrounding the ports, once again became evident—not just in New York, but around the country. Los Angeles created the Board of Harbor Commissioners in 1907,[31] and the Port of Long Beach created its own Board of Harbor Commissioners in 1917.[32] And in 1921, New York and New Jersey followed suit.

The Port Authority's essential purpose involved developing the supporting systems around the ports. In the first decade of its existence, the authority established the infrastructure to facilitate high-traffic interstate commerce. In 1927 the authority began construction on the George Washington Bridge, which opened in 1931 to connect the two states over the Hudson River. The Lincoln Tunnel came next, uniting the states below the river. Construction of the George Washington Bridge, which took four years to build and cost $59 million (roughly $1 billion in 2023 dollars),[33] was unveiled as the longest suspension bridge in the world.[34] The authority financed the construction with both state and city funds, including the issuance of $30 million in municipal bonds ($500 million in 2023).[35] The Lincoln Tunnel, also built with public funds, benefited from contributions from the New Deal's Works Progress Administration, as its costs ran to $85 million ($1.8 billion in 2023 dollars).[36] Both the bridge and tunnel were (and continue to be) tolled, generating revenue the Port Authority uses to service its debt and pay for the maintenance of its assets. The ports themselves remained entirely under private control. In the 1940s, however, that changed. The governors of both New York and New Jersey requested the Port Authority expand its focus on bridges and tunnels to include shipping. Among other reasons, the governors hoped the Port Authority could crack down on organized crime and corruption in unions at the ports. The association between New York ports and crime hurt business both reputationally and concretely, as cargo theft was on the rise.[37]

The Port Authority took a major step into shipping in 1948, when it took over operations of the Port of Newark, now known as Port Newark-Elizabeth, which had been a US Navy base but was abandoned at the end of World War II.[38] Upon taking over operations, PANYNJ announced plans to invest $11 million ($135 million in 2023 dollars) to dredge the Hudson River and modernize the port. And who did it contract to provide trucking? None other than Malcolm McLean, who had found the perfect moment to enact his plan. During the process of planning construction, he convinced PANYNJ of the viability of his containerization system and proposed building the new Waterman Terminal to be the container terminal, which his company would then lease. McLean won a contract to lease the first renovated pier at the new Port Elizabeth terminal.[39] It was from this port, operated by a McLean Industries subsidiary and reconstructed with Port Authority investment, that the first modern container ship set off for Houston. Though this was not a public-private partnership in the typical modern sense, it is nevertheless a remarkable example of the government and the private sector collaborating to introduce revolutionary infrastructure.[40]

The partnership with McLean began a new era at the Port Authority, one during which P3s began to flourish. "When containerization hit in the 1960s, we started to rely more on private partners to run our ports," Derek Utter told me, "and private shippers, some non-shippers, entrepreneurs like the Maher organization, built up one of the biggest ports at Elizabeth, New Jersey." As a result of private participation, Utter continued, "there's been a lot of experimentation and people willing to take a risk. A lot of my job is to work closely with private partners to maximize our development opportunities."

Once McLean won his contract with PANYNJ, his intermodal container system transformed everything about New York City's waterfront and its relationship to ports. The increased size of cargo ships, the great quantities of freight unloaded and processed, and the entire system for unloading and managing the containers made urban centers unsuitable locations for modern containerized ports. The new, enormous Port Elizabeth, situated on Newark Bay, an even more protected inner channel in the delta of the Hudson, offered an ideal location for large-scale operations. After containerization, PANYNJ's expansion of seaport infrastructure required migrating almost all of New York City's ports to New Jersey.

The containerization and migration of ports to New Jersey marked the beginning of the modern era of shipping in New York. Malcolm McLean's invention, and his private containership company, set in motion the rapid expansion of shipping capacity and a resultant sharp drop in shipping costs. The PANYNJ also played a central role by investing in port revitalizations and awarding a contract to an innovative company.

The ultimate origins of the structure of the Port of New York and New Jersey's management, however, trace back to a period before the birth of the United States. In precolonial times, New York Bay sheltered the canoes of the Lenape people, as well as groups of Mohawk, Iroquois, and other tribes from the larger Wappinger Native American community. When the Italian explorer Giovanni Verrazzano sailed his three-masted galleon, *La Dauphine*, into New York Bay in 1525, he became the first European to navigate the waters. Verrazzano had been engaged by the king of France, François I, to search for new trade routes through the Americas in hopes of finding an advantage over Portugal, Spain, and England in the spice trade. When he arrived in New York, after sailing up the coast from Cape Fear, North Carolina, Verrazzano described a rugged shoreline on which he could not find a suitable landing site. As one historian recounts, "after a fruitless search for some convenient harbor, he cast anchor off the shore, and landed in his boat. The timid natives . . . press[ed] forward to point out the best place for landing."[41] Though without a port, New York Bay posed challenges for large craft like *La Dauphine*, and the value of the site as a harbor was obvious: a wide, deep bay, protected from the open ocean, at the mouth of the Hudson River and the headwaters of the Delaware. The bay would make the ideal place for a sheltered port that could facilitate commerce to both the North and South. A subsequent emissary of François I, Jacques Cartier, declared the bay, along with all of North America, the property of France in 1534. As might be expected, the French claim would not be honored by the rest of Europe.

In the second half of the sixteenth century, French, Spanish, Dutch, and English explorers continued to map and settle the New World, but most development was centered in the southern United States because of its proximity to colonies in the West Indies. That would change in 1609, when the British explorer Henry Hudson sailed into New York Bay. Hudson established the beginnings of the first colony there, the first traces of what would become New York City. Like his predecessor Verrazzano, Hudson had been contracted to search for new passages to China to establish favorable trade routes. Hudson was not employed by the French or British crown, or any monarch. He was hired by a joint stock company, the Dutch East India Company.

Founded in 1602, the Dutch East India Company was the first multinational corporation.[42] Often referred to as the VOC, after its Dutch name, Veerenigde Oostindische Compagnie, the company was created by a consortium of Dutch merchants to invest in the infrastructure needed to conduct the spice trade and import other exotic goods from the Far East. Like other joint stock companies to follow, the VOC operated with a grant from the state for monopoly rights on trade in a particular sector or region, in this case in the East Indies, as Indonesia and the surrounding archipelagos were called. During the first half of the seventeenth century, the VOC outpaced its competition in England and Portugal, and the success of the joint stock enterprise contributed significantly to the rise of Holland as a major power both in Europe and the world. One of the VOC's advantages was that Holland had been a republic since 1588 and was governed not by a monarch but a *stadtholder*, an administrative steward, who allowed the merchant class an almost unprecedented degree of freedom. The VOC established trade routes and outposts throughout Indonesia in the first half of the seventeenth century and eventually secured trading relationships with China and India, as well.[43]

After Hudson asserted Dutch control over New York in 1609, the VOC began making plans to establish the first proper European settlement in New York, officially declaring the creation of New Amsterdam in 1614. But this caused some controversy back in Holland: Did the company have the right to trade there? The Dutch East India Company had a monopoly on trade in the East Indies, but not in the New World or the West Indies. Two Dutch investors, Willem Usselincx and Jessé de Forest, seized on the debate as an opportunity. Usselincx spearheaded the effort to persuade the Dutch government not to extend the East India Company's monopoly into the New World, but to give it to a competing company instead.[44] Usselincx convinced Amsterdam's stewards, and in 1621, with de Forest, won a charter for a new venture, the West India Company, which was granted monopoly rights to trade in the Americas and West Africa.[45] Usselincx put forward the bulk of the initial capital to create the company upon winning the charter, investing 130,000 Dutch florins,[46] or roughly $13 million in 2023.[47]

As an agent of the West India Company, when Peter Minuit, the third colonial governor of New Netherland, purchased the Island of Mannahatta from the Lenapes, he was founding New Amsterdam in the name of a private company rather than the Dutch government. In 1626 New Amsterdam built the first pier into the Hudson River, establishing the first infrastructure on the port of New York. Given the terms of the company's charter, not only did the pier count as a private entity, but the entire colony of New Amsterdam could be thought of as infrastructure constructed by and for the joint stock company. Though Amsterdam did contribute financing and promised military support for the new colony,[48] in the end the state backing would not materialize when the West India Company needed it most.

The roots of PANYNJ can be traced to these early origins, and the structure of the port, in which private operators manage terminals with near indifference to the state granting charters and leases, remains almost entirely intact today. Over the course of Dutch and English ownership, then regulation by state governors, the Docks Commission, then the Port Authority, the terminals of New York and New Jersey have remained almost entirely under the operating control of private companies. Across the country, ports remind us of the rich and essential relationship between infrastructure, the private sector, and smart regulatory oversight.

Private Operators at the Port in the Twenty-First Century

As a typical example of how seaport ownership works, we can look at Maher Terminal, one of the three largest terminals at Port Elizabeth. The terminal began modestly in the mid-twentieth century. Michael Maher established the beginnings of the terminal when he leased storage space from PANYNJ for lumber warehouses in 1958, but soon thereafter took possession of two piers and adapted them for containerized shipping. As business at Port Elizabeth took off, generating roughly $200 million in revenue annually, so did Maher's business.[49] After Maher's death in 1995, the family-run business renegotiated its contract with the Port Authority in 2000, signing a thirty-year lease. According to the document, Maher Terminal would pay the Port Authority $13.3 million annually. The renegotiated lease between Maher and PANYNJ also established terms regulating the transfer of the lease, including requirements that the new operator (1) be a major steamship or stevedore company, (2) have $75 million in capital as of the most recent fiscal year, (3) have positive net income over the previous five years, and (4) disclose any legal sanctions imposed on it in the previous five years.[50] The terms allowed broad latitude for transfers, permitting the greatest amount of competition among bidders and providing commissionaires with the security that they would not be locked into a long-term lease. Transfer terms were important to Maher. In 2007 the Maher Holdings Corporation sold all its assets, including the New Jersey Terminal, to RREEF, the real estate and infrastructure group of Deutsche Bank.[51] With the global financial crisis, container volumes dropped and shipping companies like CMA-CGM decided to renegotiate their contracts with the container ports, as Maher ports faced bankruptcy. Deutsche Bank took over the terminal on its balance sheet in what financial institutions call the "bad bank" (basically, the bad bank owns all the nonperforming assets) and finally opted to sell the terminal to Macquarie Group, the now-familiar Australian infrastructure investor, under the original terms of Maher's thirty-year lease. It is important to note that the bankruptcy had no impact on the Port Authority, the city, or the state. Deutsche Bank assumed the risk and addressed its losses without any intervention from the government, similar to the situation with the Indiana Toll Road.

Other terminals have similar stories. Maersk owns the APM Terminal, directly beside Maher, on a twenty-nine-year lease with annual payments to PANYNJ of $5 million. Global Container Terminals leases piers at the

Bayonne Terminal on New York Bay, as well as a separate pier at the How-land Hook Terminal Staten Island. Ports America, the largest port operator and stevedore in the country, manages four terminals through PANYNJ, as well as ports in New Orleans, Miami, Houston, Los Angeles, Seattle, and elsewhere.

Under the privatized model, the opposite is true: the private sector con-tributes to municipal budgets, a point that critics of P3s don't acknowl-edge. The Port Department of PANYNJ generated $125 million in revenue in 2021, $64 million in 2020, and $46 million in 2019.[52] The revenue from port concessions has gone toward a series of infrastructure expansions and improvements for all PANYNJ assets, from seaports to tunnels, bridges, and airports. Though port revenue tends to be lower than revenue from other sectors, including bridges, tunnels, and aviation, the benefits of privatiza-tion are not directly observable in these figures. After all, for the most part the revenue from ports does not go toward covering the operating costs of ports, as it does for other forms of transport that are managed more directly by PANYNJ. In 2021 operating expenses for the Port Authority ran to $1.6 billion for aviation, $524 million for bridges and tunnels, but only $164 mil-lion for ports, a number that has stayed steady over the last several years even as port revenue has increased.[53]

Throughout the country, the majority of ports follow roughly the same model as PANYNJ. The Port of Los Angeles and the Port of Long Beach, the second two largest ports in the country, are both landlord ports, leasing terminals to private companies, many of which are the same companies op-erating in New York and New Jersey. The ports of Houston and Miami are also landlord ports. The Port of Miami is growing in importance, as the eco-nomic activity of the port has exploded in the twenty-first century. In 2005 the port facilitated $65 billion in trade; by 2015, the value of goods passing through its piers had risen to $106 billion.[54] It provides 300,000+ jobs to the community and generates $43 billion for Miami-Dade County annually.[55]

Recently, Miami has demonstrated how ports can use more modern forms of public-private partnerships to improve operations. The expansion of the Port of Miami Tunnel, which allows for additional cargo capacity and reduces congestion, was achieved using a P3 structure, as was the con-struction of a new homeport terminal for Royal Caribbean's largest cruise vessels.[56] These P3 initiatives show that even for operator ports that do not lease terminals, the private sector can play an important role.[57] Jeb Bush, who was governor of Florida at the time, explained that the project would never have happened if not for private participation. "That infrastructure has been invaluable and without a public-private partnership, we wouldn't have been able to do it," he said.

On the whole, ports illustrate the ideal structure of public-private partnerships, and one reason there may be less controversy over privately operated ports is that the government inevitably plays a robust role even in fully privatized ports. The full power of the US Customs and Border Protection (CBP) Agency, as well as the US Coast Guard, is brought to bear on securing and regulating ports. The CBP, the largest law enforcement agency within the Department of Homeland Security, oversees imports-exports and regulates immigration. Its duties include confiscating illegal goods, monitoring for fraud (such as knock-off goods), and enforcing duty fees. In 2021 CBP levied monetary penalties of $43 million from companies charged with fraud or negligence in all ports of entry. Comparatively few travelers enter the United States by seaport—the vast majority arrive by road or plane—but there are still over a million visitors arriving by boat each year,[58] and CBP ensures they are properly registered. One of the major efforts of CBP since 2020 has been the installation of biometric sensors. These sensors, the agency predicted, would facilitate faster security processes at ports of entry everywhere. In 2021 CBP biometrically scanned 400,000 people arriving at seaports in the United States and 48 million people overall.[59]

But there are additional agencies overseeing ports. Most important is the Merchant Marines. Overseen by the US Marine Administration, a branch of the Department of Transportation, the Merchant Marines is a civilian group not associated with the military, which is responsible for ensuring safe passage for private, international cargo ships on the high seas.[60] There are Merchant Marines stationed at every port across the country from which ships sail into international waters, and every cargo ship has members of the merchant marines protecting it.[61] In addition to overseeing the Merchant Marines, the US Marine Administration promotes development of port infrastructure.

Such oversight is critical, as these security and regulatory apparatuses allow private enterprise to flourish in ports. There are also certain cases, though rare, in which the federal government does intervene in the market to a greater extent. Typically, such cases involve national security concerns. For instance, in 2006 PANYNJ and the US Congress mobilized to block the sale of ports in New York and New Jersey to DP World, a firm owned by the United Arab Emirates (UAE). In 2005 DP World acquired the British company Peninsular and Oriental Steam Navigation (P&O), along with the six terminals it operated in the United States, including a terminal at Port of Newark. The PANYNJ sued P&O for violating the terms of its lease, claiming DP World failed to meet the requirements outlined above, specifically arguing that it was not a major steamship operator.[62] Congress, too, opposed the deal, though for different and more tenuous reasons. Congressman Peter King (R-NY) worried, for instance, that DP World would be susceptible to infiltration by al-Qaeda, given that two of the 9/11 hijackers hailed from the UAE. Although President George W. Bush supported the deal, and DB World hired Senate legend Bob Dole to represent it in court,[63] the acquisition was ultimately relinquished. In the wake of the political blowback the company was forced to sell the terminals,[64] after the emir of Dubai, Sheikh Mohammed bin Rashid Al Maktoum, decided to shift away from the US market to preserve diplomatic relations.[65] Over the ensuing years, DP World invested in ports across Europe, Asia, and Latin America, becoming one of the largest shipping companies in the world. It has yet to invest in container ports in the United States. The orphaned ports of P&O, meanwhile, became Ports America after AIG acquired them in 2006.[66] Similar to Maher terminal, the terminals essentially went bankrupt in the aftermath of the 2008 global recession and had to be financially restructured.[67] In 2014 Oaktree Capital Management purchased Highstar, the successor owner to AIG. Under Oaktree, Ports America thrived, and in 2021 it was wholly sold to the Canada Pension Plan Investment Board (CPPIB), which represents twenty million contributors in Canada and has a fund of C$519 billion (US$383 billion). CPPIB purchased the shipping company and its PANYNJ terminals from Oaktree for $6 billion in 2021.[68]

Two interesting observations can be made. The first revolves around the role pension funds play, or should play, in the ownership and management of infrastructure assets. Pension funds, unlike private sector funds, may generally have a longer horizon and therefore are able to weather business cycles. It is not surprising that a pension fund such as CPPIB would want to invest in a container port with a thirty-year lease. The surprising element is that no US pension fund has invested directly in infrastructure assets to the extent Canadian pension funds have. This is a major shortcoming of our system that needs to be remedied and that should form the basis of any long-term solution for US infrastructure.[69] The second is that by denying Dubai Ports investments in the United States on spurious grounds, the country lost an opportunity to develop a strategic relationship with one of the largest port operators in the world. In this day of strategic competition, the United States has few allies that actively own and operate the critical ports that form the backbone of the global supply chain. The United States is now complaining that it has no allies in its quest to gain a presence in the global supply chain.

China's Belt and Road Initiative Takes to the Sea

The P3 model adopted in US ports has been used extensively around the world. The port authority is owned by the government, it leases container ports under long-term concessions to operators (with no regard as to whether they are privately held or government controlled), and it then manages the relationship through P3 agreements that require concessionaires to constantly invest in the asset and also require the port authority to invest in the ancillary infrastructure. Similar models can be found in Europe, Asia (including China), Australia, Canada, Latin America, Africa, and the Middle East.

It is worth dwelling for a moment on China's strategy in comparison to the United States and on what China has done in the last few decades through its port investments. China has poured at least $900 billion into its massive infrastructure investment program, the Belt and Road Initiative (BRI),[70] sometimes called the New Silk Road, and sometimes more faithfully translated from the Chinese as "One Belt One Road." The program involves enormous investment in roads, bridges, rail, renewable energy, and, perhaps most controversially, ports. Some estimate China's investment to be in the trillions, not billions: in 2021, the *South China Morning Post* projected China's investment in the BRI at as much as $5 trillion,[71] and according to the American Enterprise Institute's China Investment Tracker, the country has invested $2.27 trillion.[72] What is sure is that since 2013 China has extended over $600 billion in infrastructure-related loans, in comparison to $490 billion extended by the World Bank, Asia Development Bank (ADB), African Development Bank (AFDB), and Inter-American Development Bank (IADB) combined.[73]

Much of China's investment since 2013 has been international. One of the goals of the program, underlined by the concept of the "New Silk Road," is to expand Chinese economic influence across the globe. Many have argued that China's global infrastructure investment strategy is a key element of its aim for "geopolitical dominance." The reality, however, may be more grounded in economics. While some may find China's investments in ports adversarial, economic imperatives such as security of food supplies and key minerals to maintain economic growth have driven much of China's investments internationally. This is exactly what the United States is trying to do today with international frameworks such as the Indo-Pacific Economic Framework for Prosperity (IPEF), launched by President Biden in 2022. IPEF includes four pillars, one of which is supply chains among IPEF members.[74]

What propelled China to embark on a massive global infrastructure investment strategy? As China invested in its own infrastructure, it developed an extensive network of industrial companies in such fields as construction and manufacturing, as well as technologies to serve its new domestic infrastructure needs. As the positive multiplier effect of infrastructure investment on economic growth started to diminish, it was natural that after a thirty-year infrastructure spending boom (1980–2010), the Chinese infrastructure-industrial complex would seek new markets. The primary factor for China's international expansion was simply an economic rationale: diminishing returns in its domestic markets and greater profits in overseas markets. There is little doubt that the economic motivation was coupled with strategic considerations, including the security of supply chains—which the United States decided to pursue ten years later and after COVID—but it would be a mistake to attribute the global expansion of the last decade solely to an attempt at global control.

Take as an example the largest shipping company in China, COSCO. A state-owned entity created in 1961, COSCO grew and morphed into a large state-controlled shipping conglomerate by the 1990s. In 2009, in the aftermath of the global financial crisis, it carried over 43 million TEUs. Of those, 3.47 million (8 percent of its total volume) came from its overseas container port investment, which at the time consisted of only three container port terminals: the ports of Piraeus and Antwerp and a container port in the northern part of the Suez Canal, the most important navigation route for oil.[75] As the dominant player in China, COSCO's share of the domestic container market was over a third of total volume and therefore could not possibly grow beyond that percentage. Two years later, overseas volume had increased by 56 percent, compared to 7 percent for the domestic market, and by 2019 COSCO's overseas TEUs represented 25 percent of its total volume. COSCO by then had invested in more than a dozen container ports globally, including in the United States (Seattle's container port), Latin America, Europe, and Asia. In its annual report, COSCO stated that it was targeting investments overseas with low double-digit returns, compared to the single-digit returns from its existing investment in China.[76] In the span of a decade, COSCO transformed itself from the major domestic force in container ports to one of the largest global players, and it is listed on the Shanghai stock exchange.[77]

There is an obvious economic incentive for state-owned infrastructure companies in China to expand into the global market, independent of any ambition for global dominance. But economic growth and investment in international development carries with it inevitable political and cultural influence. Many countries around the world have accepted Chinese investment and are considered member countries of the BRI. The majority of African countries participate in the BRI, including the largest economies (Egypt, Nigeria, and South Africa), as well as nearly half the countries in South America, including the large economies of Peru, Chile, and Venezuela. A group of European countries has also joined, most notably Portugal, Poland, Czechia, and Greece.[78]

In response to the global growth of the BRI, the Trump administration cast Chinese international investment as a debt-trap scheme. According to the scholar Eyck Freymann of the Harvard University Asia Center, though, it is more likely that the global investment policy aims to create a patronage system rather than a set of debt traps.[79] Such a patronage system would produce larger, if less concrete, rewards than mere debt traps. For instance, in 2023 Saudi Arabia, a BRI country since 2018, announced it would consider conducting its oil trade in Chinese Yuan rather than American dollars.[80] Regardless of China's precise motivations, its engagement with ports around the world has created a considerable amount of worry and consternation.

The most controversial aspect of China's program is its acquisition of port terminals, and even entire ports, around the world. Domestically, China has the greatest number of ports in the world and through the BRI has won control over another one hundred ports in sixty-three foreign countries.[81] COSCO alone owns 367 berths in thirty-seven ports around the world, 220 of which are at container terminals.[82] Freymann argues that through its investment in ports, including the construction of entirely new port terminals in developing countries like Sri Lanka and Pakistan, the Chinese government is developing a "working model for a future geopolitical bloc led by China, structured along the lines of a modern tributary system."[83] Other scholars have argued the strategy of leasing ports may also serve a potential military purpose.[84]

The BRI provides China with the opportunity to cultivate loyalty from countries hungry for large infrastructure investment and paves the way for new trade routes and trade centers. The Port of Gwadar, for instance, located at the mouth of the Gulf of Oman on the southern coast of Pakistan, is owned by the Pakistani government and regulated by a state Port Authority, but it was leased to the China Overseas Port Holding company on a forty-year contract.[85] The port represents a key hub connecting the Middle East, Africa, and China. According to the Asia Society Policy Institute and others, China's maritime policies, even if they do not involve direct military involvement, amount to the "weaponization" of ports in the name of Chinese hegemony.[86] Among other things, including reaping the benefits of port tariffs on trade, Chinese ownership of ports will allow privileged and subsidized entry to global markets for Chinese state-owned companies.[87]

The Port of Piraeus in Greece offers an instructive counterexample to the way China pursues control in foreign ports through its state-owned shipping companies. The Port of Piraeus is the largest port near Athens, located some six miles to the south, and has been in operation since classical times (it is mentioned in the opening lines of Plato's *Republic*). The Greek government established the Port Authority of Piraeus in 1930, and its first container terminal opened in 1978.[88]

In 2009 Greece suffered a severe economic contraction following the global recession and accrued $400 billion in debt—126 percent of Greek GDP.[89] That year, COSCO obtained a concession for two terminals in the Port of Piraeus, paying €50 million ($73 million in 2023 dollars) up front. Overall, COSCO would pay $4.3 billion over the course of a thirty-five-year lease, with subsequent payments made as a percentage of revenue.[90] The Port Authority would retain control over only one terminal in the port.

Chinese investment in the port quickly improved port operations. In 2009 the Port of Piraeus had a capacity for 880,000 TEU containers,[91] but by 2011 capacity expanded to accommodate 1.7 million TEU, and by 2012, 2.7 million TEU. The port moved from seventy-seventh to forty-sixth in the global ranking of container ports.[92] If one wants an example of the effect of P3s on an infrastructure asset, this is the case study. With its initial leases, China had only gotten started at Piraeus. In 2010, as Greece continued to grapple with its long-running debt crisis, it accepted a $146 billion bailout from the IMF, and in exchange the country guaranteed certain austerity measures,[93] including privatizing $50 billion in state-owned assets.[94] At the time, the Port Authority of Piraeus was a publicly traded company, though the Greek state owned a majority share. In 2013 COSCO bought the majority stake in the authority for $280 million, with guarantees to invest another $300 million in exchange for an additional 15 percent of port ownership. By 2022 COSCO owned 67 percent of the Port Authority and had invested more than $1 billion in its development. As a result, Piraeus has surpassed

Valencia as the largest port in the Mediterranean. Capacity reached 7.2 million TEU, and in 2021 the Port of Piraeus Authority recorded its highest ever profit of $40 million.[95] Irrespective of ulterior motives, China invested massively in the port, which had been a highly corrupt, money-losing proposition; there is simply no doubt that putting operation of the port in private hands (albeit a state-owned body that operates as a private entity) has generated results never before seen in Piraeus. Piraeus is yet again an unambiguous example that, properly structured, a private operator can undertake reforms that a state-run entity may not have the ability or willingness to see through.

In certain cases there may be reasons for regulators and other governmental oversight agencies to impose stricter limitations on ports than are typically necessary when considering bids from private companies based in adversarial countries. But on the whole, the concerns about national security ignore the larger economic motives driving China's BRI and therefore tend to be overreactive. These concerns also draw attention away from the fact that the United States has failed to develop national infrastructure champions in multiple infrastructure sectors because it has fundamentally neglected investment in its own infrastructure—the same as airports. There is not a single US port operator that operates any significant port facilities outside the United States.

There is no clear solution to America's competitive disadvantages compared to China in infrastructure diplomacy. As Eyck Freymann states: "China is not an interloper in the global system that needs to be sidelined or boxed in. It is a long-term rival that needs to be managed and outcompeted."[96] This is a policy position the United States has embraced in the past, and it is one it can adopt again. In the United States, infrastructure policy was an integral part of foreign aid starting with the end of World War II. The creation of the World Bank as part of the Bretton Woods agreement was in fact a massive infrastructure project, as evidenced by the legal name of the World Bank still in use, The International Bank for Reconstruction and Development (IBRD). The United States had the strategic advantage over any other country as a victor in World War II, and its effective control of the Bretton Woods institutions allowed the country to leverage the new economic order to undertake massive infrastructure projects globally that aligned with US foreign policy. If the United States returns to its previous levels of investment, not just in domestic infrastructure but in ports, airports, and other sectors internationally, it can play a critical role in this era of strategic competition.

From the first European settlements, the US economy depended on privately built and managed ports, and these ports, still managed under this model, perform perfectly well. As the country embarks on a new infrastructure era, the example of a P3 ports framework indicates that strong participation by the private sector across the board can be highly beneficial. Other infrastructure sectors could look to ports as a model: privatize operations and create strong regulatory bodies to maintain the conditions for success; invite foreign investment; and extend investment (perhaps through P3s) to foreign operators, including Chinese operators (why not—they can't take it back to China). This model has the ability, if properly guided, to cope even with large strategic challenges like the one posed by China.

Though ports illustrate the viability of a large role for the private sector in infrastructure management and investment, they also show the important part government must play in regulation and facilitation. As we will see in the next chapter, there are circumstances in which government contributions to delivering infrastructure are indispensable.

eight

NEW FRONTIERS

Investing in Broadband and Emerging Technologies

DOC BROWN: "Roads? Where we're going, we don't need roads."
—*Back to the Future* (1985)

In the nineteenth century, electricity was a luxury. It was generated by privately owned power plants and sold to municipalities to light the streets, as well as to private homes and businesses that could afford to install the wiring. For a short period of time, electricity may have looked like a novelty, but soon new applications revealed the truly revolutionary nature of the technology, as electric motors were refined for factory use and home appliances like electric toasters began to appear. Life in electrified communities rapidly became more efficient and productive. At the factory, workers could rely on powered machines to lift heavy loads that would have previously required time-consuming, dangerous, and exhausting labor; at home, electric appliances sped up housework. Quickly, electricity came to look not like a luxury, but like a necessity for competing in the world. Today, we can hardly imagine living an hour without it.

As the story of containerization at seaports highlights, staying apace with technological innovation is a necessity of competition. In an interconnected world, systems that fall behind technologically risk being excluded from full participation in the economy, and as more of our infrastructure relies on digital systems, there is an even greater need to keep up with innovations and upgrades. Broadband internet is one of the primary areas of concern, and how to expand broadband access has been hotly debated for decades. Just as electricity was a novelty and luxury in its earliest days, high-speed internet has also seemed like a luxury to some—useful for watching high-def streaming video or multiplayer gaming, maybe, but not a necessity of everyday life. In the wake of the COVID-19 pandemic, that view mostly disappeared. There is now wide consensus that high-speed internet is critical to economic growth and basic quality of life. The millions of people living without access to broadband internet are as disadvantaged as those living without electricity in the early twentieth century were. The new developments in artificial intelligence (AI), as of 2023, have generated a gold rush for the infrastructure that will support the applications of AI across all aspects of life.

The infrastructure of the future relies on digital systems. In particular, our ability to fight global climate change will largely depend on how fast we adopt new technologies for the delivery of infrastructure services. In the water and wastewater sector, broadband is ensuring remote monitoring of water quality levels on a real-time basis, as opposed to periodic manual inspections. In the roads sector, new "internet of things" (IoT) technologies that combine telematics and machine learning technology are allowing us to better predict road maintenance that would require less bitumen use, a hydrocarbon product used on all roads in the world. In the port sector, the use of IoT sensors for refrigerated containers allows companies to reduce spoilage of medicine or food, such as fruit transported across the oceans. (To illustrate how central these technologies have become, the CEO of Fresh Del Monte, one of the leading US fresh food distributors, believes that in the coming years his company will become an infra-tech-based company, rather than an agricultural company.)[1] And of course wind and solar farms would not function properly without the use of internet connectivity.

In 2020 the data aggregator and internet policy expert Broadband Now estimated that 42 million Americans do not have broadband internet.[2] Microsoft, whose Airband Initiative promotes expanded access, projected the number may be as high as 162 million people, amounting to 48 percent of Americans.[3] The lack of broadband among certain populations in the country has created a "digital divide" between those who have access to high-speed internet and those who do not. Much like the electricity divide of the early twentieth century, those without broadband in the early twenty-first century overwhelmingly live in rural areas and typically earn less than those that have a high-speed connection. The Federal Communications Commission (FCC) found in 2019 that 44 percent of those earning $30,000 or less a year did not have high-speed internet.[4] It estimated that 22 percent of Americans living in rural areas do not have broadband, compared to 1.5 percent of those who live in cities.[5]

The story of broadband access offers a window into how government and the private sector manage technological advancement and reveals some of the difficulties in adopting new forms of infrastructure in general. The end of the chapter draws some comparisons between the effort to deliver high-speed internet and the push to introduce renewable energy sources. In both cases, one of the primary obstacles has been negotiating the extent to which government should be involved. Let's begin with a brief history of broadband internet and its regulation.

Broadband Policy

In 2015 the FCC defined broadband internet as any connection with a minimum speed of 25 Mbps (megabits per second). The term *broadband*, however, is imprecise, referring to any bandwidth, or data transfer capacity, greater or "broader" than dial-up internet. Twenty years earlier, the FCC had defined broadband as a connection speed of 200 kilobytes per second, and in 2010 it went up to 4 Mbps.[6] For reference, it requires 5 to 8 Mbps to stream high-definition video, and 4 Mbps for multiplayer online gaming.[7] Recently, the FCC's definition has been criticized as too slow,[8] but also as unnecessarily fast.[9]

The definition of broadband remains under debate, but throughout the 2010s there was also fierce debate about broadband's importance and its role in the economy and society at large. This debate gets to the heart of the question of how we ought to manage infrastructure. Consider this burgeoning form of infrastructure, yet to be fully adopted by the entire population, with still unsettled conventions about regulation and operation: How should we fund and manage this newly essential infrastructure system? The back and forth between policymakers underlines the uncertainty faced by private sector digital infrastructure investors and government officials.

In 2015 the FCC voted to classify broadband internet as a public utility, bringing the industry under stricter regulation by the government and subjecting it to the same oversight as traditional telecommunications companies.[10] At the FCC, where commissioners are appointed by the president of the United States, the decision did not come without a fight, split along party lines. The three Democrats in the majority—Mignon Clyburn, Jessica Rosenworcel, and Tom Wheeler—argued that the regulation would promote "net neutrality," prohibiting preferential treatment for higher paying customers, whether they are website owners or users. It prohibited service providers from blocking or throttling websites that display legal material, as well as banning "paid prioritization," which would grant higher speeds and preferential treatment to particular websites that paid the provider a fee.

The rules were inspired by activists who lobbied the FCC to prevent internet service providers from creating "fast lanes" for web services willing to pay extra. The fear among those lobbying for regulation was that the internet would come to favor the sites of established companies while deprioritizing and de-emphasizing not-for-profit, independent users who would lose traffic and visibility once relegated to the "slow lanes." This prospect betrayed the idealistic vision of the internet as a force for "democratization" and decentralized information. In essence, the fear boiled down to the idea that granting companies privileged access to high-speed service would destroy the public nature of broadband as an infrastructure. A number of towering figures from internet history lined up behind the activists, including Tim Berners-Lee, the University of Oxford and MIT professor credited with inventing the World Wide Web, as well as Steve Wozniak, the cofounder of Apple.[11] "More than anything else, the action [taken] today will preserve the reality of permission-less innovation that is the heart of the internet," Berners-Lee said after the FCC's 2015 net neutrality decision. "It's about consumer rights, it's about free speech, it's about democracy."[12]

The belief that the internet should guarantee equal access to all users dates back to the creation of the World Wide Web in 1990.[13] It gained particular traction after the uprisings in Tahrir Square during the 2011 revolution in Egypt, which was largely organized on the internet; Wael Ghonim, the moderator of a popular Facebook page that helped foment the uprising, chronicled the role of social media and the internet in Tahrir Square extensively in his book *Revolution 2.0*.[14] In 2011 the United Nations declared that the internet is integral to the exercise of human rights and called for equal access for all users.[15] It did not explicitly indicate that the internet itself is a human right, but argued that the technology was a requirement for full participation in society and thus a key element of exercising human rights in the digital age. It ruled that denying a citizen access to the internet, by censoring a legal web page, for instance, amounted to a violation of the International Covenant on Civil and Political Rights. The decision reflected the view of a majority of people around the world; according to a BBC poll conducted in 2010, almost four out of five people believed access to the internet constituted a human right.[16] Since 2011 the United Nations has developed and refined its sustainable development goals, and today technology and innovation feature prominently across most of these objectives.

On the Republican side of the FCC's decision, policymakers argued that regulation of the internet would lead to loss of investment and make internet markets less free. Ajit Pai, who led the opposition against the policy change in 2015, argued that regulation would harm small businesses in the same way the monopolization of utility companies hurt smaller competitors in the electricity sector. Pai agreed access to the internet was key to success in the modern world, but suggested regulation would in fact make expanding access more difficult. "The main complaint consumers have about the internet is not and has never been that their internet service provider is blocking access to content," he wrote. "It's that they don't have access at all or enough competition. These regulations have taken us in the opposite direction from these consumer preferences."[17] Pai argued the regulations would prevent smaller internet providers from gaining a foothold in the market and that the limitations on service provision would dampen future investment and potential growth. In short, he proposed that more regulation would block the private sector from closing the digital divide.

When Pai became chair of the FCC with the departure of President Obama and the election of President Trump, the commission reevaluated the 2015 policy change. In 2017 the FCC voted to overturn the decision, once again along party lines. Since 2017 there have been no rules in place to prevent throttling, blocking, or paid privileging. Yet the internet has not been divided into slow and fast lanes, nor is there significant evidence that throttling, or website blocking, has increased. A study by Northeastern University found that while service providers do throttle certain websites, the rate at which this occurs did not change after the policy reversal in 2017. In other words, service providers were throttling sites even under the regulations imposed in 2015, and the repeal in 2017 did not lead to an increase in that throttling.[18]

The calculus about how to manage and regulate the internet changed again in 2020, however, with the onset of the COVID-19 pandemic, the shift to remote work, and the election of President Biden. Across the country, communities that were without access to broadband fell behind dramatically. For many people in states where access to high-speed internet is minimal, working from home was not an option. The same went for telemedicine and remote learning. Remote doctor's visits during the height of the pandemic? Zoom get-togethers with friends and family? Not possible. And if the local schools wanted to go remote and children had to attend classes at home? Not possible. Teachers who did not have fast connections in their homes were unable to teach, and families who had poor internet, or none, could not participate. Figures 8.1, 8.2, and 8.3 indicate broadband use over the last two decades by level of education, community type, and race. There is a marked difference in utilization rates between college graduates and those with less than high school education, as well as between white users and Black or Hispanic users. The gap between rural and urban communities is still significant but seems to have narrowed over the last decade.

In 2020, as work and schools went remote, those without high-speed internet found themselves shut out. Particularly affected were low-income families, families of minorities, those without a college education, and those living in rural areas. The difficulties among educators and students received particular attention in the media. Across the country, children were falling behind on their education, and stories streamed in of teachers conducting lessons and students learning in cars stationed in the parking lots of schools, fast-food restaurants, and churches, where they could access fast internet.[19]

Home broadband use by education
% of US adults who say they have a broadband connection at home, by education level

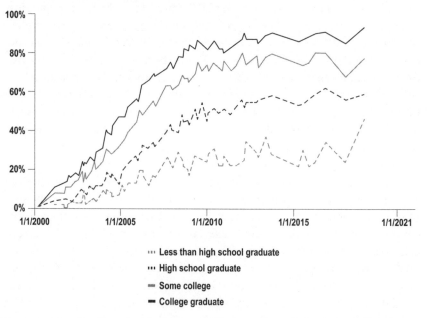

Figure 8.1. Broadband use by education, 2000–2021. *Source:* "Internet/Broadband Fact Sheet," Pew Research Center, April 7, 2021, https://www.pewresearch.org/internet/fact -sheet/internet-broadband/#panel-3109350c-8dba-4b7f-ad52-a3e976ab8c8f.

Home broadband use by community type
% of US adults who say they have a broadband connection at home, by community type

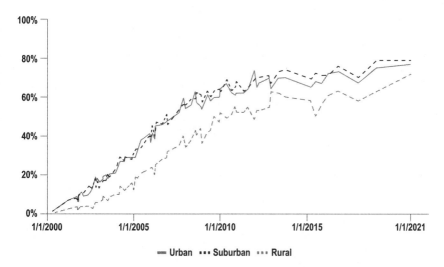

Figure 8.2. Broadband use by community type, 2000–2021. *Source:* "Internet/Broadband Fact Sheet," Pew Research Center, April 7, 2021, https://www.pewresearch .org/internet/fact-sheet/internet-broadband/#panel-3109350c-8dba-4b7f-ad52 -a3e976ab8c8f.

Many families without stable internet resorted to using smartphone Wi-Fi hotspots for education. In 2021, 15 percent of Americans were smartphone-only internet users.[20]

The lack of internet infrastructure during the pandemic resulted in significant learning loss, most pronounced in school districts that enacted remote learning, and especially in low-income communities, where there is the least broadband. According to a study conducted by the Stanford Institute for Economic Policy Research, some communities registered almost no change in test scores between 2019 and 2022, while other communities saw a dramatic drop.[21] Overall, however, fourth- and eighth-grade reading scores fell between 2019 and 2022 to levels not seen since 1992. Performance in mathematics declined more sharply, with student achievement dropping to nearly the lowest level seen since the National Center for Education Statistics began keeping track.[22] The United States is already lagging behind other developed countries, and other major economies like China,

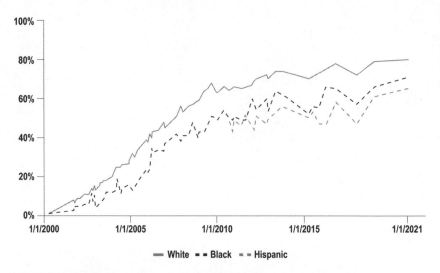

Home broadband use by race
% of US adults who say they have a broadband connection at home, by race/ethnicity

Figure 8.3. Broadband use by race, 2000–2021. *Source:* "Internet/Broadband Fact Sheet," Pew Research Center, April 7, 2021, https://www.pewresearch.org/internet /fact-sheet/internet-broadband/#panel-3109350c-8dba-4b7f-ad52-a3e976ab8c8f.

in reading and math education. In 2019 the Organization for Economic Co-operation and Development (OECD) ranked the United States thirteenth in reading, eighteenth in science, and thirty-seven in mathematics education compared to other countries.[23] The organization's report found that in the United States digital education was lacking, and that this failure spelled trouble for the future. "There is a great risk that technology will super-empower those with strong knowledge and skills while leaving those with weak foundations further behind," the report argues. As technology becomes more foundational, those without the skills to navigate the digital world will increasingly be shut out from participation entirely or will have their opportunities greatly reduced.

The consequences of learning loss are many, impacting not only individuals but also society as a whole. A separate study by the OECD estimated that students affected by remote learning in grades 1–12 could expect a 3 percent decrease in income over the course of their lives. In the long term, the cumulative effect of learning loss could result in an annual decrease in GDP of

1.5 percent.[24] In 2022, that would have amounted to roughly $375 billion in losses (based on $25 trillion GDP in 2022).[25] McKinsey estimates the overall economic cost for learning loss will be an annual drop of $128–188 billion in GDP.[26] Given that these losses are especially pronounced in mathematics, the impact will disproportionately be in the sciences and technology sectors, creating an even wider chasm and one that is particularly difficult to cross.

The problem is not unique to the pandemic; in classrooms with access to high-speed internet, teachers had already begun heavily incorporating the internet into their lesson plans before the pandemic, and students regularly learn to use the internet for research and communication. Indeed, some scholars of pedagogy argue schools should focus on providing an education in digital citizenship.[27] Those regions without broadband access will grow up without these critical twenty-first-century skills.[28]

The issue is not confined to education, either. Access to broadband also affects small businesses. In 2010, the Senate Committee on Small Business and Entrepreneurship identified access to broadband as a key to success in the twenty-first century, noting that the abilities to advertise jobs, hire new talent, and advertise oneself all depend on the internet.[29] This gives a leg up to all business conducted in places with strong internet access and leaves small businesses operating in broadband deserts, particularly in rural areas, out of luck. Even where access was available in rural areas, service remained spotty, and costs were much greater than in urban areas, again creating a strong disadvantage. The inability of rural businesses to function at the same level as urban ones leads to further decline in nonurban areas, which lose businesses and workers to regions with better opportunities—through the internet.[30] In 2016 the Obama administration released a report on the impact of broadband on local economies, pointing to pronounced, measurable advantages in the hiring and job-seeking processes. In households with internet, it found unemployed workers "were four percentage points more likely to be employed one month in the future than those in households without Internet."[31] Without better internet access, small towns struggle to diversify their economic base and have difficultly retaining skilled workers. To paint a picture, in some of these broadband deserts, it can take over five minutes simply to download a new email—an unimaginable scenario for anyone living in digital modernity, and a clear indication of how difficult slow connections make running a modern business.

The link between technology and economic development, and particularly the impact of broadband on economic growth, has long been understood. In 2009 World Bank economist Christine Qiang found that each 10 percent increase in broadband speed leads to 1.3 percent growth in GDP.[32] Yet the United States has never had a consistent approach to developing broadband technology, despite its economic importance. In part, this is because the country has never entirely decided whether broadband should be regulated as a utility or left to the private sector—as the back and forth about the net neutrality bill demonstrates. This indecision stems, however, from a more complex puzzle about broadband. While the private sector has delivered broadband to the great majority of Americans, the remaining lack of access in rural and low-income regions is evidence of market failure.

Market Failure

Though the digital divide looks like a textbook case of market failure, what has caused this failure is a matter of some debate. The simple story of stalled broadband expansion is that extending access to economically disadvantaged areas does not offer a sufficient return to justify the cost of connecting the region, and so the market has no incentive to deliver service. Even if the cost of connection is manageable, will households in the area be able to afford monthly payments for a basic internet connection? The start-up costs and risks outweigh the potential rewards. In many cases, when economically disadvantaged communities have asked providers to expand coverage, they have been denied. Where service does exist, it is often poor quality at a high price.

For many, this is evidence that the private sector has failed to sufficiently deliver a needed service. A report by the Benton Institute for Broadband and Society notes: "The persistence of these [digital] gaps demonstrates that private-sector investment alone is not closing our digital gaps. . . . As a result, broadband deployment does not emerge absent some form of public support. In less rural areas, competition is rare because return-on-investment challenges deter new investors from competing against existing monopolies and duopolies." As this quote implies, part of the disincentive is competition against monopolies and duopolies. Others have argued on this basis that the problem may not require public intervention so much as smarter regulation to promote more competition. In 2004 the economist Charles Ferguson published a provocative book, *The Broadband Problem: Anatomy of a Market Failure*, which laid out the challenges facing US internet access. The thrust of Ferguson's argument is that the impediment to expansive broadband access is the lack of competition in the market. The ultimate market failure is not a consequence of demand not met with sufficient supply, but rather of government failing to let the market find solutions. Needless to say, Ferguson's views were controversial, and many fellow researchers, including from the Brookings Institution, disagreed with him.[33] There is some truth to both Ferguson's point and that of the Benton Institute, and some of the difficulties Ferguson identified remain with us today.

American broadband and internet policy finds its explicit origins in the Telecommunications Act of 1996. More foundationally, however, the internet is governed by the Communications Act of 1934, so before discussing the 1996 act, it is worth reviewing the Communications Act briefly. The 1934 bill was passed during the New Deal era, when, as we have seen, the government sought to take control of large swaths of infrastructure. It created the FCC and brought all telephone, telegraph, and radio (and later television) communications under regulation. The rationale for creating the FCC is based on fundamentally the same arguments we have discussed across the book. Title 1 of the Communications Act states:

> For the purpose of regulating interstate and foreign commerce in communication by wire and radio so as to make available, so far as possible, to all the people of the United States a rapid, efficient, Nation-wide, and world-wide wire and radio communication service with adequate facilities at reasonable charges, for the purpose of the national defense, for the purpose of promoting safety of life and property through the use of wire and radio communication, and for the purpose of securing a more effective execution of this policy by centralizing authority heretofore granted by law to several agencies and by granting additional authority with respect to interstate and foreign commerce in wire and radio communication, there is hereby created a commission to be known as the "Federal Communications Commission.[34]

The FCC, in itself, does not dictate whether communications providers should be private or public, but only the requirements for any provider. The creation of a regulatory body is important, but again, as Keynes stated, whether the provider is public or private should not be an ideological question but a practical one, although, admittedly, sometimes it is impossible to separate the two.

Among other things, the 1934 act established rules for "common carriers," the large communications companies that had monopolies in particular areas. The bill determined these common carriers to be public utilities and regulated them as such. According to Title II of the Communications Act, the FCC would regulate communication to ensure that common carriers broadcast only what was in "the public interest, convenience, and necessity." Public interest required common carriers to furnish interstate and foreign communication connections "upon reasonable request" and impelled them to work with one another to create connections between carriers.[35]

Importantly, the bill also required companies to provide service to all citizens, even those in rural areas where the cost of connection might outweigh the return. During the debates over net neutrality, and even today, the argument is made that broadband, and internet platforms, should fall under Title II of the Communications Act in order to guarantee service.[36]

Perhaps most important with respect to broadband, the Communications Act allowed the American Telephone & Telegraph Company (AT&T), known as Ma Bell or the Bell System, to operate as a "natural monopoly," a term first brought into the mainstream by John Stuart Mill in his 1848 *Principles of Political Economy*. Mill judged a monopoly to be natural if it delivers a service of critical social value that requires the public trust; just as the field of medicine should not be opened to competition from non-doctors, certain markets can't be left open, Mill argued, but should belong only to providers approved and regulated by the government.[37] In 1921 Congress passed the Willis-Graham Act, which adopted the Senate Commerce Committee's position that "telephoning is a natural monopoly."[38] The 1934 Communications Act continued this policy, protecting AT&T from antitrust laws while imposing new requirements for the privilege of operating as a monopoly.

It was this monopolistic architecture that Congress meant to dismantle with the 1996 Telecommunications Act. The bill came on the heels of the breakup of AT&T in 1984, after an antitrust lawsuit forced the company to divest itself of its local operating companies, resulting in the separation of the national long-distance carrier AT&T and a collection of smaller networks that came to be known as the "Baby Bells."[39] According to the FCC, the law aimed "to let anyone enter any communications business—to let any communications business compete in any market against any other."[40] It repealed the notion of the natural monopoly in telecommunications.

The 1996 Telecommunications Act has had mixed results, however. Initially, the act resulted in increased consolidation of telecommunications companies. In the first five years after its enactment, the original seven Baby Bells were winnowed down to four major providers: Verizon, SBC, Bellsouth, and Qwest.[41] By 2001, these four companies supplied 95 percent of local telecommunications and broadband service in the country. At first the bill appeared actually to *reduce* competition by lifting regulations on how the Baby Bells could operate, allowing them to integrate with other companies and expand their franchises. By 2010, however, competition increased, particularly with the entry of Google into the market. Between 2010 and 2016 broadband access expanded dramatically; in 2010, only 11 percent of Americans had access to broadband, but by 2016 the figure had grown to 65 percent.[42] But while the new regulations have increased competition—in many areas, consumers have a choice of local carriers—they did not entirely put an end to virtual monopolies in many areas. In 2017 over fifty million households across the United States still had only one option for broadband service.[43] Competition among providers may have increased the number of options in high-density areas, but there is still no market incentive to extend or improve service to rural areas. It would seem that businesses stand to grow more by improving service in high-density areas than by providing service to low population regions.

This provides an opening for government to play an important role in infrastructure delivery. While the private sector should play a much larger role in US infrastructure delivery, the government has many powers that the private sector does not; the private sector cannot create new tariffs to generate capital, for instance, and government has greater capital reserves to draw from than any individual company. Wherever the market does not incentivize the private sector to invest, it is the role of government and the legislative bodies to decide whether taxpayer money should be used to fill the hole. It then becomes a policy issue, not an economic one. If a road is built that has no economic return, but a state wishes to build it anyway for other considerations, that is the role of elected officials.[44] If one is unhappy with that decision, one can vote to replace the officials.

As debate over the Biden administration's infrastructure investment plans began to heat up in 2020, Jeb Bush published an important article about broadband spending in *Slate*. Bush has been a longtime advocate of broadband expansion in Florida and around the country. "The whole telecom industry needs to be modernized," he told me in a conversation. "Not just schools, but across the board." In *Slate*, he wrote: "I admit that when I hear government spending called an investment, I get skeptical. Most government spending, even those dollars termed an "investment," is money put out the door on an annual basis. There is no expected clear-cut return, which is what an investment has to do. In this case, spending on digital infrastructure promises a real return, as it would ensure that America's technological leadership produces widely shared gains and a larger overall taxable economic base."[45] Bush draws a powerful parallel between broadband access and Eisenhower's interstate highway program, arguing that we should replicate such a program for the digital age. Just as road systems allowed commuters to work in busy cities while maintaining peaceful suburban homes, universal high-speed internet will transform our ability to live where we like without worrying about job opportunities. His vision of a future digital America is well summarized:

> Imagine if we could put every area of America on an even playing field when it comes to high-speed internet. It would be a future where you don't have to choose between a high-potential, creative job and living in a part of the country where you can still see the stars at night. Young families would be able to live in rural areas and stay there, rather than chase opportunities in the cities. Those who have to take care of aging parents would be able to have that option while still maintaining good, well-paying jobs in small towns. People from low-income households in urban areas wouldn't have to go to local coffee shops to connect to a video job interview; they could pursue their economic dreams and professional ambitions the way everyone else does—in a quiet place, where they can think and where they can be heard. And they wouldn't be priced out of their own neighborhoods, either.[46]

Building this future, he proposed, including upgrading networks in rural and underserved communities, would require a $100 billion fund and greater reliance on public-private partnership. It would also demand a Digital Infrastructure Act "to create strong incentives for telecommunications companies to support workforce training, especially in rural and underserved communities, to make sure we have the workers with the necessary skills to build and maintain our national digital highways."[47]

In addition to the national highway program of the 1950s, there is a strong precedent for such government involvement in sectors that experience similar market dynamics that do not incentive the private sector to invest. The most prominent example is the Rural Electrification Act of 1936. In the early 1930s, electricity was still primarily an urban luxury. In city centers, arc lamps had been lighting the streets since the 1870s, and electricity began illuminating buildings in New York City in 1882. By 1888 Edison General Electric had established a grid to provide all of Midtown Manhattan with power, and within the decade Philadelphia, San Francisco, and Boston, among other major hubs, had electric grids that powered businesses and residential homes.[48] However, even by 1936, 90 percent of rural homes were without electricity,[49] as were any rural businesses that could not afford to generate their own (as was fairly common among companies at the time). In 1935 President Roosevelt signed an executive order to create the Rural Electrification Administration, and a year later Congress passed the Raymond-Norris Rural Electrification Act (REA). Roosevelt highlighted that the act would not only improve quality of life for farmers, but also open opportunities for them by introducing electrified machinery that would reduce labor demands and create more efficient farming practices, including electric grain grinders and cow milkers, heat lamps, and cold storage units.

The REA allocated $410 million ($2.9 billion in 2023 dollars) to extend electric grids to cover rural areas. The Rural Electrification Administration distributed the funds in subsidized loans to private companies and local electricity cooperatives to extend coverage and create new power generation facilities.[50] The cooperatives, comprised of local community members, managed electricity generation on a not-for-profit basis, directing revenue to pay off interest on the initial government loan and for reinvestment in other local infrastructure.[51] The model roughly followed the storied Tennessee Valley Authority, which had been created as a federally operated authority by the Roosevelt administration three years earlier, in 1933, to manage electricity generation, as well as flood control and fertilizer manufacturing in Tennessee, as well as parts of Alabama, Mississippi, and Kentucky. The electricity co-ops were civilian-run nonprofits benefiting from federal subsidization, often affiliated with municipal government, but not directly connected to either local budgets or local elections.

The Rural Electrification Administration succeeded in its goals. By 1950 nearly 80 percent of farms had been electrified. The government's investment helped create 350 co-ops in forty-five states and led to the electrification of 1.5 million farms. What's more, the overall default rate of Rural Electrification Administration loans was under 1 percent as of the mid-1950s.[52] Rather than attempting to take the place of the private sector, by instead shoring up the market where it naturally produces "holes," the government played an indispensable role in generating efficiency and productivity. Many of the co-ops created under rural electrification still operate.[53]

Though the REA undoubtedly transformed the rural landscape and rural opportunities, the received wisdom that only government could have achieved this result may not be true. In *Powering American Farms: The Overlooked Origins of Rural Electrification*, historian Richard Hirsh argues that rural communities might well have seen the same transformation without government intervention. In the decade before the REA, electricity had already reached a large number of farms in communities that were working proactively with the private sector. Between 1923 and 1933 the percentage of farms with electricity in California jumped from 23 to 60 percent, and in Washington State from 18 to 52 percent. In Massachusetts during the same period, farms with electricity shot from 7 to 56 percent.[54] Hirsh does not deny the importance of the REA, but instead aims to show that the private sector also contributed to rural electrification on its own and before the Roosevelt administration directed it to do so.[55]

In 2021 the Biden administration set out to do for broadband what Roosevelt's Rural Electrification Administration did for electricity, solving approximately the same challenge: that there has been little market incentive to provide broadband to low-density and low-income areas. To a greater extent than the REA, though, the Biden administration's plan leaned on the private sector.

As part of the Infrastructure Investment and Jobs Act (IIJA), the Biden administration directed $65 billion to expand access, lower costs, and improve service for underserved communities.[56] The majority of this allocation, which won broad bipartisan support,[57] was to be dispersed to states and territories through the Broadband Equity, Access, and Deployment (BEAD) program. States and territories have invested their BEAD allocations in private companies and nonprofit co-ops through programs like ConnectALL in New York and the Governor's Broadband Development Council in Texas,[58] which work with local providers. Colorado awarded $20 million to twenty-nine rural broadband projects, mostly through contracts with private operators, and Minnesota invested $84 million in its statewide broadband initiative, drawing another $110 million in matching funds from the private sector.[59] In 2022 the state of Maine, only 85 percent of which has access to broadband, received a $28 million award from the Chamber of Commerce and $5.5 million through the BEAD program as part of nearly $250 million in total state and federal funds Maine has received since 2020 to expand broadband.[60] Governor Janet Mills announced that the BEAD money would expand its contracts with FirstLight, a fiber optic provider based in Albany, New York, to bring access to the state's remote corners.[61] Maine had an established partnership with FirstLight beginning in 2018,[62] and in 2021 it created the Maine Connectivity Authority to distribute funds and regulate the private broadband providers that receive federal and state grants.[63] On the whole, the Biden administration has enacted a massive P3 program to expand access, and states have worked closely in conjunction with the private sector.

In some cases, municipalities have constructed broadband facilities on their own, sometimes with the help of private companies. In Leeds, Maine, only fifty miles northwest of Portland, residents complained to city officials about the slow internet service for years. When local leaders requested service from Spectrum, the only major local provider, they were told no.[64] Feeling itself to be without other options, the municipal government proposed constructing a publicly owned broadband facility, which it projected would require a $2.2 million bond, and put the idea to a vote. The town approved the plan. That year, the municipality of 2,262 people joined forces with a small, local fiber optics company, Axiom, to build the facility.[65] Axiom would manage operations after construction, but the facility would remain in the town's ownership.[66] Not all towns, however, want to be responsible for funding the construction of their own facilities and would be happy to let the private sector manage it from start to finish. An hour's drive from Leeds, in Hampden, Maine, a neighboring town of Bangor at the mouth of the Penobscot River, municipal leaders put a similar proposal to a vote. The 7,709 residents opted not to invest in the facility,[67] which carried a price tag of $4.5 million.[68]

The ambivalence surrounding operations and the willingness among some municipalities to invest relatively large sums to facilitate high-speed internet creates ideal conditions for public-private coordination. The funding directed toward states continues to present an opportunity to create P3 structures, which would guarantee control over quality of service and pricing but would leave operations to private companies.

The Biden administration also awarded large grants directly to companies to expand access. While these public-private partnerships differ from the highly structured relationships between government and private entities that we saw in the transportation and water sectors, the combined investment, long-term distribution of funds, and imposition of duties and responsibilities represent the same concept as a more formal lease of an asset. Subsidies, after all, are an age-old form of public-private partnerships, so familiar as to hardly be recognizable as a P3. In his first week in office, Biden created the Interagency Working Group on Coal and Power Plant Communities and Economic Revitalization,[69] and within the month the commission adopted a sweeping plan to expand broadband access. The plan was based on a 2019 proposal by the FCC for the Rural Digital Opportunity Fund (RDOF), which was to be furnished with $20.4 billion.[70]

Biden's Interagency Working Group adopted the FCC plan with the full funding request, making an explicit comparison to rural electrification,[71] and planned to release the funds in two phases. During phase I, in 2021, RDOF allocated $9.1 billion to winning bidders, typically companies that promised to create the highest speeds.[72] The top recipient, awarded $1.3 billion,[73] was LTD Broadband, serving Minnesota, Iowa, Nebraska, South Dakota, and Wisconsin.[74] Charter Telecommunications, a Connecticut-based company serving areas throughout the Midwest and the West, came in second, receiving $1.2 billion, and the Rural Electric Cooperative Consortium was granted $1.1 billion. SpaceX, the recipient of the fourth largest grant, received $885 million in RDOF money for Starlink, the company's satellite-based internet service. During phase II, RDOF resolved to allocate an additional $11.2 billion.

The RDOF was not the first federal effort to invest in closing the digital divide, but its investment overshadowed previous programs. During the Trump administration, the FCC organized the Connect America Fund (CAF), which was also unrolled in two phases: phase I distributed $115 million,[75] and phase II issued $1.4 billion.[76] The Obama administration's stimulus plan after the 2008 financial crisis pledged $7.8 billion for broadband expansion and launched a series of programs to that end, including ConnectEd to provide service to students and ConnectALL (a national plan that still exists in states such as New York and Maine).[77] Eventually, at the end of his term in 2016, the Obama administration called for an additional $18 billion to wire every home with high-speed internet, though that agenda item was left unfulfilled. Despite all these efforts, the divide remains. And despite the larger effort by President Biden, the RDOF has hit stumbling blocks as well.

The RDOF chose a diverse assortment of recipients for its awards. The Rural Electric Cooperative represents thirty-two rural co-ops and was the first such consortium to be eligible for federal funding, receiving a CAF grant in 2018. It has a proven record of providing fiber optic service. Charter Telecommunications, similarly, has a strong track record of delivering high-speed service, and unlike the consortium of co-ops, incorporated the RDOF funding into a considerably larger capital project in broadband; the company plans to invest a total of $5 billion on expansions throughout the West and Midwest.[78] But not all grantees were as carefully considered. LTD Broadband, a privately held company based in Las Vegas, had little experience delivering fiber optic service when it won its grant,[79] which immediately caused a stir among other bidders.[80] In 2022, after reviewing the awards granted by RDOF, the FCC rejected two of the four largest awards, those granted to LTD and to SpaceX, ruling that neither company could reliably provide the service promised. "We cannot afford to subsidize ventures that are not delivering the promised speeds or are not likely to meet program requirements," the FCC explained.[81] In the case of SpaceX, the FCC worried the relevant satellite technology had not been sufficiently developed, and that funds could be more efficiently spent.

How the Biden administration's public-private investment proceeds will depend on the ability of companies and co-ops to deliver. As rural electrification proved and has been demonstrated in broadband expansion already, government subsidies can successfully fill gaps in the market, even if in an ideal world it might not be necessary. The monopoly system of the twentieth century stifled competition and resulted in low quality service; though the deregulation of the 1990s improved service quality and introduced competition, it still left holes in coverage, which government subsidies have helped to plug. Ideally, what we should have at the end of the day is a collection of well-regulated private and not-for-profit entities competing to provide the best service, in the same way government helped launch major infrastructure projects in the road sector over seventy years ago.

Toward Tech-Enabled Infrastructure

Broadband has become essential to nearly every infrastructure sector. It is used in the water industry to deliver data about consumption and quality, as well as to identify leaks in pipes and monitor wastewater. Smart meters have also begun to transform the electricity sector. Some 69 percent of electricity monitors across the country now use the internet to relay information about consumption to generators.[82] Power companies use the data to produce a more exact amount of power to meet demand, saving money, conserving energy, and guaranteeing reliable service to users. States and private companies also invest today in "smart roads," which use internet-connected sensors, cameras, and radar to measure and analyze traffic; monitor road wear; and even provide data on parking capacity. Smart traffic lights will also revolutionize surface transport by responding to changes in traffic in real time.[83] Technology companies are developing smart bridges, too, which will provide constant monitoring of a bridge's structural integrity[84]—an important improvement over the biannual inspections currently undertaken, which, as we discussed earlier, can fail to catch critical damage.

As digital technologies become increasingly enmeshed in our world, they will continue to have a sweeping impact on our critical systems. New and emerging technologies, however, have the potential both to improve and to disrupt how infrastructure assets and services are designed, built, and delivered, with technological change occurring at an ever-increasing pace.

These technologies—including IoT-based devices coupled with big data analytics, advanced machine learning capabilities, and increasing automation and robotics applied to critical processes—can enable infrastructure operators to do more with less, increasing capacity, efficiency, reliability, and resilience. New technologies can enable traditional infrastructure assets to provide higher quality and more efficient services to users, enhancing returns on traditional infrastructure investments. When such opportunities are missed, though, the coming revolution in infrastructure technology threatens to strand investments previously considered sound and resilient. Take the electric utility sector. Emerging battery and other energy storage technologies have the potential to solve the problem of intermittency in renewable energy sources and to reduce the marginal cost of energy. However, they also threaten the viability of certain traditional generation assets. Even a few batteries on the power grid can reduce the marginal cost of electric power at peak times—and therefore the total cost of energy to consumers.[85]

Though they come with risks, new technologies will on the whole improve safety, performance, and cost efficiency in many forms of infrastructure. Yet the IIJA's $100 million investment, directed through the Strengthening Mobility and Revolutionizing Transportation (SMART) program, is simply too little to realize all the potential benefits. As a reminder, the IIJA principally catches up with the absence of any serious infrastructure investments in the 1970–2022 period. The funds should be sufficient to repair and upgrade existing infrastructure but will *not* be able to invest in the coming wave of investments that will perforce focus on infra-tech-enabled infrastructure. The majority of these innovations are pursued and financed by the private sector, and there are simply no substantial funds allocated to state-owned entities to adopt such technologies. For example, because infrastructure assets are prime targets for cybercrime, and because cyberattacks can have a devastating impact on the essential services infrastructure delivers, a core component ought to be to invest in cybersecurity technology. But this sort of financing is simply not coming from government sources.[86]

As a member of the President's National Infrastructure Advisory Council, I am privy to the type of cybersecurity risks the country faces and the need for systematic investments. These cannot be addressed by the government alone, nor by the private sector alone, but will require a public-private partnership. Indeed, in *Fixing American Cybersecurity*, which has the pointed subtitle "Creating a Strategic Public-Private Partnership," the authors address the main issues with current US cybersecurity strategy and provide concrete proposals on how to integrate cybersecurity strategies into sectors like energy infrastructure in a sustained way.[87] But the debate on who pays for those new requirements continues unabated. In March 2023 the Biden administration, with bipartisan support, required states to report on cybersecurity threats to public water systems and to take action to protect assets from such risks. Basically, it appealed to states to invest in sufficient technology to protect against such attacks. Some states protested. In July 2023 the US Court of Appeals for the 8th Circuit granted a stay on the EPA's order. The American Water Works Association (AWWA) stated that they "strongly supported efforts to strengthen cybersecurity in the water sector" but argued the approach adopted by the EPA was not the right one.[88] Perhaps, but the bottom line is: Who will pay for it? Cybersecurity protection means not just adding new software but effectively upgrading the entire management system of the water utility system and adopting operational technologies (OT) to prevent attackers from physically taking control of the equipment.

The focus of this book has been primarily on the infrastructure sectors owned and operated by municipalities and states that require significant reforms and where the private sector is broadly a secondary player. I have omitted a prolonged investigation of the energy sector beyond some references in earlier chapters, principally because the energy sector is largely a liberalized sector and has been covered extensively elsewhere.[89] But in response to climate change, the energy industry is planning the logistics of one of the largest, most complex, and vital infrastructure transformations in world history. Renewable energy, and broadly the energy transition from fossil fuel generation to clean generation, will play the central role in the coming American energy infrastructure era and will affect every other sector as well.[90]

I appreciated the intersection between investments in renewables, technology, and the need for new sources of power when the Dermott Wind Farm, in Dermott, Texas, was developed by I Squared Capital. The farm, which is now fully operational, generates enough electricity to power ninety thousand homes. Fulfilling its purpose, the plant generates 90 percent of the electricity powering nearby Amazon facilities.[91] The project marked a watershed moment: Amazon's commitment to wind power indicated the development of a larger dedication in the private sector to renewable energy and a transition away from fossil fuels. Tech companies were now driving the need for digital infrastructure as well as renewables infrastructure.

The Texas renewables farm is far from unique. Over the last ten years, I have found myself investing in renewable power in the United States, Peru, the Dominican Republic, the United Kingdom, Spain, Italy, India, China, Taiwan, and Japan, among other countries, and the rate of progress has been extraordinary. This would not have been possible without new technologies that have appended basic infrastructure, as well as development in broadband infrastructure that has allowed the monitoring and operation of assets in remote areas.

Over the course of the 2010s, renewable energy infrastructure developed steadily. In 2019, for the first time, the United States produced more energy with renewable sources than with coal.[92] In 2022, 20 percent of US energy came from wind or solar,[93] an 8 percent jump from 2019. Investment in renewable energy also reached an all-time high in 2022,[94] spurred by large government injections of capital, not just in the United States but around the world.[95] And renewable energy technology continues to improve impressively; since 2000, for instance, the production capacity of a single wind turbine has improved 319 percent.[96]

The energy transition is happening now, but we are still at the beginning. For some, this transition has been too long in coming and is taking place too slowly. It is true that we have been hearing about the coming renewable energy revolution since the Carter administration. One reason for the slow ramp up of wind and solar energy is that, like broadband, start-up costs were for many years prohibitively high and the savings not attractive enough. In addition, the skills needed to service new energy technologies were rare, and so the new infrastructure typically also required new training and education programs. All this led to hesitation on the part of the private sector.

The calculus has changed, however, and the Dermott Wind Farm can be seen as a kind of canary in the coal mine (as it were). In the last five years, the price of a megawatt generated by wind power has fallen below the price to generate the same power using coal,[97] the skills for installing and maintaining wind turbines and solar panels are more common, and technology has improved as competition has heated up. Though the majority of investment has come from private companies, government subsidies have played a crucial role.

As with broadband, the United States has steadily, if tentatively, invested in renewable energy going back to the 1970s, but it has never committed to a transformative push to restructure the energy industry until the IRA. As a result, the United States has lagged behind other countries. In 2021 China generated 27 percent of its power with renewable energy; Germany and Italy generated 41 percent of their energy through renewables; Portugal hit 65 percent, and Canada 68 percent; Colombia produced 74 percent of its energy without fossil fuels, and Brazil 80 percent (mostly hydro). Norway produced 99 percent of its energy using renewable sources in 2021 (mostly hydro).[98]

In some of these cases with the highest production, government has stepped in to fund the construction of new infrastructure, but the private sector has also been extremely active in renewables internationally. Norway has invested in its leading renewable energy infrastructure primarily through a sovereign wealth fund, which draws its resources from hefty taxes on oil and gas. The fund wields $1.3 trillion in capital.[99] With the IIJA, as well as the Inflation Reduction Act (IRA), the Biden administration set the United States on course to catch up with competitors around the world, and the administration did so in a way that would maximize public-private coordination. The IIJA included an investment of $7.5 billion for electric car infrastructure, as well as $5 billion to electrify school buses. But it was the IRA that kicked the energy transition into high gear. It directed $114 billion to renewable energy over ten years, part of a total of $369 billion for climate-related infrastructure—the largest investment in wind, solar, and hydroelectric in American history.[100] Energy experts have predicted the investment will triple US renewable energy production.[101] Like the broadband investment, the investment will be distributed to bidding companies through grants to construct and operate the infrastructure.

The work of integrating new technology into infrastructure is daunting, requiring new forms of expertise, high start-up costs, and an unpredictable degree of risk.[102] It is not surprising, then, that in some cases the private sector is hesitant to embrace new, untested technologies. In these cases, it is logical and sometimes even necessary for government to grease the wheels of progress through subsidies, incentives, and partnerships. What the history of broadband access, or of the renewables sector for that matter, shows is that neither a utility monopoly nor direct government management is desirable. The success of the renewables sector, however lethargic it may have been in its infancy, provides evidence to the same end. It is easiest to embrace the future when the private sector and government work together. The next chapter discusses in greater detail a variety of models for public-private partnerships and other means of collaboration between private and government investors.

nine

REBUILDING AMERICA'S INFRASTRUCTURE

This Time Should Be Different

Federal policies [on infrastructure] mandate one-size-fits-all answers. . . .
[W]hat may work in one place may not work in another, but we're far
more likely to find real solutions if we unleash the creative potential of as
many Americans as possible.
—Senator Connie Mack (FL), Joint Economic Committee
on Privatization, 104th Cong. (February 1996)

Chapters 3 through 8 reviewed the development of infrastructure investments in diverse sectors, including water, roads, bridges, airports, ports,
and the telecom sector. The chapters demonstrated the fundamental challenges faced by infrastructure development and the roadblocks policymakers and private capital confront when it comes to securing more substantial
and longer-term investment for America's critical infrastructure systems. I
chose these sectors because I have worked in every one of them, either in
the United States or around the world. I have invested in and managed infrastructure assets in each of these areas; negotiated P3s; renegotiated P3s;
dealt with failing assets; and met with support as well as opposition by governments, state municipalities, mayors, and even presidents. By now the
following key points should have become clear:

1. The need for infrastructure investment is greater than ever, and the
   United States lags behind in a significant way.
2. There is an inability to galvanize investments in the infrastructure sectors we have reviewed (even in the wake of the IIJA), which is a result
   of the failure of the economic models to adequately provide long-term
   funding for what are long-term assets.

3. The use of privatization mechanisms has been relatively limited, despite their adoption by many economies around the world, both industrial and emerging.
4. The country's serious debate on the topic is still confused by a mix of ideology, inertia, and the absence of recently available data to inform the debate.

This chapter aims to address the last point by separating fact from ideology and demonstrating that privatization has indeed worked. New research based on panel data across the world, which in fairness was not available until recently, demonstrates convincingly that privatization has generally been successful in improving efficiency, providing greater capital to much needed infrastructure sectors, and delivering better service to consumers than nonprivatized assets. By now the reader is familiar with the thrust of my Keynesian approach: there is little question of principle when it comes to which parts of the economy should be managed by the private sector. The country should be guided by whatever works best. Privatization is one solution, but there are others as well. For example, in the highway sector, technology that allows for price differentiation, which would have been technologically challenging in the past, could significantly improve the ability to increase funding for the US highway network, as Clifford Winston has suggested.[1] Would that make road management more efficient? Not necessarily, but at least it would generate sufficient funds to reinvest in existing infrastructure through VMT and congestion charges away from the gasoline tax revenue, which is bound to dwindle in the coming decades. Creating independent authorities that compensate their employees close to private sector levels and manage infrastructure assets independent of any political influence is another step in the right direction that does not require privatization.

However, I believe the United States is ready for a renewed attempt to bring in private capital for the development of its twenty-first-century infrastructure. The country has already learned much from its past experiences and those of other countries. The Biden administration's Infrastructure Investment and Jobs Act, along with the Inflation Reduction Act and parts of the CHIPS Act, have collectively provided the foundation to pursue such a new era in US infrastructure. But this new era will still depend on the willingness of all to embrace new approaches in infrastructure delivery—those opposed to any role at all for the private sector in the provision of infrastructure services and those who believe that the road to salvation can only come from the private sector.

The debate over the role private capital should play in the delivery of public services is not new. Our current system reflects a centuries-long tug-of-war between advocates of state management and those who believe in private management. Many scratch their heads over why the energy sector, telecommunications, and seaports did not face the same fate as highways, water, and bridges. In many respects, Derek Utter of PANYNJ provided the answer when he commented rather diplomatically that much of our infrastructure policy—that is, the roles of the public and private sectors—is a result of "quirks of history." Between the New Deal and winning a war through an extraordinary mobilization of infrastructure resources, there was no incentive to revert back to private ownership of infrastructure. Throughout the decades following World War II the system worked well, and with it inertia took over, so that by the 1970s the infrastructure sectors faced path dependence: an inability to change even if the majority of policymakers recognized that something needed to change.[2] The gridlock stymying policymakers since the 1990s ensured further deterioration of our infrastructure, and our ability to sustain investments has consequently fallen dramatically, even as economies such as the European Union, Canada, Australia, and China have embarked on a well-thought-out combination of both public and private initiatives without the ideological barriers put up by the left or, more recently, the far right.

Overcoming Ideology

Let's review some of this debate to understand the deadlock the United States faces in the discourse on privatization of infrastructure so as to better formulate actionable solutions. To that end, it is illuminating to start with a review of the Joint Economic Committee of the 104th Congress: a Senate hearing on privatization that occurred over twenty-five years ago in February 1996 and was almost identical to a discussion I had with members of the Transport & Infrastructure Committee of Congress in . . . June 2023. Nearly thirty years later, we are still rehearsing the same arguments and objections.

The Joint Economic Committee, led by Senator Connie Mack of Florida and Representative Jim Saxton of New Jersey, invited several experts to advise Congress on possible solutions to the declining state of US infrastructure. Though many participated on the committee, the spirit of the debate can be captured in the confrontation between two figures who have been involved in the policy debate on infrastructure provision away from the rhetoric: the transportation expert Robert Poole, who advocates for the private sector to play a key role in infrastructure provision, and Elliot Sclar, whose work was heavily cited by those committee members skeptical of privatization, though he himself did not participate in the hearings. Poole, who is now director of transportation policy at the Reason Foundation, served as an infrastructure adviser to presidents Ronald Reagan, George H. W. Bush, Bill Clinton, and George W. Bush,[3] and in 1980 he authored the influential book *Cutting Back City Hall*, about the role the private sector could play in developing infrastructure. Elliott Sclar, currently director of the Center for Sustainable Urban Development and professor of urban planning and international affairs at Columbia University, offers a more critical view of privatization that he has developed across a number of books, beginning in the 1970s, arguing that the state must always be at the center of infrastructure provision, and reforms should occur within the state rather than outside of it.

The committee held three panels. The first was on "the opportunities privatization has to offer, as well as roadblocks the Federal Government has erected that keep state and local governments from taking advantage of those opportunities"; the second was on exploring "the practical effects that federal barriers have on state governments' initiatives"; and the third panel covered "federal barriers to state and local privatization." Speaking to the Joint Economic Committee on the third panel, Robert Poole began with the following:

> We all know by now from many, many studies that funding for infrastructure is simply not keeping pace with the needs that we can project over the next ten to twenty years, and that federal assistance is much more likely to shrink than it is to grow in the years ahead. Other countries all over the world are facing similar problems, and their response, for the most part, is to turn to the private sector and private capital for their infrastructure needs. The latest global survey that came out from the newsletter, Public Works Financing, reports that three hundred and fifty-six privatized infrastructure projects worth $146 billion had been financed and put under construction in forty-two countries during the past decade. But only a handful of these projects are in the United States. I find it ironic that USAID goes around the world telling foreign governments why they should privatize infrastructure, but the United States relies primarily on government ownership and operation for airports, highways, seaports, water supply, and wastewater treatment. Yet, there's strong evidence that

private ownership of these kinds of facilities leads to great efficiency, wiser investment decisions, and greater user-friendliness. Those types of infrastructure where the United States has relied primarily on the private sector, such as electricity and telephones, are universally acknowledged to be the world standard in those fields. But we cannot honestly say the same thing about the US's quality of airports, highways, seaports, water supply or waste disposal facilities. The most advanced infrastructure in those fields is in places like Britain, France, Italy, Japan, and Hong Kong, where long-term private franchises or outright private ownership are the order of the day and becoming increasingly standard. Why does the United States lag so far behind in this field?[4]

The following exchanges in the committee proceedings should be highlighted also, if only to remind ourselves of how little progress has been made and to get a more concise sense of the shape of the debate:

MR. POOLE: There's $5 trillion in US pension fund assets, for example, as one possible source that could be mobilized to invest in rebuilding America's infrastructure. Not with somebody's economically targeted coercion from government, but on a voluntary basis because it could make good commercial sense to do so.

SENATOR MACK: And why don't they invest now?

MR. POOLE: They don't invest now because all infrastructure today, when it's owned by Government is funded with tax-exempt bonds or direct tax money. Pension funds don't have any reason to buy tax-exempt bonds because they don't pay taxes. So, if we shifted to a financing system based on taxable investments, then it would be an economically attractive proposition for pension funds to invest in this kind of infrastructure. . . .

SENATOR MACK: So far, we've identified a couple of things [that privatization can bring]—innovation, efficiencies . . . , and the capital needs. And what both of you said in your statements [referring to Poole and the second speaker, Ronald Lauder, chairman of New York State Research Council on Privatization and CEO of Estée Lauder], in essence, was that over a certain period of time, there is estimated a tremendous capital need for infrastructure in the country. And neither of you see the politicians willing to step forward and say, in order to finance that, we've either got to cut entitlement programs, or, as I would be quickly reminded by others, to reduce the rate of growth in entitlement programs. If we're not willing to do that or to raise taxes, then what we're saying, in a very quiet way, is what the people in the country are going to feel in the future is a deterioration in the infrastructure of the nation, whether that's water or sewer or whether that's airports or roads or major highways or bridges. . . .

MR. POOLE: The opportunity [for the private sector] to earn a profit by providing services that people want and need [will attract them to invest in US infrastructure]. It's not just a matter of theory. We already know that in the United States, we have the best electricity system in the world. And that's largely because that is mostly a private enterprise, investor-owned industry. The desire to earn a profit by delivering good service is precisely what will attract people into the water supply business, the airport business, the highway business. And that is going to have the benefit not only of preventing deterioration, but of making services better and more user-friendly. . . .

There are going to be some situations where you have what's today a public-sector monopoly that will be replaced, for all practical purposes, with a private sector monopoly. For example, a city's water system. It's unlikely that there is going to be a competitive water system to that. In some cities, there really is only one airport that's big enough in a reasonable period of time, at least, to serve air carriers. Let's say Kansas City or Wichita. So, what do you do in those cases? There, I think it's important that we understand that government will retain, and needs to retain, some kind of a consumer protection regulatory role. But that's a very different role from being the owner and operator of the facility itself. Just as we, for the most part, don't have government in the electricity business in the United States, we do have government where there's electricity monopoly service regulating that monopoly in the interest of protecting consumers. And likewise, in those few cases where we do have investor-owned water companies, we have government playing a regulatory role. . . .

SENATOR MACK: So, what we're in essence saying is that in areas like highways and bridges and airports, water plants. . . . We ought to look at them similar to how we have in the past looked at, I guess, telephones and electricity.

MR. POOLE: That's right. Exactly.

SENATOR MACK: That the interest of the public at large has been served through a combination of private investment, private operation, with a regulatory oversight.[5]

Another important witness at the hearings was Al Bilik, the president of the Public Employee Department of the AFL-CIO (American Federation of Labor and Congress of Industrial Organizations), who took a more critical view of privatization. Bilik was the son of immigrants and enlisted in the navy at the age of nineteen. He served as a medical corpsman on the USS *Hyde* in the Pacific theater of World War II, earning a Bronze Star.[6] He made his position very clear from the outset:

> Our members provide public services on a daily basis. They know that privatization can serve as a panacea only for the financially near-sighted and is a disguise for poor management of our infrastructure's assets. And that's the essential question. It is not public versus private. It's good and bad management. And you find examples of both in both. We all have the same objective: to improve the quality of our infrastructure and our public services, generally. But our citizens should be warned, in my view. Privatization promises a simple, compelling solution to the complex, multifaceted, chronic fiscal crisis which now plagues American governments. I urge the Committee to set aside ideology, look at the facts and seek alternative solutions. Proponents argue that privatization can provide state and local government significant savings. As Richard Hebdon of Cornell notes in his review of the Lauder report, which we heard much of this afternoon, "unfortunately, ideology still seems to be the guiding principle of privatization research." Hebdon, who reviews the academic literature contained within the Lauder report, finds that the study's cost data is twenty to thirty years old. The report primarily relies upon one article from 1984, which fails to present the full results of that author's statistical analysis. In addition, the article's intent is to simply promote privatization, not to provide objective analysis. . . . Estimates, nevertheless, of privatization savings range widely, anywhere from, among the figures we've seen, sixteen to seventy-seven percent. Local governments frequently target, for example, mass transit for privatization. However, research by Columbia University Professor Elliott Sclar shows that while some initial incremental savings may be found after contracting out, by the second round of contracting, those savings disappear.[7]

Later in the hearing he commented:

> When President [George H. W.] Bush issued his Executive Order 12803, urging states and local governments to privatize, there were responses from various sources, the AFL-CIO issued a statement that placed the 13-million-member federation in strong opposition. We said that privatization of public assets is a recipe for disaster at a time when the Nation's infrastructure is in a state of severe decline. It is bad policy for the government to turn over public facilities to private operators that place a top priority on making money, not serving the public.

Bilik concluded:

> I think putting America's infrastructure on the auction block will only serve to harm ordinary Americans, businesses and communities. Low-income households would be particularly harmed. Although the privatizers say that the facilities should continue to be used for its original purpose, they don't specify who is to determine how long a facility will be needed. Privatized facilities such as recycling centers, water treatment plants, hospitals, schools could be converted to other uses. And in the event that a private firm cannot make a profit, it may be forced into bankruptcy, and under such circumstances, all of us, the taxpayers, will be liable. We could end up with a situation much like the savings and loan debacle. The public employee department believes that the federal government should put a stop to any further efforts to privatize public facilities. We urge the Congress to reject legislation such as H.R. 1907 and S. 1063, which value private profit over public service. We would ask President Clinton to rescind the Bush Executive Order 12803, and this action would be more in the public interest than enacting any legislation that would expand and codify the Bush Executive Order.[8]

Chairman Mack's concluding statement attempted to reconcile these views. "No one," Senator Mack said, "is saying that all government assets and services should be privatized. Ideally, America should be simultaneously trying at least fifty different approaches to solving our most pressing problems. Yet many federal policies mandate one-size-fits-all answers. Sure, what may work in one place may not work in another, but we're far more likely to find real solutions if we unleash the creative potential of as many Americans as possible."[9] Senator Mack's recommendations were not heeded, and privatization, as we have seen, has continued only in fits and starts. Mack retired from the Senate in 2001.

This debate continues unabated in the United States. Proponents of privatization believe that in the long run, markets are efficient, and full privatization will provide the best solutions. Failing wholesale privatization, Poole argues for a utility-based model, or even a model relying on independently run, state-owned authorities, as a second best. Infrastructure investment and management are better off if they are separate from political decision-making, and full privatization offers the strongest version of this.[10] These arguments have also been made extensively by others, most recently by Clifford Winston and Trevor Gallon.

By contrast, in *You Don't Always Get What You Pay For: The Economics of Privatization* and more recent work, Sclar takes a highly critical view of privatization.[11] The "near conventional folk wisdom [that] privatization almost invariably represents improvement . . . is simply not true," he writes.[12] His concern is in identifying the metrics for determining which method of provision is best, but he disagrees that the market will always provide the best outcomes if permitted, arguing that sometimes markets do not end up serving society itself. "Contracts and markets in the public service do work fine at times," he writes. "It is sometimes a toss-up as to which is better. Hence, if one starts from the assumption that markets must serve society and not the other way around, the critical question is can we do a better job of knowing which is better and in which situations?"[13] How can we determine when the private sector is appropriate and when government is a better choice of owner or manager? Sclar outlines the obstacles and drawbacks to privatization as follows: "The question of how government should organize to provide public service is prominent on the policy agenda. In the US political context, this question is characterized as 'privatization.' The term as used here describes initiatives to introduce market relationships into the bureaucratic production of public services. The intention is to *force* public bureaucracies to be governed by the same competitive forces that make private markets socially beneficial."[14]

A prerequisite for establishing this trust between public agencies and private ownership or private management is the establishment of clearly delineated roles. This has been broadly achieved in the electricity sector, for example, where utility companies that are listed on the stock exchange are regulated by public utility commissions (PUCs). Private companies accept the regulatory role of PUCs in exchange for having the monopoly right to operate. The problem is that such arrangements do not exist in the context of transport infrastructure services such as roads, airports, or the delivery of utilities such as water and sewage. Whereas proponents of privatization argue that if P3s are encouraged and properly structured, they can deliver better outcomes, opponents are more pessimistic, proposing that this is only true exceptionally and only when combined with parallel development of more robust public agencies. "Expanding reliance on contracting only works when it is part of a comprehensive reform strategy that simultaneously strengthens not diminishes public agency performance. Such enhancement means that agencies can regulate more effectively and deliver services better. Ideological privatization proponents seek the polar opposite of this outcome: diminished capacity to deregulate."[15] But as we saw in the UK water sector, the government created an independent regulator, Ofwat, that oversees private operators who own the assets outright, as Jonson Cox explained, or the airport regulatory authorities created at the time of the UK airport privatization, or NHAI in India, which regulates the P3 toll roads; these have broadly succeeded in their regulatory obligations.

Macky Tall's experience at Caisse de Dépôt et Placement du Quebec (CDPQ), a state pension fund, also offers a good example of how such partnerships can work today to ensure benefits for all parties. In the development of a new transit system in Montreal, the province teamed up with the state pension fund to create an innovative P3 model. The province of Quebec and the city of Montreal had been trying for years, and failing, to solve the puzzle of how to construct a transit system between the airport and the downtown area, one of the most heavily congested sections of the city and not easy to build in. CDPQ won a contract to develop, construct, operate, and own the transit system, but under strict guidance by the city. "The government's role was clearly to protect the public interest, by defining objectives, setting standards for required performance, and making sure that costs would be competitive compared to other alternatives in the public domain. And the role and responsibility of CDPQ, as the partner, was to take those guidelines and come up with the best solutions. We led every phase, investing meaningful resources and bringing in the best experts in the world to crack what was a difficult challenge," Tall said.[16] The ability to enter into a long-term contract involving construction and operation of an urban transport system leads to significant asymmetric information between parties. Given the asymmetrical information between the city and the privately run CDPQ, the contract might have led to an outcome that benefited the private operator disproportionately—as Sclar might have predicted would be the case. The structure of the deal, however, prevented this. CDPQ's return on investment was publicly shared from the start, and the rate of return was determined not by either CDPQ or Montreal but by independent third parties. "We put in place an independent process with third parties," Tall said, "to establish the risk we were taking in building this system and calculate an appropriate market return based on that risk." Independent third parties can ensure that such contracts are both fair and transparent. Having an open dialogue and the ability to develop such projects hand-in-hand certainly enhances the outcome for both the city and the private operator. In many respects, this is the same approach that the Port Authority of New York and New Jersey adopted in the expansion of its terminals at JFK airport.

But the dialogue breaks down because while proponents of privatization believe it is possible to establish a strong relationship between the state as regulator and private capital as operator-cum-owner, opponents of infrastructure privatization ultimately do not believe that such a relationship can ever be widely applied. The inherent pursuit of profits in a contractual structure in which there is asymmetric information in favor of the private operator facing a public entity means that "P3s are too narrow a public finance platform for solving society's pressing issues in a satisfactory and timely manner and should be used in limited circumstances."[17] Critics such as Sclar provide a serious assessment of infrastructure privatization that has helped advance the debate, and others such as Poole and Geddes provide a serious counterpoint.[18] More recently, there has also been a backlash against privatization from the far right, but for different reasons. The opposition is based on the fear that P3s will involve multinational corporations that are part of the international rules-based system, with little accountability. Terri Hall, the founder of the advocacy group Texas Uniting for Reform and Freedom, argues that "when there is only one way to get where you need to go and the state pushes that road in the hands of a private corporation who controls the toll rates. . . . [T]hat's not free choice nor free market—it's tyranny."[19] As I have explained, almost all P3s do not set the prices on their own but have a regulatory framework that dictates what the prices should be, and that pricing mechanism is set by the state authority *before* a P3 is bid out. But the fact remains that opposition to public infrastructure has been expressed in different manners from the far left and more recently the far right.[20]

In the aftermath of the global financial crisis of 2008, there was a renewed attempt at revisiting privatization of infrastructure assets.[21] The US government deficit had ballooned to 10 percent of GDP in 2009, the highest since 1945, and alternative funding methods were reexamined once more.[22]

The inspector general of the Department of Transportation issued a report in 2011 analyzing privatization in the delivery of infrastructure services, following up some fifteen years after Congress's joint committee report. The Office of Inspector General, which has bureaus in every major government department, works to ensure efficient use of state resources and to protect against unlawful practices across the government, essentially acting as the largest public watchdog. Its 2011 report concluded that P3s would cost more than traditionally funded projects, but toward the end of the report, in its summary, it also made the following comment:

> PPPs offer an alternative means for the completion of transportation infrastructure projects. However, PPPs can only provide additional funds for transportation investments to the extent that the private sector can achieve efficiencies large enough to offset the disadvantages of PPP financing. For highway projects, efficiencies in construction and revenue generation are potentially of sufficient scale to provide such an offset. The determination of whether PPP or traditional financing offers greater value must be made on a case-by-case basis because of each project's unique properties. Our analysis focused exclusively on the financial trade-offs between PPPs and traditional financing. Any decision about whether to use a PPP or a traditional public project delivery method should include consideration of factors such as risk allocation and expediency of project delivery.[23]

The report did little to advance the discussion since it lacked any empirical data. (The FHWA offered a response to the report that included a more measured analysis of the issue.)[24] Yes, if it is cheaper for the government to build a project on its own, then it should always do so. But cheap today doesn't mean cheap tomorrow, as we will discuss later. The report also perpetuates the wrongly held view that it is cheaper for municipalities to fund their infrastructure projects because they benefit from tax-exempt financing through the municipal bond market. But the only reason it is cheaper is that the government subsidizes municipal bonds, as we discussed in chapter 2, and those subsidies are still ultimately paid for by someone, in this case the taxpayers. The cost is not eliminated, only shunted to a third party. A proper analysis of such projects should account for those subsidies.

The Congressional Budget Office (CBO) picked up this point in a report it issued in 2012 on the same issue,[25] offering a more balanced view. The report indicated that between 1992 and 2012, there were twenty-one P3 projects in the United States with a total value of $16 billion, or just 0.5 percent of the total investments made during that period. Less than 1 percent of investment in infrastructure was made through P3s. The report's basic conclusion is that P3s can be an important source of funding road projects. Interestingly, the CBO also brings up loss of control as an issue:

> A drawback of a [P3] arrangement for the public sector, however, can be its loss of control of a project. Contracts for public-private partnerships may in some cases turn over some toll-setting authority to the private sector. Higher tolls are likely to result in an outcome that may conflict with other public-sector goals. A loss of control may also lead to conflicts about and renegotiations of the terms of the contract, which may be costly for the public sector. More generally, less control of a project by the public partner over the long run may make attainment of the government's future objectives more costly; it may also complicate efforts to adhere to a contract written many years—or even decades—earlier and still protect the public's interests.[26]

The loss of control refers indirectly to loss of revenue, loss of the ability to change prices, and ultimately loss of the ability to change public policy. Let's examine the first loss. To the extent that the government received payment up front, there is no loss of revenue but rather up-front capital in lieu of future payment. The question is then: What ought the municipality do with the up-front capital? But this has nothing to do per se with the concession mechanism. The second is a loss of control over determining tolls, which we have previously discussed. The third is more complex. Yes, once you privatize an infrastructure asset, you have potentially locked yourself into a long-term obligation. But the terms of such a concession need not be restrictive and can easily include mechanisms that allow the state to change the policy setting. In addition, a strong statewide regulatory framework such as the one in the electric sector would provide the required long-term flexibility that policymakers may need.

Ultimately, the question is whether we believe that government is better at *managing* or *regulating* such monopolies, not whether such monopolies ought to exist or be completely sold to a private entity. If we believe that government is more efficient at managing the asset and regulating it at the same time, then there is no role for the private sector. But if we believe the private sector *could* manage the asset more efficiently so long as the government *regulates* it, then we should encourage private investment in those sectors.

What we have not learned from this ongoing debate is whether or not P3s have in fact performed as expected and whether that performance was superior to the performance of assets managed by the state. Have P3s in fact outperformed conventionally funded infrastructure? This may be the most salient question when determining the value of P3s for the United States. It is, not surprisingly, a difficult question to answer given the lack of data for the United States that go beyond individual cases. However, recent literature has provided steady evidence that P3s have indeed performed across multiple metrics.

Have P3s Performed?

The question we seek to answer is the following: How have privatized assets performed? Was the choice to privatize rather than maintain assets as government managed the optimal one? There are different ways to answer these questions,[27] but making any such comparison is difficult because no two infrastructure assets are the same. The first approach to answering the question is to analyze the performance of the privatized asset (P3 or otherwise) relative to its ex ante, or forecasted, objectives. Did the P3 end up achieving its projected goals? Since the more recent P3s are generally selected based on a Value for Money (VfM) methodology compared to the status quo, to the extent that a P3 does achieve its stated goals, one could argue that P3 did outperform the same asset had it been undertaken through a public procurement process. But the opposite is not necessarily true. To the extent a P3 project fails to meet its objectives, it is not clear that a state procurement process would have performed better, unless we are able to gather the VfM differential and compare it to its actual performance.[28]

Another method of analysis compares privatized infrastructure assets to *other* nonprivatized assets. This attempts to address the question of how, for instance, a water utility company would have performed had it not been privatized. Since we can't measure that outcome (because we can only have one of the two scenarios, not both), the analysts use data on existing state-owned infrastructure projects and compare them to assets that have been privatized. Such an analysis requires sample datasets about both types of projects that can be directly compared as if they were the same type of project. There are limitations to this analysis. If one finds two wastewater projects in the United States, one privatized and the other still managed by the municipality, and compares them, would that provide valuable information?

It depends, but most likely the result would be, at best, two case studies that would tell you two stories that might be comparable in some areas but could not be generalized in a way that would produce meaningful conclusions. This simplistic method has been used mostly by critics of P3s.[29] For example, if all the best-performing assets were kept by the municipality, or the most complex and expensive projects undertaken by a P3, then the sample would be biased, and it would not be easy to compare the two. The analyst must therefore conduct the research by controlling for these differences.

In the 1990s a whole field of econometric measurement was developed to measure causal inference in observational studies using nonprametric methods, based on the work of Rubin and others.[30] In a perfect world, one would randomly assign some projects to be privatized and others to keep within state management and then measure their performance after a few years. That unfortunately is somewhat difficult to do.[31] The most robust analysis is therefore to obtain a large sample and match the privatized assets against the nonprivatized assets along different criteria, then isolate the privatization effect and measure the variables you wish to evaluate.[32]

Water

A study conducted by researchers at the World Bank analyzed the performance of private sector participation (including both fully privatized assets and P3-style concessions) in electric and water distribution.[33] The study covered the two sectors in all developing regions as defined by the World Bank: Europe, East Asia and the Pacific, Central Asia and South Asia, Latin America and the Caribbean, the Middle East, and North Africa and sub-Saharan Africa. To address the counterfactual question, the authors identified state-owned companies in the same sectors and countries. The ultimate sample, which covered the period from 1973 to 2005, included 250 electricity companies in fifty-three countries and 977 water utilities in forty-eight countries across the years, building one of the most extensive panel data collections of its type. So, what do the results show? Controlling for all other factors, with private participation, residential water connections increased by 12 percent compared to state-owned water companies. That is, privately managed water companies were able to reach more households than a publicly run water company. How efficient were these companies? Compared to state entities, privatized companies saw an increase of 54 percent in connections per worker and an increase of 18 percent in the amount of water supplied per worker. These are (statistically) significant differences and can be attributed to privatization. A 54 percent increase in water connections

relative to the publicly run equivalent water company is a meaningful difference. This should not be surprising; the underlying thesis regarding privatization has been that, in general, privately managed assets tend to be more
efficiently run. The same result was obtained for the electric distribution
sector. This evidence should convince US policymakers to seriously consider involving the private sector in US water infrastructure. Was there any
downside? Yes, employment decreased by 22 percent. To some, that would
be a big negative. Mr. Bilik testified in 1996 that his concern was a loss of
jobs. But the choice should precisely not be one or the other, since employment targets could be achieved through different policies than maintaining
an underperforming water company.

Brendan Ballou, in his book *Plunder*, describes how private equity failed
to manage the water systems in Middletown, Pennsylvania, and Bayonne,
New Jersey, which were given to KKR, a private equity manager, to operate under a P3 structure.[34] The author uses these examples as evidence that
private capital cannot be involved in the operations of infrastructure assets;
private capital seeks to maximize profits at any cost and will ultimately produce higher fees for consumers and lower employment. Cities are forced to
enter into such agreements because they are short of money and have no
other alternative but to lease out their assets. What is not discussed is that
many public infrastructure services have for years charged rates that are not
sufficiently high to cover operating expenses, let alone the capital expenditure needed to maintain and upgrade the infrastructure.

The solution some have proposed is to increase state taxes or increase
federal grants, which indirectly means higher taxes. But irrespective of the
desire to subsidize a service, to run the water system efficiently and provide the right incentives to the operator (whether state or private), the business should be run in a way that at least covers its operating expenses as
well as long-term capital expenditure to maintain, upgrade, innovate, and
generate a profit to ensure efficient allocation of capital, even if that profit
is distributed to the state or reinvested in the water company. If the state
wishes to subsidize water rates for some, that can be done through efficient targeting mechanisms rather than by subsidizing the whole system,
which is simply not sustainable, as events over recent decades have demonstrated. After all, this is what US policy recommendation has been for the
last forty years to emerging economies, as Poole aptly identifies! The P3
concession in Bayonne or Middletown could easily have mandated no price
increases at all but then would have required a subsidy paid to the operator
to cover the expenses. Ballou mentions, for example, that the operator was

not allowed to increase prices for a number of years except if the volume demand dropped below a certain threshold level. No one forced the city to propose those terms. These types of clauses in P3s could easily have been negotiated out with the careful structuring of a P3. The price increase was not necessary if the city was willing to cover the differential, which it would have covered anyway, either in the form of subsidies or simply by delaying any capital expenditures that were undertaken by the private operator. At the core are some fundamental questions of public policy, which need to be addressed first by decision-makers before embarking on these kinds of arrangements. But as the World Bank study shows, the private sector did operate water companies more efficiently and, yes, water tariffs did go up because they had to cover the additional capital expenditure undertaken.

Roads

I discussed extensively the example of India and how it managed to develop a comprehensive P3 program. The size of the investments has been staggering, but how did these P3s perform? In the most comprehensive study to date on the performance of P3s in roads, edited by Stefan Verweij and others,[35] the authors bring together a series of studies that provide an objective assessment using robust methodologies. They conclude that

> one message to public policymakers and PPP practitioners is to consider developing infrastructure through PPPs, not so much for their financial benefits, but more so for their ability to increase public service delivery in terms of policy outcomes such as improved road safety, healthy healthcare, and education. Much of the attention goes to the cost performance of PPPs. In many countries, especially countries that are faced with budget deficits and deteriorating infrastructure—economic or social infrastructure alike, inviting private sector into the development of infrastructure indeed makes a lot of sense. Improved cost performance of infrastructure delivery through PPP's then becomes a core rationale. However, in many developed countries where budgets are not the problem, per se, it seems to us that the core rationale should be improved service quality and, ultimately, increased public value.[36]

The study analyzes how P3s performed relative to non-P3 projects in Indian toll roads, similarly to the study on water.[37] They build a data sample of toll road projects between 1996 and 2017 that consists of 997 projects: 481 developed through public procurement and 516 through P3s. Their conclusion?

P3 projects completed the construction phase faster than state-procured projects and, while there were no major differences on cost overruns, P3 projects did cost more. But the postconstruction operations and maintenance as well as quality indicators were superior to state-operated roads. This finding is corroborated by other studies that revealed that travel time reduction ranged from 30 to 50 percent on P3 roads compared to non-P3-managed roads, and there was an improvement in fuel mileage of 30 percent.[38] The chapter also refers to reports provided by the comptroller and auditor general of India (an independent watchdog), who indicated that most of the government projects were generally deficient in quality, whereas most of the P3 projects were deemed to be satisfactory.[39]

Another study analyzes the safety performance of P3s in Spain versus state-owned roads.[40] It uses panel data econometric models, as did the study on the water sector, to determine the difference with respect to road safety, a key qualitative variable. Using a sample of P3 projects across fifty Spanish regions over the period 2003–2019, the researchers come to a startling conclusion: P3-managed roads have statistically significant lower accident rates than state-managed roads.[41] Because the authors control for all variables that could influence the causal relation, the link is clear: compared to state-managed roads, P3-managed roads, *on average*, are better managed, have stricter controls, and have clearer penalties that incentivize the operator to maintain the highest possible environmental health and safety standards. Are there P3-managed roads with a higher-than-average incidence of accidents? Certainly. The point is that introducing P3-managed roads in the United States is not just about economics, but also about quality of service.

Airports

I argued earlier that private management could help improve the state of US airports. I showed examples of attempts to bring in the private sector that failed either because of uninformed opposition based on fear of losing control or unfounded claims, as Emilio Gonzalez described. Setting aside these objections, how have privatized airports performed? We saw individual cases of success and also of poor management after privatization, but can we infer anything from just a few cases? Any frequent user of Gatwick Airport and London City airports knows that the service was vastly improved thanks to the great efforts of Bayo Ogunlesi and his team, who run the private equity fund that owned and managed these airports. A research paper produced by the National Bureau of Economic Research (NBER) in 2022 provides an analysis very much in line with the ones mentioned earlier for

other sectors, based on a dataset of over twenty-four hundred airports operating in 217 countries.[42] Of those, 437 airports had been privatized, and the
authors were able to conduct a panel data analysis comparing privatized airports versus nonprivatized airports across a series of efficiency parameters.
This is probably the first comprehensive study conducted on airport privatization. Unlike the study on roads, which was confined to India, or those on
water and utilities, which were mostly focused on emerging economies, the
airport study covers countries around the world. The researchers were able
to get such information on airports because the sector tends to have much
more available information as a result of various disclosure requirements,
both at the level of agencies that control these airports (e.g., the FAA) and
in terms of overall performance metrics required by international bodies.
The results, which cover the period 1996 to 2019, suggest that privatization
has improved airport performance. In the case of traffic volume (which is a
primary concern for airports), the number of passengers per flight, a key efficiency metric that enables the airport to serve more people with the same
infrastructure, there was a material and statistically significant increase relative to nonprivatized airports—as much as 20 percent. Another metric the
study measures is the number of routes served by the airport. The data again
show that the number of international routes increased by 46 percent compared to nonprivatized airports. The data also show there is a significant decline in flight cancellations at airports run by the private sector compared to
nonprivatized airports. To measure the quality of service, the study uses as
a proxy the number of Airport Council International awards, which recognize airport excellence in customer experience through service. The authors
find that there was a greater probability of getting such awards in privatized
airports versus nonprivatized ones. They conclude: "[Our] results suggest
that privatizations, especially by private equity funds, do well both for their
investors and for the general public. They increase the fees they charge airlines but despite these higher fees, also increase the number of passengers
flying through them. They appear to accomplish this by providing better
service, offering passengers nonstop flights to more places, lower cancella-
tion rates, and better amenities inside the airports."[43]

Other Data

Other studies using the same analytic framework as those mentioned here
arrive at similar conclusions. For example, a study on Portuguese P3 hospitals suggests P3-operated hospitals provide the same level of health care as
public hospitals, if not better.[44] The study observed 2,660 hospitals, 2,380

of which were public and the remainder of which were managed through P3s. While P3-run hospitals seemed to perform better in key metrics, both types exhibited inefficiencies. For example, the rate of hip surgeries in the first forty-eight hours after a fracture should approach 100 percent; while P3s outperformed public hospitals, both failed to reach the targeted goal.

It is important to briefly mention an earlier generation of studies. In an often-quoted study, published in 2007 by Infrastructure Partnerships Australia and conducted by the University of Melbourne and Allen Consulting Group,[45] researchers analyzed various differences across a sample of twenty-one P3 projects and thirty-three traditional projects. The study concluded that traditionally procured projects versus P3s had a cost overrun of 35.3 percent compared to 11.6 percent from the period of original approval to final delivery. If one examined only the contracting period, contractors ended up having cost overruns of 14.8 percent, compared to 1.2 percent for P3 projects. As expected from the first conclusion, time overrun for the full period was 25.6 percent for traditional projects versus 13.2 percent for P3s, and during the full construction period, the time overrun was 23.5 percent, while for P3 projects the construction came in under the expected time by 3.4 percent. While these studies used simple averages to compare the two pools of projects, they provided an important groundwork for the debate about the benefits of P3s at the time.

Finally, an often-quoted argument is that P3s are inherently inefficient because they tend to be entered into when the state is short on funds and is willing to accept onerous contractual agreements out of desperation and therefore agrees to onerous terms, like the city of Bayonne in New Jersey. This argument has some merit, especially because in many cases the treatment of P3s from an accounting perspective is deemed to be off-balance sheet for the municipality or the state and therefore will not show up as a direct debt obligation, thus providing some relief from the capital markets and the rating agencies. A 2017 study of infrastructure finance in France used an innovative way to test whether P3s were selected by French municipalities for off-balance sheet reasons,[46] that is, because they did not have enough money in their budgets to invest in infrastructure and were not willing to cut their budgets. The hypothesis to test is whether governments are more likely to use P3s when financially constrained. The novel aspect of this research was that the researchers leveraged a 2010 French law that required all P3s to be recognized on the balance sheet to compare municipalities that undertook P3s before and after the new law. Because the decision made by the government was exogenous to municipalities' decision-making prior to the law, the before-and-after comparison should provide an unbiased analysis. What the study shows very clearly is that French mayors continued to choose P3s even under conditions of budget constraints and under the new law, in which they would have to recognize the liabilities associated with the P3s. Evidence suggests that one of the reasons French mayors considered P3s is that they believe them to be a more efficient choice than state provision of infrastructure.[47]

P3 Performance Relative to Its Base Case

What about P3's performance relative to their initial objectives? Did they meet their goals even if, as the evidence suggests, P3s perform better than non-P3 projects in sectors such as water, electric distribution, and airports? Did they deliver what they said they would deliver? The World Bank conducted a comprehensive analysis of its own P3 projects in infrastructure. While the bank has been a proponent of P3s, there are also those within the organization who have questioned the approach.[48] A study prepared by the World Bank in 2015 reviews the performance of P3s in its portfolio of loans through both the bank itself as well as the International Finance Corporation (IFC), the private sector investment arm of the World Bank.[49] The IFC was created in 1956 to work with the private sector in developing commercial projects in countries where there would be an advantage in supporting private sector investments. The IFC has had an opportunity over the years to play a critical role in encouraging private investments in emerging markets, in particular infrastructure, and has devoted a considerable amount of time and resources to development and investment through P3s. The IFC and the World Bank have a rich dataset that allows a partial analysis of the performance of P3s. Unlike the previous studies, which compared P3 projects to non-P3 projects, this study compares the ex ante objectives with ex post performance across multiple parameters, such as cost efficiency. Between 2002 and 2012 the IFC invested in 176 P3s, amounting to $6.2 billion in original commitments. Those P3 projects represented approximately 41 percent of the total investments in infrastructure and about 9 percent of total IFC investments.[50] According to the IFC scoring methodology, P3s have been successful when measured against their original, ex ante objectives. The way the IFC measures this is through project completion, loan disbursement, business performance, environmental quality, and other key metrics. The analysis demonstrates that P3s undertaken by the IFC have largely been successful, with more than 60 percent of these projects rated satisfactory. Since the IFC and the World Bank have their own respective portfolios of P3s, the data show that 83 percent of the projects undertaken by the IFC were rated as satisfactory or better, compared to 66 percent for the World Bank; also interestingly, P3s in infrastructure outperform other infrastructure investments by 69 percent versus 61 percent, respectively. The report suggests that the objective of improving access to infrastructure was achieved for the large majority of investments for which data are available (93 percent for World Bank projects and 66 percent for IFC investments). In addition, it would seem that quality indicators for these projects were positive; for example, in water projects the ex ante water quality objectives were achieved relative to their original benchmark. Since all these projects were approved following a VfM evaluation that concluded that in the particular projects, a P3 is more advantageous than undertaking a strictly governmental procurement process, it is a fair assumption that by meeting or exceeding their original targets, the P3s also would have performed better than had the project been undertaken by the government entity.

In a similar study conducted on French P3s,[51] the authors collected information on P3 performance in France by conducting a survey of public authorities to determine whether they were satisfied with the achievement of P3 objectives. Using a sample of thirty P3s, the survey points out that 97 percent of those P3s reviewed had faced a renegotiation of the contract, but over 70 percent of the state authorities considered themselves very satisfied with the results of the renegotiations, which were by and large done in a cooperative way. State authorities also indicated that in 90 percent of the projects reviewed, they were able to confirm the cost of work was satisfactory and met the initial objectives. In addition, in terms of delivery on time, 77 percent indicated that the projects were delivered on time or better, and in terms of the quality of the end result, 67 percent declared themselves satisfied or very satisfied. The novel aspect of the project is that they were able to survey projects well past their construction phase. Over 80 percent of the projects seem to have respected their operational maintenance expenses, and there were no higher maintenance costs than expected. These results seem to confirm the study conducted by Price Waterhouse Coopers in 2011.[52]

As the recent evidence shows, P3s work. In the water sector, evidence using panel data demonstrates that water and wastewater projects under privatized systems can deliver better results than similar assets managed by the government. The same was demonstrated for toll roads in India and in Spain, as well as for airports that had been privatized compared to those still managed by government entities. None of these studies have a particular axe to grind, and all have used sound statistical methodologies. The ability to compare in the social sciences a treatment (privatized vs. not privatized) and its effect has always been hampered by the lack of data on both types of treatment. In addition, it is only in the last decade that statistical methods on causal inference were more widely used in the area of applied economics and in the context of privatization. Since the United States has had few privatizations, except for a limited number of studies, the majority of studies have focused on markets in other OECD economies as well as high-growth economies. But there are no particular reasons why the results of these studies would not apply to the United States with respect to the question of whether privatization of infrastructure assets result in better outcomes. This should therefore be a serious option for US states to consider in the coming years. Do voters agree?

I'm Mad as Hell, and I'm Not Gonna Take It Anymore!

As I was researching this book, I tried to find surveys that had been conducted in the context of the debate over the IIJA. While many lobbying groups undertook various surveys, none addressed the questions I wanted answered: Are people satisfied with the state of their infrastructure service? What do they care about? Are they willing to pay for better service? And which services? Do they feel strongly about the private sector operating any of the infrastructure services they use in their daily lives? I asked these questions of Chicagoans so I could understand how they felt about what had happened there fifteen years earlier. But I also wanted to know about the rest of the nation. In the summer of 2022 I conducted a survey of 1,025 adults;[53] the results are available on the website of the Development Research Institute (DRI) at NYU.[54] What are the key takeaways?

Approximately 40 percent felt they were not satisfied with the state of their infrastructure, another 40 percent said they were, and 20 percent were undecided. But when the responses are broken down by income, interesting nuances emerge. Working-class families are not happy with the state of their infrastructure, but middle-class families are the most unhappy about the state of their infrastructure service. How did respondents feel about privatization? Americans are open to more private sector management of infrastructure. Federal, state, and local governments would meet with little resistance and much support—and potentially could upgrade infrastructure quality—if they were to make public-private partnerships a bigger part of the infrastructure equation. Rather than ask about increasing rates without context, the survey asked if respondents would accept increased rates if that meant helping the environment. A significant portion of the US population cares deeply about the environment, enough to potentially pay more in user fees to improve it, and they also stand behind efforts on the part of policy-makers to fix the nation's crumbling infrastructure, as long as it's done in a way that benefits both society and the planet.

For most types of infrastructure, more Americans—across demographics—support private sector involvement in public infrastructure than are opposed to it. And in many cases, the preference for private sector involvement is pronounced. Figure 9.1 provides further details. For example, when it comes to water systems, 41 percent of Americans said private sector management should be allowed (only 33 percent said it shouldn't). For public transport, a greater portion (44 percent) supports private sector management (only 28 percent said no), and 41 percent are in favor of private sector management of airports (with only 29 percent saying no). Interestingly, there was a slight preference for not having the private sector operate toll roads (36 percent), compared to 35 percent who supported private management of toll roads.

But let's look at this in more detail. Generally, low-income households have a very strong preference for private sector management of water resources. Of those earning between $30,000 and $40,000 annually, 44 percent are in favor of private operation, compared to 28 percent who are not, and this increases to 47 percent for the next income bracket. This is also true for those earning above $150,000, of whom 55 percent support private management of water resources. Airports have the same profile: increasing support as income increases. For roads, lower income households are not in favor of private management of toll roads, but higher income brackets are very much in favor. Notably, support for private management of infrastructure is generally equally strong across income groups and Democrats or Republicans. Interestingly, Millennials are particularly open to private sector management of infrastructure: 49 percent of Millennials are in favor of private management of public transit (versus 38 percent and 42 percent respectively for Gen X and Baby Boomers); 48 percent are in favor of it for water systems (compared to 39 percent and 37 percent, respectively, for Gen X and Baby Boomers); 47 percent are in favor of private management for airports (versus 38 percent for both Gen X and Baby Boomers). When it comes to private management of toll roads, 38 percent of Millennials support it, compared with 30 percent of Gen X and 31 percent of Baby Boomers. This

Do you believe that private companies should be allowed to manage these various types of infrastructure?

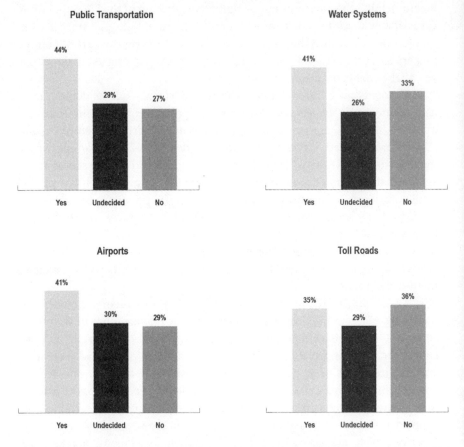

Note: For "Yes," survey respondents indicated "definitely yes" or "probably yes"; for "Undecided," they indicated "might or might not"; for "No," they indicated "definitely not" or "probably not." See Americans and Infrastructure: Results of a National Survey 2022 on the Development Research Institute at NYU's website for the survey methodology and more findings. https://static1.squarespace.com/static/5605cc76e4b082983-2a5b0a4/t/64b16da4fcd58c734866db82/1689349541119/AMERICANS+AND+INFRASTRUCTURE_RESULTS+OF+A+NATIONAL+SURVEY+-%28Released+November+2022%29.pdf

Figure 9.1. Americans' attitudes toward private management of infrastructure. *Source:* Sadek Wahba, "Americans and Infrastructure: Results of a National Survey (Released November 2022)." New York University Development Research Institute, November 2022, https://static1.squarespace.com/static/5605cc76e4b0829832a5b0a4/t/64b16da4fcd58c734866db82/1689349541119/AMERICANS+AND+INFRASTRUCTURE_RESULTS+OF+A+NATIONAL+SURVEY+%28Released+November+2022%29.pdf.

is the same trend we saw in Chicago. Interestingly and importantly, African Americans favor private company management of US infrastructure to a significantly greater degree than the rest of the adult population. For respondents who identify as Black or African Americans, 53 percent are open to private operation of public transit, versus only 44 percent of the survey sample as a whole; 51 percent support private management of water systems, versus 41 percent of the overall sample; 50 percent support private management of airports, versus 41 percent of the whole sample; and 45 support private management of toll roads, versus 34 percent of the overall sample. Why are we not surprised? Those most impacted in Flint, Michigan, and other towns across the United States that suffer from poor water service have been African American households. If someone can provide better service, they don't care if it is the private sector that does it, as long as they have access to safe and clean water. Any increase in tariffs faced by those families could then be more efficiently targeted through subsidies, given the technology available today.

Not only are Americans supportive of private companies managing infrastructure, but they also think private companies will do a better job. Overall, 44 percent of Americans reported they believe the private sector could do a better job than government in managing toll roads, public transit, water systems, and airports. Republicans (54 percent), non-white Americans (51 percent, versus 42 percent for white Americans), people with household incomes over $100,000 (50 percent) and Millennials (50 percent) are most likely to believe private companies would outperform government at managing infrastructure.

The survey also asked how respondents would feel about applying the UK model to their own infrastructure. Nearly half of Americans reported that the UK system of privatization—in which water systems and airports are privately run and regulated by the government—could work in their state or local community. The vast majority of Americans indicated they'd be willing to help pay for infrastructure improvements—better transit, roads, water, for instance—if those projects were guaranteed to have a positive environmental and climate impact. More specifically, 45 percent of Americans reported they would be willing to spend more on tolls and sales taxes for environmentally positive infrastructure improvements; 29 percent weren't sure, and only 26 percent said they would not be willing to pay more. And 94 percent of Americans believed that it is important for new infrastructure projects to be climate friendly, a number that increased among non-white Americans (98 percent) and Democrats (99 percent). Millennials are more willing than other generational groups to pay for infrastructure improvements that benefit the climate: 51 percent of Millennials said they'd pay more, and only 18 percent said they wouldn't, whereas 47 percent of Gen Xers said they would pay more, and only 36 percent of Baby Boomers said they would pay more.

Further, Blacks/African Americans are markedly more committed to infrastructure projects with climate and environmental benefits than are white Americans: 57 percent of respondents who identified as Black or African American reported that they'd be willing to pay more (only 16 percent were unwilling), compared to 43 percent of white respondents who were willing (and 28 percent who were not).[55]

There is a high willingness to pay more for infrastructure improvements that benefit the climate, but this differs among political parties and community type. Notably, 59 percent of Democrats said they are willing to pay more for infrastructure improvements that benefit the climate (13 percent not willing), versus 35 percent of Republicans (38 percent not willing). Support for the notion is somewhat greater among suburban (47 percent willing) and urban (49 percent willing) residents than rural residents (39 percent willing). This survey shows strong desire for change across income levels and socioeconomic groups, and across political parties, in every region of the country.

I propose three categories of solutions.[56] The first relates to the nature of P3 agreements. Much of the debate surrounding P3s, apart from the political rhetoric, has been about the design, enforceability, and monitoring of these agreements. So what can be done to improve those structures and make them more acceptable? The second category relates to states' and municipalities' capacity to execute these privatization processes and then to establish the appropriate monitoring mechanism. The third category is funding. How can the country establish, alongside privatization mechanisms, complementary funding that can ensure that those who are not willing to privatize assets (voters ultimately choose, not policymakers) have sufficient funds to guarantee America can continue to invest in infrastructure in ways that encourage greater efficiency, without waiting another forty years for the next IIJA?

How to Construct Efficient P3s

While recent research has demonstrated that privatization has outper-formed its equivalent state-managed alternative, the fact remains that P3s are complex legal contracts that have shortcomings. Over the last decade a rich and innovative body of work has developed over P3 constructs that provides several practical and implementable solutions.

Many researchers have examined the performance of P3s from a contrac-tual perspective in the context of contract theory and have suggested vari-ous modifications. An entire special issue of the *Journal of Economic Policy Reform*,[57] published in 2022, contains a series of relevant articles on P3s.[58] Augusto de la Torre, chief economist of the World Bank at the time, wrote a summary based on the large body of research conducted by the World Bank, *The Seven Sins of Flawed Public-Private Partnerships*, which provides a straightforward recipe for how to construct P3s.[59] Veronica Vecchi and colleagues published a book on public private partnerships, *Principles of Sustainable Contracts*.[60] My point is simple: those who object to P3s on the basis of contractual deficiencies or inability to structure appropriate solu-tions should find answers to their questions in the most recent literature, which has focused on providing practical solutions.

Ballou criticizes the role of the private sector in the delivery of infrastruc-ture services but offers no practical solutions except a severe curtailment of the role of private capital overall (see his chapter 12). My argument is that cities like Bayonne and Middletown would benefit from a detailed analysis of the value of a P3; if they then decided to proceed, they could develop a carefully structured P3 that meets their *policy objectives*. Cities must also ask themselves whether they have the internal capacity to monitor and ex-ecute such agreements. If the answer is no, then entering into such agree-ments would be a very bad idea indeed. But to blame private capital solely is simply not correct.

Let's examine some of the structural elements of P3s and proposed solu-tions to recurring issues.

Improving VfM Technology

The core of any P3 decision has been the calculation of the cost of the alter-native, namely having the state embark on that project as opposed to enter-ing into a P3 agreement. Much literature has been written about improving VfM methodologies, and the US DoT has developed a strong set of tools to account for recent changes in measuring both observables, as well as the means to estimate unobservables, in evaluating whether to engage in P3s. A VfM methodology also needs to account for the new contractual aspects of the underlying P3 itself. One of the cardinal sins of P3s is that they do not undertake sufficient market tests on the merits of the arrangement. The availability of public information before and after awarding a P3 is of critical importance. But since municipalities have few resources to undertake this type of work, and the financial advisors hired to help are constrained by time and the need to generate immediate fees, I advocate the development of an information-sharing platform (ISP) to be made available to all participants, both public and private. The ISP could ensure the use of real-time data on P3 projects as well as recent improvements in VfM methodologies that could be accessed by all.[61] No city or state should embark on developing a P3 program without a thorough review of its objectives and how they translate in the design of an optimal P3, as well as an assessment of the city's monitoring capabilities.

Improving Procurement Processes for P3s and DBBs

In the United States, highway procurement is traditionally executed by the Department of Transportation (DoT) in every state. These projects are funded by a combination of federal and state transfers, debt, and toll revenues.[62] How are these funds invested in actual projects? A DoT prepares the design of a selected project and then puts it out for bids from independent contractors who can build the project (DBB model).[63] As Poole has argued, "The DBB process focuses on the wrong cost target; it minimizes the *initial* cost at the expense of considerably higher total *life-cycle cost*."[64] The DBB model forces DoTs to go for the cheapest bid by absolute cost to avoid issues of corruption. Contractors are therefore incentivized to use change orders, which can increase the cost; they push out deferred maintenance or simply do not account for it in terms of quality of equipment and material when bidding the contract. There is, in addition, a tendency among DoTs to select projects that may be politically motivated. The DBB process emerged from a desire to avoid the corruption that had been prevalent in the municipal construction sector. But as many have argued, bidding for the lowest possible price kills any possible innovation, because any deviation from the bid would automatically disqualify the bidder. Cost overruns present a major challenge to such contracts in general. Poole refers to a study produced in 2003 by a group of Danish economists that explored why megaprojects tended to have cost overruns;[65] it found that government-managed projects are particularly prone to such overruns. The group concluded that "the conventional procurement approach in which government is the project promoter and financer and the private sector is limited to design and construction creates perverse incentives to create optimistic scenarios . . . which puts the risk on the shoulder of the taxpayers."[66]

P3s tend to operate over a long duration, and the concessionaire is therefore responsible for the risk of any major maintenance costs as well as any construction cost overruns. Moreover, the selection process of P3s is fundamentally different than in the traditional model. Overall, P3s have a multifactor selection process, the first factor being the technical ability of the consortium bidding on the P3 to meet project qualifications. It is not necessarily the lowest cost that wins, but a weighted average score based on different criteria that allows the concession bidders to come up with different, novel ideas, rather than simply the cheapest plan. This leads to a longer process, but overall, in principle, the P3 should result in a better outcome.[67]

Nevertheless, the nature of the P3 contract, being long term and tying the state to certain parameters identified ex ante (thereby assuming that public policy will remain static, for example, for ninety-nine years), is indeed problematic. When considering contracts over such a long period, the institutional, legal, and financial frameworks in which each party operates, as well as information availability, become critical. Since the late 1990s, economics has developed into several key branches, one of which is contract theory, which essentially studies the theory and writing of contracts between state and private actors. Contract theory is about how economic agents interact under a legal contract, either with perfect information or, as may generally be the case in the delivery of infrastructure services, with imperfect information. I had the pleasure of studying under Eric Maskin, who received the Nobel Prize in 2007, and Oliver Hart, who received the Nobel Prize in 2016, both for work in contract theory. While this is not the place to review contract theory, suffice it to say that in many respects it has revolutionized the way contracts are developed, both in bidding processes and in the work of drafting complex license agreements between the state and the private sector (telecom licenses provide a textbook example). Over the last few decades, extraordinary work has been done on evaluating P3s specifically and, not surprisingly, almost all this research has come from either European or Chinese universities. This is because they have been at the forefront of public and private partnerships and have had sufficient experience over the years to improve such contracts in a way that addresses the serious criticisms leveled at P3 contracts.

Much of the contract theory literature applied to infrastructure investment has focused on two broad issues: the asymmetrical nature of the contract (incomplete contract) and the principal-agent issues associated with the procurement process. Whether we are referring to a P3 or to a DBB process, the issue exists in both. In the case of a P3 process, the issue is made more complex, however, because both parties sign a contract on day one that will last for a long period. Dejan Makovsek and Adrian Bridge provide a survey of the issues associated with procurement in the context of infrastructure contracts.[68] Their view is that contract and auction theory can provide a useful framework to help rethink not only how to develop procurement projects of the DBB type but also how to design P3s.

While the studies mentioned in the previous section show that P3s can be superior to state-managed investments, they are silent about costs to the state as a result of entering into suboptimal procurement processes. One of the recent articles that does address this issue is a study on procurement for highway projects in California.[69] The focus is on what the authors call "adaptation costs," which they define as costs "incurred by disruptions to the normal flow of work that could have been avoided with adequate planning in advance. Renegotiating the contract also generates adaptation costs in the form of haggling, dispute resolution, and opportunistic behavior." The value of this study is that it provides a dollar value to the adaptation costs. The authors collected data from publicly available bid sources as well as final payment forms, bidding date location, the number of firms that participated, and the number of wins on projects that were procured by California transport (Caltrans) in the period 1999–2005. The article also includes the estimated project cost to establish a baseline of what would have been a fair price ex ante. Two conclusions come out of their analysis. The first is that the system adopted by Caltrans generally promotes competition. This is measured by the possible markup relative to the benchmark and suggests that markup to be modest at best. The real issue is change orders: changes in objectives by Caltrans generate adaptation costs that range from $0.55 to $2 for every dollar in change. As the authors argue, "Since the source of these costs is the incompleteness of project design and specifications, an obvious policy implication is to consider increasing the ex ante costs and efforts put into estimating and specifying projects before they are left out for bidding." In contrast to the public sector, private sector buyers allow for mechanisms other than competitive bidding to select a contractor. A related article finds that in private sector contracts, open competitive bidding is only used in 18 percent of the contracts, and 44 percent of the contracts are negotiated.[70] Those negotiated contracts are more commonly used for projects that appear to be more complex, for which ex post changes in plans and specifications are likely. A perceived advantage of negotiated contracts is that they allow the architect, buyer, and contractor to discuss the project plans so that the contractor can point out pitfalls and suggest modifications to the project design before work begins. Furthermore, negotiated contracts often are based on cost plus compensation.

Other studies suggest that some of the poor incentives associated with cost plus contracts could be compensated for by the ability to renegotiate terms, because these contracts allow for renegotiation as the contractor presents its receipts for the additional expenses and is reimbursed, which avoids tension among the parties and litigation.[71] That is precisely what P3 structures are for. In many respects, any additional cost or modification is priced accordingly with observables, including a known return on equity. When critics argue that P3s cost more, what they have not accounted for is the actual cost incurred in DBB projects after the contract is awarded, and after construction, to account for differences in operating expenses, as Poole has argued. A more radical solution is to develop a statewide regulator for the water sector and another for transport, which would eliminate the need to negotiate the need for a separate P3 every time.

Renegotiation Risk

The risk in renegotiation of P3 contracts has been identified as an important weakness.[72] Because of the incomplete nature of these contracts, critics of P3s point to the high propensity to renegotiate them as evidence of P3 failure. Structuring the right contract and having a strong counterparty to the private operator are critical, as we have indicated. In a study conducted in France on the renegotiation outcomes of P3, the majority of government officials were satisfied with the outcomes of those renegotiations.[73] The fact is that early versions of P3s did face some renegotiation, and I witnessed it myself in Chile, when many P3 concessionaires, who were also undertaking the construction, anticipated in their base case the "renegotiation" premium, which invariably juiced up their returns.[74] Part of this was due to the fact that the Chilean DoT had not yet developed the sophistication it developed later on.[75] Joaquim Sarmento and Luc Renneboog provide a useful review of P3 structures.[76] They point out that P3s have certain characteristics that make them more susceptible to renegotiation. The long-term, complex nature of these incomplete contracts—as well as the fact that they tend to operate in politically sensitive sectors with monopolistic characteristics and the need for a high level of capital expenditure, or capex, determined up front—makes it difficult to formulate them properly. The authors' broad conclusion is the need for an independent P3 arbitrator, to ensure best practices and improvement in P3s have been implemented in the following generations of P3s. A 2021 study by Daniel Danau and Annalis Vinella provides recommendations on how to deal with this principal-agent risk.[77]

A related strand of literature examines the incentives one needs to include in the P3 selection process to ferret out the low productivity investor who would be incentivized to renegotiate and seek additional government support, versus the productive investor who might potentially be more expensive but would avoid any future renegotiation.[78] Once again, recent research has tried to address these concerns and has come up with ways to design P3s that account for those risks. Ultimately, as de la Torre and Rudolph stress in *Seven Sins of Flawed Public-Private Partnerships*: do not provide excessive government guarantees, and do not fall into the trap of renegotiation. The new generation of P3s attempts to do just that. Policymakers should use them.[79] But once more, undertaking P3s without appropriate resources to manage and monitor them over their lifetimes could be a worse outcome than maintaining the status quo.

Concession Length

The length of a concession has been mostly a political issue rather than an economic one. The economics of the concession length are pretty simple. The longer the concession, the greater the up-front proceeds for the state. The longer the concession, the more it amounts to a sale or outright privatization of the asset. When the Indiana Toll Road and Chicago Skyway undertook concessions well in excess of thirty years, there was an outcry because critics felt the state was actually selling the assets outright. And they were right, in a way: in some cases the length of the concession is akin to an almost outright sale. I write "almost" because in nearly every case P3s give the right to the state to take over the concession if the private operator defaults on certain terms and the concessionaire is not able to remedy the default. What is the optimal concession length? Again, solid research exists on that question and related issues.[80] If the state needs funds up front to cover a deficit or invest in other needs, then a longer concession will increase the proceeds but face more resistance. In my experience, the most politically palatable and economically feasible P3 on a stand-alone basis is one with a

twenty-year duration. A twenty-year concession offers a reasonable horizon; the majority of those who saw the asset go into a P3 structure will see
it revert to the state at the end of the concession life. Longer concessions
would require revenue-sharing mechanisms to ensure alignment of interest
and to reduce principal-agent issues. These revenue-sharing mechanisms
could take several forms: maintain a minority ownership, an earn-out if the
asset is sold during its lifetime, or a share of the profits above a certain level.

How does a twenty-year concession stack up against full privatization à
la the United Kingdom? While the surveys I conducted have clearly shown
that those surveyed do not object to such privatization—especially Millennials—I do not believe that full privatizations will ever be a popular solution in the short term. As a first step, a P3 with a term of up to twenty years
is simply a more politically acceptable model. Moreover, as another recent
study shows, P3 projects have a greater chance of success if the infrastructure asset is returned back to the state, compared to an outright sale. Nothing stops the state from retendering the asset into a new P3 at the end of the
concession life, which would be akin to a full sale.[81]

User Fee Mechanisms in P3s

In 2018, Poole published a book entitled *Rethinking America's Highways: A
21st Century Vision for Better Infrastructure.* In addition to providing a comprehensive assessment of our transport sector, he reminds the reader that
the FHWA, which manages most of the highways across the United States,
has for all intents and purposes not been functioning the way it should for
a long time.[82] The failure of the FHWA calls into question precisely the ability of government agencies to be at the center of infrastructure delivery.
There is an agreement by all parties, whether on the left or the right, that
the "gas tax" system of the FHWA is not sustainable, and it has not changed
in thirty years. Poole identifies four reasons for this insufficiency. First, federal policy has imposed more and more strict fuel economy mandates for
new vehicles, which means that vehicles become more efficient in terms
of consumption of gas for the same amount of distance, and since the tax
is levied on the amount of gas one consumes, the revenue coming from
fuel consumption has come down over time. Second, fuel tax rates are not
indexed to inflation, but the fuel tax revenues are used to upgrade lanes,
maintain safety on highways, and upgrade bridges—all expenses that are
very highly correlated with inflation. Third, it has become politically impossible for elected officials to increase any rates because they are criticized
for increasing "taxes" (when in fact they really are increasing user fees).[83]

And fourth, the introduction of electric vehicles, if taken to the extreme by eliminating all combustion engines on the road, would reduce the revenues of the FHWA essentially to zero and in the transition make the gasoline tax more regressive.[84] The gasoline tax should therefore be replaced sooner or later with a new mechanism. The most straightforward one is simply to increase toll rates depending on the demand for that particular highway. This doesn't require a P3 or any privatization mechanisms. P3s could generate additional revenues for the state by having the private operator manage the rate increase the state desires.

But the price setting in a P3 concession has been controversial. The price for delivering an infrastructure service should reflect the true cost of operating, for instance, a wastewater treatment plant or major road, including the long-term capital expenditure requirement—the cost of installing and operating smart infrastructure—while providing the operator with an acceptable rate of return, irrespective of who the operator is. This has generally not been the case for state-owned infrastructure assets. The pricing mechanism adopted in P3s is generally based on the existing price that has been charged historically, with an upfront adjustment followed by inflation adjustments. Clifford Winston has argued that efficient pricing is the best way to pay for infrastructure.[85] In an article for the *Journal of Macroeconomics*, Winston and his coauthor Trevor Gallen use an applied general equilibrium model, which is a good way to illustrate the whole impact of a particular policy as opposed to looking at it in a partial equilibrium. For example, an increase in revenue or an increase in capital expenditure for transport infrastructure would obviously have a positive impact through employment and other economic benefits that are associated with building a highway. On the other hand, what this partial analysis does not take into account is the reliance on tax increases to fund that capex. How does that impact the rest of the economy, and what is the net effect of that policy? That generally can only be calculated in a general equilibrium framework. Using this type of model, Winston demonstrates that efficient pricing could be an extremely effective tool for managing highway investments.[86] He points out that efficient pricing can be more beneficial than simply increasing spending on highways through taxation. His point addresses the fact that, all things being equal, we do not need to spend one full dollar on capital expenditure but can reduce that dollar with more efficient pricing. In many economies, the concession charges a price to the municipality that is higher than what the municipality charges consumers. That is true for waste water treatment in China, certain toll roads in India, and many other infrastructure sectors.

Exit Mechanisms in P3s

Another challenge with P3s, especially those that monetize existing operating assets, such as the Indiana Toll Road, has been the fact that in almost all concessions, the concessionaire is allowed to sell the concession. Suppose a private operator enters into a P3 to upgrade an existing road that had a toll, and under the concession agreement the operator would be entitled to increase the tolls after it has invested an up-front amount, including the operation and maintenance of the road during the life of the concession. If the initial investment the operator made is $100, and it expects a 10 percent return on equity, then if the company sells the concession after seven years, it could expect to have doubled its investment. If it sells it for more than double, because the risk profile of the remaining life of the concession is attractive relative to other investments, that profit accrues to the concessionaire, not the state. In the eyes of the public, this seems wholly unfair, even though the P3 concessionaire pays taxes on the capital gains and has taken all the risk. In hindsight one could argue that $100 was too low and the price paid should have been higher. But there is nothing unfair about the situation if the $100 paid to the state was a market price at the time. Unfortunately the market price for a highway concession has unique characteristics and is difficult to fully determine. That is why having the right VfM technology and the scoring mechanism we discussed is critical. In many cases, municipalities set a reservation price below which they will not undertake a P3. Nevertheless, the public simply cannot help but feel cheated. In the United States specifically, this has caused much harm to the reputation of P3s. There are several solutions that have been used across the board, and ultimately they will depend on the primary objective of the state. One solution is simply to retain a minority ownership in the P3, as mentioned earlier. This provides transparency, since being in the shareholder structure confers information rights at the very least, and in the event of a profitable sale at some point during the life of the concession, the municipality would also benefit. Conversely, if the sale is a failure because the concessionaire underestimated what it would cost to build or upgrade the infrastructure asset and it cost much more than $100, or the traffic simply did not materialize, the state would lose on its retained ownership. Another mechanism used by NHAI is to prolong or shorten the concession life depending on how well it performs. If the concession performs better than expected, one can reduce the concession life, and conversely, if it underperforms, it is possible to allow the concessionaire to extend it. A third mechanism is to seek a premium over and above a certain threshold. In the example we gave, if the sale generated three times the initial investment, the municipality could share in any return that is more than double the initial investment. All these mechanisms are easily executable but require the municipality to think carefully about its objectives and to specify them up front.

Exits do not just occur at the time of sale. In the event of sustained losses, the P3 concessionaire could walk away from a concession. While typical P3s include penalties, given that the public sector would need to take over the concession and manage it or bid it out to another third party, the cost could be high for municipalities. Once more, researchers have examined that issue and how one can modify P3s to maximize the value for the municipality.[87]

P3s and Exogenous Risks

In many cases P3s address all the risks we have identified except those that are totally exogenous to either the state or the private operator. An example is commodity risk. One study reviewed an integrated desalination plant that entered into an agreement to supply water for twenty-five years. The project was linked to another project in power generation (the most important cost in a desalination plant). The project ultimately failed and had to be restructured, not because of the procurement process or technology or operational risks, but purely because of commodity risk.[88] This example points to the need to create more flexible P3 agreements to account for risks that are totally out of the control of the state or the private operator. The public agency can ask the private operator to take on that risk, similar to interest rate risk, refinancing risk in the capital markets, and so forth, but while those risks can to a large extent be hedged and appropriately modeled, commodity risks, or natural disaster risks, are difficult to manage. Many projects have entered into long-term fixed-price commodity supply agreements. But to the extent the risk cannot be hedged, either the risk can be taken on by the P3 operator (and higher risk can then be introduced to the project that is not adequately priced by either party), or the project will not happen. In Chile, in the early period of P3 projects, the government offered currency swaps to address currency risk volatility because the project revenues were all in Chilean pesos and most of the investors were foreign investors looking to the US dollar or euro as their base currency. If the currency depreciated by more than 10 percent, the ministry of finance would provide protection, and if the currency appreciated by more than 10 percent, the ministry of finance reaped the benefit. The private operators could bid with or without the swap agreement. Such mechanisms should be introduced in P3s for risk that cannot be properly hedged by any party, or else the risk should be absorbed by the state. But the state should be limited to provide the smallest number of guaranties. In the development of the Miami Tunnel, connecting the Port of Miami to the mainland, the city provided a guarantee against dredging risk and hurricane events that facilitated the successful conclusion of the selection process. Without the city keeping these risks, few investors would have undertaken the project. But that risk would have been borne by the city anyway in a traditional DBB process.

P3 and Smart Infrastructure

Infrastructure needs to become smart and adopt technology in ways that have not happened on any significant scale yet. For example, the IIJA focuses on traditional infrastructure repair, with some funds associated with smart urban infrastructure development. But the investments needed to make infrastructure smart will be considerable over the coming decades. Can P3s provide a mechanism to encourage private investment in these technologies—especially in urban contexts, where the smart city is the future? Carlos Cruz and Joaquim Sarmento discuss precisely this point.[89] They surmise that traditional P3s will not work, and a new type of P3 will need to be developed that is more dynamic, one that allows for state entities to modify procurement laws to account for "innovative partnerships [like] the EU is undertaking, and a dynamic regulatory framework presumably with a different regulator to account for the inherent risk in the adoption of technologies." P3 are best positioned to implement these technological innovations, because they are incentivized to improve performance. In contrast, New York City, where all the toll roads are controlled by the state and the FHWA, introduced E-ZPass in 1997, but only introduced e-tolls in 2020. The same technology was introduced in Italy in 1989. In the case of congestion charges, which also require the implementation of monitoring and billing technology, after navigating the byzantine process of reviews and approvals, congestion charging in NYC was finally approved. As Bryan Walsh wrote in an article in Vox, "What if I told you there was a fairly simple policy initiative that would reduce auto traffic by 15 to 20% in the heart of America's most congested city, raise $1 billion annually for the country's biggest mass transit system at a time when such services are on the edge of the financial death spiral, and improve air quality for urban neighborhoods that have long suffered disproportionately from pollution?"[90] Bryan noted that New York arrived at this point seventeen years after Mayor Michael Bloomberg first proposed the idea, when it was promptly turned down by the state legislature. A small correction, however: congestion pricing was first suggested for the New York subway system by William Vickrey, a Nobel Prize winner in economics and a leading researcher in public policy, some *seventy-one years* earlier, in 1952.[91] Has this story finally found a happy ending? Unfortunately, no. A few weeks after the announcement, the state of New Jersey sued the Biden administration over its congestion charge proposal. The congestion charge would discriminate against New Jersey commuters and would force them to seek alternate routes, which would reduce the revenues from tolls collected by New Jersey.[92] A P3 process would have greater flexibility in developing an entire congestion charge policy with a proper implementation, given the time and resources required to develop such a system.

Capacity Building

Having a well-structured P3 is one thing, but having the ability to monitor, adjust whenever necessary, impose fines, or take over P3s is another matter altogether. As Amanda Girth, a professor of public affairs at Ohio State University and an expert on management processes and accountability in public-private procurement processes, writes: "Although well-written contracts with specified performance measures are critical first steps towards accountability, *they are virtually worthless without vigilant execution*" (emphasis added).[93] There are two issues. The first concerns the implementation of a DBB-P3 procurement process: Who has the ability to research, adopt new processes, and implement them? Second, who can monitor, renegotiate, and enforce P3s?

The hesitancy to explore alternatives to the federal and state tax-revenue-funded infrastructure model arises in no small part from the inherently complex nature of P3s. Public-private partnerships are complicated and multifaceted, and many state and municipal leaders do not have the experience needed to assess whether a P3 would be appropriate for their assets, even as awareness about the issue grows. A former governor put this in very practical terms. If a governor has the choice between raising debt and adding investment to the regular budget for an infrastructure project or else spending four years or more developing a P3 that requires a lot of explaining, the choice is an easy one. According to the Brookings-Rockefeller Project on State and Municipal Innovation, many local governments hesitate to implement innovative financing solutions for infrastructure because they lack the necessary expertise.[94] In comparing the outcomes for Indiana, Chicago, and New York, all of which negotiated quite different contracts with private entities, it is clear that from the perspective of municipal governance, when it comes to public-private partnerships or outright privatization, the devil is in the details.[95]

One of the best ways to guarantee successful P3 contracts is to enact enabling laws that will standardize some of the terms for both public and private partnerships, as India and other countries have done. One of the factors that led to the failure of the Pennsylvania Turnpike privatization was the lack of state laws governing how P3s ought to be structured. Because Pennsylvania did not have such laws, confusion and uncertainty proliferated. Lawmakers and administrators often do not have the information they need to determine if privatization would be a viable option for their state or city. A study published in the *Journal of Law and Economics* found that one of the best predictors of a successful public-private partnership is whether the state has established such enabling laws for negotiating contracts.[96] Today, thirty-six states have enabling laws on the books, and those states, at least anecdotally, have an easier time attracting private investment and convincing public officials that P3s will benefit their constituents.[97] Indiana, for instance, enacted such laws in 2006, just before the privatization of its toll road. In every chapter of this book we have encountered uncertain investors and politicians who might have been more easily swayed had a tested framework been approved by the government.

Our review of the P3 experience points out the need for a strong regulator, a theme that has cut across this book. There is a unanimous view that this is a condition sine qua non for a successful public-private partnership. A weak regulator or corrupt regulator could make outcomes worse than if an infrastructure project were executed solely by a state entity. The key to securing strong regulation lies in the contract writing process. Eric Maskin and Jean Tirole provide important research on applying contract theory to P3s.[98] One of the crucial aspects is their analysis of the way governments enter into P3s as a way to evade budgetary rules and/or provide particular incentives to private operators—that is, corrupt behavior on the part of the government or the concessionaire.[99] Even with a solid contract and good-faith government participation, things can go wrong. A concrete example of failed regulation is discussed in a novel analysis by Gianluca Delfino, who examined government influence in the crash of the cable car in Cavalese, Italy, in which twenty people died.[100] It turned out that gross negligence on the part of the private company operating the cable car was responsible for the accident. The negligence occurred during the pandemic period, when all cable car activities were canceled across Italy, which caused a complete loss of revenue. After lobbying by operators, the tourism board, and others, the government agreed to defer maintenance costs and then reopen the cable cars. While the terms of the contract were unambiguous regarding supervisory work conducted by the local authorities and the requirement to maintain the facility in good order, the green light to defer maintenance costs meant that the fatal accident was only a matter of time.

The issue of accountability is not limited to P3s but extends more broadly to government contracting as well, including the DBB model that we discussed earlier between the government and a private contractor.[101] Another example (regrettably in Italy again) is the collapse of the Morandi Bridge, which garnered international attention when forty-three people died. Because of the importance of P3s in Italy as a means to fund infrastructure, researchers went straight to work to understand what had failed in the P3 structure itself and what lessons could be learned. The analysis of the Morandi Bridge collapse (irrespective of who was at fault) is a case study in how politicians have used P3s to either take credit for or distance themselves quickly from these mechanisms. In many respects, politicians were quick to accuse the P3 structure itself of failure rather than accuse the operator or reflect on their own failure to monitor appropriately.[102]

An analysis was recently conducted of the international experience of P3s from a supervisory perspective. The analysis confirms that the success of P3s relies in large part on the ability to institute a strong supervisory role over the P3. Chile is often mentioned as an example of strong regulatory oversight in sectors such as water and the electric transmission and distribution business. While at Morgan Stanley, I invested in an electric transmission and distribution business, SAESA. The regulatory framework was elaborate and complex but clearly implementable. The same could be said for the water sector, but not for the toll roads. It took some time for the Ministry of Transportation in Chile to fully appreciate the design of P3 contracts. At the time, the objective was to identify construction companies that could build the highways and institute toll systems. The P3s bundled the construction and management of the concession into one, but the companies bidding were essentially construction companies seeking to win contracts more than to manage the roads for the long run. That inherent conflict caused the P3 concessionaire to focus solely on civil works and how to extract maximum value, including through renegotiation. Not to be outdone, Chilean policymakers (historically educated at the University of Chicago's famed department of economics) caught on, and Chile modified its P3 laws in 2010, which allowed for greater transparency through an independent supervisory board that would evaluate the merits of renegotiating P3s. Another example of weak regulatory oversight has been in Mexico, where despite ten years of P3s, the government failed to devote sufficient resources to the monitoring of P3 concessions.[103] In these scenarios, enabling legislation and strong regulation are the key to success.

The first step for the United States is to establish enabling legislation that governs P3s in each state. That is definitely necessary, but it is certainly not sufficient, as a number of studies indicate.[104] My proposed solution is to clearly separate management from regulation, whether management of infrastructure assets is conducted by the state or the private sector. An independent and strong regulator like NHAI for the Indian toll roads or Ofwat for the UK water sector is necessary and very much feasible. Figure 3.1 shows an integrated regulatory system responsible for UK water. Each sector and each state would require its own independent regulator or public commission for roads, water, airports and so forth. This means that in addition to the contractual arrangement, one would need an overarching regulatory framework that would dictate the specific broad terms of the P3s, or if the market is deep enough, move to a whole-regulatory system that encompasses the general terms of the P3, making it more akin to the PUC that regulates the electric generation and distribution companies for every state. For example, one could create a thirty-year concession framework for water companies and manage them under a unified regulatory regime (basically a mega-P3 for the whole sector).[105] Performance would be measured across the board as in the Chilean water system; outperformers would be compensated, and underperformers would be penalized with lower allowed returns. The public water commission for the state would develop standards for P3s that meet the state's own requirements and objectives. The commission would help not only in designing the P3 framework, but also in designing the bidding process, the cost recovery mechanism, and the nature of the P3 contract, accounting for the shortcomings discussed earlier.[106]

The nature of P3s makes formulating the right type of incentives complex. At the federal level, the country would need to invest in research similar to what the World Bank has undertaken over the last few decades. What the IFC has done for infrastructure P3 programs across the world, America should do across all fifty US states.[107] Much work has been done on VfM methodology, which is critical to the decision-making process. The disappointing aspect of the debate in the United States is how little knowledge there is of the work that has been done over the last decade to refine and improve the P3 technology.[108] This type of applied research is absent from the current discourse in the United States but very much alive in the European Union in the aftermath of COVID and the realization of the urgent need to develop sustainable technology in the delivery of basic infrastructure services.[109]

The United States is simply too far behind other economies, not just in terms of investments, but also in research and development relating to the best way to develop and fund its infrastructure, and this must be rectified. The federal government could take on the role of trusted adviser to state entities in the development of P3 standards, across multiple sectors. The United States has the human capital to design P3s that include all the elements discussed here, as well as to development of VMT and congestion charges. The country needs to attract American technology companies that are in the vanguard of new innovations that integrate technology within infrastructure, whether to optimize traffic lights and congestion in an urban setting or logistics technologies that manage entire fleets of trucks or intermodal equipment that provides the backbone of the supply chain system. Right now, all that work rests on the shoulders of individual departments in every state, which simply do not have the resources, budgets, or incentives to undertake all that is required of them, however dedicated they are.[110] Rosabeth Moss Kanter, in *Move: How to Rebuild and Reinvent America's Infrastructure*, suggests creating an office in the US Treasury Department to provide the necessary technical assistance when states or cities look to develop such structures.[111] Whether this capacity building should reside at the Treasury level, with the DoT when it comes to transport infrastructure, or in a Federal Infrastructure Bank can be debated. For example, in 2023 the National Infrastructure Advisory Council issued a report, *Preparing United States Critical Infrastructure for Today's Evolving Water Crises*, which addresses the need for federal coordination.[112] One of its key recommendations is the need for a national water strategy and the possible creation of a Federal Department of Water. Interestingly, the report suggests looking at how China runs its water infrastructure, with one possibility being to create, in addition to the various state entities, a Federal Infrastructure Bank.

Alternative Funding Mechanisms

In 2021 I published an article entitled "The US Needs an Infrastructure Bank That Models the World Bank,"[113] arguing that the United States needs to learn to develop P3s and evaluate them. To ensure the message was clear, I stated: "The analogy is disturbingly apt—our infrastructure sector is in need of long-term development help, similar to Europe when it needed a Marshall Plan in the aftermath of WWII." Just as the World Bank has provided a general guide to P3s, a centralized US infrastructure bank could offer more specific guidance for particular states and municipalities in a more detailed and case-by-case manner. The World Bank has a world-renowned applied research department that feeds into its lending programs. The concept of a National Infrastructure Bank has been discussed for many years.[114] Without going too far back in history, one can argue that in our postwar era, the largest infrastructure bank created was the World Bank. As we indicated earlier, the World Bank was principally created to support the European countries that were devastated during World War II and help rebuild their infrastructure. Since then, a series of institutions have been created at both national and multilateral levels, the most recent of which, and by far the largest, is the Asia Infrastructure Investment Bank, created by China and headquartered in Beijing. The story of the AIIB is worth summarizing here.[115] It is a multilateral investment bank with 103 members. Its aim is to provide financing for sustainable infrastructure development. Between its launch in 2014 and the end of 2019, the AIIB approved funding for sixty-three global infrastructure projects totaling $12.04 billion. It has committed $8.37 billion and has disbursed $2.89 billion.[116] Interestingly, the AIIB has adopted some of the most stringent environmental and, more broadly, environmental, social, and governmental (ESG) criteria. An early assessment of the AIIB suggests that, with over $25 billion in investments and over one hundred projects, it is taking a cautious and conservative approach to investment, and that there is much less overlap with BRI projects than expected.

The US response to the creation of the AIIB was to combat China's global infrastructure expansion, but with no defined objective. When, in 2015, the United States chose not to participate in the AIIB and failed to persuade its European allies to withdraw as well, former treasury secretary Lawrence Summers wrote in the *Washington Post*: "This past month may be remembered as the moment the United States lost its role as the underwriter of the global economic system. . . . I can think of no evidence since Bretton

Woods comparable to the combination of China's effort to establish a major new institution and the failure of the United States to persuade dozens of its traditional allies, starting with Britain, to stay out."[117] Officially, the United States stated:

> The United States and many major global economies all agree there is a pressing need to enhance infrastructure investment around the world. We believe any new multilateral institution should incorporate the high standards of the World Bank and the regional development banks. Based on many discussions, we have concerns about whether the AIIB will meet these high standards, particularly related to governance, and environmental and social safeguards. . . . The international community has a stake in seeing the AIIB complement the existing architecture, and to work effectively alongside the World Bank and Asian Development Bank.[118]

The United States at one time had its own version of an infrastructure bank, the Public Works Administration (PWA), but that was more a funding vehicle created by the Roosevelt administration to fight the Great Depression. A comprehensive report on the subject was published in 2019 by the Global Infrastructure Hub, which was created by the G-20 group to ensure that available information on infrastructure investment opportunities,[119] as well as alternative funding mechanism, are available for governments (including the United States).[120] The key parameters for an infrastructure bank are purpose, ownership, governance, and capital treatment. An infrastructure bank can have a variety of purposes. Some were created to invest in long-term infrastructure projects where capital markets were nonexistent; some were created to complement private finance infrastructure by filling a gap that could exist in capital markets. Some have had the specific purpose of supporting municipal projects in disadvantaged areas. And some have looked to accomplish all of that or some combination thereof. Traditionally, infrastructure banks have been owned by the state as a specialized development bank to support the development of infrastructure. Others have been indirectly owned by the state with an implicit guarantee, and some have later been privatized by the government. Most of these banks have had their capital treated as part of the government's balance sheet, but not always. The PWA, created in 1933 as part of the New Deal, fit in the category of development bank owned by the state, but it was not a bank in the strict sense because it issued grants. The PWA ended up investing $6 billion and invested in infrastructure projects by subcontracting to the private sector, which would build the bridge or canal or dam using the DBB model. It was terminated at the start of World War II, but the IIJA could be seen as a modern version of the PWA.

The idea of a proper US infrastructure bank has been revived many times. In more recent periods, lawmakers have introduced several legislative proposals, starting with the Obama administration.[121] Obama proposed a bank that would take the form of a state-owned entity, with a board appointed by the president and Congress, that would be active in lending to projects whether public or private. It was not clear whether it could invest in equity or offer subordinated loans to support projects. In 2021 the IIJA included provisions for an Infrastructure Finance Authority (IFA), which had been proposed earlier by Senator Mark Warner (D-VA) and others through the Reinventing Economic Partnerships and Infrastructure Redevelopment (REPAIR) Act,[122] but this program was removed at the eleventh hour for no clear reason (I know from personal experience). The purpose of the legislation was to create an independent federal institution that would be under the direct supervision of Congress to extend small loans to projects with a focus on infrastructure projects in rural areas.

A private bank, rather than one owned and directly managed or supervised by the government, would ensure the ability of the United States to continue to invest in infrastructure well after the IIJA has accomplished its mission. There are two fundamental objectives. The first is to provide capital for long duration projects that would be difficult to fund without the state providing a guaranty, either directly or indirectly through the issuance of general obligation bonds or revenue bonds that are linked to the municipality's creditworthiness. The bank should focus on nonrecourse financing without an implicit or explicit guarantee by any state entity. In addition, the bank should focus on investing equity either directly or through subordinated loans or provide guarantees to P3 projects on risks that the state should not keep and the private sector could not underwrite. Figure 9.2 presents the two opposing views of what an infrastructure bank should look like.

IRA Funding Mechanism

One proposal to raise funds for infrastructure projects is the use of dedicated IRAs.[123] As I argued on Infrastructure Investor:

> Congress should modify section 408 of the internal revenue code to allow for a new type of individual retirement account that invests solely

Comparison of House Infrastructure Bills Private Bank vs. Government Owned Entities

Infrastructure Bank for America Act of 2020 H.R. 7231 (IBA)	Government Owned Infrastructure Bank Proposals House Bills H.R. 658, 4780, 6422
Structure - IBA is a private Delaware Bank Holding Company with a wholly owned Bank subsidiary established as a GSE. Sec. 2	**Structure** - All three established as Government owned and controlled corporations under US Code commonly known as the "Government Corporation Control Act" or similar statute.
Funding & Guarantees - IBA is privately owned, managed and funded, like the FHLB and Farm Credit System. IBA will receive no funds or guarantees from the US Government. Sec. 10	**Funding & Guarantees** - All three are Government funded, all or in most part. Their securities will carry a full US Government guarantee as wholly owned US Corporations.
Management & Governance - The IBA will have 7 Directors all elected by the shareholders. Management is appointed by the Board. Sec. 2	**Management & Governance** - All Directors will be appointed by the President with the consent of the Senate, with nominations from Congress, Labor and others.
Oversight & Reporting - The IBA Holding Company and Bank shall be regulated and supervised by the Federal Reserve, Treasury and the SEC, all of which have Congressional oversight. Sec.6	**Oversight & Reporting** - All are regulated by and report to the President and to Congress and must at all times operate in a manner consistent with the legislation which creates them.

Figure 9.2. Two opposing visions for an infrastructure bank. *Source:* "Comparison of House Infrastructure Bills: Private Bank vs. Government Owned Entity," Federal Infrastructure Bank, accessed April 15, 2023, https://federalinfrastructurebank.com/wp-content/uploads/Bill-Comparison-Summary-Private-vs.-Government-Owned-Proposals-07-15-20-v2.pdf.

in infrastructure development. Taxpayers would be able to make tax-deductible contributions of up to $5,000 each year, even after making the maximum allowable contributions to a 401(k) plan or a traditional or Roth IRA. The only available investment for this IRA would be for US infrastructure. The IRA investment could be locked in for at least 10 years. During that period, participants would not change investments or take withdrawals from the IRA. However, as with a traditional IRA, investment earnings would be tax-deferred. Today, there are over 30 million IRA accounts, with over $7 trillion in assets. If a third of IRA account holders opened the new IRA account, we could raise $50 billion annually, contributed by Americans happy to earn a steady return and proud to invest their retirement capital to improve our roads and airports.[124]

This could create greater household awareness of the importance of infrastructure and the pricing of basic infrastructure services, and possibly greater accountability.

Conclusion

I have attempted in this chapter to provide an overview of the issues surrounding privatization of infrastructure. America's inability to find innovative solutions to the problems facing infrastructure (the IIJA notwithstanding) is symptomatic of the deterioration of political discourse in the United States in the last few decades and the desire to maintain control of infrastructure assets. But the solutions are clear, are implementable, and have the support of the population. Whoever can deliver the best services should do the job within the rules of the monopolistic market that characterizes public services. Privatization through outright sale and P3s with proper regulatory oversight are useful tools that the United States has not availed itself of; as a result it has fallen far behind other countries in terms of serving its citizens, improving productivity, and competing efficiently with the rest of the world. As Governor Rendell asked: "How is it that we've come to this state of affairs in our infrastructure? Why have we let this happen?" I hope this book provides answers to these questions and indicates some of the solutions we should look to implement over the coming decade.

ACKNOWLEDGMENTS

The ideas discussed in this book began to take shape when I first started working on infrastructure projects some thirty years ago. Growing up in the 1970s and 1980s, I remember the global inflation crisis, when the US ten-year treasury bond reached 15 percent under Chairman of the Federal Reserve Paul Volcker, and the 1982 debt crisis, during which "third world" countries faced structural adjustment programs that required the privatization of their national companies, including infrastructure assets. The UK privatization wave of the 1980s was a shock to any economics student, and combined with the beginning of the Chinese miracle, which I encountered on my first visit to China in the winter of 1987, the period marked the start of significant global economic transformation. When I undertook a PhD in economics, focused on measuring causal relations in observational studies, I wanted to understand the arc that linked my academic interest with these larger policy issues; later, these connections would become central to my professional work on financing infrastructure projects. My desire to connect international finance with policy issues never left me; this book is in some sense the fruit of that reflection.

Over the years, I have had the pleasure of discussing policy issues related to US infrastructure with a wide range of people who have helped me formulate many of the ideas discussed in this book; to them I am grateful for all these conversations. In researching this book, many kindly agreed to be interviewed and quoted, and others provided insights while preferring to remain anonymous given their current positions in government. Former governor Jeb Bush of Florida, Jonson Cox, David Gadis, Emilio Gonzalez, Dana Levenson, Harikishan Reddy, former governor Ed Rendell of Pennsylvania, Kent Rowey, Macky Tall, and Derek Utter provided their time and shared their views on infrastructure policy in the United States. To them I am truly grateful.

Jamil Baz read the manuscript and, as always, provided precise comments and suggestions. I would like to recognize the support of the New York University Development Research Institute (DRI), which provided access to NYU's extensive resources. Rajeev Dehejia, director of the institute, read the full manuscript and provided suggestions as well as corrections. I am also grateful to the Wilson Center in Washington, DC, for help and support; in particular, I thank Ambassador Mark Green, president and CEO, and Mark Kennedy, director of the Wahba Institute for Strategic Competition (WISC), for their input and suggestions.

My thanks also go to my colleagues at I Squared Capital, who have provided invaluable support over the last decade. I would like to thank Harsh Agarwal, Gautam Bhandari, and Mohamed El-Gazzar for our long conversations over many years on infrastructure investments across sectors and regions covering the world.

Hilary Claggett, my editor at Georgetown University Press, played an invaluable role, first by enthusiastically accepting the book for publication and then by offering helpful advice and support in completing the writing. Four anonymous reviewers commented on an early version as well as the final version of the manuscript and provided useful suggestions and identified errors and omissions, which much improved the book.

David Baum, Frank Sommerfield, and MJ Romano helped to organize and transcribe the interviews I conducted, carry out research, and review the manuscript as well as help in the design of the cover. Jeremy Butman, who was the development editor, played a crucial role and always displayed a most positive attitude over long conversations.

Last but not least, I would like to thank my family for their patience and support. Both my children made contributions to the book: my daughter, Victoria, appears in the preface, and my son, Charles, had the idea to integrate relevant quotations from movies into the book. To him goes the credit for the quotations included in every chapter; my only condition was that we had to have seen the movie together, which meant many long nights watching several movies to understand the context. Josephine Wahba (aka my mother) dutifully read the manuscript and pointed out many inconsistencies. This book would not have happened without the constant support of my wife and partner in life, Suzy. She read the manuscript many times, provided edits, and corrected mistakes, improving the flow of the book substantially, and was always patient as I spent my weekends writing. To her I am always deeply grateful.

The usual caveat applies: all remaining mistakes are regrettably mine alone, and the views and opinions expressed in this book do not necessarily reflect those of I Squared Capital, the DRI at NYU, the Wilson Center, the President's National Infrastructure Advisory Council, or anyone quoted in the book.

NOTES

Chapter One

1. Fu et al., *Reform of China's Urban Water Sector*, 207–15.
2. Fu et al.
3. Meng, *Politics of Chinese Media*, 19.
4. Nallathiga and Shah, "Public Private Partnerships in India."
5. "National Highways to Be Expanded by 25,000 km in 2022–3: FM," *Times of India*, February 1, 2022, https://timesofindia.indiatimes.com/business/india-business/national-highways-to-be-expanded-by-25000-km-in-2022-23-fm/articleshow/89269754.cms.
6. Tim Starks and David DiMolfetta, "Court Temporarily Dunks Water Cybersecurity Initiative," *Washington Post*, July 13, 2023, https://www.washingtonpost.com/politics/2023/07/13/court-temporarily-dunks-water-cybersecurity-rule/.
7. Blinken, "Foreign Policy for the American People."
8. Wahba, "Integrating Infrastructure in U.S. Policy."
9. See Freymann, *One Belt One Road*; and Economy, *Third Revolution*.
10. See Sparrow, *Warfare State*.
11. Rendell, *Nation of Wusses*, 180.
12. Arrow and Kurz, *Public Investment*; Barro, "Government Spending in a Simple Model," 103–25; and Barro and Salai-Martin, *Economic Growth*.
13. Gaspar et al., "Public Investment for the Recovery."
14. Aschauer, "Is Public Expenditure Productive," 177–200; and Munnell, "Policy Watch," 189–98. See also Munnell, "Why Has Productivity Growth Declined?," 3–22.
15. Ramey, "Macroeconomic Consequences of Infrastructure Investment," 219–68.
16. Bivens, "Potential Macroeconomic Benefits."
17. Calderón and Servén, "Infrastructure, Growth and Inequality"; and Timilsina, Hochman, and Song, "Infrastructure, Economic Growth, and Poverty."
18. Hooper, Peters, and Pintus, "Can Long-Term Investment Reduce Inequality." Comparing debt securities and loans issued by states as a percentage of state

281

and local government receipts, that ratio went from 112 percent in 1947 to over 145 percent in 2021. When compared to total GDP, that percentage jumps from 6.5 to 13.6 percent for the same period.

19. Timilisina et al., "Infrastructure, Economic Growth, and Poverty."

20. Campbell, *Pivot*, 53.

21. "More public infrastructure may yield diminishing returns if pushed too far. The returns may even become negative if infrastructure investment crowds out private sector activity. This 'crowding out effect' may take a variety of forms. First, preferential lending for government-supported infrastructure projects can lead to inefficiency in resource use when projects are not subject to market discipline. Second, development of infrastructure can drive up the cost of inputs and cause dislocations. . . . Third, for road infrastructure, beautiful roads with no traffic or accompanying private sector development do not yield productive outcomes. Moreover, for road infrastructure, building one road may be productive, but building more may largely divert existing traffic . . . [and] fourth, lagging regions may lack the absorptive capacity to take advantage of large amounts of infrastructure investment." Shi, Guo, and Sun, "Infrastructure in China's Regional Growth," 38. See also an interesting case study by Banerjee, Duflo, and Qian, "On the Road."

22. Badlam et al., "CHIPS and Science Act."

23. Badlam et al., "Inflation Reduction Act."

24. "2021 Report Card for America's Infrastructure." Brookings finds a similar number; see Tomer, Kane, and Puentes, "$1 Trillion Infrastructure Program?"

25. "2021 Report Card for America's Infrastructure."

26. "Trucking Industry Congestion."

27. "Bipartisan Infrastructure and Job Act."

28. Zhang et al., "Causes and Statistical Characteristics of Bridge Failures," 388–406.

29. "InfoBridge."

30. Black, "2022 Bridge Report."

31. "2021 Report Card for America's Infrastructure."

32. "World Development Indicators."

33. Shelby Simon, "How Many People Die from Car Accidents Each Year?," *Forbes*, October 10, 2022, https://www.forbes.com/advisor/legal/auto-accident/car-accident-deaths/#:~:text=In%20the%20United%20States%2C%20the,Fatality%20Analysis%20Reporting%20System's%20history.

34. "World Development Indicators."

35. AQUASTAT.

36. Thatcher, "Speech to Conservative Women's Conference."

37. The first, in 2021, surveyed one thousand US consumers over the age of eighteen. The survey sample was stratified to match census representation for region, age, gender, and ethnicity. The survey was fielded using the Qualtrics Insight Platform, and the panel was sourced from Lucid. Fielding was executed from

July 6, 2021 to July 9, 2021. The second iteration, in 2022, surveyed one thousand US consumers age eighteen years or older. The survey sample was stratified to match census representation for region, age, gender, and ethnicity. The survey was fielded using the Qualtrics Insight Platform and the panel was sourced from Lucid. Fielding was executed from August 22, 2022 to August 25, 2022. Wahba, "Americans and Infrastructure (2021)"; and Wahba, "Americans and Infrastructure (2022)."

38. For a review of the various actors involved in infrastructure assets, see Goldsmith, "Actors and Innovations in the Evolution of Infrastructure Services."

39. *Public Private Partnerships.*

40. "Value for Money Analysis."

41. Robert W. Poole Jr., makes a case for privatizing American roadways in *Rethinking America's Highways.*

42. Roth, *Street Smart*, 327.

43. "About Us."

44. *Chiffres Cles.*

45. Caon, "What Role Can Private Investors Play."

46. Caon.

47. Fair, "U.S. Infrastructure."

48. "China—Country Commercial Guide."

49. AQUASTAT.

50. While the construction of new dams has been highly controversial, 97 percent of the eighty thousand dams in the United States do not generate power. See Johnson, "Damned If You Don't."

51. "Share of Renewables in Electricity Production."

52. "Share of Renewables in Electricity Production."

53. Jeb Bush, interview with the author, March 23, 2023. All quotes from Bush are from this interview.

54. Gravely, *Reframing America's Infrastructure*, 474.

55. Estrin and Pelletier, "Privatization in Developing Countries," 65–102.

56. David Gadis, interview with the author, March 1, 2023. All quotes from Gadis are from this interview.

57. Macky Tall, interview with the author, February 22, 2023. All quotes from Tall are from this interview.

58. Thatcher, *Downing Street Years*, 676.

59. Thatcher, *Margaret Thatcher*, 619.

60. "Jonson Cox, Chairman of the Water Industry Regulator."

61. Jonson Cox, interview with the author, November 23, 2022. All quotes from Cox are from this interview.

62. A selection of examples: "The Guardian View on Privatisation: The God That Failed," *Guardian*, June 22, 2022, https://www.theguardian.com /commentisfree/2022/jun/22/the-guardian-view-on-privatisation-the-god-that

-failed; Matthew Lawrence, "The Wretched State of Thames Water Is One of the Best Arguments for Public Ownership We Have," *Guardian*, June 28, 2023, https://www.theguardian.com/commentisfree/2023/jun/28/thames-water-public-ownership-water-privatisation-england-and-wales-executives-shareholders; and Obsidian Adebayo, "Has Privatisation Failed the UK?," *Rolling Stone UK*, accessed July 31, 2023, https://www.rollingstone.co.uk/politics/features/has-privatisation-failed-uk-politics-thatcher-rollingstone-13151/.

63. "It's Time for Real Change."

64. Reagan, "Statement on the President's Commission on Privatization."

65. "Green New Deal."

66. See Wahba, "Estimation of Causal Effects in Observational Studies."

67. See Angrist and Pischke, *Mostly Harmless Econometrics*; Imbens and Rubin, *Causal Inference for Statistics and Biomedical Sciences*; and Angrist, "Empirical Strategies in Economics," 2509–39. This same econometric framework has been used to evaluate the effectiveness of privatization.

68. Stiglitz, *Economic Role of the State*, 57.

69. Keynes, *Collected Writings*, 19:695.

70. Coase, "Lighthouse in Economics," 357–76.

71. Mill, *Principles of Political Economy*, 364.

72. See Wahba, "Future of U.S. Infrastructure," 92–98.

Chapter Two

1. "FY 2022 Company Profile."

2. *Hearing Before the . . . Subcommittee on Railroads, Pipelines, and Hazardous Materials*, testimony of William Flynn.

3. Vranich, *Derailed*.

4. "Federal Grants to Amtrak."

5. "USDOT, Biden Administration Deliver $4.3 Billion in Funding."

6. Lin, Saat, and Barkan, "Quantitative Causal Analysis of Passenger Train Accidents," 4.

7. Burrows, Burd, and McKenzie, *Commuting by Public Transportation in the United States*.

8. O'Toole, "Amtrak's Big Lie."

9. "Majority of Americans Want More Investment in Passenger Rail."

10. Villa, "92% of Americans Support High Speed Rail."

11. See Gravely, *Reframing America's Infrastructure*, ch. 2.

12. "Documentary History of American Waterworks: Boston."

13. "Documentary History of American Waterworks: Providence."

14. "Documentary History of American Waterworks: Providence."

15. Wood, *Turnpikes of New England*, 3.

16. Wood, 5.

17. Kirby, "Nineteenth-Century Patterns of Railroad Development," 157–70.

18. Turnbull, *John Stevens*, 383.

19. "Beginnings of American Railroads and Mapping."

20. Turnbull, "John Stevens," 454.

21. Turnbull, 454.

22. Williams, *Great and Shining Road*, 28.

23. Rohatyn, *Bold Endeavors*, 57.

24. Rohatyn, 57.

25. Williams, *Great and Shining Road*, 29.

26. Williams, 58.

27. Williams, 242.

28. Duran, "First US Transcontinental Railroad," 181.

29. De Luca, "Infrastructure Financing in Medieval Europe."

30. De Luca, 183.

31. Goldsmith, "Actors and Innovations in the Evolution of Infrastructure Services," 84.

32. Goldsmith, 44–45.

33. Leonhardt, *Account of the Grisons*, 37.

34. Lorenzini, "Infrastructure Financing in the Early Modern Age."

35. Lorenzini.

36. Goldsmith, "Actors and Innovation in the Evolution of Infrastructure Services," 43.

37. Baskin and Miranti, *History of Corporate Finance*, 90.

38. Dale, *First Crash*, 98.

39. Jon Moen, "John Law and the Mississippi Bubble," *Mississippi History Now*, October 2001, https://www.mshistorynow.mdah.ms.gov/issue/john-law-and-the-mississippi-bubble-1718-1720.

40. Baskin and Miranti, *History of Corporate Finance*, 102.

41. Reghizzi, "Finance of Local Public Goods at the Onset of the Industrial Revolution."

42. Lorenzini, "Infrastructure Financing in the Early Modern Age."

43. Pinkney, *Napoleon III and the Rebuilding of Paris*, 177.

44. Pinkney, 177.

45. Goldsmith, "Actors and Innovations in the Evolution of Infrastructure Services."

46. "History of Chester."

47. "Quick Facts: Chester, Pennsylvania."

48. Anderson, "New Minimal Cities," 1118–1227.

49. "Chester City Act 47 Exit Plan."

50. "Chester City Act 47 Exit Plan."

51. "County of Chester, 2022 Approved Budget."

52. Lorenzini, "Infrastructure Financing in the Early Modern Age," 30.

53. Lorenzini, 31.

54. "Beaver Creek Dam Rehabilitation Project."

55. "New Deal Worked." See also Fishback, "How Successful Was the New Deal?," 1435–85.

56. Keynes, *General Theory of Employment, Interest, and Money*, 128.

57. Stiglitz, *Economic Role of the State*, 13.

58. Jenkins, *Bonds of Inequality*, 8.

59. Sbragia, *Debt Wish*, 159.

60. Jenkins, *Bonds of Inequality*, 8.

61. "Federal Reserve Economic Data."

62. *Report on the Municipal Securities Market*; and "State of State (and Local) Tax Policy."

63. "Economic Research."

64. Joffe, "Doubly Bound."

65. "Public Spending on Transportation and Water Infrastructure, 1956 to 2017."

66. "State and Local Backgrounders."

67. "Public Spending on Transportation and Water Infrastructure, 1956 to 2017."

68. Kent Rowey, interview with the author, December 22, 2022. All quotes from Rowey are from this interview.

69. Jenkins, *Bonds of Inequality*, 128.

70. Jenkins, 18.

71. Deye, "US Infrastructure PPPs."

72. See Bakke, *Grid*.

73. "Electricity 101."

74. For a comprehensive description of this early period see Hirsh, *Power Loss*.

75. "Changing Structure of the Electric Power Industry," 111.

76. "Electricity Prices by Year and Adjusted for Inflation."

77. Poole, *Rethinking America's Highways*.

Chapter Three

1. Julia Lurie, "Meet the Mom Who Helped Expose Flint's Toxic Water Nightmare," *Mother Jones*, January 21, 2016, https://www.motherjones.com/politics/2016/01/mother-exposed-flint-lead-contamination-water-crisis/.

2. Michael Wines, Patrick McGeehan, and John Schwartz, "Digging Further into a Water Problem," *New York Times*, March 26, 2016, https://www.nytimes.com/2016/03/27/us/digging-further-into-a-water-problem.html.

3. The French multinational Veolia is among the largest investors in infrastructure in forty-eight countries worldwide, operating in water management, wastewater management, and energy services.

4. Stanley, "Emergency Manager," 38–40.

5. "Sanitation and Drinking Water."

6. "Waterborne Disease in the United States."

7. Allaire, Wu, and Lall, "National Trends in Drinking Water Quality Violations."

8. See Clark, *Poisoned City*; and Evan Osnos, "The Crisis in Flint Goes Deeper Than the Water," *New Yorker*, January 20, 2016, https://www.newyorker.com/news/news-desk/the-crisis-in-flint-goes-deeper-than-the-water.

9. *Preparing United States Critical Infrastructure*.

10. Jessica Glenza, "Pittsburgh Officials May Have Deflected Attention from Lead-Contaminated Water," *Guardian*, July 25, 2017, https://www.theguardian.com/us-news/2017/jul/25/pittsburgh-lead-drinking-water-flint-epa.

11. Josiah Bates, "Newark Officials Providing Bottled Water to 15,000 Homes over Lead Contamination Concerns: Here's What You Need to Know about the City's Water Crisis," *Time*, August 27, 2019, https://time.com/5653115/newark-water-crisis/.

12. Geoff Pender, "Another Lawsuit over Jackson Water Crisis," *Mississippi Today*, September 19, 2022, https://mississippitoday.org/2022/09/19/another-lawsuit-filed-over-jackson-water-crisis/.

13. "Biden-Harris Lead Pipe and Paint Action Plan."

14. *Preparing United States Critical Infrastructure*, 7.

15. McGillis, "Jackson Water Crisis and the Urgency of Climate Adaptation."

16. Glen MacDonald, "Beyond the Perfect Drought: California's Real Water Crisis," *Yale Environment 360*, June 15, 2015, https://e360.yale.edu/features/beyond_the_perfect_drought_californias_real_water_crisis.

17. "World of Change."

18. Gabrielle Canon, "NASA Images Show Extreme Withering of Lake Mead over 22 Years," *Guardian*, July 21, 2022, https://www.theguardian.com/environment/2022/jul/21/nasa-images-lake-mead-drought.

19. See Green, *Moving Water*.

20. Maggie Wade, "Lumumba: It Would 'Literally' Cost a Billion Dollars to Replace Jackson's Entire Water System," *WLBT 3*, February 19, 2021, https://www.wlbt.com/2021/02/19/lumumba-it-would-literally-cost-billion-dollars-replace-jacksons-entire-water-system/.

21. "Building a Better America."

22. "US EPA: Fiscal Year 2022."

23. "About DWSD."

24. "Documentary History of American Waterworks: Detroit."

25. Rossi, "Regionalizing the Detroit Water and Sewerage Department."

26. Lurie, "Meet the Mom."

27. Stanley, "Emergency Manager," 16–18.

28. Scorsone and Bateson, *Long-Term Crisis and Systemic Failure*.

29. "Quick Facts: Flint City, Michigan."

30. Stanley, "Emergency Manager," 16.

31. Pauli, *Flint Fights Back*, 72–76.

32. Pauli, 87.

33. "State and Local Backgrounders."

34. Pauli, *Flint Fights Back*, 1.

35. Fisher, "Infrastructure Investment and Financing for the 2019 Incoming Gubernatorial Administration."

36. Fair, "U.S. Infrastructure."

37. The argument that municipal leaders are wary of public-private partnerships and other innovative solutions to production difficulties because of ideological commitments and, occasionally, corrupt motives, is outlined well in Lerusse and Van de Walle, "Local Politicians' Preferences in Public Procurement," 1–24.

38. Mark Kennedy, interview with the author, March 3, 2023. All quotes from Kennedy are from this interview.

39. Pauli, *Flint Fights Back*, 43–45.

40. Larusse and Van der Walle, "Local Politicians Preferences in Public Procurement," 3.

41. Pauli, *Flint Fights Back*, 168.

42. Jordan Chariton and Jenn Dize, "The Flint Cover Up," Intercept, July 21, 2021, https://theintercept.com/2021/07/21/flint-water-crisis-rick-snyder/.

43. Monica Davey and Mitch Smith, "Emails Reveal Early Suspicion of Flint Link to Legionnaires Disease," *New York Times*, February 4, 2016, https://www.nytimes.com/2016/02/05/us/emails-reveal-early-suspicions-of-a-flint-link-to-legionnaires-disease.html.

44. Pauli, *Flint Fights Back*, 6.

45. Pauli, 55.

46. "Flint Water Crisis Fast Facts," CNN, January 14, 2021, https://www.cnn.com/2016/03/04/us/flint-water-crisis-fast-facts/.

47. Ron Fonger, "Superiors Pushed Flint's Switch to River Water Despite Problems at Plant, Witness Says," MLive, April 25, 2022, https://www.mlive.com/news/flint/2022/04/superiors-pushed-flints-switch-to-river-water-despite-problems-at-plant-witness-says.html.

48. Rossi, "Regionalizing the Detroit Water and Sewerage Department."

49. John Wisely and Joe Guillen, "Great Lakes Water Authority Okays Lease of Detroit System," *Detroit Free Press*, June 12, 2015, https://www.freep.com/story/news/local/michigan/detroit/2015/06/12/regional-water-vote/71088638/.

50. "Indianapolis Water Company."

51. "Truth about Private Water in Indianapolis, IN."

52. Mike Hudson, "Misconduct Taints the Water of Some Privatized Systems," *Los Angeles Times*, May 29, 2006, https://www.latimes.com/archives/la-xpm-2006-may-29-me-privatewater29-story.html.

53. Rebecca Thiele, "Lake Station Joins other Cities in Privatizing Drinking Water," PBS, October 23, 2019, https://www.wfyi.org/news/articles/lake-station-joins-other-cities-in-privatizing-drinking-water.

54. *Trends in Water Privatization.*

55. Al Sullivan, "Decade Old Water Deal Still Making Waves," *Tap into Bayonne*, February 2, 2022, https://www.tapinto.net/towns/bayonne/sections /government/articles/decade-old-bayonne-water-deal-still-making-waves."

56. Brenda Flanagan, "Bayonne Water Rates Spike After Privatization," *NJ Spotlight News*, January 5, 2017, https://www.njspotlightnews.org/video/bayonne -water-rates-spike-privatization/.

57. Nina Lahkani, "Pennsylvania Community Halts Largest Sewer Privatisation Deal in US History," *Guardian*, September 8, 2022, https://www.theguardian.com /us-news/2022/sep/08/pennsylvania-water-sewer-system-privatisation-fails.

58. Carey L. Biron, "Baltimore Votes to Become First Large U.S. City to Ban Water Privatization," Reuters, November 7, 2018, https://www.reuters.com/article /us-usa-water-cities/baltimore-votes-to-become-first-large-u-s-city-to-ban-water -privatization-idUSKCN1NC2O4.

59. Ballou, *Plunder*, 178.

60. *Preparing United States Critical Infrastructure*, 13.

61. *Preparing United States Critical Infrastructure*, 19–20.

62. Goldsmith, "Actors and Innovations in the Evolution of Infrastructure Services," 58.

63. Millward, "1940s Nationalizations in Britain," 210.

64. Lobina and Hall, "UK Water Privatization."

65. *Development of the Water Industry in England and Wales*, 2.

66. Richard Seymour, "A Short History of Privatisation in the UK: 1979–2012," *Guardian*, March 29, 2012, https://www.theguardian.com/commentisfree/2012 /mar/29/short-history-of-privatisation.

67. "2020 Population and Housing State Data."

68. *Economic Regulation of the Water Sector.*

69. Dore, Kushner, and Zumer, "Privatization of Water in the UK and France," 1.

70. *Economic Regulation of the Water Sector.*

71. Dore, Kushner, and Zumer, "Privatization of Water in the UK and France," 41–50.

72. Gill Plimmer and Ella Hollowood, "England's Water Groups Slashed Investment in Sewage Networks in Recent Decades," *Financial Times*, December 22, 2021, https://www.ft.com/content/86ac79f2-1169-4c2e-b28c-b18ff74aac10.

73. Marin, *Public-Private Partnerships for Urban Water Utilities.*

74. Galiani, Gertler, and Schargrodsky, "Water for Life," 83–120.

75. "Kirchner le Rescindió el Contrato a Aguas Argentinas," *La Nacion*, March 22, 2006, https://www.lanacion.com.ar/economia/kirchner-le-rescindio -el-contrato-a-aguas-argentinas-nid790872/.

76. Wahba, "Commentary."

77. Al-Madfaei, "Impact of Privatisation on the Sustainability of Water Resources."

78. Tudor, "Sewage Pollution in England's Waters."

79. Helena Horton, "Ofwat Chief Defends Water Companies over Lack of New Reservoirs," *Guardian*, August 16, 2022, https://www.theguardian.com /environment/2022/aug/16/ofwat-chief-defends-water-companies-over-lack -of-new-reservoirs.

80. Zoe Conway, "Sewage Regularly Dumped Illegally in England and Wales Rivers," BBC News, January 19, 2022, https://www.bbc.com/news/uk-60040162.

81. Helena Horton, "Sewage Monitors Faulty at Seaside Spots in England and Wales, Data Shows," *Guardian*, August 22, 2022, https://www.theguardian.com /environment/2022/aug/22/seaside-sewage-monitors-england-environment -agency.

82. Matt Oliver, "Britain Runs Dry as Wasteful Water Company Springs a Leak," *Telegraph*, July 19, 2022, https://www.telegraph.co.uk/business/2022/07/19/britain -runs-dry-wasteful-water-industry-springs-leak/.

83. Editorial, "The Guardian View on Water Companies: Nationalise a Flawed Private System," *Guardian*, August 10, 2022, https://www.theguardian.com /commentisfree/2022/aug/10/the-guardian-view-on-water-companies-nationalise -a-flawed-private-system; Greg Heffer, "Trade Union Leaders Demand Nationalisation of Energy Firms in Face of Cost-of-Living Crisis . . . on Same Day Starmer Abandons Labour's Pledge to Take Energy, Rail, Mail and Water into Public Ownership," *Daily Mail*, July 25, 2022, https://www.dailymail.co.uk/news /article-11045711/Labour-DITCHES-plan-nationalise-rail-energy-water-Starmer -abandons-Corbyns-promises.html; and Natalie Crookham, "Poll Result: England Urged to 'Take Back Control' of Water System," *Express*, August 21, 2022, https:// www.express.co.uk/news/uk/1657962/water-nationalisation-england-water -system-hosepipe-ban-poll-result-spt.

84. James Phillips, "Boss of Water Regulator Ofwat Denies Network Is in Meltdown as He Blames New Pipes for Leaks That Have Doubled in Heatwave," *Daily Mail*, August 16, 2022, https://www.dailymail.co.uk/news/article-11116869/Boss -water-regulator-Ofwat-denies-network-meltdown-blames-new-pipes-leaks .html.

85. Colvile, "Knee-Jerk Nationalisers Have No Idea."

86. See, for instance, John Cassidy, "The Economic Case for and Against Thatcherism" *New Yorker*, April 9, 2013, https://www.newyorker.com/news/john -cassidy/the-economic-case-for-and-against-thatcherism.

87. AQUASTAT.

88. Chin, "Dating Nanjing Man," 947.

89. Honey, "Before Dragons Coiled and Tigers Crouched," 15–25; and "History of Nanjing."

90. Musgrove, *China's Contested Capital*, 4.

91. Tsui, *China's Conservative Revolution*.

92. This comparison is somewhat controversial, but apt insofar as China has also leaned on heavy investment to create markets that will lead to growth, just as

the United States did in Europe and Japan after World War II. See Freymann, *One Belt One Road*, 36–38.

93. Yu and Danqing, "Privatization of Water Supply in China."

94. Zheng, Jiang, and Sugden, "People's Republic of China."

95. *Development of PPP in China.*

96. *Development of PPP in China.*

97. *China's Economic Rise.*

98. "China Pollution: Over 80% of Rural Water in North-East 'Undrinkable,'" BBC News, April 12, 2016, https://www.bbc.com/news/world-asia-china -36022538.

99. *Online Source Water Quality Monitoring.*

100. Wahba, "Americans and Infrastructure (2022)."

101. "Reorganization Plan No. 3 of 1970."

102. "Environmental Protection Agency."

103. "EPA Organization Chart."

104. "US Water Supply and Distribution Factsheet."

105. "US EPA: Fiscal Year 2022."

106. "Applicants Selected for FY 2022 Brownfields Assessment."

107. Allaire, Wu, and Lall, "National Trends in Drinking Water Quality Violations," 2078–83.

108. Bryan Walsh, "The GOP's Hidden Debt-Deal Agenda: Gut the EPA," *Time*, August 2, 2011, https://content.time.com/time/health/article/0,8599,2086421,00 .html.

109. Arthur Neslen, "Donald Trump Taking Steps to Abolish Environmental Protection Agency," *Guardian*, February 1, 2017, https://www.theguardian.com/us -news/2017/feb/02/donald-trump-plans-to-abolish-environmental-protection -agency.

110. Alan Liptak, "Supreme Court Limits E.P.A.'s Ability to Restrict Power Plant Emissions," *New York Times*, June 30, 2022, https://www.nytimes.com/2022/06/30 /us/epa-carbon-emissions-scotus.html.

111. *Sackett et ux. v. Environmental Protection Agency et al.*, 598 U.S. 651 (2022).

112. See, for example, Lima, Brochado, and Marques, "Public-Private Partnerships in the Water Sector."

Chapter Four

1. Spirou and Rudd, *Building the City of Spectacle*, 137–39.

2. *City of Chicago Comprehensive Annual Financial Report.*

3. "Richard M. Daley's 22 Years as Mayor," *Chicago Tribune*, April 30, 2011, https://www.chicagotribune.com/news/ct-xpm-2011-04-30-ct-met-daley -timeline-special-section20110430-story.html.

4. Daley, "Inaugural Address."

5. Neal Gabler, "The Secret Shame of Middle-Class Americans," *Atlantic*, May 2016, https://www.theatlantic.com/magazine/archive/2016/05/my-secret-shame/476415/.

6. "Infrastructure Case Study: Chicago Skyway Bridge."

7. See Poole, *Rethinking America's Highways*, 31. For a review of the history of toll roads in the United States, see Poole, ch. 3.

8. "Project Profile: Chicago Skyway."

9. "Bridges: Condition and Capacity."

10. *Rough Roads Ahead.*

11. "Goethals Bridge Replacement."

12. Eric Jaffe, "From $250 Million to $6.5 Billion: The Bay Bridge Cost Overrun," *Bloomberg*, October 13, 2015, https://www.bloomberg.com/news/articles/2015-10-13/how-the-cost-of-remaking-the-san-francisco-bay-bridge-soared-to-6-5-billion.

13. Situ, "Costs of Megaprojects."

14. "Bipartisan Infrastructure and Job Act."

15. "Bridges: Condition and Capacity."

16. Cook, Barr, and Halling, "Bridge Failure Rate."

17. Gregory Korte, Mark Niquette, and Skylar Woodhouse, "How the I-95 Bridge Reopened Just 12 Days after Fiery Collapse," *Bloomberg*, June 28, 2023, https://www.bloomberg.com/news/articles/2023-06-28/resurrection-of-i-95-in-just-two-weeks-is-dubbed-small-miracle.

18. "Bridges: Condition and Capacity."

19. "Expressways."

20. Heise and Edgerton, *Chicago, Center for Enterprise*, 67–70.

21. "Burnham Plan."

22. Kennedy, *Illinois Highway Improvement Bluebook.*

23. "William G. Edens, Roads Promoter: Chicago Banker for Whom Expressway Near City Was Named Dies at 93," *New York Times*, November 16, 1957, https://www.nytimes.com/1957/11/16/archives/william-g-edens-roads-promoter-chicago-banker-for-whom-expressway.html; and Kennedy, *Illinois Highway Improvement Bluebook*, 2.

24. Kennedy, *Illinois Highway Improvement Bluebook*, 2.

25. "William G. Edens, Roads Promoter."

26. Dyble, "Chicago and Its Skyway," 191.

27. Dyble, 191.

28. Dyble.

29. Dyble, 193.

30. Dyble.

31. Dyble, 197.

32. Dyble, 198.

33. Dyble, 194.

34. Dyble, 200.

35. "South Side."

36. Dyble, "Chicago and Its Skyway," 198.

37. Dyble.

38. Dyble, 193.

39. Dyble, 201.

40. Dyble, 193.

41. Dyble, 197.

42. "President Finds End of City Crisis, with Dip in Crime," *New York Times*, March 5, 1973, https://www.nytimes.com/1973/03/05/archives/president-finds -end-of-city-crisis-with-dip-in-crime-in-radio.html.

43. Harvey, "From Managerialism to Entrepreneurialism," 3–17.

44. See, for instance, Judd and Ready, "Entrepreneurial Cities and New Politics of Economic Development," 209–47; and Eisinger, *Rise of the Entrepreneurial State*.

45. Jessup and Sum, "Entrepreneurial City in Action," 2287–2313.

46. Richard Florida, "How Chicago Became the 'City of Spectacle,'" *Bloomberg*, December 22, 2016, https://www.bloomberg.com/news/articles/2016-12 -22/how-richard-m-daley-turned-chicago-into-a-spectacle.

47. Justin Fox, "'Alternatives' Isn't a Dirty Economic Word," *Harvard Business Review*, August 1, 2013, https://hbr.org/2013/08/alternatives-isnt-a-dirty-economic -word.

48. Ebenstein, *Milton Freidman*, 208.

49. Spirou and Rudd, *Building the City of Spectacle*, 44.

50. See Spirou and Rudd.

51. Banks, "Attention Economy of Authentic Cities," 195–209.

52. Dyble, "Chicago and Its Skyway," 202.

53. "Making Millennium Park."

54. Laura Vanderkam, "Parks and Re-creation: How Private Citizens Saved New York's Public Spaces," *City Journal*, Summer 2011, https://www.city-journal .org/html/parks-and-re-creation-13401.html.

55. Dyble, "Chicago and Its Skyway," 202.

56. Dyble, 204.

57. Dyble, 198.

58. Dyble, 202.

59. "Lawsuit Charges Chicago Skyway Tolls Violate Federal Law," The Bond Buyer, April 24, 2000, https://www.bondbuyer.com/news/lawsuit-charges-chicago -skyway-tolls-violate-federal-law.

60. Dyble, "Chicago and Its Skyway," 204.

61. "Infrastructure Case Study: Chicago Skyway Bridge."

62. "Project Profile: Chicago Skyway."

63. *City of Chicago Comprehensive Annual Financial Report*, 27.

64. "Infrastructure Case Study: Chicago Skyway Bridge."

65. Molly Ball, "The Privatization Backlash," *Atlantic*, April 23, 2014, https://www.theatlantic.com/politics/archive/2014/04/city-state-governments-privatization-contracting-backlash/361016/.

66. Daniel Mihalopoulos and Gary Washburn, "Group Is Wary of Skyway Spending," *Chicago Tribune*, December 2, 2004, https://www.chicagotribune.com/news/ct-xpm-2004-12-02-0412020313-story.html.

67. Shruti Singh, "Chicago Seeks Approval for $4.4 Billion in Borrowing in 2022," *Bloomberg*, October 14, 2021, https://www.bloomberg.com/news/articles/2021-10-14/chicago-seeks-authority-to-sell-4-4-billion-in-bonds-next-year#xj4y7vzkg.

68. Wahba, "Chicagoans and Infrastructure Survey, 2023."

69. Dutzik, Imus, and Baxandall, "Privatization and the Public Interest."

70. "Public Private Partnerships."

71. Enright, *Chicago Skyway Sale*.

72. Joseph S. Pete, "New Owner Takes Majority Stake in Chicago Skyway," *NWI Times*, September 15, 2022, https://www.nwitimes.com/business/local/new-owner-takes-majority-stake-in-chicago-skyway/article_475382c1-1135-5622-9946-8eec88e37727.html.

73. Enright, *Chicago Skyway Sale*.

74. Fran Spielman, "Chicago Skyway Sold—Again—Generating Windfall for Beleaguered Taxpayers," *Chicago Sun-Times*, September 13, 2022, https://chicago.suntimes.com/city-hall/2022/9/13/23351264/chicago-skyway-sold-pension-plans-australian-toll-road-daley-99-year-lease.

75. Dana Levenson, "Should Chicago Consider More Public-Private Partnerships?," *Crain's Chicago Business*, February 16, 2022, https://www.chicagobusiness.com/opinion/chicago-should-consider-more-public-private-partnerships-city-owned-assets.

76. "Our History."

77. Smith, *Wealth of Nations*, 310.

78. Coase, "Lighthouse in Economics," 357–76.

79. Smith, *Wealth of Nations*, 311.

80. Smith, 311.

81. "Canadian Pension Funds Buy Chicago Skyway for $2.8 Billion," *Chicago Tribune*, November 13, 2015, https://www.chicagotribune.com/business/ct-chicago-skyway-operator-sold-20151113-story.html.

82. Chris Bourke and Amy Bainbridge, "Australian Firm Defies Top Investor, Buys Chicago Skyway Stake from Canada Pensions," *Bloomberg*, September 12, 2022, https://www.bloomberg.com/news/articles/2022-09-12/atlas-arteria-agrees-to-buy-2-billion-stake-in-chicago-skyway#xj4y7vzkg.

83. Spielman, "Chicago Skyway Sold—Again."

84. Spielman.

85. The research surveyed 1,025 respondents age eighteen and older living in the Chicago DMA. The survey sample was stratified to match census representation for age, gender, and ethnicity. The survey was fielded using the Qualtrics Insight Platform, and the panel was sourced from Lucid. Fielding was executed from January 18, 2023 to January 25, 2023.

86. Monica Davey, "Bridge's Private Ownership Raises Concerns," *New York Times*, October 12, 2007, https://www.nytimes.com/2007/10/12/us/12bridge.html.

87. Like most US infrastructure, bridges in the nineteenth century were almost all privately owned and operated. Typically, these bridges still pay for upkeep through a toll, though some have learned to turn their privately owned status into an attraction, like Dingmans Bridge in Delaware, a favorite local anomaly that the press has praised as a sort of historic landmark.

88. Joann Muller, "Why One Rich Man Shouldn't Own an International Bridge," *Forbes*, January 12, 2012, https://www.forbes.com/sites/joannmuller/2012/01/12/why-one-rich-man -shouldnt-own-an-international-bridge/?sh=2d5f91c96c18.

89. "Bridge Facts."

90. Lowenstein, *Warren Buffett*, 212.

91. Louis Aguilar, "Buffett: Post-Bankrupt Detroit Appealing to Investors," *Detroit News*, September 18, 2014, https://www.detroitnews.com/story/business/2014/09/18/buffett-touts -post-bankrupt-detroit/15840269/.

92. Yvette Brend, "Ambassador Bridge Owner Wants to Mend Relations with Canada in Wake of Blockade," Canadian Broadcasting Corporation, March 12, 2022, https://www.cbc .ca/news/business/ambassador-bridge-mathew-moroun-convoy-1.6380486.

93. "Modernising New York's Transport Infrastructure."

94. "Modernising New York's Transport Infrastructure."

95. "Major Bridge P3 Program."

96. "Major Bridge P3 Program."

97. "Connecting Industries in Norway."

98. "Connecting Industries in Norway."

99. Nissen and Rotne, "Getting the Balance Right," 417–26.

100. "Vasco da Gama Bridge."

101. "Confederation Bridge."

102. See "Second Vivekananda Bridge Tollway Company Private Limited."

103. Siemiatycki, "Public-Private Partnerships in Canada," 343–62.

104. Inderst, "Pension Fund Investment in Infrastructure," 40–47.

105. Inderst, 44.

106. Wahba, "Commentary."

107. Wahba.

108. "National Data."

109. Inderst, "Pension Fund Investment in Infrastructure," 45.

Chapter Five

1. "2021 Report Card for America's Infrastructure: Roads."

2. Fernald, "Roads to Prosperity?"

3. Sharma and Bisht, "Carrying Capacity Assessment and Sustainable Tourism Management," 401.

4. "I Squared Capital Signs Agreement to Acquire Toll Road in India."

5. Niall McCarthy, "Report: India Lifted 271 Million People Out of Poverty in a Decade," *Forbes*, July 12, 2019, https://www.forbes.com/sites/niallmccarthy/2019/07/12/report-india-lifted-271-million-people-out-of-poverty-in-a-decade-infographic/?sh=60de55912284.

6. Shuriah Niazi, "India Tops World in Road Deaths, Injuries," *AA*, November 21, 2021, https://www.aa.com.tr/en/asia-pacific/india-tops-world-in-road-deaths-injuries/2425908.

7. "Why India's Roads Are so Deadly," *Economist*, August 5, 2022, https://www.economist.com/asia/2022/08/05/why-indias-roads-are-so-deadly.

8. India Infrahub, "Green Highways: NHAI Plants 2.2 Crore Trees along National Highways since FY 2018," *Swarajya*, December 2, 2021, https://swarajyamag.com/insta/green-highways-nhai-plants-over-22-crore-trees-along-national-highways-since-fy-2018.

9. Sain-Baird, "How Central Park Keeps New York City Healthy."

10. Garg and Dayal, "Road Learnings," 2488–2510.

11. Jyotsna Singh, "India en Route for Grand Highways," BBC News, May 26, 2003, http://news.bbc.co.uk/2/hi/south_asia/3043235.stm.

12. Kancharla, "Data: By March 2019."

13. Nallathiga and Shah, "Public Private Partnerships in Roads Sector in India."

14. "Public Road and Street Mileage in the United States."

15. "The Total Length of Highways in China Reached 5,28 Million Kilometers," *Railly News*, April 26, 2022, https://raillynews.com/2022/04/cindeki-karayollarinin-toplam-uzunlugu-528-milyon-kilometreye-ulasti/.

16. "About NHDP."

17. K. Vinay Pratap, "Indian Infrastructure: The Road Sector Shows the Path," *Financial Express*, June 20, 2022, https://www.financialexpress.com/opinion/the-road-sector-shows-the-path/2565904/.

18. Harikishan Reddy, interview with author, January 16, 2023. All quotes from Reddy in are from this interview.

19. See Wahba, "Americans and Infrastructure (2021)"; and "Americans and Infrastructure (2022)."

20. Brooks and Liscow, "Can America Reduce Highway Spending?," 107–50.

21. See Clifford Winston comment in Brooks and Liscow; Winston, *Last Exit*; Winston, "On the Performance of the US Transportation System," 773–824; and Winston, *Gaining Ground*.

22. Ed Rendell, interview with the author, March 2, 2023. All quotes from Rendell are from this interview.

23. Rendell, *Nation of Wusses*, 173.

24. Rendell, 10.

25. Daniel B. Klein, "Private Toll Roads in America—The First Time Around," *Access Magazine*, Spring 1993, https://www.accessmagazine.org/spring-1993 /private-toll-roads-in-america-the-first-time-around/.

26. "William Bingham." See also Landis, "History of the Philadelphia and Lancaster Turnpike," 235–58.

27. Mires, "Turnpikes."

28. Newspaper articles detailing these changes appear in "Montgomery Avenue Toll House."

29. Kidd, "It Was America's First Superhighway."

30. "PA Turnpike History."

31. Longfellow, "Back in Time."

32. Hoffer, "Pennsylvania Turnpike."

33. Dakelman and Schorr, *Pennsylvania Turnpike*, 20; and "Early Years."

34. "Early Years."

35. Shieh, "Building of the Great Pennsylvania Turnpike."

36. "Safety Focused, Customer Driven."

37. Kidd, "It Was America's First Superhighway."

38. "Leasing the Pennsylvania Turnpike."

39. Even in 2021, as President Biden toured the country promoting the IIJA, a bridge outside Pittsburgh collapsed. See Hannah Sarisohn and Jay Croft, "Pennsylvania Officials Agree to Spend $25 Million to Replace a Pittsburgh Bridge One Week after It Collapsed," CNN, February 4, 2022, https://www.cnn.com/2022/02 /04/us/pennsylvania-bridge-repair/index.html.

40. "Governor Rendell Proposes Budget with No Tax Increase."

41. Alter et al., "Pennsylvania."

42. Hall and Green, "Beyond Unemployment."

43. Carlson, "Illinois Unemployment Rate Is Worst in US."

44. "Regional and State Unemployment."

45. Hymowitz, "In the Rendell Era, City's Image Rose."

46. Quehl, "Bottom Line . . . and Beyond."

47. Mortimer Sellers, "Another Philadelphia Story," *Washington Post*, February 1, 1998, https://www.washingtonpost.com/archive/entertainment/books/1998/02 /01/another-philadelphia-story/aab21640-1d90-4f12-acd3-19043cbd0bda/.

48. Bissinger, *Prayer for the City*, 24.

49. Dale Russakoff, "U.S. Seizes Philadelphia Public Housing Authority," *Washington Post*, May 21, 1992, https://www.washingtonpost.com/archive/politics /1992/05/21/us-seizes-philadelphia-public-housing-authority/4af685c1-06df -4f67-a54a-8c02448e7c4a/.

50. Simon Van Zuylen-Wood, "How Tom Corbett Made Us All Losers in the Pennsylvania Lottery," *Philadelphia Magazine*, January 16, 2013, https://www.phillymag.com/news/2013/01/16/lottery-privatization-draft/.

51. Bissinger, *Prayer for the City*, 36.

52. "Mayor Rendell Cleans Up City Hall," *Prescott Courier*, March 16, 1992, https://news.google.com/newspapers?nid=886&dat=19920316&id=zm9LAAAAIBAJ&sjid=q3oDAAAAIBAJ&pg=6826,3799673.

53. Van Zuylen-Wood, "How Tom Corbett Made Us All Losers in the Pennsylvania Lottery."

54. Jacob Weisberg, "Philadelphia Story," *New York Magazine*, May 2, 1994, 30–32, https://books.google.com/books?id=OeQCAAAAMBAJ&printsec=frontcover&source=gbs_ge_summary_r&cad=0#v=onepage&q&f=false.

55. Lopez, "Nursing Home Privatization."

56. Scott Farmelant, "Nursing Suspicions," *City Paper*, December 7, 1995, https://mycitypaper.com/articles/113095/article005.shtml.

57. "Philadelphia Museum of Art Strike Ends with Worker Victory," *ArtForum*, October 17, 2022, https://www.artforum.com/news/philadelphia-museum-of-art-strike-ends-with-worker-victory-89439#:~:text=Unionized%20employees%20of%20the%20Philadelphia,then%20ratified%20on%20October%2016.

58. Edelman and Edelman, *CMA Report*.

59. "City of Philadelphia Closing Philadelphia Nursing Home."

60. Bissinger, *Prayer for the City*, 106.

61. Bissinger, 106.

62. Bissinger, 108.

63. "Philadelphia City Workers Go on Strike," *Los Angeles Times*, October 6, 1992, https://www.latimes.com/archives/la-xpm-1992-10-06-mn-495-story.html.

64. "Philadelphia's Municipal Strike Ends," UPI, October 6, 1992, https://www.upi.com/Archives/1992/10/06/Philadelphias-municipal-strike-ends/2785718344000/.

65. "Philadelphia's Municipal Strike Ends."

66. Osborne and Gaebler, *Reinventing Government*.

67. The most controversial privatizations were of nursing homes. See Edelman and Edelman, *CMA Report*.

68. Hymowitz, "In the Rendell Era, City's Image Rose."

69. John L. Micek and John M.R. Bull, "Rendell Budget Full of 'Painful' Cuts: He Aims to Unveil Alternative, but GOP Ready to OK Plan No. 1," *Morning Call*, March 5, 2003, https://www.mcall.com/news/mc-xpm-2003-03-05-3451633-story.html.

70. "Rendell's Budget in Place for Clear Sailing in Senate," *Pocono Record*, March 10, 2003, https://www.poconorecord.com/story/news/2003/03/11/rendell-s-budget-in-place/50984470007/.

71. "Driven by Dollars."

72. "Driven by Dollars," 10. In its 2018 report card for the state of Pennsylvania (the most recent with full state data), the ASCE projected an investment gap of $7.2 billion by 2020. Part of the discrepancies might be accounted for by the introduction in 2016 of income tax hikes. See "2018 Report Card for Pennsylvania's Infrastructure," 91.

73. Paul Nussbaum, "Turnpike Lease Plan Sent to Pa. Legislature," *Philadelphia Inquirer*, May 22, 2007, https://www.inquirer.com/philly/news/homepage/20070522_Turnpike_lease_plan_sent_to_Pa__legislature.html.

74. "Act 44 Plan."

75. Paul Nussbaum, "I-80 Toll Plan Is Kicked Back," *Philadelphia Inquirer*, December 14, 2007, https://www.inquirer.com/philly/news/homepage/20071214_I-80_toll_plan_is_kicked_back.html.

76. FreightWaves Staff, "Rendell Chooses Morgan Stanley."

77. Though working at Morgan Stanley at the time, I was not involved in the process. The advisory was run by the municipal department, and as a private equity fund within Morgan Stanley, Infrastructure Partners' involvement would have resulted in a conflict.

78. "Driven by Dollars," 14.

79. "For Whom the Road Tolls."

80. Mark Scolforo, "House Democratic Study Criticizes Idea of Leasing Pa. Turnpike," *Pocono Record*, March 3, 2008, https://www.poconorecord.com/story/news/traffic/2008/03/03/house-democratic-study-criticizes-idea/52437775007/.

81. "Driven by Dollars," 16.

82. "FDI Statistics."

83. Poole, *Rethinking America's Highways*, 117.

84. Wahba, "Americans and Infrastructure (2022)."

85. Poterba, "Is the Gasoline Tax Regressive," 145–64; and Santos and Rojey, "Distributional Impacts of Road Pricing," reject the view that road pricing is always regressive.

86. Joan Gralla, "Pennsylvania Bid to Lease Turnpike Ends for Now," Reuters, October 1, 2008, https://www.reuters.com/article/pennsylvania-turnpike/pennsylvania-bid-to-lease-turnpike-ends-for-now-idUSN3034541720080930.

87. Gilroy, "Feds to Reject PA Turnpike Commission's 1-80 Toll Plan."

88. "PA Turnpike Makes Final $450 Million Payment."

89. "Act 44 Plan."

90. "PA Turnpike Makes Final $450 Million Payment."

91. "World Development Indicators."

92. Poole and Samuel, "Return of Private Toll Roads."

93. Poole and Samuel.

94. "2021 Report Card for America's Infrastructure: Roads."

95. "It's Been 28 Years since We Last Raised the Gas Tax."

96. See Atkinson, "Letter Regarding Vehicle Miles Traveled (VMT) Tax."

97. Clifford Winston, "The Little-Known Provision That Could Revolutionize Highway Travel," *New York Times*, July 6, 2023, https://www.nytimes.com/2023/07/06/opinion/infrastructure-investment-jobs-act-climate-change-electric-vehicle.html.

98. "Business: Private Toll Roads Show the Way," *Time*, February 28, 1955, https://content.time.com/time/subscriber/article/0,33009,861259-1,00.html.

99. "Business."

100. "Alaska: End Sought for 'Bridge to Nowhere,'" *New York Times*, September 22, 2007, https://www.nytimes.com/2007/09/22/us/22brfs-ENDSOUGHT FOR_BRF.html.

101. Casale, "New Report Spotlights Wasteful Highway Boondoggles."

102. Andy Sullivan, "In Alabama, Infrastructure Dollars Revive a 'Zombie' Highway," Reuters, March 30, 2022, https://www.reuters.com/world/us/alabama-infrastructure-dollars-revive-zombie-highway-2022-03-30/.

103. "Conversation on the Indo-Pacific Economic Framework."

104. Peter McGuire, "Climbing Costs Drive State to Pass Up 12 More Road and Bridge Projects," *Portland Press Herald*, May 9, 2019, https://www.pressherald.com/2019/05/09/maine-dot-cuts-59-million-from-construction-plan/.

105. "Country Case Study: The United States."

106. Renner and Nulton, 2022 *Public-Private Partnership Trends Report*.

107. Tom Coyne, "Australian Company Buys Bankrupt Indiana Toll Road Vendor," *Indianapolis Star*, March 11, 2015, https://www.indystar.com/story/news/politics/2015/03/11/australian-company-buys-bankrupt-indiana-toll-road-vendor/70161160/.

108. Madeline Buckley, "Toll Road Bankruptcy Reignites Old Debate about Privatization," *South Bend Tribune*, September 23, 2014, https://www.southbendtribune.com/story/news/local/2014/09/23/oll-road-bankruptcy-reignites-old-debate-about-privatizatio/46399889/.

109. Zwalf, "From Turnpikes to Toll Roads," 103–20.

110. Peter Boyle, "WestConnex Privatisation Is 'Highway Robbery on a Massive Scale,'" *Greenleft*, September 29, 2021, https://www.greenleft.org.au/content/westconnex-privatisation-highway-robbery-massive-scale.

111. Boyle.

112. Boyle.

113. "Improving Public Private Partnerships."

114. John Kehoe, "WestConnex Sale to Add $13b to NSW Generations Fund," *Financial Review*, August 9, 2021, https://www.afr.com/policy/economy/westconnex-sale-to-add-13b-to-nsw-generations-fund-20210809-p58h1e.p58h1e.

115. Montoya and Ismay, "Issues Backgrounder."

116. Montoya and Ismay.

117. "Understanding the Debate around Motorway Concessions in France."

118. Abiven, "Spain's Empty Highways Lead to Bankruptcy."

119. Baeza and Vassallo, "Private Concession Contracts for Toll Roads in Spain," 299–304.

120. Moraleja, Blanc-Brude, and Whittaker, "Take the Next Exit."

121. "Urban Highway Concessionaires in Santiago, Chile."

Chapter Six

1. *Aircraft Accident Report.*

2. "Public Law 104-264."

3. Clinton, "Statement on Signing the Federal Aviation Reauthorization Act of 1996."

4. "Airport Investment Partnership Program."

5. "Air Transport, Passengers Carried—United States."

6. "2001 Report Card for America's Infrastructure."

7. "2001 Report Card for America's Infrastructure."

8. James C. McKinley Jr., "Security Is Tightened at Nation's Airports," *New York Times*, August 10, 1995, https://timesmachine.nytimes.com/timesmachine/1995/08/10/676695.html?pageNumber=14.

9. "Timeline of FAA and Aerospace History."

10. "Timeline of FAA and Aerospace History."

11. "Critical Infrastructure Protection in the Digital Age."

12. "Critical Infrastructure Protection in the Digital Age."

13. "Airport Infrastructure Funding."

14. "1998 Report Card for America's Infrastructure."

15. "2001 Report Card for America's Infrastructure."

16. Poole and Edwards, "Privatizing US Airports."

17. *Airport System Development*, 209.

18. Winston, *Last Exit*, 9.

19. Poole and Edwards, "Privatizing US Airports."

20. "Downtown Garment District Coming Back to Life."

21. Nicholas Phillips, "How Should Downtown St. Louis Move Forward?," *St. Louis Magazine*, March 19, 2020, https://www.stlmag.com/longform/how-can-st-louis-build-on-its-recent-momentum/.

22. Phillips.

23. Corinne Ruff, "St. Louis Mayor Krewson Pulls Plug on Airport Privatization Process," *St. Louis on the Air*, St. Louis Public Radio, December 20, 2019, https://news.stlpublicradio.org/show/st-louis-on-the-air/2019-12-20/st-louis-mayor-krewson-pulls-plug-on-airport-privatization-process#stream/0.

24. Jeanette Cooperman, "Should the City Turn Over Operation of St. Louis Lambert International Airport?," *St. Louis Magazine*, October 4, 2019, https://www.stlmag.com/news/should-the-city-turn-over-operation-of-st-louis-lambert-inte/.

25. "Fitch Affirms Lambert-St. Louis Int'l Airport (MO) at 'BBB+.'"

26. *Comprehensive Annual Financial Report, 2018.*

27. Ruff, "Krewson Pulls Plug on Airport."

28. Tim Jones and Charles Babcock, "Rex Sinquefield's Crusade against Income Taxes," *Bloomberg*, March 29, 2012, https://www.bloomberg.com/news/articles/2012-03-29/rex-sinquefields-crusade-against-income-taxes?leadSource=uverify%20wall.

29. "Rex Sinquefield."

30. Harold Dondis and Patrick Wolff, "The Chess Hall of Fame Is Saved," *Boston Globe*, June 14, 2010, http://archive.boston.com/ae/games/articles/2010/06/14/the_chess_hall_of_fame_is_saved/.

31. "Rex Sinquefield, the Chess Mogul," *Real Sports*, HBO, https://www.youtube.com/watch?v=nbvrDspsGNU.

32. Francis Slay, "We Should Explore Airport's Untapped Potential," *St. Louis Post-Dispatch*, February 2, 2018, https://www.stltoday.com/opinion/columnists/we-should-explore-airports-untapped-potential/article_73dd1218-520a-52e7-ac9d-e2b2ca98f055.html.

33. "Group Blasts Survey of St. Louis Residents on Lambert as Pro-privatization," St. Louis Public Radio, September 23, 2018, https://news.stlpublicradio.org/economy-business/2018-09-13/group-blasts-survey-of-st-louis-residents-on-lambert-as-pro-privatization.

34. "St. Louis Not for Sale."

35. Stokes, "Privatization of the Saint Louis Water Utility."

36. Interestingly, on the front page of the group's website it claims Veolia managed Flint's infrastructure during the crisis, which we know from chapter 3 is incorrect.

37. "Group Blasts Survey of St. Louis Residents."

38. Wahba, "Americans and Infrastructure (2022)."

39. Taylor Tiamoyo Harris, "St. Louis Extends Orders for Homeless Encampment," *St. Louis Post-Dispatch*, July 4, 2022, https://www.stltoday.com/news/local/crime-and-courts/st-louis-extends-order-for-homeless-encampment-under-highway/article_2df98b31-ddd0-5f39-9332-12c9d0ae25a7.html.

40. "St. Louis to Participate in Airport Privatization Pilot Program."

41. Once again, this is not an issue specific to P3; the same could easily happen to a government procurement process. If states are serious about governance, such roles should be banned for a number of years.

42. Cooperman, "Should the City Turn Over Operation."

43. Jeremy Kohler, "Lawsuit Alleges Airport Working Group Violated Sunshine Law, with Closed-Door Meetings" *St. Louis Post-Dispatch*, December 6, 2019, https://www.stltoday.com/news/local/govt-and-politics/lawsuit-alleges-airport-working-group-violated-sunshine-law-with-closed-door-meetings/article_b5d75e59-14ad-5169-939e-7f94cb2b7e66.html.

44. Steve Vockrodt, "Tapes Show St. Louis' Failed Quest to Privatize Lambert Airport Was Riddled with Secrecy," St. Louis Public Radio, March 25, 2022, https://news.stlpublicradio.org/government-politics-issues/2022-03-25/tapes -show-st-louis-failed-quest-to-privatize-lambert-airport-was-riddled-with -secrecy.

45. Kohler, "Lawsuit Alleges Group Violated Sunshine Law."

46. "Sunshine Law."

47. Cooperman, "Should the City Turn Over Operation."

48. Krewson, "Mayor's Letter to Airport Working Group."

49. Ruff, "Krewson Pulls Plug on Airport."

50. "City of St. Louis Ends Fiscal Year 2022 with $49 Million Surplus"; and "City of St. Louis Ends Fiscal Year 2021 with $32 Million Surplus."

51. Jim Erickson, "Privatization Discussed as Concept for Lambert Airport," *Mid-Rivers News Magazine,* September 7, 2021, https://www.midriversnews magazine.com/news/privatization-discussed-as-concept-for-lambert-airport /article_fc08e6bc-2d59-5481-bbf9-4ad8f1747ead.html.

52. Ruff, "Krewson Pulls Plug on Airport."

53. "MIA Ranked America's Biggest Airport."

54. Emilio Gonzalez, interview with the author, December 22, 2022. All quotes from Gonzalez are from this interview.

55. Scribner, "Reforming the Airport Investment Partnership Program."

56. Poole and Edwards, "Privatizing US Airports."

57. Winston, "On the Performance of the US Transportation System," 790.

58. "Overview: What Is AIP & What Is Eligible?"

59. Green, "Airports and Economic Development."

60. *Airport Privatization: Limited Interest,* 41.

61. "Airport Infrastructure Funding."

62. "Airport Infrastructure Funding."

63. "Fiscal Year 2022–2023 Proposed Budget."

64. Rachel King, "Inside the New Delta Air Lines Terminal at New York City's LaGuardia Airport," *Fortune,* June 4, 2022, https://fortune.com/2022/06/04/delta -air-lines-terminal-new-york-city-laguardia-airport/; "American Airlines Celebrates Unveiling"; and Skylar Woodhouse, "LaGuardia's $4 Billion Revamping Terminal Is Finally Opening," *Bloomberg,* June 1, 2022, https://www.bloomberg .com/news/articles/2022-06-01/laguardia-shows-off-revamped-delta-terminal -as-travel-picks-up.

65. "2021 Report Card for America's Infrastructure."

66. "Independent Research Highlights the Need to Increase the PFC," 6.

67. David Shepardson, "US Awards Nearly $1 Billion to Airports in Infrastructure Grants," Reuters, February 27, 2023, https://www.reuters.com/world/us/us -awards-nearly-1-billion-airports-infrastructure-grants-2023-02-27/.

68. *Airport Privatization: Limited Interest.*

69. Douglas, "Midway Privatization in Final Phase."

70. John Byrne, Jeff Coen, and Hal Dardick, "Emanuel Halts Midway Privatization Bidding," *Chicago Tribune*, September 6, 2013, https://www.chicagotribune.com/politics/chi-emanuel-halts-midway-lease-talks-20130905-story.html.

71. "AOPA Attacks Plan to Privatize New Orleans Lakefront Airport."

72. Podkul, "New Orleans Drops Plan to Privatise Airport."

73. *Airport Privatization: Issues and Options*, 7.

74. "'Airport Lease-to-Pay-Down-Municipal-Debt' Argument."

75. *Airport Privatization: Issues and Options.*

76. Davis, "Study Commissioned by Congress Recommends."

77. Davis.

78. Miller et al., "US Airport Infrastructure Funding and Financing."

79. *Airport Privatization: Limited Interest.*

80. "British Pound Has Lost 70% of Its Value since 1987."

81. Kost, "British Model."

82. Elliott, Ong, and Cuttle, "Coming Down to Earth."

83. "Airports Group Europe Raises Offer for Vienna Airport Stake."

84. Elliot, Ong, and Cuttle, "Coming Down to Earth."

85. Graham, "Airport Privatisation."

86. De la Peña, "Tale of Two Airports."

87. "Case Study on Commercialization."

88. "French Airport Privatisation," *Aviation Strategy*, April 2005, https://aviationstrategy.aero/newsletter/Apr-2005/2/French_airport_privatisation.

89. "French Airport Privatization."

90. "Shareholders."

91. "Backlash Builds in France over Privatization of Airports Operator," Reuters, December 4, 2019, https://www.reuters.com/article/us-france-privatisation-adp/backlash-builds-in-france-over-privatization-of-airports-operator-idUSKBN1Y810S.

92. Parker, "Performance of BAA before and after Privatisation," 133–45.

93. Isla Binnie, Andres Gonzalez, and Pamela Barbaglia, "Heathrow Owner Ferrovial Studies Options for Stake in Britain's Biggest Airport—Sources," Reuters, August 9, 2022, https://www.reuters.com/business/aerospace-defense/exclusive-heathrow-owner-ferrovial-studies-options-stake-britains-biggest-2022-08-09/; and "Ferrovial to Sell Its 25% Stake in London's Heathrow for $3 Billion," Reuters, November 29, 2023, https://www.reuters.com/markets/deals/ferrovial-sell-its-25-stake-londons-heathrow-3-billion-2023-11-28/.

94. Luke Peters, "What's the Latest with London Heathrow Airport's Third Runway?," *Simple Flying*, May 26, 2022, https://simpleflying.com/london-heathrow-airport-third-runway-latest/.

95. Elliot, Ong, and Cuttle, "Coming Down to Earth."

96. "Heathrow Apologises for Poor Service, Could Ask for More Flight Cuts," *Reuters*, July 11, 2022, https://www.reuters.com/world/uk/heathrow-apologises -poor-service-could-ask-more-flights-cuts-2022-07-11/.

97. "Puerto Rico Considering Privatization of Aguadilla Airport," *Aviation Week Network*, June 15, 1998, https://aviationweek.com/puerto-rico-considering -privatization-aguadilla-airport.

98. Bram, Martínez, and Steindel, "Trends and Developments in the Economy of Puerto Rico."

99. Palmer, "J&J Investing $225 Million in 4 Puerto Rico Plants."

100. "Puerto Rico."

101. Michelle Kaske and Jim Wyss, "Puerto Rico Is Out of Bankruptcy after a $22 Billion Debt Exchange," *Bloomberg*, May 14, 2022, https://www.bloomberg .com/news/articles/2022-03-15/puerto-rico-bankruptcy-set-to-end-with-22 -billion-debt-exchange.

102. "Infrastructure Case Study: San Juan Airport."

103. "Project Profile: Luis Muñoz Marín International Airport."

104. "Puerto Rico Public-Private Partnerships Authority."

105. "Puerto Rico."

106. "Infrastructure Case Study: San Juan Airport."

107. Brent Tasugi, interview with the author, January 20, 2023. All quotes from Tasugi are from this interview.

108. "Whole New LGA Nears Completion."

109. Derek Utter, interview with the author, January 26, 2023. All quotes from Utter are from this interview.

110. "Governor Hochul Announces Groundbreaking of $9.5 Billion New Terminal One."

111. "John F. Kennedy International Airport New Terminal One Redevelopment."

112. "John F. Kennedy International Airport New Terminal One Redevelopment."

113. "John F. Kennedy International Airport New Terminal One Redevelopment."

Chapter Seven

1. *Handbook of Statistics 2023*, 75.

2. Nagurney, "Brief History of the Shipping Container."

3. Jacob Gronholt-Pederson, "Top Container Ships Maersk, MSC to End Alliance from 2025," *Reuters*, January 25, 2023, https://www.reuters.com/business /autos-transportation/top-container-shippers-maersk-msc-end-alliance-2025 -2023-01-25/#:~:text=MSC%2C%20privately%20owned%20by%20the,share%20 the%20last%20eight%20years.

4. "Top Ten: The Largest Shipping Lines in the World," *Container News*, August 27, 2021, https://container-news.com/top-10-the-largest-shipping-lines -in-the-world/.

5. Placek, "Leading Ship Operator's Share of the World Liner Fleet."

6. "Ports Primer."

7. Campanelli, "Deep Dive on America's Ports."

8. "Survey Shows Ports Plan Big Infrastructure Investments."

9. "Ports."

10. "Biden-Harris Administration Announces Historic Investment."

11. "Biden-Harris Administration Announces More Than $703 Million to Improve Port Infrastructure."

12. "Global Container Freight Rate Index."

13. "Record Year for America's Ports."

14. "Record Year for America's Ports."

15. Wolfgang Saxon, "M.P. McLean, 87, Container Shipping Pioneer," *New York Times*, May 29, 2001, https://www.nytimes.com/2001/05/29/nyregion/m-p-mclean-87-container-shipping-pioneer.html.

16. Levinson, "Container Shipping and the Decline of New York," 49–80.

17. Levinson, *Box.*

18. Nagurney, "Brief History of the Shipping Container."

19. Levinson, *Box*, 15.

20. Bruno, "Ever Alot Breaks Record for World's Largest Containership."

21. Gresser, "PPI's Trade Fact of the Week."

22. Levinson, *Box*, 49.

23. Levinson.

24. Thompson, "History of the Shipping Container Created in 1956."

25. "Port History."

26. "Port of New York."

27. Their names were John T. Agnew, Wilson G. Hunt, William Wood, R. M. Henry, and Hugh Smith.

28. "The Charter Election," *New York Times*, December 1, 1868, https://timesmachine.nytimes.com/timesmachine/1868/12/02/79361808.html?pageNumber=1.

29. "Boss Tweed."

30. "The Department of Docks," *New York Times*, December 6, 1871, https://timesmachine.nytimes.com/timesmachine/1871/12/06/79006291.html?pageNumber=4.

31. "History," Port of Los Angeles.

32. "Port of Long Beach History Timeline."

33. "George Washington Bridge."

34. "Building the George Washington Bridge."

35. "Municipal Loans: Port of New York Authority," *New York Times*, October 23, 1929, https://timesmachine.nytimes.com/timesmachine/1929/10/23/96005553.html?pageNumber=48.

36. "Lincoln Tunnel—New York to New Jersey."

37. Levinson, "Container Shipping and the Decline of New York."

38. "History," Port Authority of New York & New Jersey.

39. Levinson, "Container Shipping and the Decline of New York."

40. George Cable Wright, "Authority Spurs Port Elizabeth," *New York Times*, March 22, 1962, https://timesmachine.nytimes.com/timesmachine/1962/03/23 /90160416.html?pageNumber=66.

41. Greene, *Life and Voyages of Verrazzano*, 8.

42. Clulow and Mostert, *Dutch and English East India Companies*, 13.

43. Clulow and Mostert, 14.

44. Clulow and Mostert.

45. "Charter of the Dutch West India Company."

46. Jameson, *Willem Usselincx*, 197.

47. Israel, *Dutch Republic*, 326.

48. Den Heijer, "Public and Private Dutch West India Interest," 161.

49. Peter Buxbaum, "Port Elizabeth's Maher Terminals to Be Sold by Deutsche Bank," *Global Trade*, April 25, 2016, https://www.globaltrademag.com/port -elizabeths-maher-terminals-to-be-sold-by-deutsche-bank/.

50. "Agreement of Lease Between Port Authority of New York and New Jersey and Maher Terminals."

51. "Deutsche Bank's US Real Estate Arm to Buy Maher Terminals," Reuters, March 20, 2007, https://www.reuters.com/article/rreef-takeover/deutsche-banks -u-s-real-estate-arm-to-buy-maher-terminals-idUSWNAS451220070320.

52. "Financial Statements."

53. "Financial Statements."

54. "Connectivity."

55. "Port Miami."

56. Parker, "Ports Ponder Public Private Partnerships."

57. I was involved in the bidding for the construction of the Miami Tunnel as part of a consortium that included Morgan Stanley Infrastructure Partners and a Spanish construction company specializing in tunnels. Unfortunately, we lost.

58. *CBP Trade and Travel Report*, 6.

59. *CBP Trade and Travel Report*, 7.

60. "§ 1.92 The Maritime Administration."

61. Hutchison, "Everything You Need to Know about the Merchant Marine."

62. Jeffery Gold, "New York Port Authority Sues to Block UAE Takeover," *Spokesman-Review*, February 25, 2006, https://www.spokesman.com/stories/2006 /feb/25/new-york-port-authority-sues-to-block-uae-takeover/.

63. Jeffrey H. Birnbaum, "Role of Sen. Dole's Husband at Issue," *Washington Post*, February 24, 2006, https://www.washingtonpost.com/archive/politics /2006/02/24/role-of-sen-doles-husband-at-issue/1e2b4f08-7ca0-49af-b53d -26b3c70590fa/.

64. David E. Sanger, "Under Pressure, Dubai Company Drops Port Deal," *New York Times*, March 10, 2006, https://www.nytimes.com/2006/03/10/politics /under-pressure-dubai-company-drops-port-deal.html.

65. FreightWaves Staff, "DP World Sells U.S. Terminals to AIG."

66. FreightWaves Staff.

67. "AIG-Highstar Raise $3.5 bln Infrastructure Fund," Reuters, October 30, 2007, https://www.reuters.com/article/aig-fund/aig-highstar-raise-3-5-bln -infrastructure-fund-idUSN3013933020071030.

68. "CPP Investments to Acquire Ports America Interest from Oaktree."

69. Sadek Wahba, "Pension Funds Can Launch a New Infrastructure Era," *Pensions & Investments*, June 2, 2021, https://www.pionline.com/industry-voices /commentary-pension-funds-can-launch-new-infrastructure-era.

70. Tom Phillips, "The $900bn Question: What Is the Belt and Road Initiative?," *Guardian*, May 11, 2017, https://www.theguardian.com/world/2017/may/12/the -900bn-question-what-is-the-belt-and-road-initiative.

71. Cary Huang, "Who Picks up the Trillion-Dollar Tab for China's Belt and Road?," *South China Morning Post*, May 14, 2017, https://www.scmp.com/week -asia/opinion/article/2094156/whos-picking-trillion-dollar-tab-chinas-belt-and -road.

72. "China Global Investment Tracker."

73. "China's Involvement in Global Infrastructure."

74. See "Pillar II—Supply Chains."

75. "2009 Final Results Press Conference."

76. "Annual Report 2019."

77. Sections of the preceding four paragraphs appear in Wahba, "Integrating Infrastructure in U.S. Domestic and Foreign Policy."

78. Sacks, "Countries in China's Belt and Road Initiative."

79. Freymann, *One Belt One Road*, 18–20.

80. Summer Said and Stephen Kalin, "Saudi Arabia Considers Accepting Yuan Instead of Dollars for Chinese Oil Sales," *Wall Street Journal*, March 15, 2022, https://www.wsj.com/articles/saudi-arabia-considers-accepting-yuan-instead -of-dollars-for-chinese-oil-sales-11647351541.

81. *China's Belt and Road Initiative in the Global Trade, Investment and Finance Landscape.*

82. "About CSP."

83. Freymann, *One Belt One Road*, 20.

84. Isaac Kardon, "China's Geopolitical Gambit in Gwadar," *Asia Dispatches*, October 20, 2020, https://www.wilsoncenter.org/blog-post/chinas-geopolitical -gambit-gwadar.

85. Kardon.

86. "Weaponizing the Belt and Road Initiative."

87. Lew et al., "China's Belt and Road."

88. "Port of Piraeus."

89. "Greece National Debt."

90. Van der Putten, "Chinese Investment in the Port of Piraeus, Greece."

91. "Greece's Piraeus Port Vitalized under BRI Cooperation."

92. Van der Putten, "Chinese Investment in the Port of Piraeus, Greece."

93. "Greece's Debt Crisis."

94. Angeliki Koutantou, "China's COSCO Hopes for Greek Deal on Piraeus Despite Delay—Official," Reuters, May 28, 2021, https://www.reuters.com/article/us-cosco-ship-hold-greece-piraeus/chinas-cosco-hopes-for-greek-deal-on-piraeus-despite-delay-official-idUSKCN2D91H7.

95. Van der Putten, "Chinese Investment in the Port of Piraeus, Greece."

96. Freymann, *One Belt One Road*, 242.

Chapter Eight

1. Mohamed Abou Ghazalah, CEO of Fresh Del Monte, interview with the author, October 3, 2022. All quotes from Ghazalah are from this interview.

2. The FCC estimated there were twenty-one million people without broadband in 2022, but its methodology was shown to be flawed. Busby, Tanberk, and BroadbandNow Team, "FCC Reports Broadband Unavailable to 21.3 Million Americans."

3. Stauffer et al., *How States Are Expanding Broadband Access.*

4. Federal Communications Commission, Broadband Deployment Advisory Council, *Increasing Broadband Investment in Low-Income Communities Working Group.*

5. "Broadband."

6. Cooper, "FCC Definition of Broadband."

7. "Broadband Speed Guide."

8. Nathaniel Mott, "FCC's Definition of Broadband Is Too Slow, US Watchdog Says," *PC Mag*, July 8, 2021, https://www.pcmag.com/news/fccs-definition-of-broadband-is-too-slow-us-watchdog-says.

9. Cooper, "FCC Definition of Broadband."

10. Rebecca R. Ruiz and Steve Lohr, "F.C.C. Approves Net Neutrality Rules, Classifying Broadband Internet Service as a Utility," *New York Times*, February 26, 2015, https://www.nytimes.com/2015/02/27/technology/net-neutrality-fcc-vote-internet-utility.html.

11. Dominic Rushe, "Net Neutrality Activists Score Landmark Victory in Fight to Govern the Internet," *Guardian*, February 26, 2015, https://www.theguardian.com/technology/2015/feb/26/net-neutrality-activists-landmark-victory-fcc.

12. Rushe.

13. "Short History of the Web."

14. Ghonim, *Revolution 2.0.*

15. La Rue, *Report on Promotion and Protection of the Right to Freedom of Opinion and Expression.*

16. "Internet Access Is 'a Fundamental Right,'" BBC News, March 8, 2010, http://news.bbc.co.uk/2/hi/8548190.stm.

17. "Statement of Chairman Ajit Pai Re: Restoring Internet Freedom."

18. Khalida Sarwari, "Northeastern University Researcher Finds That Wireless Networks Are Throttling Video Streaming 24/7," *Northeastern Global News*, August 27, 2019, https://news.northeastern.edu/2019/08/27/northeastern-university -researcher-finds-that-wireless-networks-are-throttling-video-streaming-24-7/.

19. Chambers, "Internet Deserts Prevent Remote Learning During COVID-19."

20. "Internet/Broadband Fact Sheet."

21. Spector, "Digging Deeper on the Pandemic Learning Loss."

22. "National Assessment of Educational Progress."

23. Schleicher, "PISA 2018 Insights and Interpretations."

24. Hanushek and Woessman, "Economic Impacts of Learning Losses."

25. "Gross Domestic Product, Fourth Quarter and Year 2022 (Advance Estimate)."

26. Dorn et al., "COVID-19 and Education."

27. Choi, Cristol, and Gimbert, "Teachers as Digital Citizens," 143–63.

28. Technological illiteracy is a wider challenge. We are already beginning to see that a generation raised with digital technology may not inherently have the skills needed to succeed in the technology sector. Though Generation Z may have been raised with smartphones and iPads, many nevertheless lack basic technological know-how—even the ability to create a spreadsheet. According to Pew Research, only 17 percent of Americans are "digitally ready," meaning they have the capacity to resolve a technological malfunction. See Vogels, "Millennials Stand Out for Their Technology Use."

29. *Report: The Impact of Broadband Speed and Price on Small Business.*

30. Ben Casselman, "Rural Areas Are Looking for Workers: They Need Broadband to Get Them," *New York Times*, May 17, 2021, https://www.nytimes.com/2021 /05/17/business/infrastructure-rural-broadband.html.

31. "Digital Divide and Economic Benefits of Broadband Access."

32. Qiang, "Broadband Infrastructure Investment in Stimulus Packages."

33. Crandall, "Charles Ferguson and the 'Broadband Problem.'"

34. "Communications Act of 1934."

35. "Communications Act of 1934."

36. Thayer, "FCC's Legal Authority to Regulate Platforms as Common Carriers."

37. Mill, *Principles of Political Economy*, 348.

38. Loeb, "Communications Act Policy Toward Competition," 14.

39. John, *Network Nation*, 360.

40. "Telecommunications Act of 1996."

41. Brotman, "Was the 1996 Telecommunications Act Successful."

42. Brotman.

43. Brodkin, "50 Million US Homes Have Only One 25Mbps Internet Provider."

44. Unfortunately, it also means funding roads to nowhere.

45. Jeb Bush, "Broadband Internet Is an Imperative, Not a Luxury," *Slate*, October 2, 2020, https://slate.com/technology/2020/10/jeb-bush-broadband-internet-investment.html.

46. Bush, "Broadband Internet Is an Imperative."

47. Bush.

48. Freeburg, *Age of Edison*, 18.

49. McBride, "Celebrating the 80th Anniversary of the Rural Electrification Administration."

50. McBride.

51. Rural Electrification Administration, *Guide for Members of Cooperatives*.

52. Today, there are 831 co-ops, which serve forty-two million Americans and provide electricity to 92 percent of US counties that suffer persistent poverty. Malone, "Rural Electrification Administration."

53. "Electric Co-op Facts & Figures."

54. Hirsh, *Powering American Farms*, 2.

55. In my view, given that the power market has become highly efficient, I am not sure these cooperatives should not be privatized.

56. "Department of Commerce's Use of Bipartisan Infrastructure Deal Funding."

57. Levin, "Broadband Bipartisanship."

58. "Governor Hochul Announces New York State ConnectALL Office Achieves Critical Milestone"; and "Governor's Broadband Development Council."

59. Stauffer et al., *How States Are Expanding Broadband Access*.

60. "ConnectMaine Receives Major Award"; "Biden-Harris Administration Awards More Than $5.5 Million to Maine"; and "Our View: Corporate Giant Tries to Kill Small Maine Town's Broadband Plans," *Portland Press Herald*, November 23, 2021, https://www.pressherald.com/2021/11/23/our-view-corporate-giant-tries-to-kill-a-small-maine-towns-broadband-plans/.

61. Ramona du Houx, "Public-Private Partnership Will Bring Fiber Broadband to Five Maine Communities," *Maine Insights*, February 4, 2022, https://maineinsights.com/2022/02/19/public-private-partnership-will-bring-fiber-broadband-to-five-maine-communities/.

62. Fischer, "FirstLight Takes Fiber into the Wilds of Maine."

63. "Maine Connectivity Authority."

64. "Our View."

65. "Leeds Town, Androscoggin County, Maine."

66. "Tale of Two Cities in Maine."

67. "Hampden Town, Penobscot County, Maine."

68. "Tale of Two Cities in Maine."

69. "Background."

70. "FCC Proposes $20.4 Billion Rural Digital Opportunity Fund."

71. "Opportunity: What RDOF Means for Electric Co-Ops."

72. Hardesty, "Biggest RDOF Winner LTD Broadband Responds to Naysayers."

73. Hardesty.

74. Cooper, "Rural Digital Opportunity Fund (RDOF)."

75. "Connect America Fund (CAF) Phase I."

76. "Connect America Fund Phase II FAQs."

77. Stauffer et al., *How States Are Expanding Broadband Access.*

78. "Charter Communications Launches Multiyear, Multibillion-Dollar Initiative."

79. Walker Orenstein, "The Feds Just Announced over $400 Million for Rural Broadband in Minnesota—Three Quarters of It Is Going to One Small Company with Limited Fiber Optic Experience," *Minneapolis Post,* December 10, 2020, https://www.minnpost.com/greater-minnesota/2020/12/the-feds-just-announced-over-400-million-for-rural-broadband-in-minnesota-three-quarters-of-it-is-going-to-one-small-company-with-limited-fiber-optic-experience/.

80. Hardesty, "Biggest RDOF Winner LTD Broadband Responds to Naysayers."

81. "FCC Rejects LTD Broadband."

82. "Frequently Asked Questions."

83. "Smart Roads Start with Smart Infrastructure."

84. "Smart Bridge Campaign."

85. Wiser et al., "Impacts of Variable Renewable Energy."

86. The preceding two paragraphs appear in Wahba, *Measuring Risk-Adjusted Returns.*

87. Clinton, *Fixing American Cybersecurity.*

88. Tim Starks and David Di Molfetta, "Court Temporarily Dunks Water Cybersecurity Initiative," *Washington Post,* July 13, 2023, https://www.washingtonpost.com/politics/2023/07/13/court-temporarily-dunks-water-cybersecurity-rule/.

89. See, for example, Bakke, *Grid;* Keeley, *Sustainable;* Edwards, *Energy Trading and Investing;* and Raiker and Adamson, *Renewable Energy Finance.*

90. Wahba, "Accelerating Sustainable Infrastructure"; and Sadek Wahba, "Can the Private Sector Bring about the 'Greening' of Infrastructure?," *Forbes,* August 17, 2021, https://www.forbes.com/sites/forbesfinancecouncil/2021/08/17/can-the-private-sector-bring-about-the-greening-of-infrastructure/?sh=29447ac84ebe.

91. Pomerantz, "Amazon Turns to Wind to Power Its Business."

92. "US Renewable Energy Factsheet."

93. Benjamin Storrow, "U.S. Renewable Energy Will Surge Past Coal and Nuclear by Year's End," *Scientific American,* November 22, 2022, https://www.scientificamerican.com/article/u-s-renewable-energy-will-surge-past-coal-and-nuclear-by-years-end/.

94. Hall, "These Charts Show Record Renewable Energy Investment in 2022."

95. "Renewable Power's Growth Is Being Turbocharged."

96. *Wind Market Reports: 2022 Edition.*

97. Pomerantz, "Amazon Turns to Wind to Power Its Business."

98. "Share of Renewables in Electricity Production."

99. "Norway Wealth Fund Invests Further in Renewable Energy," *Barron's*, January 17, 2023, https://www.barrons.com/news/norway-wealth-fund-invests-further-in-renewable-energy-01673957295.

100. Michael Schoeck, "IRA to Drive $114 Billion in US Renewable Energy Investments by 2031, Report Says," *PV Magazine*, January 19, 2023, https://pv-magazine-usa.com/2023/01/19/ira-to-drive-114-billion-in-u-s-renewable-energy-investments-by-2031-report-says/.

101. "US Inflation Reduction Act."

102. For an interesting analysis of the future of infrastructure see Gravely, *Reframing America's Infrastructure*, ch. 6.

Chapter Nine

1. Winston, *Gaining Ground*; and Winston, *Government Failure vs Market Failure.*

2. The question of path dependence is a complex topic that has been studied across the social science disciplines. For an interesting article, see Page, "Path Dependence."

3. "Robert Poole."

4. *Federal Barriers to State and Local Privatization*, 87.

5. *Federal Barriers to State and Local Privatization*, 13, 15, 19.

6. "Obituary: Albert Bilik."

7. *Federal Barriers to State and Local Privatization*, 40–41.

8. *Federal Barriers to State and Local Privatization*, 44.

9. *Federal Barriers to State and Local Privatization*, 70.

10. Poole, *Cutting Back City Hall*, 149–50.

11. Sclar, *You Don't Always Get What You Pay For*; and Sclar, "Political Economics of Investment Utopia," 1–15.

12. Sclar, *You Don't Always Get What You Pay For*, 5.

13. Sclar, xii.

14. Sclar, 4–5.

15. Sclar, 94.

16. Macky Tall, interview with the author, January 5, 2023. Additional quotations from Tall in this chapter are also from this interview.

17. Sclar, "Political Economics of Investment Utopia," 13.

18. Geddes, *Road to Renewal.*

19. Quoted in Poole, *Rethinking America's Highways*, 142.

20. See, for example, the leader of the far right movement Rasssemblement National, Marine Le Pen's, view on privatization of the French airport company ADP, in Alexandra Saint Pierre, "Pourquoi Marine Le Pen s'oppose aux privatisations,"

Boursier.com, June 18, 2018, https://www.boursier.com/actualites/economie/pourquoi-marine-le-pen-s-oppose-aux-privatisations-39024.html.

21. See, for example, Kim, "Can Alternative Service Delivery Save Cities."

22. "Federal Budget Deficit for 2011."

23. "Financial Analysis of Transportation-Related Public-Private Partnerships."

24. "Financial Analysis of Transportation-Related Public-Private Partnerships."

25. *Using Public-Private Partnerships to Carry Out Highway Projects.*

26. *Using Public-Private Partnerships to Carry Out Highway Projects.*

27. Many reviews of the performance of P3s were written in the late 1990s or the first decade of the twenty-first century and tend to conflate P3s with private finance initiatives (PFIs), which are mostly a UK phenomenon and under our definition are *not* P3s, because in a PFI almost all of the risk is borne by the state. The debate about whether PFIs performed better than the state or even met their own targets is a legitimate one, but this book does concern itself with PFIs and does not consider them as part of the privatization discussed here. I was never a supporter of PFI projects, which are principally an off-balance sheet means of financing state projects, but if one is interested, the literature is ample in terms of evaluating those types of projects.

28. For more detail see, for example, Yescombe and Farquharson, *Public-Private Partnerships for Infrastructure.*

29. See, for example, Shaoul, Stafford, and Stapleton, "Fantasy World of Private Finance for Transport." For a broad review see also Hodge and Greve, "Public-Private Partnerships: An International Performance Review," 545.

30. See Imbens and Rubin, *Causal Inference for Statistics, Social, and Biomedical Sciences*; Wahba, "Estimation of Causal Effects in Observational Studies"; and Dehejia and Wahba, "Causal Effects in Nonexperimental Studies."

31. For an intriguing exception, see Barrera-Osorio et al., "Impact of Public-Private Partnerships on Private School Performance," 429–69.

32. Dehejia and Wahba, "Propensity Score Matching Methods for Non-Experimental Causal Studies," 151–61; and Dehejia, "Experimental and Non-Experimental Methods in Development Economics," 47–69.

33. Gassner, Popov, and Pushak, "Does Private Sector Participation Improve Performance."

34. See Ballou, *Plunder*, ch. 9.

35. Verweij, van Meerkerk, and Casady, *Assessing the Performance Advantage of Public Private Partnerships.*

36. Verweij, van Meerkerk, and Casady, 221.

37. Deep, Nayyer, and Rajan, "Performance of PPP and Publicly Procured Road Projects," 156–83.

38. Deep, Nayyer, and Rajan, 176.

39. Deep, Nayyer, and Rajan, 177.

40. Albalate, Bel, and Bel-Piñana, "Evaluation of the Safety Performance of PPPs."

41. For a comprehensive study on highway tolls that includes similar results, see Samuel, "Putting Customers in the Driver's Seat."

42. Howell et al., "All Clear for Takeoff."

43. Howell et al., 5–6.

44. Ferreira and Marques, "Public-Private Partnerships in Health Care Services."

45. Duffield and Raisbeck, *Performance of PPPs and Traditional Procurement in Australia.*

46. Buso, Marty, and Tran, "Public-Private Partnerships from Budget Constraints," 56–84.

47. While not directly related to the off-balance sheet incentive, an interesting study suggests that municipalities tend to enter into P3 between election cycles and avoid them right before elections. See De la Higuera-Molina et al., "Political Hourglass."

48. James Leigland provides an excellent summary of the recent critiques of PPP away from the ideologically based arguments in "Public-Private Partnerships in Developing Countries," 103–34. He provides a summary of the major criticism leveled against PPP based on evidence and data but would not have accounted for some of the recent studies mentioned here. See also Klein, "Public-Private Partnerships."

49. *World Bank Group Support to Public Private Partnerships.*

50. *World Bank Group Support to Public Private Partnerships*, 70.

51. Saussier and Tran, "L'efficacité des contrats de partenariat en France," 81–110.

52. *Étude sur la performance des contrats de partenariat.*

53. I surveyed 1,025 respondents age eighteen and older living in the Chicago DMA. The survey sample was stratified to match census representation for age, gender, and ethnicity. The survey was fielded using the Qualtrics Insight Platform, and the panel was sourced from Lucid. Fielding was executed from January 18 to 25, 2023.

54. Wahba, "Americans and Infrastructure (2022)."

55. There has been some literature on trying to measure consumer perception of pricing of toll roads, and more recently of alternative methods of financing infrastructure. See, for example, Mostafavi, Abraham, and Vives, "Exploratory Analysis of Public Perceptions," 10–23.

56. See also Engel, Fischer, and Galetovic, "Public-Private Partnerships," for similar suggestions.

57. See Siemiatycki, Reeves, and Palcic, "Editorial: Unresolved Nature of Public-Private Partnerships," 81–84.

58. For further examples, see Silaghi and Sarkar, "Agency Problems in Public-Private Partnerships Investment Projects," 1174–91; Iossa and Martimort, "Risk Allocation and Public-Private Partnerships," 442–74; Iossa and Martimort, "Simple Microeconomics of Public-Private Partnerships," 4–48; Irwin, "Public Money for Private Infrastructure"; Irwin, "Government Guarantees"; and Martimort and Pouyet, "To Build or Not to Build," 393–411.

59. De la Torre and Rudolph, *Seven Sins of Flawed Public-Private Partnerships*.

60. Vecchi et al., *Public-Private Partnerships*.

61. See Zhao et al., "Public-Private Partnerships"; Yescombe and Farquharson, *Public-Private Partnerships for Infrastructure*; Santandrea, Bailey, and Giorgino, "Infrastructure Funding and Financing"; and Lucas and Montesinos, "Fair Value Approach for Valuing Public Infrastructure Projects."

62. Haughwout, "Infrastructure Investment as Automatic Stabilizer," 132.

63. Poole, *Rethinking America's Highways*, 149–50.

64. Poole, 149–50.

65. Flyvbjerg, Bruzelius, and Rothengatter, *Megaprojects and Risk*.

66. Flyvbjerg, Bruzelius, and Rothengatter, 102.

67. Poole, *Rethinking America's Highways*, 150.

68. Makovsek and Bridge, "Procurement Choices and Infrastructure Costs."

69. Bajari, Houghton, and Tadelis, "Bidding for Incomplete Contracts," 1288–1319.

70. Bajari, McMillan, and Tadelis, "Auction versus Negotiations in Procurement," 372–99.

71. Bajari and Tadelis, "Incentives versus Transaction Costs," 387–407.

72. Guasch, Laffont, and Straub, "Concessions of Infrastructure in Latin America," 1267–94.

73. Saussier and Tran, "L'efficacité des contrats de partenariat en France," 81–110.

74. Engel, Fischer, and Galetovic, "Public-Private Partnerships."

75. Sarmento and Renneboog, "Renegotiating Public-Private Partnerships."

76. Sarmento and Renneboog, "Anatomy of Public-Private Partnerships."

77. Danau and Vinella, "Under/Over-Investment and Early Renegotiation."

78. Russo et al., "Renegotiation in Public-Private Partnerships," 949–79.

79. Sometimes the renegotiation goes the other way when states can no longer afford to honor the terms of the P3s. See Reis and Sarmento, "'Cutting Costs to the Bone.'"

80. See Jin et al., "Determining Concession Periods and Minimum Revenue Guarantees," 512–24.

81. Mansaray et al., "Residual Government Ownership."

82. Poole, *Rethinking America's Highways*, 149–50.

83. Incidentally, that is one of the reasons the city of Chicago pushed to privatize its parking meters: it did not have the political will or ability to increase rates,

and doing so through a public-private partnership allowed the city to reap the benefit of rate hikes without paying a political price for increasing "taxes."

84. Glaeser, Gorback, and Poterba, "How Regressive Are Mobility-Related User Fees and Gasoline Taxes?"

85. Gallen and Winston, "Transportation Capital and Its Effects on the US Economy"; see also Trevor S. Gallen and Clifford Winston, "The Wrong Way to Pay for Infrastructure," *Barrons*, July 7, 2021, https://www.barrons.com/articles/the-wrong-way-to-pay-for-infrastructure-51625606077.

86. There needs to be a greater use of applied general equilibrium models to study the full effect of changes in user fees. As a side note, during my work at the World Bank I developed an applied general equilibrium model with John Whalley and Ngee-Choon Chia to study the consequences of structural adjustment policies on household income distribution. That kind of analysis could only happen in the context of an applied general equilibrium model. See Chia, Wahba, and Whalley, "Poverty Reducing Targeting Programmes," 309–38.

87. Buso, Dosi, and Moretto, "Do Exit Options Increase the Value," 721–42.

88. Phang, "Convergence of Water, Electricity and Gas Industries."

89. Cruz and Sarmento, "Reforming Traditional PPP Models," 94–114.

90. Bryan Walsh, "New York's Long and Winding Road to Congestion Pricing," *Vox*, July 5, 2023, https://www.vox.com/future-perfect/2023/7/5/23784467/new-york-city-congestion-pricing-traffic-environmental-review-climate-change-traffic-air-pollution.

91. "William Vickrey (1914–1996)." See also Vickrey, "Congestion Theory and Transport Investment."

92. David Shepardson, "New Jersey Sues to Block New York Traffic Congestion Plan," Reuters, July 21, 2023, https://www.reuters.com/legal/stuck-somewhere-jersey-nj-sues-block-new-york-city-congestion-plan-2023-07-21/.

93. Girth, "Closer Look at Contract Accountability," 317–48.

94. Istrate and Puentes, "Moving Forward on Public Private Partnerships." See also Schleicher, *In a Bad State*, 163.

95. See Baxandall, Wohlschlegel, and Dutzik, *Private Roads, Public Costs*.

96. Albalate, Bel, and Geddes, "Public-Private Partnership-Enabling Laws," 46–47.

97. Marin and Sarad, "Public Private Partnerships: USA."

98. Maskin and Tirole, "Public-Private Partnerships and Government Spending Limits," 412–20.

99. See also Schomaker, "Conceptualizing Corruption in Public Private Partnerships," 807–20.

100. Delfino, "Can Politicians Jeopardize Public-Private Partnerships," 1192–97.

101. For more analysis on accountability issues see, for example, Agyenim-Boateng, Stafford, and Stapleton, "Role of Structure in Manipulating PPP Accountability," 119–44; Forrer et al., "Public-Private Partnerships and the Public

Accountability Question," 475–84; and Girth, "Closer Look at Contract Accountability," 317–48.

102. Cusumano, Siemiatycki, and Vecchi, "Politicization of Public-Private Partnerships Following a Mega-Project Disaster," 173–89.

103. Fuentes et al., "Public-Private Partnerships in Mexico," 35–52.

104. Geddes and Reeves, "Favorability of US PPP Enabling Legislation and Private Investment," 157–65.

105. For a similar view see Marques, "Why Not Regulate PPPs?," 141–46.

106. An interesting study on wastewater treatments in Spain suggests there
is greater benefit for small communities to team up under one larger procurement system than to undertake privatization. Bel and Gradus, "Privatisation,
Contracting-out and Inter-municipal Cooperation."

107. Various platforms for infrastructure investment have been developed, such
as the Global Infrastructure Hub, created by the G20 (which includes the United
States).

108. Yescombe and Farquharson, *Public-Private Partnerships for Infrastructure*; Engel, Fischer and Galetovic, *Economics of Public-Private Partnership*. See
also Zhao et al., "Public-Private Partnerships"; Santandrea, Bailey, and Giorgino,
"Infrastructure Funding and Financing"; and Lucas and Montesinos, "Fair Value
Approach for Valuing Public Infrastructure Projects."

109. See Vecchi et al., *Public-Private Partnerships*.

110. See Sadek Wahba, "The US Needs an Infrastructure Bank that Models the
World Bank," *The Hill*, August 4, 2021, https://thehill.com/opinion/finance
/566307-the-us-needs-an-infrastructure-bank-that-models-the-world-bank/.

111. Kanter, *Move*, 223–41.

112. *Preparing United States Critical Infrastructure.*

113. Wahba, "US Needs an Infrastructure Bank."

114. See Kanter, *Move*, 251.

115. The following two paragraphs appear in Wabha, "Integrating Infrastructure
in U.S. Domestic and Foreign Policy."

116. "2019 Annual Report."

117. Lawrence Summers, "The World—Including China—Is Unprepared for the
Rise of China," *Washington Post*, November 8, 2015, https://www.washingtonpost
.com/opinions/the-world—including-china—is-unprepared-for-the-rise-of
-china/2015/11/08/70aa6c70-84ab-11e5-8ba6-cec48b74b2a7_story.html.

118. Peng and Tok, "AIIB and China's Normative Power," 736–53.

119. The twenty members are Argentina, Australia, Brazil, Canada, China,
France, Germany, India, Indonesia, Italy, Japan, Republic of Korea, Mexico, Russia,
Saudi Arabia, South Africa, Türkiye, the United Kingdom, the United States, and
the European Union.

120. "Guidance Notes on National Infrastructure Banks."

121. Brad Plumer, "How Obama's Plan for an Infrastructure Bank Would Work," *Washington Post*, September 19, 2011, https://www.washingtonpost.com/business /economy/how-obamas-plan-for-infrastructure-bank-would-work/2011/09/19 /gIQAfDgUgK_story.html.

122. "Warner, Blunt, Colleagues Reintroduce Bipartisan Bill."

123. I would like to thank my friend Michael Kumar for stimulating conversations about the IRA and alternative means to fund infrastructure.

124. Wahba, "US Infra Funding Needs More Than Just a Tax Hike."

BIBLIOGRAPHY

Abiven, Katell. "Spain's Empty Highways Lead to Bankruptcy." Phys.org. October 28, 2012. https://phys.org/news/2012-10-spain-highways-bankruptcy.html.
"About CSP: Corporate Profile." COSCO Shipping. Accessed January 15, 2023. https://ports.coscoshipping.com/en/AboutCSP/CorporateProfile/Overview/.
"About DWSD." City of Detroit. Accessed July 24, 2023. https://detroitmi.gov/departments/water-and-sewerage-department/dwsd-resources/about-dwsd#:~:text=DWSD%20has%20a%20rich%20history,1973%20under%20Detroit's%20City%20Charter.
"About NHDP." National Highways Authority of India. May 31, 2017. https://nhai.gov.in/#/about-nhdp.
"About Us." Autostrade per l'italia. Accessed July 24, 2023. https://www.autostrade.it/en/chi-siamo.
"Acts and Resolves: At the General Assembly of the Governor and Company of the English Colony of Rhode-Island and Providence Plantations in New-England in America, Begun and Held at South-Kingstown Within and for Said Colony." Water Works History. Accessed July 24, 2023. http://www.waterworkshistory.us/RI/Providence/FieldsFountainSociety1772.pdf.
"Act 44 Plan." Pennsylvania Turnpike. Accessed October 15, 2022. https://www.paturnpike.com/about-us/investor-relations/act-44-plan.
"Agreement of Lease Between the Port Authority of New York and New Jersey and Maher Terminals, Inc." Port Authority of New York & New Jersey. October 1, 2000. https://www.panynj.gov/corporate/en/transparency/port-leases.html.
Agyenim-Boateng, Cletus, Anne Stafford, and Pamela Stapleton. "The Role of Structure in Manipulating PPP Accountability." *Accounting, Auditing & Accountability Journal* 30, no. 1 (2017): 119–44.
"Air Transport, Passengers Carried—United States." World Bank. Accessed July 24, 2023. https://data.worldbank.org/indicator/IS.AIR.PSGR?locations=US.
Aircraft Accident Report. National Transportation Safety Board. August 23, 2000. https://www.ntsb.gov/investigations/AccidentReports/Reports/AAR0003.pdf.

"Airport Infrastructure Funding." Airports Council International. Accessed December 6, 2022. https://airportscouncil.org/advocacy/airport-infrastructure-funding/.

"Airport Investment Partnership Program, Formerly Airport Privatization Pilot Program." Federal Aviation Administration. August 5, 2022. https://www.faa.gov/airports/airport_compliance/privatization.

"The 'Airport Lease-to-Pay-Down-Municipal-Debt' Argument Surfaces Again—This Time in Baltimore." CAPA Centre for Aviation. February 9, 2022. https://centreforaviation.com/analysis/reports/the-airport-lease-to-pay-down-municipal-debt-argument-surfaces-again—this-time-in-baltimore-596276.

Airport Privatization: Issues and Options for Congress. Congressional Research Service. March 11, 2011. https://crsreports.congress.gov/product/pdf/R/R43545/14.

Airport Privatization: Limited Interest despite FAA's Pilot Program. US Government Accountability Office. November 2014. https://www.gao.gov/assets/gao-15-42.pdf.

Airport System Development. US Congress Office of Technology Assessment. August 1984. https://ota.fas.org/reports/8403.pdf.

"Airports Group Europe Raises Offer for Vienna Airport Stake." Airport Technology. September 27, 2022. https://www.airport-technology.com/news/airports-group-europe/.

Albalate, Daniel, Germà Bel, and Paula Bel-Piñana. "Evaluation of the Safety Performance of PPPs versus Publicly Funded and Managed Motorways in Spain." In *Assessing the Performance Advantage,* edited by Stefan Verweij, Ingmar van Meerkerk, and Carter B. Casady, 184–205. Cheltenham, UK: Edward Elgar Publishing, 2022.

Albalate, Daniel, Germà Bel, and R. Richard Geddes. "Do Public-Private Partnership-Enabling Laws Increase Private Investment in Transportation Infrastructure?" *Journal of Law and Economics* 63, no.1 (February 2020): 43–70.

Allaire, Maura, Haowei Wu, and Upmanu Lall. "National Trends in Drinking Water Quality Violations." *Proceedings of the National Academy of Sciences* 115, no. 9 (February 2018): 2078–83. https://www.pnas.org/doi/full/10.1073/pnas.1719805115#executive-summary-abstract.

Al-Madfaei, Mohammed Yousef. "The Impact of Privatisation on the Sustainability of Water Resources." IWA Publishing. Accessed July 24, 2023. https://www.iwapublishing.com/news/impact-privatisation-sustainability-water-resources.

Alter, Theodore R., Theodore E. Fuller, Vanessa Rickenbrode, Gretchen Seigworth, and Alexander Riviere. "Pennsylvania: Great Recession to Recovery?" Center for Economic and Community Development, Penn State University College of Agricultural Studies. July 2016. https://aese.psu.edu/research/centers/cecd/publications/economic-trends/pennsylvania-great-recession-to-recovery.

"American Airlines Celebrates Unveiling of New Concourse at New York's LaGuardia Airport." American Airlines. November 29, 2018. https://news.aa .com/news/news-details/2018/American-Airlines-Celebrates-Unveiling-of -New-Concourse-at-New-Yorks-LaGuardia-Airport/default.aspx.

Anderson, Michelle Wilde. "The New Minimal Cities." *Yale Law Journal* 123, no. 5 (March 2014): 1118–1227.

Angrist, Joshua. "Empirical Strategies in Economics: Illuminating the Path from Cause to Effect." *Econometrica* 90, no. 6 (November 2022): 2509–39.

Angrist, Joshua and Jörn-Steffen Pischke. *Mostly Harmless Econometrics: An Empiricist's Companion.* Princeton, NJ: Princeton University Press, 2009.

"Annual Report 2019." COSCO Shipping. Accessed July 3, 2023. https:// ports.coscoshipping.com/en/Investors/IRHome/FinancialReports/.

"AOPA Attacks Plan to Privatize New Orleans Lakefront Airport." AOPA. May 29, 2003. https://www.aopa.org/news-and-media/all-news/2003/may/29 /aopa-attacks-plan-to-privatize-new-orleans-lakefront-airport-(2).

"Applicants Selected for FY 2022 Brownfields Assessment, RLF, Cleanup (ARC) Grants and RLF Supplemental Funding." US Environmental Protection Agency. Accessed September 15, 2022. https://www.epa.gov/brownfields/applicants -selected-fy-2022-brownfields-assessment-rlf-cleanup-arc-grants-and-rlf#: ~:text=Today%20we%20are%20announcing%20that,Fund%2C%20and %20Cleanup%20Grant%20funding.

AQUASTAT. Food and Agriculture Organization of the United Nations. Accessed August 14, 2022. http://www.fao.org/nr/water/aquastat/data/query/index .html?lang=en.

Arrow, Kenneth, and Mordecai Kurz. *Public Investment, the Rate of Return and Optimal Fiscal Policy.* Baltimore, MD: Johns Hopkins University Press, 1970.

Aschauer, David A. "Is Public Expenditure Productive?" *Journal of Monetary Economics* 23 (March 1989): 177–200.

Atkinson, Robert. "Letter to House and Senate Transportation Committee Leaders Regarding Vehicle Miles Traveled (VMT) Tax." Information Technology & Innovation Foundation. March 3, 2021. https://itif.org/publications /2021/03/03/letter-house-and-senate-transportation-committee-leaders -regarding-vehicle/.

"Background." Interagency Working Group on Coal & Power Plant Communities & Economic Revitalization. Accessed January 15, 2023. https://energy communities.gov/background/.

Badlam, Justin, Stephen Clark, Suhrid Gajendragadkar, Adi Kumar, Sara O'Rourke, and Dale Swartz. "The CHIPS and Science Act: Here's What's in It." McKinsey & Company. October 4, 2022. https://www.mckinsey.com /industries/public-and-social-sector/our-insights/the-chips-and-science-act -heres-whats-in-it.

Badlam, Justin, Jared Cox, Adi Kumar, Nehal Mehta, Sara O'Rourke, and Julia Silvis. "The Inflation Reduction Act: Here's What's in It." McKinsey & Company. October 24, 2022. https://www.mckinsey.com/industries/public -and-social-sector/our-insights/the-inflation-reduction-act-heres-whats -in-it.

Baeza, María de los Ángeles, and José Manuel Vassallo. "Private Concession Contracts for Toll Roads in Spain: Analysis and Recommendations." *Public Money and Management* 30, no. 5 (2010): 299–304.

Bajari, Patrick, and Steven Tadelis. "Incentives versus Transaction Costs: A Theory of Procurement Contracts." *Rand Journal of Economics* 32, no. 3 (Autumn 2001): 387–407.

Bajari, Patrick, Stephanie Houghton, and Steven Tadelis. "Bidding for Incomplete Contracts: An Empirical Analysis of Adaptation Costs." *American Economic Review* 104, no. 4 (April 2014): 1288–1319.

Bajari, Patrick, Robert McMillan, and Steven Tadelis. "Auction versus Negotiations in Procurement: An Empirical Analysis." *Journal of Law, Economics, and Organization* 25, no. 2 (2009): 372–99.

Bakke, Gretchen. *The Grid: The Fraying Wires between Americans and Our Energy Future.* New York: Bloomsbury, 2017.

Ballou, Brendan. *Plunder: Private Equity's Plan to Pillage America.* New York: PublicAffairs, 2023.

Banerjee, Abhijit, Esther Duflo, and Nancy Qian. "On the Road: Access to Transportation Infrastructure and Economic Growth in China." *Journal of Development Economics* 145 (June 2020): 102442. https://doi.org/10.1016/j.jdeveco .2020.102442.

Banks, David A. "The Attention Economy of Authentic Cities: How Cities Behave Like Influencers." *European Planning Studies* 30, no. 1 (2022): 195–209.

Barrera-Osorio, Felipe, Pierre De Galbert, James Habyarimana, and Shwetlena Sabarwal. "The Impact of Public-Private Partnerships on Private School Performance: Evidence from a Randomized Controlled Trial in Uganda." *Economic Development and Cultural Change* 68, no. 2 (January 2020): 429–69.

Barro, Robert. "Government Spending in a Simple Model of Endogenous Growth." *Journal of Political Economy* 98, no. 5 (1990): 103–25.

Barro, Robert, and Xavier Salai-Martin. *Economic Growth.* Cambridge, MA: MIT Press, 2004.

Baskin, Jonathan Barron, and Paul J. Miranti Jr. *A History of Corporate Finance.* Cambridge: Cambridge University Press, 1997.

Baxandall, Phineas, Kari Wohlschlegel, and Tony Dutzik. *Private Roads, Public Costs: The Facts about US Toll Road Privatization and How to Protect the Public.* US PIRG Education Fund. Spring 2009. https://pirg.org/wp-content /uploads/2012/02/Private-Roads-Public-Costs-Updated_1.pdf.

"Beaver Creek Dam Rehabilitation Project." Chester County, Pennsylvania. March 2012. https://www.chesco.org/2173/CCWRA–Beaver-Creek-Dam -Rehabilitation-.

"The Beginnings of American Railroads and Mapping." Library of Congress. Accessed December 15, 2023. https://www.loc.gov/collections/railroad-maps -1828-to-1900/articles-and-essays/history-of-railroads-and-maps/the -beginnings-of-american-railroads-and-mapping/.

Bel, Germà, and Raymond Gradus. "Privatisation, Contracting-out and Inter-municipal Cooperation: New Developments in Local Public Service Delivery." *Local Government Studies* 44, no. 1 (2018): 11–21.

"Biden-Harris Administration Announces Historic Investment to America's Port and Waterway Infrastructure." White House. January 19, 2022. https://www .whitehouse.gov/briefing-room/statements-releases/2022/01/19/fact-sheet -biden-harris-administration-announces-historic-investment-to-americas -port-and-waterway-infrastructure/.

"Biden-Harris Administration Announces More Than $703 Million to Improve Port Infrastructure, Strengthen National Supply Chains, Lower Costs." US Department of Transportation Maritime Administration. October 28, 2022. https://www.maritime.dot.gov/newsroom/biden-harris-administration -announces-more-703-million-improve-port-infrastructure.

"Biden-Harris Administration Awards More Than $5.5 Million to Maine in 'Internet for All' Planning Grants." BroadbandUSA, National Telecommunications and Information Administration. December 8, 2022. https://broad bandusa.ntia.doc.gov/news/latest-news/biden-harris-administration-awards -more-55-million-maine-internet-all-planning.

"The Biden-Harris Lead Pipe and Paint Action Plan." White House. December 16, 2021. https://www.whitehouse.gov/briefing-room/statements-releases/2021 /12/16/fact-sheet-the-biden-harris-lead-pipe-and-paint-action-plan/.

"Bipartisan Infrastructure and Job Act." White House. August 2, 2021. https:// www.whitehouse.gov/briefing-room/statements-releases/2021/08/02 /updated-fact-sheet-bipartisan-infrastructure-investment-and-jobs-act/.

Bissinger, Buzz. *A Prayer for the City*. New York: Random House, 1997.

Bivens, Josh. "The Potential Macroeconomic Benefits of Increasing Infrastructure Investment." Economic Policy Institute. July 18, 2017. https://www.epi.org /publication/the-potential-macroeconomic-benefits-from-increasing -infrastructure-investment/.

Black, Dr. Alison Premo. "2022 Bridge Report." American Road & Transportation Builders Association. 2022. https://artbabridgereport.org/reports/2022 -ARTBA-Bridge-Report.pdf.

Blinken, Antony. "A Foreign Policy for the American People." State Department. March 3, 2021. https://www.state.gov/a-foreign-policy-for-the-american -people/.

"Boss Tweed." In *Britannica*. Accessed January 30, 2023. https://www.britannica .com/biography/Boss-Tweed.

Bram, Jason, Francisco E. Martínez, and Charles Steindel. "Trends and Developments in the Economy of Puerto Rico." *Current Issues in Economics and Finance* 14, no. 2 (2008). https://ssrn.com/abstract=1116247.

"Bridge Facts." Ambassador Bridge. Accessed July 24, 2023. https://www .ambassadorbridge.com/bridge-facts/.

"Bridges: Condition and Capacity." ASCE Infrastructure Report Card. 2022. https://infrastructurereportcard.org/cat-item/bridges-infrastructure.

"The British Pound Has Lost 70% of Its Value since 1987." CPI Inflation Calculator. Accessed December 6, 2022. https://www.in2013dollars.com/uk/inflation/1987.

"Broadband." US Department of Agriculture. Accessed January 15, 2023. https:// www.usda.gov/broadband.

"Broadband Speed Guide." Federal Communications Commission. July 18, 2022. https://www.fcc.gov/consumers/guides/broadband-speed-guide.

Brodkin, Jon. "50 Million US Homes Have Only One 25Mbps Internet Provider or None at All." Ars Technica. June 30, 2017. https://arstechnica.com/information -technology/2017/06/50-million-us-homes-have-only-one-25mbps-internet -provider-or-none-at-all/.

Brooks, Leah, and Zachary D. Liscow. "Can America Reduce Highway Spending? Evidence from the States." In *Economic Analysis and Infrastructure Investment*, edited by Edward L. Glaeser and James M. Poterba, 107–50. Chicago: University of Chicago Press, 2021.

Brotman, Stuart N. "Was the 1996 Telecommunications Act Successful in Promoting Competition?" Brookings Institution. February 8, 2016. https://www .brookings.edu/articles/was-the-1996-telecommunications-act-successful-in -promoting-competition/.

Bruno, Margherita. "Ever Alot Breaks Record for World's Largest Containership." Port Technology International. June 27, 2022. https://www.porttechnology.org /news/ever-alot-breaks-record-for-worlds-largest-containership/.

"Building a Better America: President Biden's Bipartisan Infrastructure Law Is Delivering in Mississippi." White House. July 2022. https://www.whitehouse.gov /wp-content/uploads/2022/08/Mississippi-BIL-Fact-Sheet.pdf.

"Building the George Washington Bridge: Washington Heights NYC." Washington Heights. October 30, 2020. https://www.washington-heights.us/george -washington-bridge/.

"Burnham Plan." In *Encyclopedia of Chicago*. 2005. http://www.encyclopedia .chicagohistory.org/pages/191.html.

Burrows, Michael, Charlynn Burd, and Brian McKenzie. *Commuting by Public Transportation in the United States: 2019*. US Census Bureau. April 2021. https://www.census.gov/content/dam/Census/library/publications/2021/acs /acs-48.pdf.

Busby, John, Julia Tanberk, and BroadbandNow Team. "FCC Reports Broadband Unavailable to 21.3 Million Americans, BroadbandNow Study Indicates 42 Million Do Not Have Access." BroadbandNow Research. May 6, 2022. https://broadbandnow.com/research/fcc-underestimates-unserved-by-50-percent.

Buso, Marco, Cesare Dosi, and Michele Moretto. "Do Exit Options Increase the Value for Money of Public-Private Partnerships?" *Journal of Economic Management Strategy* 30, no. 4 (Winter 2021): 721–42.

Buso, Marco, Frederic Marty, and Phuong Tra Tran. "Public-Private Partnerships from Budget Constraints: Looking for Debt Hiding?" *International Journal of Industrial Organization* 51 (March 2017): 56–84.

Butman, John, and Simon Targett. *New World, Inc.: The Making of America by England's Merchant Adventurers*. New York: Little, Brown, 2018.

Calderón, Cesar, and Luis Servén. "Infrastructure, Growth and Inequality: An Overview." Policy Research Working Paper no. 7034, World Bank Group, October 14, 2014. https://elibrary.worldbank.org/doi/abs/10.1596/1813-9450 -7034.

Campanelli, Bryce. "A Deep Dive on America's Ports." *Bipartisan Policy Center* (blog), July 27, 2017. https://bipartisanpolicy.org/blog/a-deep-dive-on-americas -ports/.

Campbell, Kurt. *The Pivot: The Future of American Statecraft in Asia*. New York: Hachette Book Group, 2016.

Campbell, Richard J. "Weather-Related Power Outages and Electric System Resiliency." Congressional Research Service. August 28, 2012. https://www .ourenergypolicy.org/wp-content/uploads/2016/02/R42696.pdf.

Caon, Viola. "What Role Can Private Investors Play in the US's Aviation Rebound?" Private Banker International. May 27, 2022. https://www .privatebankerinternational.com/infrastructure/what-role-can-private -investors-play-in-the-uss-aviation-rebound/.

Carlson, Justin. "Illinois Unemployment Rate Is Worst in US." Illinois Policy. October 23, 2022. https://www.illinoispolicy.org/illinois-unemployment-rate-is -worst-in-nation/.

Casale, Matt. "New Report Spotlights Wasteful Highway Boondoggles across the Country." US PIRG Education Fund. September 8, 2022. https://pirg.org /edfund/media-center/new-report-spotlights-wasteful-highway-boondoggles -across-the-country/.

"Case Study on Commercialization, Privatization and Economic Oversight of Airports and Air Navigation Services Providers: France." International Civil Aviation Organization. August 6, 2013. https://www.icao.int/sustainability /CaseStudies/France.pdf.

Cassis, Youssef, Guisseppe De Luca, and Massimo Florio, eds. *Infrastructure Finance in Europe: Insights from the History of Water, Transport, and Telecommunications*. Oxford: Oxford University Press, 2016.

CBP Trade and Travel Report. US Customs and Border Protection. April 2022. https://www.cbp.gov/sites/default/files/assets/documents/2022-Apr /FINAL%20FY2021_%20Trade%20and%20Travel%20Report%20%28508 %20Compliant%29%20%28April%202022%29_0.pdf.

Chambers, Lauren. "Internet Deserts Prevent Remote Learning during COVID-19." ACLU Data for Justice Project. May 13, 2020. https://data.aclum .org/2020/05/13/internet-deserts-prevent-remote-learning-during-covid-19/.

Chambers, Matthew, and Mindy Liu. "Maritime Trade and Transportation by the Numbers." Bureau of Transportation Statistics. March 7, 2013. https:// www.bts.gov/archive/publications/by_the_numbers/maritime_trade_and _transportation/index#figure_01.

"The Changing Structure of the Electric Power Industry: An Update." Energy Information Administration. December 1996. https://www.eia.gov/electricity /archive/056296.pdf.

"Charter Communications Launches New Multiyear, Multibillion-Dollar Initiative to Expand Broadband Availability to Over 1 Million New Customer Locations." Charter Communications. February 1, 2021. https://corporate .charter.com/newsroom/charter-communications-launches-new-multiyear -multibilliondollar-initiative-to-expand-broadband-availability-to-over-1 -million-new-customer-locations.

"Charter of the Dutch West India Company: 1621." Yale Law School Lillian Goldman Law Library. Accessed January 15, 2023. https://avalon.law.yale.edu/17th _century/westind.asp.

"Chester City Act 47 Exit Plan." Commonwealth of Pennsylvania. 2018. https:// dced.pa.gov/download/chester-city-act-47-exit-plan-adopted-2018-10-10 /?wpdmdl=88894.

Chia, Ngee-Choon, Sadek Wahba, and John Whalley. "Poverty-Reducing Targeting Programmes: A General Equilibrium Approach." *Journal of African Economies* 3, no. 2 (October 1994), 309–38.

Chiffres Cles: 2022 Key Figures. ASFA. Accessed July 24, 2023. https://www .autoroutes.fr/FCKeditor/UserFiles/File/ASFA_ChiffresCles_2022.pdf.

Chin, Gilbert. "Dating Nanjing Man." *Science* 291, no. 5506 (2001): 947.

"China—Country Commercial Guide." International Trade Administration. January 4, 2022. https://www.trade.gov/country-commercial-guides/china -environmental-technology.

"China Global Investment Tracker." American Enterprise Institute. 2022. https:// www.aei.org/china-global-investment-tracker/.

China's Belt and Road Initiative in the Global Trade, Investment and Finance Landscape. OECD Business and Finance Outlook. 2018. https://www.oecd.org /finance/Chinas-Belt-and-Road-Initiative-in-the-global-trade-investment -and-finance-landscape.pdf.

China's Economic Rise: History, Trends, Challenges and Implications for the United States. Congressional Research Service. June 25, 2019. https://sgp.fas.org/crs /row/RL33534.pdf.

"China's Involvement in Global Infrastructure." Construction Market Trends. November 30, 2019. https://www.globaldata.com/store/report/chinas -involvement-in-global-infrastructure/.

Choi, Monson, Dean Cristol, and Belinda Gimbert. "Teachers as Digital Citizens: The Influence of Individual Backgrounds, Internet Use and Psychological Characteristics on Teachers' Levels of Digital Citizenship." *Computer and Education* 121 (June 2018): 143–61. https://www.sciencedirect.com/science/article /abs/pii/S0360131518300587.

City of Chicago Comprehensive Annual Financial Report. City of Chicago. 2003. https://www.chicago.gov/content/dam/city/depts/fin/supp_info/CAFR/2003 /CAFR_2003.pdf.

"City of Indianapolis Sells Water and Wastewater Utilities to Citizens Energy Group." Faegre Drinker. August 2011. https://www.faegredrinker.com/en/services /experience/2011/8/city-of-indianapolis-sells-water-and-wastewater-ut.

"City of Philadelphia Closing Philadelphia Nursing Home." City of Philadelphia. June 14, 2022. https://www.phila.gov/2022-06-14-city-of-philadelphia-closing -philadelphia-nursing-home/.

"City of St. Louis Ends Fiscal Year 2021 with $32 Million Surplus." City of St. Louis. August 27, 2021. https://www.stlouis-mo.gov/government/departments /comptroller/news/fy21-year-end.cfm.

"City of St. Louis Ends Fiscal Year 2022 with $49 Million Surplus." City of St. Louis. September 9, 2022. https://www.stlouis-mo.gov/government /departments/comptroller/news/city-fiscal-year-2022-surplus.cfm.

Clark, Anna. *The Poisoned City.* New York: Metropolitan Books, 2018.

Clinton, Larry, ed. *Fixing American Cybersecurity: Creating a Strategic Public-Private Partnership.* Washington, DC: Georgetown University Press, 2023.

Clinton, William J. "Statement on Signing the Federal Aviation Reauthorization Act of 1996." October 9, 1996. The American Presidency Project. Accessed July 24, 2023. https://www.presidency.ucsb.edu/documents/statement-signing -the-federal-aviation-reauthorization-act-1996.

Clulow, Adam, and Tristan Mostert, eds. *The Dutch and English East India Companies: Diplomacy, Trade and Violence in Early Modern Asia.* Amsterdam: Amsterdam University Press, 2018.

Coase, Ronald. "The Lighthouse in Economics." *Journal of Law and Economics* 17, no. 2 (October 1974): 357–76.

Colvile, Robert. "Knee-Jerk Nationalisers Have No Idea How the Water Industry Actually Works." CAPX. August 15, 2022. https://capx.co/knee-jerk -nationalisers-have-no-idea-how-the-water-industry-actually-works/.

"Communications Act of 1934, The." Federal Communications Commission. 1934. https://www.nsa.gov/portals/75/documents/news-features/declassified -documents/friedman-documents/reports-research/FOLDER_047 /41786769082578.pdf.

"Comparison of House Infrastructure Bills: Private Bank v. Government Owned Entities." Federal Infrastructure Bank. 2020. https://federalinfrastructurebank .com/wp-content/uploads/Bill-Comparison-Summary-Private-vs. -Government-Owned-Proposals-07-15-20-v2.pdf.

Comprehensive Annual Financial Report, 2018. City of St. Louis. 2018. https:// www.stlouis-mo.gov/government/departments/comptroller/documents /upload/CityofStLouisMO_CAFR-FY18.PDF.

"Confederation Bridge." Vinci Concessions. Accessed October 14, 2022. https:// www.vinci-concessions.com/en/infrastructure/confederation-bridge.

"Connect America Fund (CAF) Phase I." Federal Communications Commission. July 26, 2012. https://www.fcc.gov/reports-research/maps/connect-america -fund-caf-phase-i/.

"Connect America Fund Phase II FAQs." Federal Communications Commission. December 30, 2019. https://www.fcc.gov/consumers/guides/connect-america -fund-phase-ii-faqs.

"Connecting Industries in Norway through Sustainable Infrastructure." Macquarie. Accessed October 14, 2022. https://www.macquarie.com/us/en /impact/case-studies/connecting-norway-industries-through-sustainable -infrastructure.html.

"Connectivity." Miami-Dade Beacon Council. Accessed July 24, 2023. https://www .beaconcouncil.com/data/economic-overview/connectivity/.

"ConnectMaine Receives Major Award to Connect Dozens of Rural Communities." Maine Department of Economic & Community Development. February 25, 2022. https://www.maine.gov/decd/about/news/connectmaine-receives -major-award-connect-dozens-rural-communities.

"A Conversation on the Indo-Pacific Economic Framework with Secretary of Commerce Gina Raimondo." The Wilson Center. July 25, 2023. https://www .wilsoncenter.org/event/conversation-indo-pacific-economic-framework -secretary-commerce-gina-raimondo.

Cook, Wesley, Paul J. Barr, and Marvin W. Halling. "Bridge Failure Rate." *Journal of Performance of Constructed Facilities* 29, no. 3 (2015). https://doi.org/10.1061 /(ASCE)CF.1943-5509.0000571.

Cooper, Tyler. "The FCC Definition of Broadband: Analysis and History." BroadbandNow Research. February 10, 2018. https://broadbandnow.com/report/fcc -broadband-definition/.

———. "Rural Digital Opportunity Fund (RDOF)—Map, Auction and Analysis." BroadbandNow Research. February 9, 2021. https://broadbandnow.com/report /rural-digital-opportunity-fund/.

"Country Case Study: The United States." Public-Private Partnership Infrastructure Advisory Facility. March 2009. https://ppiaf.org/sites/ppiaf.org/files /documents/toolkits/highwaystoolkit-russian/6/pdf-version/us.pdf.

"County of Chester, 2022 Approved Budget." County of Chester Finance Department. December 16, 2021. https://www.chesco.org/DocumentCenter/View /67474/County-of-Chester-2022-Approved-Budget.

Cox, Jonson. *Reflections on the Regulation of the UK Water Sector*. Water Services Regulation Authority (Ofwat). July 2018.

"CPP Investments to Acquire Ports America Interest from Oaktree." CPP Investments. Accessed July 24, 2023. https://www.cppinvestments.com/public -media/headlines/2021/cpp-investments-to-acquire-ports-america-interest -from-oaktree/.

Crandall, Robert W. "Charles Ferguson and the 'Broadband Problem.'" Brookings Institution. May 15, 2004. https://www.brookings.edu/research/charles -ferguson-and-the-broadband-problem/.

"Critical Infrastructure Protection in the Digital Age." *Federal Register*, October 18, 2001. https://www.govinfo.gov/content/pkg/FR-2001-10-18/pdf/01-26509.pdf.

Cruz, Carlos Oliveira, and Joaquim Miranda Sarmento. "Reforming Traditional PPP Models to Cope with the Challenges of Smart Cities." *Competition and Regulation in Network Industries* 18, nos. 1–2 (2017): 94–114.

Cudahy, Richard D. "Return on Investment and Fairness in Regulation." *Public Utilities Fortnightly* 123, no. 3 (February 1989): 19–23.

Cusumano, Niccolò, Matti Siemiatycki, and Veronica Vecchi. "The Politicization of Public-Private Partnerships Following a Mega-Project Disaster: The Case of the Morandi Bridge Collapse." *Journal of Economic Policy Reform* 25, no. 2 (2022): 173–89.

Dahl, Robert. *Who Governs? Democracy and Power in an American City*. New Haven, CT: Yale University Press, 1961.

Dakelman, Mitchell E., and Neal A. Schorr. *The Pennsylvania Turnpike*. Chicago: Arcadia, 2004.

Dale, Richard. *The First Crash: Lessons from the South Sea Bubble*. Princeton, NJ: Princeton University Press, 2004.

Daley, Richard M. "Mayor Richard M. Daley Inaugural Address, 2003." Chicago Public Library. May 5, 2003. https://www.chipublib.org/mayor-richard-m -daley-inaugural-address-2003/.

Danau, Daniel, and Annalisa Vinella. "Under/Over-Investment and Early Renegotiation in Public-Private Partnerships." *Journal of Industrial Economics* 69, no. 4 (2021): 923–66.

Davis, Jeff. "Study Commissioned by Congress Recommends Increasing Airport PFC Cap by $3 per Passenger." Eno Center for Transportation. January 16, 2020. https://www.enotrans.org/article/study-commissioned-by-congress -recommends-increasing-airport-pfc-cap-by-3-per-passenger/.

de la Higuera-Molina, Emilio J., Marc Esteve, Ana M. Plata-Díaz, and José L. Zafra-Gómez. "The Political Hourglass: Opportunistic Behavior in Local Government Policy Decisions." *International Public Management Journal* 25, no. 5 (2022): 767–84. http://doi.org/10.1080/10967494.2021.1905117.

De la Peña, Eduardo. "A Tale of Two Airports: Public vs. Private." *World Bank Blogs*, October 25, 2018. https://blogs.worldbank.org/ppps/tale-two-airports -public-vs-private.

De la Torre, Augusto and Heinz Rudolph. *The Seven Sins of Flawed Public-Private Partnerships.* Washington, DC: World Bank, 2020.

De Luca, Guisseppe. "Infrastructure Financing in Medieval Europe: On and Beyond 'Roman Ways.'" In *Infrastructure Finance in Europe: Insights from the History of Water, Transport, and Telecommunications*, edited by Youssef Cassis, Guisseppe De Luca, and Massimo Florio, 39–60. Oxford: Oxford University Press, 2016.

DeCotis, Paul A. "PURPA Reform Implications for Utilities and Climate Change." *Natural Gas & Electricity* 36, no. 4 (2019): 17–20. https://doi.org/10.1002/gas .22144.

Deep, Akash, Mojahedul Islam Nayyer, and Thillai Rajan. "The Performance of PPP and Publicly Procured Road Projects: Evidence from India." In *Assessing the Performance Advantage of Public Private Partnerships: A Comparative Perspective*, edited by Stefan Werweij, Ingmar van Meerkerk, and Carter B. Casady, 156–83. Cheltenham, UK: Elgar, 2022.

Dehejia, Rajeev. "Experimental and Non-Experimental Methods in Development Economics: The Porous Dialectic." *Journal of Globalization and Development* 6, no. 1 (2015): 47–69.

Dehejia, Rajeev H., and Sadek Wahba. "Causal Effects in Nonexperimental Studies: Reevaluating the Evaluation of Training Programs." *Journal of American Statistical Association* 94, no. 448 (1999): 1053–62.

———. "Propensity Score Matching Methods for Nonexperimental Causal Studies." *Review of Economics and Statistics* 84, no. 1 (2002): 151–61.

Delfino, Gianluca F. "Can Politicians Jeopardize Public-Private Partnerships: The Case of the Mottarone Cable Car Crash." *Public Administration Review* 82, no. 6 (2022): 1192–97.

den Heijer, Henk. "A Public and Private Dutch West India Interest." In *Dutch Atlantic Connections, 1680–1800*, edited by Gert Oostindie and Jessica V. Roitman, 159–82. Leiden: Brill, 2014. https://doi.org/10.1163/9789004271319 _009.

"Department of Commerce's Use of Bipartisan Infrastructure Deal Funding to Help Close the Digital Divide." US Department of Commerce. November 10, 2021. https://www.commerce.gov/news/fact-sheets/2021/11/fact-sheet -department-commerces-use-bipartisan-infrastructure-deal-funding.

Development of PPP in China: Infancy to Prevalence. PwC Internal Report. November 2022.

The Development of the Water Industry in England and Wales. Ofwat. 2006. https://www.ofwat.gov.uk/wp-content/uploads/2015/11/rpt_com _devwatindust270106.pdf.

Deye, Andrew. "US Infrastructure PPPs: Ready for Takeoff?" World Bank. September 25, 2015. https://www.worldbank.org/en/news/opinion/2015/09/25/us -infrastructure-ppps-ready-for-takeoff.

"The Digital Divide and Economic Benefits of Broadband Access." White House Council of Economic Advisers. March 2016. https://obamawhitehouse .archives.gov/sites/default/files/page/files/20160308_broadband_cea_issue _brief.pdf.

"Documentary History of American Waterworks: Boston, Massachusetts." Water Works History. Accessed July 24, 2023. http://www.waterworkshistory.us/MA /Boston/.

"Documentary History of American Waterworks: Detroit, Michigan." Water Works History. Accessed March 14, 2023. http://www.waterworkshistory.us /MI/Detroit/#:~:text=Wells%20completed%20the%20works%2C%20which ,Hydraulic%20Company%2C%20probably%20in%201829.

"Documentary History of American Waterworks: Providence, Rhode Island." Water Works History. Accessed September 4, 2022. http://www.waterworks history.us/RI/Providence/.

Dore, Mohammed H. I., Joseph Kushner, and Klemen Zumer. "Privatization of Water in the UK and France—What Can We Learn?" *Utilities Policy* 12, no. 1 (2004): 41–50.

Dorn, Emma, Bryan Hancock, Jimmy Sarakatsannis, and Ellen Viruleg. "COVID-19 and Education: The Lingering Effects of Unfinished Learning." McKinsey & Company. July 27, 2021. https://www.mckinsey.com/industries /education/our-insights/covid-19-and-education-the-lingering-effects-of -unfinished-learning.

Douglas, Rebecca. "Midway Privatization in Final Phase." Airport Improvement. January/February 2009. https://airportimprovement.com/article/midway -privatization-final-phase.

"Downtown Garment District Coming Back to Life." City of St. Louis. May 22, 2018. https://www.stlouis-mo.gov/government/departments/sldc/news /downtown-garment-district-coming-back-to-life.cfm.

"Driven by Dollars." Pew Center on the States. 2009. https://www.pewtrusts .org/-/media/legacy/uploadedfiles/wwwpewtrustsorg/reports/state_policy /paturnpikefinalwebpdf.pdf.

Duffield, Colin, and Colin Raisbeck. *Performance of PPPs and Traditional Procurement in Australia: Final Report to Infrastructure Partnerships Australia.*

The Allen Consulting Group and University of Melbourne. 2007. https://
infrastructure.org.au/wp-content/uploads/2016/12/IPA_PPP_FINAL.pdf.

Duran, Xavier. "The First US Transcontinental Railroad: Expected Profits and
Government Intervention." *Journal of Economic History* 73, no. 1 (March 2013):
177–200.

Dutzik, Tony, Brian Imus, and Phineas Baxandall. "Privatization and the Public
Interest." Frontier Group. October 1, 2009. https://frontiergroup.org/resources
/privatization-and-public-interest/.

Dyble, Louise Nelson. "Chicago and Its Skyway: Lessons from an Urban Mega-
Project." In *Infrastructure and Land Policies*, edited by Gregory K. Ingram and
Karin L. Brandt, 189–211. New York: Columbia University Press, 2013.

"Early Years." Pennsylvania Turnpike. Accessed October 15, 2022. https://www
.pahighways.com/toll/PATurnpike.html.

Ebenstein, Lanny. *Milton Freidman: A Biography*. New York: Palgrave Macmillan,
2007.

The Economic Regulation of the Water Sector. UK National Audit Office. October 14, 2015. https://www.nao.org.uk/wp-content/uploads/2014/07/The
-economic-regulation-of-the-water-sector.pdf.

"Economic Research." Federal Reserve of St. Louis. Accessed March 14, 2023.
https://fred.stlouisfed.org/.

Economy, Elizabeth C. *The Third Revolution: Xi Jinping and the New Chinese
State*. Oxford: Oxford University Press, 2019.

Edelman, T., and M. Edelman. *CMA Report: Privatization of County-Owned Nursing Facilities Is Not Good for Residents, Staff, or States*. Center for Medicare
Advocacy. October 21, 2021. https://medicareadvocacy.org/cma-report
-privatization-10-2022/.

Edwards, Davis. *Energy Trading and Investing: Trading, Risk Management, and
Structuring Deals in the Energy Market*. New York: McGraw, 2017.

Eisinger, Peter K. *The Rise of the Entrepreneurial State: State and Local Economic
Development in the United States*. Madison: University of Wisconsin Press,
1988.

"Electric Co-op Facts & Figures." NRECA. April 28, 2022. https://www.electric
.coop/electric-cooperative-fact-sheet.

"Electricity 101." Department of Energy. Accessed June 29, 2023. https://www
.energy.gov/oe/information-center/educational-resources/electricity-101#who
%20owns%20the%20electric%20system.

"Electricity Prices by Year and Adjusted for Inflation." US Inflation Calculator. Accessed July 24, 2023. https://www.usinflationcalculator.com/inflation
/electricity-prices-adjusted-for-inflation/.

Elliott, Dan, Annabelle Ong, and Chris Cuttle. "Coming Down to Earth." Frontier Economics. 2019. https://www.frontier-economics.com/uk/en/news-and
-articles/articles/article-i6391-coming-down-to-earth/.

Engel, Eduardo, Ronald Fischer, and Alexander Galetovic. *The Economics of Public-Private Partnerships: A Basic Guide*. Cambridge: Cambridge University Press, 2014.

———. "Public-Private Partnerships: Some Lessons after 30 Years." Cato Institute. Fall 2020. https://www.cato.org/regulation/fall-2020/public-private-partnerships-some-lessons-after-30-years.

———. "Soft Budgets and Endogenous Renegotiations in Transport PPPs: An Equilibrium Analysis." *Economics of Transportation* 17 (March 2019): 40–50.

Enright, Dennis J. *The Chicago Skyway Sale: An Analytical Review*. International Bridge, Tunnel & Turnpike Association. 2006. https://www.ibtta.org/sites/default/files/unrestricted/38250_Section1.pdf.

"Environmental Protection Agency." USAspending.gov. September 29, 2022. https://www.usaspending.gov/agency/environmental-protection-agency?fy=2022.

"EPA Organization Chart." US Environmental Protection Agency. Accessed July 24, 2023. https://www.epa.gov/aboutepa/epa-organization-chart.

Estrin, Saul, and Adeline Pelletier. "Privatization in Developing Countries: What Are the Lessons of Recent Experience?" *World Bank Research Observer* 33, no. 1 (2018): 65–102. https://doi.org/10.1093/wbro/lkx007.

Étude sur la performance des contrats de partenariat. PriceWaterHouseCoopers, 2011.

"Expressways." In *Encyclopedia of Chicago*. 2005. http://www.encyclopedia.chicagohistory.org/pages/440.html.

Fair, Ray C. "U.S. Infrastructure: 1929–2019." Discussion Paper No. 2187, Cowles Foundation, July 2019. https://papers.ssrn.com/sol3/papers.cfm?abstract_id=3432670.

"FCC Proposes $20.4 Billion Rural Digital Opportunity Fund." Federal Communications Commission. August 2, 2019. https://www.fcc.gov/document/fcc-proposes-204-billion-rural-digital-opportunity-fund-0.

"FCC Rejects LTD Broadband, Starlink Bids for Broadband Subsidies." Federal Communications Commission. August 10, 2022. https://www.fcc.gov/document/fcc-rejects-ltd-broadband-starlink-bids-broadband-subsidies.

"FDI Statistics: An Overview of Foreign Direct Investment Trends Happening in PA." Pennsylvania Department of Community and Economic Development. Accessed March 14, 2023. https://dced.pa.gov/business-assistance/international/fdi-statistics/.

Federal Barriers to State and Local Privatization: Hearing Before the Joint Economic Committee, 104th Cong. (1996). https://www.jec.senate.gov/reports/104th%20Congress/Federal%20Barriers%20to%20State%20and%20Local%20Privatization%20(1661).pdf.

"The Federal Budget Deficit for 2011—$1.3 Trillion." Congressional Budget Office. October 7, 2011. https://www.cbo.gov/publication/42532.

Federal Communications Commission, Broadband Deployment Advisory Council. *Increasing Broadband Investment in Low-Income Communities Working Group.* December 2020. https://www.fcc.gov/sites/default/files/bdac-low-income-communities-approved-rec-12172020.pdf.

"Federal Grants to Amtrak." US Department of Transportation, Federal Railroad Administration. March 14, 2023. https://railroads.dot.gov/grants-loans/directed-grant-programs/federal-grants-amtrak.

"Federal Reserve Economic Data." Federal Reserve of St. Louis. Accessed March 14, 2023. https://fred.stlouisfed.org/series/SLGSDODNS.

Feigenbaum, Baruch, and Mae Baltz. *2022 Annual Privatization Report: Surface Transportation.* Reason Foundation. May 2022. https://reason.org/wp-content/uploads/annual-privatization-report-2022-surface-transportation.pdf.

Fernald, John G. "Roads to Prosperity? Assessing the Link between Public Capital and Productivity." *American Economic Review* 89, no. 3 (June 1999): 619–38.

Ferreira, D. C., and R. C. Marques. "Public-Private Partnerships in Health Care Services: Do They Outperform Public Hospitals Regarding Quality and Access? Evidence from Portugal." *Socio-Economic Planning Sciences* 73 (February 2021). https://doi.org/10.1016/j.seps.2020.100798.

"Financial Analysis of Transportation-Related Public-Private Partnerships." Office of Inspector General, Department of Transportation. July 28, 2011. https://www.oig.dot.gov/sites/default/files/PPP%20Final%20Report%207-28-2011%20508%20PDF.pdf.

"Financial Statements." Port Authority of New York & New Jersey. Accessed July 24, 2023. https://www.panynj.gov/corporate/en/financial-information/financial-statement.html.

"Fiscal Year 2022–2023 Proposed Budget." Los Angeles World Airports. June 2, 2022. https://www.lawa.org/lawa-investor-relations.

Fischer, Karen. "FirstLight Takes Fiber into the Wilds of Maine." Fierce Telecom. December 12, 2022. https://www.fiercetelecom.com/broadband/firstlight-takes-fiber-wilds-maine.

Fishback, Price. "How Successful Was the New Deal? The Microeconomic Impact of New Deal Spending and Lending Policies in the 1930s." *Journal of Economic Literature* 55, no. 4 (December 2017): 1435–85.

Fisher, Ronald C. "Infrastructure Investment and Financing for the 2019 Incoming Gubernatorial Administration." White Paper, Michigan State University. 2018. https://www.canr.msu.edu/michiganpolicyguide/uploads/files/11-21%20infrastructure-fischer%20final.pdf.

"Fitch Affirms Lambert-St. Louis Int'l Airport (MO) at 'BBB+'; Outlook Revised to Positive." Fitch Ratings. November 7, 2016. https://www.fitchratings.com/research/us-public-finance/fitch-affirms-lambert-st-louis-int-l-airport-mo-at-bbb-outlook-revised-to-positive-07-11-2016.

Flyvbjerg, Bent, Nils Bruzelius, and Werner Rothengatter. *Megaprojects and Risk: An Anatomy of Ambition*. Cambridge: Cambridge University Press, 2003.

"For Whom the Road Tolls: Corporate Asset or Public Good; An Analysis of Financial and Strategic Alternatives for the Pennsylvania Turnpike." Pennsylvania House of Representatives, Democratic Caucus, 2008.

Forrer, John, James E. Kee, Kathryn E. Newcomer, and Eric J. Boyer. "Public-Private Partnerships and the Public Accountability Question." *Public Administration Review* 70, no. 3 (2010): 475–84.

Fox-Penner, Peter S. "Regulating Independent Power Producers: Lessons of the PURPA Approach." *Resources and Energy* 12, no. 1 (April 1990): 117–41.

Freeburg, Ernest. *The Age of Edison: Electric Light and the Invention of Modern America*. New York: Penguin, 2014.

FreightWaves Staff. "DP World Sells U.S. Terminals to AIG." FreightWaves. March 2, 2019. https://www.freightwaves.com/news/dp-world-sells-u-s-terminals-to-aig.

———. "Rendell Chooses Morgan Stanley to Advise on Turnpike Sale." American Shipper, March 30, 2007. https://www.freightwaves.com/news/rendell-chooses-morgan-stanley-to-advise-on-turnpike-sale.

"Frequently Asked Questions." US Energy Information Administration. November 8, 2022. https://www.eia.gov/tools/faqs/faq.php?id=92&t=4#:~.

Freymann, Eyck. *One Belt One Road: Chinese Power Meets the World*. Cambridge, MA: Harvard University Asia Center, 2020.

Fu, Tao, Zhong Chang, Lijin Miao, Michael Sievers, Sven-Uwe Geissen, and Movva Reddy. *Reform of China's Urban Water Sector*. London: International Water Association Publishing, 2008.

Fuentes, Hugo J., Gustavo Mendoza, Miguel A. Montoya, and Ismael Aguilar. "Public-Private Partnerships in Mexico: Challenges and Opportunities at Local Level." *Competition and Regulation in Network Industries* 22, no. 1 (2021): 35–52.

"FY 2022 Company Profile." Amtrak. September 30, 2022. https://www.amtrak.com/content/dam/projects/dotcom/english/public/documents/corporate/nationalfactsheets/Amtrak-Company-Profile-FY2022-072523.pdf.

Galiani, Sebastian, Paul Gertler, and Ernesto Schargrodsky. "Water for Life: The Impact of Privatization of Water Services on Child Mortality." *Journal of Political Economy* 113, no. 1 (2005): 83–120.

Gallen, Trevor S., and Clifford Winston. "Transportation Capital and Its Effects on the US Economy: A General Equilibrium Approach." *Journal of Macroeconomics* 69 (2021). https://doi.org/10.1016/j.jmacro.2021.103334.

Garg, Swapnil, and Madhukar Dayal. "Road Learnings: Evolution of Public-Private Partnerships in the Indian Highway Sector." *Transportation Research Procedia* 48 (2020): 2488–2510.

Gaspar, Vitor, Paolo Mauro, Catherine Pattillo, and Raphael Espinoza. "Public Investment for the Recovery." *International Monetary Fund Blog*, October 5, 2020. https://www.imf.org/en/Blogs/Articles/2020/10/05/blog-public -investment-for-the-recovery.

Gassner, Katharina, Alexander Popov, and Nataliya Pushak. "Does Private Sector Participation Improve Performance in Electricity and Water Distribution?" World Bank. 2009. https://openknowledge.worldbank.org/server/api/core /bitstreams/859c9379-5254-5c7b-b4f7-0e2206f13f36/content.

Geddes, R. Richard. *The Road to Renewal: Private Investment in U.S. Transportation Infrastructure.* Washington, DC: American Enterprise Press, 2011.

Geddes, R. Richard, and Eoin Reeves. "The Favorability of US PPP Enabling Legislation and Private Investment in Transportation Infrastructure?" *Utilities Policy* 48 (October 2017): 157–65.

"George Washington Bridge: Historical Overview." George Washington Bridge. Accessed January 15, 2023. http://www.nycroads.com/crossings/george -washington/.

Ghonim, Wael. *Revolution 2.0.* New York: Houghton Mifflin Harcourt, 2012.

Gilroy, Leonard. "Feds to Reject PA Turnpike Commission's 1-80 Toll Plan." Reason Foundation. September 10, 2008. https://reason.org/commentary/feds -to-reject-pa-turnpike-com/.

Girth, Amanda M. "A Closer Look at Contract Accountability: Exploring the Determinants of Sanctions for Unsatisfactory Contract Performance." *Journal of Public Administration Research and Theory* 24, no. 2 (2014): 317–48.

Glaeser, Edward L., Caitlin S. Gorback, and James M. Poterba. "How Regressive Are Mobility-Related User Fees and Gasoline Taxes?" *Tax Policy and the Economy* 37 (2023). http://doi.org/10.3386/w30746.

"Global Container Freight Rate Index from January 2019 to November 2022." Statista. December 7, 2022. https://www.statista.com/statistics/1250636/global -container-freight-index/ (site discontinued).

"Global Infrastructure Hub." Global Infrastructure Hub. Accessed April 11, 2023. https://www.gihub.org/.

"Goethals Bridge Replacement—Staten Island, NY to Elizabeth, NJ." Parsons. Accessed July 24, 2023. https://www.parsons.com/project/goethals-bridge -replacement-staten-island-ny-elizabeth-nj/.

Goldsmith, Hugh. "Actors and Innovations in the Evolution of Infrastructure Services." In *Economics of Infrastructure Provisioning: The Changing Role of the State*, edited by Arnold Picot, Massimo Florio, Nico Grove, and Johann Kranz, 23–93. Cambridge, MA: MIT Press, 2015.

"Governor Hochul Announces Groundbreaking of $9.5 Billion New Terminal One in a Major Step Forward for Port Authority's JFK Transformation." Governor Kathy Hochul. September 22, 2022. https://www.governor.ny.gov/news

/governor-hochul-announces-groundbreaking-95-billion-new-terminal-one
-major-step-forward-port.

"Governor Hochul Announces New York State ConnectALL Office Achieves Critical Milestone with $7 Million in Federal Grants." New York State Office of the Governor. December 12, 2022. https://www.governor.ny.gov/news/governor -hochul-announces-new-york-state-connectall-office-achieves-critical -milestone-7.

"Governor Rendell Proposes Budget with No Tax Increase, More Money for Public Schools, Strategy for Jobs, Plan to Address Future Deficits." Pennsylvania Office of the Governor. February 9, 2010. https://www.prnewswire.com /news-releases/governor-rendell-proposes-budget-with-no-tax-increase-more -money-for-public-schools-strategy-for-jobs-plan-to-address-future-deficits -83890207.html.

"Governor's Broadband Development Council." Texas Economic Development. Accessed July 24, 2023. https://gov.texas.gov/business/page/governors -broadband-development-council.

Graham, Anne. "Airport Privatisation: A Successful Journey?" *Journal of Air Transportation Management* 89 (October 2020). https://doi.org/10.1016/j .jairtraman.2020.101930.

Gravely, Marc. *Reframing America's Infrastructure: A Ruins to Renaissance Playbook.* Vancouver, BC: Sutton Hart Press, 2022.

"Greece National Debt." Country Economy. Accessed July 24, 2023. https:// countryeconomy.com/national-debt/greece?year=2009.

"Greece's Debt Crisis." Council on Foreign Relations. Accessed July 24, 2023. https://www.cfr.org/timeline/greeces-debt-crisis-timeline.

"Greece's Piraeus Port Vitalized under BRI Cooperation." People's Republic of China National Development and Reform Commission. December 30, 2021. https://en.ndrc.gov.cn/news/mediarusources/202112/t20211231_1311182 .html.

Green, Amy. *Moving Water: The Everglades and Big Sugar.* Baltimore, MD: Johns Hopkins University Press, 2021.

Green, Richard K. "Airports and Economic Development." *Real Estate Economics* 35, no. 1 (2007): 91–112. https://doi.org/10.1111/j.1540-6229.2007.00183.x.

"The Green New Deal." Bernie Sanders. Accessed March 14, 2023. https:// berniesanders.com/issues/green-new-deal/.

Greene, George Washington. *The Life and Voyages of Verrazzano.* Cambridge, MA: Folsom, Wells, and Thurston, 1837.

Gresser, Ed. "PPI's Trade Fact of the Week: World Shipping Container Capacity Has Grown Six-Fold Since 2000." *PPI* (blog), July 13, 2022. https://www .progressivepolicy.org/blogs/ppis-trade-fact-of-the-week-world-shipping -container-capacity-has-grown-six-fold-since-2000/.

"Gross Domestic Product, Fourth Quarter and Year 2022 (Advance Estimate)." Bureau of Economic Analysis. January 26, 2023. https://www.bea.gov/news/2023/gross-domestic-product-fourth-quarter-and-year-2022-advance-estimate.

Guasch, J. Luis, Jean-Jacques Laffont, and Stéphane Straub. "Concessions of Infrastructure in Latin America: Government Led Renegotiation." *Journal of Applied Econometrics* 22, no. 7 (2007): 1267–94.

"Guidance Notes on National Infrastructure Banks and Similar Financing Facilities." Global Infrastructure Hub and Cambridge Economic Policy Associates. April 2019. https://www.gihub.org/nibs.

Hall, Keith, and Robert Green. "Beyond Unemployment: Pennsylvania's Sluggish Labor Market." Mercatus Center. June 12, 2013. https://www.mercatus.org/publications/urban-economics/beyond-unemployment-pennsylvanias-sluggish-labor-market.

Hall, Stephen. "These Charts Show Record Renewable Energy Investment in 2022." World Economic Forum. July 7, 2022. https://www.weforum.org/agenda/2022/07/global-renewable-energy-investment-iea/.

"Hampden Town, Penobscot County, Maine." US Census Bureau. 2022. https://data.census.gov/profile?g=0600000US2301930795.

Handbook of Statistics 2023. United Nations Conference on Trade and Development. December 14, 2023. https://unctad.org/system/files/official-document/tdstat48_en.pdf.

Hanushek, Eric A., and Ludger Woessman. "The Economic Impacts of Learning Losses." OECD. September 2020. https://www.oecd.org/education/The-economic-impacts-of-coronavirus-covid-19-learning-losses.pdf.

Hardesty, Linda. "The Biggest RDOF Winner LTD Broadband Responds to Naysayers." Fierce Telecom. February 11, 2021. https://www.fiercetelecom.com/telecom/biggest-rdof-winner-ltd-broadband-responds-to-naysayers.

Harvey, David. "From Managerialism to Entrepreneurialism: The Transformation in Urban Governance in Late Capitalism." *Geografiska Annaler* 71, no. 1 (1989): 3–17.

Haughwout, Andrew. "Infrastructure Investment as Automatic Stabilizer." Hamilton Project. May 16, 2019. https://www.hamiltonproject.org/papers/infrastructure_investment_as_an_automatic_stabilizer.

Hearing Before the US House of Representatives Committee on Transportation & Infrastructure Subcommittee on Railroads, Pipelines, and Hazardous Materials. 116th Cong. (2020). Testimony of William Flynn, President and Chief Executive Officer National Railroad Passenger Corporation. https://www.amtrak.com/content/dam/projects/dotcom/english/public/documents/corporate/testimony/2020/Amtrak-CEO-Flynn-House-Railroads-Testimony-COVID19-090920.pdf.

Heise, Kenan, and Michael Edgerton. *Chicago, Center for Enterprise: An Illustrated History.* Woodland Hills, CA: Windsor Press, 1982.

Hirsh, Richard F. *Power Loss: The Origins of Deregulation and Restructuring in the American Electric Utility System*. Cambridge, MA: MIT Press, 2002.

———. *Powering American Farms: The Overlooked Origins of Rural Electrification*. Baltimore, MD: Johns Hopkins University Press, 2022.

"History." Port Authority of New York & New Jersey. Accessed January 15, 2023. https://www.panynj.gov/port/en/our-port/history.html.

"History." The Port of Los Angeles. Accessed January 15, 2023. https://www.portoflosangeles.org/about/history.

"History of Chester." City of Chester, Pennsylvania. Accessed March 14, 2023. https://www.chestercity.com/about/.

Hodge, Graeme A., and Carsten Greve. "Public-Private Partnerships: An International Performance Review." *Public Administration Review* 67, no. 3 (May 2007): 545–558.

Hoffer, Ann Kramer. "The Pennsylvania Turnpike." Gardner Digital Library. Accessed October 15, 2022. http://gardnerlibrary.org/encylopedia/pennsylvania-turnpike.

Honey, David B. "Before Dragons Coiled and Tigers Crouched: Early Nanjing in History and Poetry." *Journal of the American Oriental Society* 115, no. 1 (1995): 15–25.

Hooper, Emma, Sanjay Peters, and Patrick Pintus. "To What Extent Can Long-Term Investment in Infrastructure Reduce Income Inequality." Working Paper Series no. 624, Banque de France, March 27, 2017. https://dx.doi.org/10.2139/ssrn.2952365.

Howell, Sabrina T., Yeejin Jang, Hyeik Kim, and Michael S. Weisbach. "All Clear for Takeoff: Evidence from Airports on the Effects of Infrastructure Privatization." Working Paper 30544, National Bureau of Economic Research, October 2022. http://www.nber.org/papers/w30544.

Hutchison, Harold C. "Everything You Need to Know about the Merchant Marine." Military.com. March 16, 2020. https://www.military.com/off-duty/2020/03/16/everything-you-need-know-about-merchant-marine.html.

Hymowitz, Kay S. "In the Rendell Era, City's Image Rose, But Key Problems Remained." Manhattan Institute. December 30, 1999. https://www.manhattan-institute.org/html/rendell-era-citys-image-rose-key-problems-remained-0524.html.

"I Squared Capital Signs Agreement to Acquire a 109 km Operational Toll Road in India from IJM Corporation." BusinessWire. December 8, 2014. https://www.businesswire.com/news/home/20141208005284/en/I-Squared-Capital-Signs-Agreement-to-Acquire-a-109-km-Operational-Toll-Road-in-India-from-IJM-Corporation.

Imbens, Guido W., and Donald B. Rubin. *Causal Inference for Statistics, Social, and Biomedical Sciences: An Introduction*. Cambridge: Cambridge University Press, 2015.

"Improving Public Private Partnerships—Lessons from Australia." DLA Piper. May 29, 2020. https://www.dlapiper.com/en/australia/insights/publications /2020/05/improving-public-private-partnerships–lessons-from-australia/.

"Independent Research Highlights the Need to Increase the PFC." Airports Council International. January 23, 2020. https://airportscouncil.org/news /independent-research-highlights-the-need-to-increase-the-pfc/.

Inderst, Georg. "Pension Fund Investment in Infrastructure: Lessons from Australia and Canada." *Rotman International Journal of Pension Management* 7, no. 1 (2014): 40–47.

"Indianapolis Water Company." In *Encyclopedia of Indianapolis.* Accessed March 14, 2023. https://indyencyclopedia.org/indianapolis-water-company/.

"InfoBridge: Data." US Department of Transportation Federal Highway Administration. August 16, 2022. https://infobridge.fhwa.dot.gov/Data/Dashboard.

"Infrastructure Case Study: Chicago Skyway Bridge." Center for Innovative Finance Support at the US Department of Transportation. Accessed July 24, 2023. https://www.fhwa.dot.gov/ipd/value_capture/case_studies/chicago _skyway_bridge.aspx.

"Infrastructure Case Study: San Juan Airport." Bipartisan Policy Center. 2016. https://bipartisanpolicy.org/download/?file=/wp-content/uploads/2016/10 /BPC-Infrastructure-San-Juan-Airport.pdf.

"Internet/Broadband Fact Sheet." Pew Research Center. April 7, 2021. https://www .pewresearch.org/internet/fact-sheet/internet-broadband/#panel-3109350c -8dba-4b7f-ad52-a3e976ab8c8f.

Iossa, Elisabetta, and David Martimort. "Risk Allocation and the Costs and Benefits of Public-Private Partnerships." *Rand Journal of Economics* 43, no. 3 (2012): 442–74.

———. "The Simple Microeconomics of Public-Private Partnerships." *Journal of Public Economic Theory* 17, no. 1 (2015): 4–48.

Irwin, Timothy. "Government Guarantees: Allocating and Valuing Risk in Privately Financed Infrastructure Projects." World Bank. 2007. http://hdl.handle .net/10986/6638.

———. "Public Money for Private Infrastructure: Deciding When to Offer Guarantees, Output-Based Subsidies, and Other Fiscal Support." Working Paper no. 10, World Bank, 2003. http://hdl.handle.net/10986/15117.

Israel, Jonathan I. *The Dutch Republic: Its Rise, Greatness, and Fall 1477–1806.* Oxford: Clarendon Press, 1995.

Istrate, Emilia, and Robert Puentes. "Moving Forward on Public Private Partnerships: US and International Experience with PPP Units." Brookings-Rockefeller. December 2011. https://www.brookings.edu/wp-content/uploads/2016/06 /1208_transportation_istrate_puentes.pdf.

"It's Been 28 Years Since We Last Raised the Gas Tax, and Its Purchasing Power Has Eroded." *Peter G. Peterson Foundation* (blog), March 16, 2021. https://www

.pgpf.org/blog/2021/03/its-been-28-years-since-we-last-raised-the-gas-tax
-and-its-purchasing-power-has-eroded.

"It's Time for Real Change: Manifesto of the Labour Party 2019." The Labour Party.
2019. https://labour.org.uk/wp-content/uploads/2019/11/Real-Change-Labour
-Manifesto-

Jameson, John Franklin. *Willem Usselincx: Founder of the Dutch and Swedish West
India Company*. New York: G. P. Putnam's Sons, 1887.

Jenkins, Destin. *The Bonds of Inequality: Debt and the Making of the American
City*. Chicago: University of Chicago Press, 2021.

Jessup, Bob, and Ngai-Ling Sum. "An Entrepreneurial City in Action: Hong Kong's
Emerging Strategies in and for (Inter)Urban Competition." *Urban Studies* 37,
no. 12 (2000): 2287–2313.

Jin, Hongyu, Shijing Liu, Jide Sun, and Chunlu Liu. "Determining Concession Periods and Minimum Revenue Guarantees in Public-Private-Partnership Agreements." *European Journal of Operational Research* 291, no. 2 (2021): 512–24.

Joffe, Marc. "Doubly Bound: The Costs of Issuing Municipal Bonds." Haas Institute. December 16, 2015. https://belonging.berkeley.edu/sites/default/files
/haasinstituterefundamerica_doublybound_cost_of_issuingbonds_publish.pdf.

John, Richard R. *Network Nation*. Cambridge, MA: Belknap Press, 2015.

"John F. Kennedy International Airport New Terminal One Redevelopment:
Senior Debt—Confidential Information Memorandum." JFK International Airport. December 12, 2021.

Johnson, Kristina. "Damned If You Don't: Why the US Will Lose Big without
Investing in Hydropower." General Electric. September 28, 2016. https://www
.ge.com/news/reports/dammed-dont-us-will-lose-big-without-investing
-hydropower.

"Jonson Cox, Chairman of the Water Industry Regulator Ofwat and the Property
Company Harrworth Group." University of Cambridge Judge Business School.
July 21, 2015. https://www.jbs.cam.ac.uk/insight/2015/jonson-cox-chairman
-of-ofwat/.

Judd, Dennis, and R. L. Ready. "Entrepreneurial Cities and the New Politics of
Economic Development in the United States." In *Reagan and the Cities*, edited
by G. E. Peterson and C. W. Riley. Washington, DC: Urban Institute Press,
1986.

Kancharla, Bharath. "Data: By March 2019, Surfaced Roads Constituted 65% of
the Total Road Length in India." Factly. August 8, 2022. https://factly.in/data
-by-march-2019-surfaced-roads-constituted-65-of-the-total-road-length-in
-india/.

Kanter, Rosabeth Moss. *Move: How to Rebuild and Reinvent America's Infrastructure*. New York: W. W. Norton, 2016.

Keeley, Terrence. *Sustainable: Moving Beyond ESG to Impact Investing*. New York:
Columbia Business School, 2022.

Kennedy, Laura, ed. *Illinois Highway Improvement Bluebook*. Chicago: Illinois
    Highway Improvement Association, 1919. https://ia600704.us.archive.org/18
    /items/illinoishighwayi00illiilli/illinoishighwayi00illiilli.pdf.
Keynes, John Maynard. *Collected Writings of John Maynard Keynes*. Vol. 19, *Ac-
    tivities 1922–1929: The Return to Gold and Industrial Policy*. Edited by Donald
    Moggridge. New York: Macmillan, 1981.
———. *The General Theory of Employment, Interest, and Money*. New York:
    Houghton Mifflin Harcourt, 2016.
Kidd, David. "It Was America's First Superhighway. Now Much of It Sits Aban-
    doned." *Governing*, August 20, 2018. https://www.governing.com/archive/gov
    -pennsylvania-turnpike.html.
Kim, Yunji. "Can Alternative Service Delivery Save Cities after the Great Reces-
    sion? Barriers to Privatisation and Cooperation." *Local Government Studies* 44,
    no. 1 (2018): 44–63.
Kirby, Russell S. "Nineteenth-Century Patterns of Railroad Development on the
    Great Plains." *Great Plains Quarterly* 3, no. 3 (Summer 1983): 157–70.
Klein, Michael. "Public-Private Partnerships: Promise and Hype." Policy Research
    Working Paper 7340, World Bank, 2015. http://hdl.handle.net/10986/22223.
Koch, Charles H., Jr. "Collaborative Governance in the Restructured Electricity
    Industry." *Wake Forest Law Review* 40 (2005): 589–615.
Kost, John M. "The British Model." Mackinac Center for Public Policy. October 1,
    1988. https://www.mackinac.org/6365.
Krewson, Lyda. "Mayor's Letter to Airport Working Group." City of St. Louis Mis-
    souri. December 20, 2019. https://fly314.com/wp-content/uploads/2019/12
    /Mayors-Letter-to-Airport-Working-Group-Dec-20-2019.pdf.
La Rue, Frank. *Report of the Special Rapporteur on the Promotion and Protection
    of the Right to Freedom of Opinion and Expression*. United Nations Human
    Rights Council. May 16, 2011. https://digitallibrary.un.org/record/706331
    ?ln=en.
Landis, Charles I. "History of the Philadelphia and Lancaster Turnpike: The First
    Long Turnpike in the United States." *Pennsylvania Magazine of History and
    Biography* 42, no. 3 (1918): 235–58.
"Leasing the Pennsylvania Turnpike: Frequently Asked Questions." Common-
    wealth Foundation for Public Policy Alternatives. May 2008. https://reason
    .org/wp-content/uploads/files/d9a092bd0e9f1689b79bc1054b686a3c.pdf.
"Leeds Town, Androscoggin County, Maine." US Census Bureau. 2021. https://
    data.census.gov/profile?g=0600000US2300138565.
Leigland, James. "Public-Private Partnerships in Developing Countries: The
    Emerging Evidence-Based Critique." *World Bank Research Observer* 33, no. 1
    (2018): 103–34.
Leonhardt, John. *An Account of the Grisons or, A Description of the Free and In-
    dependent Commonwealth of the Three Rhætish Leagues*. London: J. Downing,

1711. Digitized by Library of Babel. https://babel.hathitrust.org/cgi/pt?id=uc1
.aa0001505973&view=1up&seq=41.

Lerusse, Amandine, and Steven Van de Walle. "Local Politicians' Preferences
in Public Procurement: Ideological or Strategic Reasoning?" *Local Government Studies* 48, no. 4 (2022): 680–703. http://doi.org/10.1080/03003930.2020
.1864332.

Levin, Blair. "Broadband Bipartisanship: How Did It Happen and Will It Continue?" Brookings Institution, *Commentary* (blog), April 18, 2022. https://www
.brookings.edu/blog/the-avenue/2022/04/18/broadband-bipartisanship-how
-did-it-happen-and-will-it-continue/.

Levinson, Marc. *The Box: How the Shipping Container Made the World Smaller
and the Economy Bigger.* Princeton, NJ: Princeton University Press, 2006.

———. "Container Shipping and the Decline of New York, 1955–1975." *Business
History Review* 80, no. 1 (2006): 49–80.

Lew, Jacob, Gary Roughead, Jennifer Hillman, and David Sacks. "China's Belt and
Road: Implications for the United States." Council on Foreign Relations. March
2021. https://www.cfr.org/report/chinas-belt-and-road-implications-for-the
-united-states/.

Lima, Sónia, Ana Brochado, and Rui Cunha Marques. "Public-Private Partnerships in the Water Sector: A Review." *Utilities Policy* 69 (April 2021). http://doi
.org/10.1016/j.jup.2021.101182.

Lin, Chen-Yu, Mohd Rapik Saat, and Christopher P. L. Barkan. "Quantitative
Causal Analysis of Mainline Passenger Train Accidents in the United States."
*Proceedings of the Institution of Mechanical Engineers, Part F: Journal of Rail
and Rapid Transit* 234, no. 8 (2020): 869–84.

"Lincoln Tunnel—New York to New Jersey." The Living New Deal. Accessed
January 15, 2023. https://livingnewdeal.org/projects/lincoln-tunnel-new-york
-to-new-jersey/.

Lobina, Emanuele, and David Hall. "UK Water Privatization—a Briefing." Public Services International Research Unit. February 2001. http://www.archives
.gov.on.ca/en/e_records/walkerton/part2info/partieswithstanding/pdf
/CUPE18UKwater.pdf.

Loeb, G. Hamilton. "The Communications Act Policy toward Competition: A Failure to Communicate." *Duke Law Journal* 1978, no. 1 (1978): 1–56.

Longfellow, Rickie. "Back in Time: The Abandoned Pennsylvania Turnpike." US
Department of Transportation, Federal Highway Administration. June 27, 2017.
https://www.fhwa.dot.gov/infrastructure/back1007.cfm.

"The Loop." In *Encyclopedia of Chicago.* 2005. http://www.encyclopedia.chicago
history.org/pages/764.html.

Lopez, Steven H. "Nursing Home Privatization: What Is the Human Cost." Key-
stone Research Center. March 2015. https://inthepublicinterest.org/wp-content
/uploads/2015/03/krc_nursing_home_priv.pdf.

Lorenzini, Marcella. "Infrastructure Financing in the Early Modern Age: The Beginning of a 'Little Divergence.'" In *Infrastructure Finance in Europe: Insights from the History of Water, Transport, and Telecommunications*, edited by Youssef Cassis, Guisseppe De Luca, and Massimo Florio, 61–80. Oxford: Oxford University Press, 2016.

Lowenstein, Roger. *Warren Buffett: The Making of an American Capitalist.* New York: Random House, 2008.

Lucas, Deborah, and Jorge Jimenez Montesinos. "A Fair Value Approach for Valuing Public Infrastructure Projects and the Risk Transfer in Public-Private Partnerships." In *Economic Analysis and Infrastructure Investment*, edited by Edward L. Glaeser and James M. Poterba, 369–402. New York: Macmillan, 2021.

"Maine Connectivity Authority." Maine Connectivity Authority. Accessed July 24, 2023. https://www.maineconnectivity.org/.

"Major Bridge P3 Program." Pennsylvania Department of Transportation. Accessed July 24, 2023. https://www.penndot.pa.gov/ProjectAndPrograms/p3forpa /Pages/Major-Bridges.aspx.

"Majority of Americans Want More Investment in Passenger Rail." Rail Passengers Association. March 21, 2022. https://www.railpassengers.org/happening-now /news/releases/new-poll-78-of-americans-want-increased-investments-in -passenger-rail-in-the-u.s/.

"Making Millennium Park: Teaching Case Study." Lincoln Institute of Land Policy. March 2022. https://www.lincolninst.edu/publications/multimedia/making -millennium-park-teaching-case-study.

Makovsek, Dejan, and Adrian Bridge. "Procurement Choices and Infrastructure Costs." In *Economic Analysis and Infrastructure Investment*, edited by Edward L. Glaeser and James M. Poterba, 277–327. Chicago: University of Chicago Press, 2021.

Malone, Laurence J. "Rural Electrification Administration." Economic History Association. Accessed July 24, 2023. https://eh.net/encyclopedia/rural -electrification-administration/.

Mansaray, Alhassan, Simeon Coleman, Ali Ataullah, and Kavita Sirichand. "Residual Government Ownership in Public-Private Partnership Projects." *Journal of Government and Economics* 4 (Winter 2021). https://doi.org/10.1016/j.jge.2021 .100018.

Marin, Fernando J. Rodriguez, and Nicolai J. Sarad. "Public Private Partnerships: USA." *Lexology* (blog), October 1, 2021. https://bracewell.com/insights/public -private-partnerships-usa.

Marin, Philippe. *Public-Private Partnerships for Urban Water Utilities: A Review of Experiences in Developing Countries.* World Bank and Public-Private Infrastructure Advisory Facility. 2009. https://ppp.worldbank.org/public-private -partnership/sites/ppp.worldbank.org/files/ppp_testdumb/documents/FINAL -PPPsforUrbanWaterUtilities-PhMarin.pdf.

Marques, Rui Cunha. "Why Not Regulate PPPs?" *Utilities Policy* 48 (October 2017): 141–46.

Martimort, David, and Jerome Pouyet. "To Build or Not to Build: Normative and Positive Theories of Public-Private Partnerships." *International Journal of Industrial Organization* 26, no. 2 (2008): 393–411.

Maskin, Eric, and Jean Tirole. "Public-Private Partnerships and Government Spending Limits." *International Journal of Industrial Organization* 26, no. 2 (2008): 412–20.

McBride, Brandon. "Celebrating the 80th Anniversary of the Rural Electrification Administration." *US Department of Agriculture* (blog), May 20, 2016. https:// www.usda.gov/media/blog/2016/05/20/celebrating-80th-anniversary-rural -electrification-administration.

McGillis, Jordan. "The Jackson Water Crisis and the Urgency of Climate Adaptation." Manhattan Institute. September 16, 2022. https://www.manhattan -institute.org/the_jackson_water_crisis_and_the_urgency_of_climate _adaptation.

Meng, Bingchun. *The Politics of Chinese Media: Consensus and Contestation.* New York: Springer, 2018.

"MIA Ranked America's Biggest Airport." Miami International Airport. April 13, 2022. https://news.miami-airport.com/mia-ranked-americas-busiest -international-airport/.

Mill, John Stuart. *Principles of Political Economy.* Oxford: Oxford University Press, 1994.

Miller, Benjamin M., Debra Knopman, Liisa Ecola, Brian Phillips, Moon Kim, Nathaniel Edenfield, Daniel Schwam, and Diogo Prosdocimi. "US Airport Infrastructure Funding and Financing." RAND Corporation. 2020. https://www .rand.org/pubs/research_reports/RR3175.html.

Millward, Robert. "The 1940s Nationalizations in Britain: A Means to an End or the Means of Production." *Economic History Review* 50, no 2 (1997): 210.

"Modernising New York's Transport Infrastructure." Macquarie Asset Management. Accessed July 24, 2023. https://www.macquarie.com/au/en/insights /modernising-new-yorks-transport-infrastructure.html.

"Montgomery Avenue Toll House, 1910." Friends of Narberth History. Accessed March 14, 2023. https://narberthhistory.org/views/toll-house.

Montoya, Daniel, and Laura Ismay, "Issues Backgrounder: Privatisation in NSW." New South Wales Parliamentary Research Service. June 2017. https://www.parliament.nsw.gov.au/researchpapers/Documents /Privatisation%20in%20NSW%20-%20a%20timeline%20and%20key %20sources.pdf.

Moraleja, Silvia Garcia, Frédéric Blanc-Brude, and Tim Whittaker. "Take the Next Exit: A Case Study of Road Investments Gone Wrong, Spain, 1998–2018." EDHEC Infrastructure Institute-Singapore. March 2018. https://edhec

.infrastructure.institute/paper/take-the-next-exit-a-case-study-of-road
-investments-gone-wrong-spain-1998-2018/.

Mostafavi, Ali, Dulcy Abraham, and Antonio Vives. "Explanatory Analysis of Public Perceptions of Innovative Financing for Infrastructure Systems in the US." *Transportation Research Part A: Policy and Practice* 70 (December 2014): 10–23.

Munnell, Alicia. "Policy Watch: Infrastructure Investment and Public Growth." *Journal of Economic Perspectives* 6, no. 4 (1992): 189–98.

———. "Why Has Productivity Growth Declined? Productivity and Public Investment Period." *New England Economic Review* (January 1990): 3–22.

Muraoka, Taishi, and Claudia N. Avellaneda. "Do the Networks of Inter-Municipal Cooperation Enhance Local Government Performance?" *Local Government Studies* 47, no. 4 (2021): 616–36.

Musgrove, Charles. *China's Contested Capital: Architecture, Ritual and Response in Nanjing.* Honolulu: University of Hawai'i Press, 2013.

Mires, Charlene. "Turnpikes." In *Pennsylvania Encyclopedia.* Accessed March 14, 2023. https://philadelphiaencyclopedia.org/essays/turnpikes/.

Nagurney, Anna. "A Brief History of the Shipping Container." Maritime Executive. September 30, 2021. https://www.maritime-executive.com/editorials/a-brief -history-of-the-shipping-container.

Nallathiga, Ramakrishna, and Mona N. Shah. "Public Private Partnerships in Roads Sector in India." Paper presented at the International Conference on Public Private Partnerships: The Need of the Hour, Institute of Public Enterprise, January 2014.

"History of Nanjing." In *Encyclopedia Britannica.* Accessed July 24, 2023. https:// www.britannica.com/place/Nanjing-China/History.

"National Assessment of Educational Progress." National Center for Education Statistics. February 8, 2023. https://nces.ed.gov/nationsreportcard/.

"National Data." Public Plans Data. Accessed March 14, 2023. https://public plansdata.org/quick-facts/national.

"The New Deal Worked." The Living New Deal. Accessed January 15, 2023. https:// livingnewdeal.org/the-new-deal-worked/.

"1998 Report Card for America's Infrastructure." American Society of Civil Engineers. 1998. https://infrastructurereportcard.org/wp-content/uploads/2016 /10/1998-ASCE-Report-Card-for-Americas-Infrastructure.pdf.

Nissen, Jørgen, and Georg Rotne. "Getting the Balance Right: The Øresund Bridge—Design Concept." Paper presented at the IABSE Conference: Cable-Stayed Bridges—Past, Present and Future. Malmö, Sweden, 1999. https:// structurae.net/en/literature/conference-paper/getting-the-balance-right-the -oresund-bridge-design-concept.

"Notice of Ofwat's Decision to Impose a Financial Penalty on Thames Water Utilities Limited." Ofwat. December 6, 2021. https://www.ofwat.gov.uk/wp-content

/uploads/2021/12/Notice_Ofwats_Decision_Financial_Penalty_Thames_Water
_Utilities_Limited.pdf.
"Number of Scheduled Passengers Boarded by the Global Airline Industry from
2004 to 2022." Statista. Accessed April 25, 2023. https://www.statista.com
/statistics/564717/airline-industry-passenger-traffic-globally.
"Obituary: Albert Bilik." Dignity Memorial. Accessed December 30, 2023. https://
www.dignitymemorial.com/obituaries/washington-dc/albert-bilik-6948093.
Online Source Water Quality Monitoring. US Environmental Protection Agency.
September 2016. https://www.epa.gov/sites/default/files/2016-09/documents
/online_source_water_monitoring_guidance.pdf.
"The Opportunity: What RDOF Means for Electric Co-Ops." Rural Digital Opportunity Fund (RDOF). Accessed January 30, 2023. https://rdof.com/the
-opportunity.
Osborne, David E., and Ted Gaebler. *Reinventing Government: How the Entrepre-
neurial Spirit Is Transforming the Public Sector.* New York: Penguin, 1993.
O'Toole, Randal. "Amtrak's Big Lie." Cato Institute. January 14, 2020. https://www
.cato.org/commentary/amtraks-big-lie.
"Our History." City Bridge Trust. Accessed July 24, 2023. https://www.citybridge
trust.org.uk/about-us/history/.
"Overview: What Is AIP & What Is Eligible?" Federal Aviation Administration.
August 2, 2022. https://www.faa.gov/airports/aip/overview.
"PA Turnpike History." Pennsylvania Turnpike. Accessed October 15, 2022. https://
www.paturnpike.com/about-us/turnpike-history.
"PA Turnpike Makes Final $450 Million Transit Payment to PennDOT Today."
Pennsylvania Turnpike. July 28, 2021. https://www.paturnpike.com/news
/details/2021/09/14/20210728144102.
Page, Scott E. "Path Dependence." *Quarterly Journal of Political Science* 1, no. 1
(2006): 87–115.
Palmer, Eric. "J&J Investing $225 Million in 4 Puerto Rico Plants." Fierce Pharma.
October 2, 2012. https://www.fiercepharma.com/supply-chain/j-j-investing
-225-million-4-puerto-rico-plants.
Parker, Barry. "Ports Ponder Public Private Partnerships." Maritime Logistics Pro-
fessional. May/June 2017. https://2015.maritimeprofessional.com/magazine
/story/201705/ponder-private-partnerships-528179.
Parker, David. "The Performance of BAA before and after Privatisation: A DEA
Study." *Journal of Transport Economics and Policy* 33, no. 2 (May 1999): 133–45.
Pauli, Benjamin J. *Flint Fights Back.* Cambridge, MA: MIT Press, 2019.
Peng, Zhongzhou, and Sow Keat Tok. "The AIIB and China's Normative Power in
International Financial Governance Structure." *Chinese Political Science Review*
1 (2016): 736–53.
Peterson, G. E., and C. W. Riley, eds. *Reagan and the Cities.* Washington, DC: Ur-
ban Institute Press, 1986.

Phang, Sock-Yong. "The Convergence of Water, Electricity and Gas Industries: Implications for PPP Design and Regulation." *Competition and Regulation in Network Industries* 21, no. 4 (2020): 380–95.

"Pillar II—Supply Chains." US Department of Commerce. Accessed August 1, 2023. https://www.commerce.gov/ipef/pillar-ii.

Pinkney, David. *Napoleon III and the Rebuilding of Paris.* Princeton, NJ: Princeton University Press, 1958.

Placek, Martin. "Global Container Shipping Rates 2023." Statista. May 10, 2023. https://www.statista.com/statistics/1250636/global-container-freight-index/ (site discontinued).

———. "Leading Ship Operator's Share of the World Liner Fleet 2023." Statista. June 12, 2023. https://www.statista.com/statistics/198206/share-of-leading -container-ship-operators-on-the-world-liner-fleet/.

Podkul, Cezary. "New Orleans Drops Plan to Privatise Airport." Infrastructure Investor. October 22, 2010. https://www.infrastructureinvestor.com/new-orleans -drops-plan-to-privatise-airport/.

Pomerantz, Dorothy. "Amazon Turns to Wind to Power Its Business." GE. October 19, 2017. https://www.ge.com/news/reports/amazon-turns-ge-wind -turbines-power-business.

Poole, Robert, Jr. *Cutting Back City Hall.* New York: Universe Books, 1980.

———. *Rethinking America's Highways: A 21st Century Vision for Better Infrastructure.* Chicago: University of Chicago Press, 2018.

———. "Study: Leasing 31 US Airports Would Generate $131 Billion to Fund Other Infrastructure and Pay Debt." Reason Foundation. August 26, 2021. https:// reason.org/policy-study/study-leasing-31-us-airports-would-generate-131 -billion-to-fund-other-infrastructure-and-pay-debt/.

Poole, Robert, Jr., and Chris Edwards. "Privatizing US Airports." *Cato Institute Tax & Budget Bulletin*, November 2016. https://www.cato.org/sites/cato.org /files/pubs/pdf/tbb-76_1.pdf.

Poole, Robert, Jr., and Peter Samuel. "The Return of Private Toll Roads." US Department of Transportation, Federal Highway Administration. March/April 2006. https://highways.dot.gov/public-roads/marchapril-2006/return-private -toll-roads.

"Port History." Port Authority of New York & New Jersey. Accessed July 2, 2023. https://www.panynj.gov/port-authority/en/about/History/port-history-history -about.html.

"Port Miami." Miami-Dade County. 2023. https://www.miamidade.gov/portmiami/.

"Port of Long Beach History Timeline." Port of Long Beach. Accessed July 24, 2023. https://polb.com/port-info/timeline/.

"Port of New York." World Port Source. Accessed July 24, 2023. http://www .worldportsource.com/ports/review/USA_NY_Port_of_New_York_68.php.

"Port of Piraeus." World Port Source. Accessed July 24, 2023. http://www.world portsource.com/ports/review/GRC_Port_of_Piraeus_1041.php.

"Ports." In *2021 Infrastructure Report Card*, American Society of Civil Engineers. Accessed July 12, 2022. https://infrastructurereportcard.org/wp-content /uploads/2017/01/Ports-2021.pdf.

"Ports Primer: 3.1 Port Operations." US Environmental Protection Agency. Accessed June 27, 2022. https://www.epa.gov/community-port-collaboration /ports-primer-31-port-operations.

Poterba, James. "Is the Gasoline Tax Regressive." *Tax Policy and the Economy* 5 (1991): 145–64.

Pratap, Kumar V., and Rajesh Chakrabarti. *Public-Private Partnerships in Infra-structure: Managing the Challenges*. Singapore: Springer Nature, 2017.

Preparing United States Critical Infrastructure for Today's Evolving Water Crises. National Infrastructure Advisory Council. June 2023. https://www.cisa.gov /sites/default/files/2023-06/NIAC%20Water%20Security%20Report%20 -%20Draft.pdf.

Private Participation in Infrastructure (PPI): 2021 Annual Report. World Bank. June 21, 2022. https://documents.worldbank.org/en/publication/documents -reports/documentdetail/099920006212228192/p1616740725f490c0090 db0b25cd05ad7ea.

"Project Profile: Chicago Skyway." US Department of Transportation, Federal Highway Administration, Center for Innovative Finance Support. Accessed September 19, 2022. https://www.fhwa.dot.gov/ipd/project_profiles/il_chicago _skyway.aspx.

"Project Profile: Luis Muñoz Marín International Airport Privatization." US Department of Transportation, Federal Highway Administration, Center for Innovative Finance Support. Accessed September 19, 2022. https:// www.fhwa.dot.gov/ipd/project_profiles/pr_lmm_airport_privatization .aspx.

"Public Law 104-264." US Congress. October 9, 1996. https://www.congress.gov /104/plaws/publ264/PLAW-104publ264.pdf.

Public Private Partnerships: A Reference Guide Version 3. World Bank Group. April 27, 2017. https://ppp.worldbank.org/public-private-partnership/library /ppp-reference-guide-3-0-full-version.

"Public Road and Street Mileage in the United States by Type of Surface." US Department of Transportation, Bureau of Transportation Statistics. 2021. https:// www.bts.gov/content/public-road-and-street-mileage-united-states-type -surfacea.

"Public Spending on Transportation and Water Infrastructure, 1956 to 2017." *Congressional Budget Office*. October 15, 2018. https://www.cbo.gov/publication /54539.

"Public Private Partnerships." Chicago Department of Finance. Accessed October 14, 2022. https://www.chicago.gov/city/en/depts/fin/supp_info/public_private_partnerships.html.

"Puerto Rico: Factors Contributing to the Debt Crisis and Potential Federal Actions to Address Them." US Government Accountability Office. May 2018. https://www.gao.gov/assets/gao-18-387.pdf.

"Puerto Rico Public-Private Partnerships Authority." Accessed July 12, 2023. https://www.p3.pr.gov/.

Qiang, Christine Zhen-Wei. "Broadband Infrastructure Investment in Stimulus Packages: Relevance for Developing Countries." World Bank. 2010. https://documents1.worldbank.org/curated/en/154041468339016052/pdf/490970WP0Broad10Box338941B01PUBLIC1.pdf.

Qin, Shikun, Weijie Luo, and Yaling Wang. "Policy Uncertainty and Firm-Level Investment: Evidence from Public Private-Partnership Market in China." *Applied Economics Letters* 29, no. 8 (2022): 669–75.

Quehl, Scott. "The Bottom Line . . . and Beyond: Financial Plans Guided Philadelphia and New Haven to Recovery." Brookings Institution. June 1, 2000. https://www.brookings.edu/articles/the-bottom-line-and-beyond-financial-plans-guided-philadelphia-and-new-haven-to-recovery/.

"Quick Facts: Chester, Pennsylvania." US Census Bureau. Accessed August 23, 2022. https://www.census.gov/quickfacts/chestercitypennsylvania.

"Quick Facts: Flint City, Michigan." US Census Bureau. 2022. Accessed March 14, 2023. https://www.census.gov/quickfacts/flintcitymichigan.

Raiker, Santosh, and Seabron Adamson. *Renewable Energy Finance: Theory and Practice*. Cambridge, MA: Academic Press, 2019.

Ramey, Valerie. "The Macroeconomic Consequences of Infrastructure Investment." In *Economic Analysis and Infrastructure Investment*, edited by Edward L. Glazer and James M. Poterba, 219–68. Chicago: University of Chicago Press, 2021.

Reagan, Ronald. "Statement on the President's Commission on Privatization." Ronald Reagan Presidential Library and Museum. September 3, 1987. https://www.reaganlibrary.gov/archives/speech/statement-presidents-commission-privatization.

"Record £90m Fine for Southern Water Following EA Prosecution." Environment Agency. July 9, 2021. https://www.gov.uk/government/news/record-90m-fine-for-southern-water-following-ea-prosecution.

"A Record Year for America's Ports and a Look to the Year Ahead." White House. January 20, 2022. https://www.whitehouse.gov/nec/briefing-room/2022/01/20/a-record-year-for-americas-ports-and-a-look-to-the-year-ahead/.

Reghizzi, Olivier Crespi. "The Finance of Local Public Goods at the Onset of Industrialization: Water in Paris 1807–1925." In *Infrastructure Finance in Europe: Insights into the History of Water, Transport, and Telecommunications*, edited by Youssef Cassis, Giuseppe De Luca, and Massimo Florio, 123–49. Oxford: Oxford University Press, 2016.

"Regional and State Unemployment, 2008 Annual Averages." US Department of Labor, Bureau of Labor Statistics. February 27, 2009. https://www.bls.gov/news .release/archives/srgune_02272009.pdf.

Reis, Ricardo Ferreira, and Joaquim Miranda Sarmento. "'Cutting Costs to the Bone': The Portuguese Experience in Renegotiating Public Private Partnerships Highways during the Financial Crisis." *Transportation* 46 (2019): 285–302.

Rendell, Ed. *A Nation of Wusses: How America's Leaders Lost the Guts to Make Us Great.* Hoboken, NJ: Wiley, 2012.

"Renewable Power's Growth Is Being Turbocharged as Countries Seek to Strengthen Energy Security." IEA. December 6, 2022. https://www.iea.org /news/renewable-power-s-growth-is-being-turbocharged-as-countries-seek -to-strengthen-energy-security.

Renner, Charles, and Will Nulton. *2022 Public-Private Partnership Trends Report.* Husch Blackwell. March 2022. https://www.p3edu.com/wp-content/uploads /2022/03/2022-Public-Private-Partnership-Trends-Report.pdf.

"Reorganization Plan No. 3 of 1970." EPA Archive. Accessed July 24, 2023. https:// archive.epa.gov/epa/aboutepa/reorganization-plan-no-3-1970.html.

Report: The Impact of Broadband Speed and Price on Small Business. US Senate Committee on Small Business & Entrepreneurship. November 16, 2010. https://www.sbc.senate.gov/public/index.cfm/2010/11/report-the-impact-of -broadband-speed-and-price-on-small-business.

Report on the Municipal Securities Market. US Securities and Exchange Commission. July 31, 2012. https://www.sec.gov/news/studies/2012/munireport073112 .pdf.

"Rex Sinquefield." World Chess Hall of Fame. Accessed December 15, 2023. https://worldchesshof.org/hof-inductee/rex-sinquefield.

"Robert Poole." Reason Foundation. Accessed March 23, 2023. https://reason.org /author/robert-poole/.

Rohatyn, Felix. *Bold Endeavors: How Our Government Built America, and Why It Must Rebuild Now.* New York: Simon & Schuster, 2011.

Rossi, Anna. "Regionalizing the Detroit Water and Sewerage Department, the Effects of Privatization on Metro Detroit Residents and the Importance of Community Control." *Journal of Law Society* 17, no. 2 (2016): 59–65.

Roth, Gabriel, ed. *Street Smart: Competition, Entrepreneurship, and the Future of Roads.* Oakland, CA: Independent Institute, 2006.

Rough Roads Ahead: Fix Them Now or Pay for It Later. American Association of State Highway and Transportation Officials. May 2009. https://www.civfed.org /roughroadsreport_may2009.pdf.

Rural Electrification Administration. *A Guide for Members of Cooperatives.* US Department of Agriculture. September 1939.

Russo, Julio Cezar, Marco Antonio Guimarães Dias, André Barreira da Silva Rocha, and Fernando Luiz Cyrino Oliveira. "Renegotiation in Public-Private Partnerships: An Incentive Mechanism Approach." *Group Decision and Negotiation* 27 (2018): 949–79.

Sackett et ux. v. Environmental Protection Agency et al., 598 U.S. 651 (2022). https://www.supremecourt.gov/opinions/22pdf/598us2r28_5h26.pdf.

Sacks, David. "Countries in China's Belt and Road Initiative: Who's In and Who's Out." Council on Foreign Relations, *Asia Unbound* (blog), March 24, 2021. https://www.cfr.org/blog/countries-chinas-belt-and-road-initiative-whos-and -whos-out.

"Safety Focused, Customer Driven." Pennsylvania Turnpike. Accessed October 4, 2022. https://www.paturnpike.com/.

Sain-Baird, Jessica. "How Central Park Keeps New York City Healthy." Central Park Conservancy. April 25, 2017. https://www.centralparknyc.org/articles /park-city-healthy#:~:text=Central%20Park%20is%20home%20to,Yorkers %20breathe%20a%20little%20easier.

Samuel, Peter. "Putting Customers in the Driver's Seat: The Case for Tolls." Reason Public Policy Institute. 2000. https://reason.org/wp-content/uploads/files /9b293208d9cd841ca0c806da4c5bc19b.pdf.

"Sanitation and Drinking Water." Environmental Performance Index. Yale University. Accessed July 10, 2023. https://epi.yale.edu/epi-results/2020/component /h2o.

Santandrea, Martina, Stephen J. Bailey, and Marco Giorgino. "Infrastructure Funding and Financing: Safeguarding Value for Money in Public-Private Partnerships." In *Economics of Infrastructure Provisioning: The Changing Role of the State*, edited by Arnold Picot, Massimo Florio, Nico Grove, and Johann Kranz, 121–44. Cambridge, MA: MIT Press, 2015.

Santos, Georgina, and Laurent Rojey, "Distributional Impacts of Road Pricing: The Truth Behind the Myth," *Transportation* 31, no. 1 (2004): 21–42.

Sarmento, Joaquim Miranda, and Luc Renneboog. "Anatomy of Public-Private Partnerships: Their Creation, Financing and Renegotiations." *International Journal of Managing Projects in Business* 9, no. 1 (2016): 94–122.

———. "Renegotiating Public-Private Partnerships." Finance Working Paper no. 416/2016, European Corporate Governance Institute, 2016. https://dx.doi.org /10.2139/ssrn.2737858.

Saussier, Stéphane, and Phuong Tra Tran. "L'efficacité des contrats de partenariat en France: Une première évaluation quantitative." *Revue d'Economie Industrielle*, no. 140 (2012): 81–110.

Sbragia, Alberta M. *Debt Wish: Entrepreneurial Cities, US Federalism, and Economic Development*. Pittsburgh: University of Pittsburgh Press, 1996.

Schleicher, Andreas. "PISA 2018 Insights and Interpretations." OECD. 2019. https://www.oecd.org/pisa/PISA%202018%20Insights%20and%20 Interpretations%20FINAL%20PDF.pdf.

Schleicher, David. *In a Bad State: Responding to State and Local Budget Crises.* Oxford: Oxford University Press, 2023.

Schomaker, Rahel M. "Conceptualizing Corruption in Public Private Partnerships." *Public Organization Review* 20, no. 4 (2020): 807–20.

Sclar, Elliott. "The Political Economics of Investment Utopia: Public–Private Partnerships for Urban Infrastructure Finance." *Journal of Economic Policy Reform* 18, no. 1 (2015): 1–15.

———. *You Don't Always Get What You Pay For: The Economics of Privatization.* Ithaca, NY: Cornell University Press, 2001.

Scorsone, Eric, and Nicolette Bateson. *Long-Term Crisis and Systemic Failure: Taking the Fiscal Stress of America's Older Cities Seriously.* Case Study: Flint, Michigan. Michigan State University Extension. September 2011. https://cityofflint.com/wp-content/uploads/Reports/MSUE_FlintStudy2011.pdf.

Scribner, Marc. "Reforming the Airport Investment Partnership Program." Reason Foundation. September 26, 2022. https://reason.org/commentary/reforming-the-airport-investment-partnership-program/.

"Second Vivekananda Bridge Tollway Company Private Limited." SVBTC. Accessed April 10, 2023. https://www.svbtc.in/.

"§ 1.92 The Maritime Administration." Code of Federal Regulations. https://www.ecfr.gov/on/2017-01-01/title-49/subtitle-A/part-1/subpart-D/section-1.92.

"Senators Applaud FERC's Final Rule to Modernize PURPA, Protect Electricity Customers." James E. Risch, US Senate. Press release, July 16, 2020. https://www.risch.senate.gov/public/index.cfm/2020/7/senators-applaud-ferc-s-final-rule-to-modernize-purpa-protect-electricity-customers.

Shaoul, Jean, Anne Stafford, and Pam Stapleton. "The Fantasy World of Private Finance for Transport via Public Private Partnerships." Discussion Paper No. 2012-6, presented to the Roundtable on Public Private Partnerships for Funding Transport Infrastructure: Sources of Funding, Managing Risk and Optimism Bias, at University of Manchester Business School, September 27–28, 2012. https://www.itf-oecd.org/sites/default/files/docs/dp201206.pdf.

"Share of Renewables in Electricity Production." In *Enerdata World Energy & Climate Statistics—Yearbook 2022.* Accessed July 24, 2023. https://yearbook.enerdata.net/renewables/renewable-in-electricity-production-share.html.

"Shareholders." Groupe ADP. November 30, 2022. https://www.parisaeroport.fr/en/group/finance/aeroports-de-paris-shares/shareholders-structure.

Sharma, Vishwa Raj, and Kamal Bisht. "Carrying Capacity Assessment and Sustainable Tourism Management in Agra City, Uttar Pradesh (India)." *GeoJournal of Tourism and Geosites* 25, no. 2 (2019): 399–407.

Shi, Yingying, Shen Guo, and Puyang Sun. "The Role of Infrastructure in China's Regional Growth." *Journal of Asian Economics* 49 (April 2017): 26–41.

Shieh, Pauline. "The Building of the Great Pennsylvania Turnpike." Pennsylvania Center for the Book. Spring 2009. https://pabook.libraries.psu.edu/literary

-cultural-heritage-map-pa/feature-articles/building-great-pennsylvania
-turnpike.

Shiwakoti, Dinesh, and Devayan Dey. "The Hybrid Annuity Model for Public-Private Partnerships in India's Road Sector: Lessons for Developing Asia." South Asia Working Paper Series 94, ADB, August 2022. https://dx.doi.org /10.22617/WPS220344-2.

"A Short History of the Web." CERN. Accessed January 15, 2023. https://home .cern/science/computing/birth-web/short-history-web.

Siemiatycki, Matti. "Public-Private Partnerships in Canada: Reflections on Twenty Years of Practice." *Canadian Public Administration* 58, no. 3 (September 2015): 343–62.

Siemiatycki, Matti, Eoin Reeves, and Dónal Palcic. "Editorial: The Unresolved Nature of Public-Private Partnerships." *Journal of Economic Policy Reform* 25, no. 2 (2022): 81–84.

Silaghi, Florina, and Sudipto Sarkar. "Agency Problems in Public-Private Partnerships Investment Projects." *European Journal of Operational Research* 290, no. 3 (2015): 1174–91.

Singla, Akheil, Jason Shumberger, and David Swindell. "Paying for Infrastructure in the Post-Recession Era: Exploring the Use of Alternative Funding and Financing Tools." *Journal of Urban Affairs* 43, no. 4 (2021): 526–48.

Situ, Helen. "The Costs of Megaprojects: An Analysis of the Hong Kong-Zhuhai-Macau Bridge." *Viterbi Conversations in Ethics* 6, no. 1 (Spring 2022). https:// vce.usc.edu/volume-6-issue-1/the-costs-of-megaprojects-an-analysis-of-the -hong-kong-zhuhai-macau-bridge/.

"Smart Bridge Campaign: Open Restricted Bridges." Intelligent Structures. Accessed March 16, 2023. https://intellistruct.com/smart-bridge/.

"Smart Roads Start with Smart Infrastructure." Intel. Accessed March 16, 2023. https://www.intel.com/content/www/us/en/transportation/smart-road -infrastructure.html.

"The Smartphone Generation Needs Computer Help." *Atlantic Re:think* (blog), November 2019. https://www.theatlantic.com/sponsored/grow-google-2019 /smartphone-generation-computer-help/3127/.

Smil, Vaclav. *Power Density: A Key to Understanding Energy Sources and Uses.* Cambridge, MA: MIT Press, 2016.

Smith, Adam. *Wealth of Nations.* New York: Penguin Books, 2000.

"South Side." In *Encyclopedia of Chicago.* 2005. http://www.encyclopedia .chicagohistory.org/pages/1177.html.

Sparrow, James. *Warfare State: WWII Americans and the Age of Big Government.* Oxford: Oxford University Press, 2013.

Spector, Carrie. "Digging Deeper on the Pandemic Learning Loss." Stanford Institute for Economic Policy Research. October 28, 2022. https://siepr.stanford .edu/news/digging-deeper-pandemic-learning-loss.

Spirou, Costas, and Dennis R. Rudd. *Building the City of Spectacle: Mayor Richard M. Daley and the Remaking of Chicago.* Ithaca, NY: Cornell University Press, 2016.

"St. Louis Not for Sale." STL Not for Sale. Accessed March 14, 2023. https://stlnotforsale.com/.

"St. Louis to Participate in Airport Privatization Pilot Program." City of St. Louis. April 24, 2017. https://www.stlouis-mo.gov/government/departments/mayor/news/st-louis-to-particpate-in-airport-privatization-pilot-program.cfm.

Stanley, Jason. "The Emergency Manager: Strategic Racism, Technocracy, and the Poisoning of Flint's Children." *The Good Society* 25, no. 1 (2016): 1–45.

"State and Local Backgrounders." Urban Institute. 2022. https://www.urban.org/policy-centers/cross-center-initiatives/state-and-local-finance-initiative/state-and-local-backgrounders/state-and-local-expenditures.

"The State of State (and Local) Tax Policy." Tax Policy Center. 2020. https://www.taxpolicycenter.org/briefing-book/what-are-municipal-bonds-and-how-are-they-used.

"Statement of Chairman Ajit Pai Re: Restoring Internet Freedom." WC Docket No. 17-108. Federal Communications Commission. Accessed July 24, 2023. https://docs.fcc.gov/public/attachments/FCC-17-166A2.pdf.

Stauffer, Anne, Kathryn de Wit, Anna Read, and Dan Kitson. *How States Are Expanding Broadband Access.* Pew Charitable Trusts. February 27, 2020. https://www.pewtrusts.org/en/research-and-analysis/reports/2020/02/how-states-are-expanding-broadband-access.

Stiglitz, Joseph. *The Economic Role of the State.* New York: Blackwell Publishing, 1989.

Stokes, David. "Privatization of the Saint Louis Water Utility." Show-Me Institute. May 17, 2010. https://showmeinstitute.org/publication/privatization/privatization-of-the-saint-louis-water-utility/.

"Sunshine Law." Missouri Attorney General of Missouri. Accessed January 15, 2023. https://ago.mo.gov/missouri-law/sunshine-law.

"Survey Shows Ports Plan Big Infrastructure Investments through 2025." American Association of Port Authorities. April 29, 2020. https://www.aapa-ports.org/advocating/PRDetail.aspx?ItemNumber=22686.

"A Tale of Two Cities in Maine: Municipal Broadband and Misinformation." Community Networks. December 7, 2021. https://muninetworks.org/content/tale-two-cities-maine-municipal-broadband-and-misinformation.

"Telecommunications Act of 1996." Federal Communications Commission. June 20, 2013. https://www.fcc.gov/general/telecommunications-act-1996.

Thatcher, Margaret. *The Downing Street Years.* London: HarperCollins, 1993.

———. *Margaret Thatcher: The Autobiography.* New York: HarperPerennial, 2010.

———. "Speech to Conservative Women's Conference, May 25, 1985." Margaret Thatcher Foundation. Accessed July 24, 2023. https://www.margaretthatcher.org/document/106056.

Thayer, Joel. "The FCC's Legal Authority to Regulate Platforms as Common Carriers." Federalist Society, *FedSoc Blog*, March 29, 2021. https://fedsoc.org /commentary/fedsoc-blog/the-legal-authority-for-the-fcc-to-regulate -platforms-as-a-common-carrier.

Thompson, Ben. "The History of the Shipping Container Created in 1956." *Inco-Docs* (blog). August 31, 2018. https://incodocs.com/blog/history-of -shipping-container-1956-world-trade/.

"Timeline of FAA and Aerospace History." Federal Aviation Administration. Accessed January 15, 2023. https://www.faa.gov/about/history/timeline.

Timilsina, Govinda, Gal Hochman, and Ze Song. "Infrastructure, Economic Growth, and Poverty: A Review." Policy Research Working Paper no. 9258, World Bank Group, May 2020. https://openknowledge.worldbank.org /bitstream/handle/10986/33821/Infrastructure-Economic-Growth-and -Poverty-A-Review.pdf?sequence=1&isAllowed=y.

Tomer, Adie, Joseph W. Kane, and Robert Puentes. "How Historic Would a $1 Trillion Infrastructure Program Be?" Brookings Institution, *Commentary* (blog). May 12, 2017. https://www.brookings.edu/blog/the-avenue/2017/05/12/how -historic-would-a-1-trillion-infrastructure-program-be/.

Trends in Water Privatization: The Post-Recession Economy and the Fight for Public Water in the United States. Food and Water Watch. November 2010. https://www.inthepublicinterest.org/wp-content/uploads/Trends-in -Water-Privatization.pdf.

"Trucking Industry Congestion Costs Now Top $74 Billion Annually." American Trucking Research Institute. 2018. https://truckingresearch.org/2018/10 /trucking-industry-congestion-costs-now-top-74-billion-annually.

"The Truth about Private Water in Indianapolis, IN." National Association of Water Companies. Accessed March 14, 2023. http://truthfromthetap.com/wp -content/uploads/2015/03/TruthFromTheTap_CaseStudy_INDIANAPOLIS _032715.pdf.

Tsui, Brian. *China's Conservative Revolution: The Quest for a New Order, 1927–1949.* Cambridge: Cambridge University Press, 2018.

Tudor, Sarah. "Sewage Pollution in England's Waters." UK Parliament House of Lords Library. June 30, 2022. https://lordslibrary.parliament.uk/sewage -pollution-in-englands-waters/.

Turnbull, Archibald Douglas. "John Stevens." *North American Review* 233, no. 832 (1926): 446–54.

———. *John Stevens: An American Record.* New York: The Century Co., 1928.

"2018 Report Card for Pennsylvania's Infrastructure." American Society of Civil Engineers. Accessed October 15, 2022. https://www.pareportcard.org /PARC2018/downloads/ASCE-PA-report_2018.pdf.

"2019 Annual Report." Asian Infrastructure Investment Bank. Accessed April 13, 2023. https://www.aiib.org/en/news-events/annual-report/2019/_common/pdf /2019-aiib-annual-report-and-financials.pdf.

"2020 Population and Housing State Data." US Census Bureau. August 12, 2021. https://www.census.gov/library/visualizations/interactive/2020-population -and-housing-state-data.html.

"2021 Report Card for America's Infrastructure: A Comprehensive Assessment of America's Infrastructure." American Society of Civil Engineers. 2021. https:// infrastructurereportcard.org/wp-content/uploads/2020/12/National_IRC _2021-report.pdf.

"2021 Report Card for America's Infrastructure: Roads." American Society of Civil Engineers. 2021. https://infrastructurereportcard.org/wp-content/uploads /2017/01/Roads-2021.pdf.

"2009 Final Results Press Conference." COSCO SHIPPING Ports Limited. Accessed July 3, 2023. https://ports.coscoshipping.com/en/Investors/IRHome /CorporatePresentations/.

"2001 Report Card for America's Infrastructure." American Society of Civil Engineers. 2001. https://infrastructurereportcard.org/wp-content/uploads/2016/10 /2001-ASCE-Report-Card-for-Americas-Infrastructure.pdf.

"U.S.-International Freight Trade by Transportation Mode." US Bureau of Transportation Statistics. Accessed November 1, 2023. https://www.bts.gov/browse -statistical-products-and-data/freight-facts-and-figures/us-international -freight-trade.

"Understanding the Debate around Motorway Concessions in France." Vinci. February 25, 2015. https://www.vinci.com/vinci.nsf/en/news-update/pages /understanding_the_debate_around_motorway_concessions_in_france .htm.

"Urban Highway Concessionaires in Santiago, Chile." Public-Private Infrastructure Advisory Facility. 2009. https://ppiaf.org/sites/ppiaf.org/files/documents /toolkits/highwaytoolkit/6/pdf-version/chile.pdf.

"US EPA: Fiscal Year 2022." Environmental Protection Agency. May 2021. https:// www.epa.gov/sites/default/files/2021-05/documents/fy-2022-congressional -justification-all-tabs.pdf.

"US Inflation Reduction Act: Impacts on Renewable Energy." UL Solutions. September 14, 2022. https://www.ul.com/news/us-inflation-reduction-act-impacts -renewable-energy.

"US Renewable Energy Factsheet." Center for Sustainable Systems, University of Michigan. 2021. https://css.umich.edu/publications/factsheets/energy/us -renewable-energy-factsheet.

"US Water Supply and Distribution Factsheet." Center for Sustainable Systems, University of Michigan. Accessed March 14, 2023. https://css.umich.edu /publications/factsheets/water/us-water-supply-and-distribution-factsheet#:~: text=Approximately%20152%2C000%20publicly%20owned%20water,to%2079 %25%20of%20the%20population.

"USDOT, Biden Administration Deliver $4.3 Billion in Funding to Amtrak in Year One of Bipartisan Infrastructure Law." USDOT FRA. November 30, 2022.

https://railroads.dot.gov/about-fra/communications/newsroom/press-releases
/usdot-biden-administration-deliver-43-billion-0.

Using Public-Private Partnerships to Carry Out Highway Projects. Congressional
Budget Office. January 2012. https://www.cbo.gov/sites/default/files/112th
-congress-2011-2012/reports/01-09-PublicPrivatePartnerships.pdf.

"Value for Money Analysis." US Department of Transportation, Federal Highway
Administration. February 8, 2016. https://www.fhwa.dot.gov/ipd/pdfs/p3/p3
_value_2.0_session_2.pdf.

Van der Putten, Frans-Paul. "Chinese Investment in the Port of Piraeus, Greece:
The Relevance for the EU and the Netherlands." Netherlands Institute of
International Relations. February 14, 2014. https://www.clingendael.org/sites
/default/files/pdfs/2014%20-%20Chinese%20investment%20in%20Piraeus
%20-%20Clingendael%20Report.pdf.

"Vasco da Gama Bridge: General Information." Lusoponte. Accessed July 24, 2023.
https://www.lusoponte.pt/vasco-da-gama/informacoes-gerais.

Vecchi, Veronica, Francesca Casalini, Niccolò Cusumano, and Velia M. Leone.
Public-Private Partnerships: Principles for Sustainable Contracts. New York:
Palgrave Macmillan, 2021.

Verweij, Stefan, Ingmar van Meerkerk, and Carter B. Casady, eds. *Assessing the
Performance Advantage of Public Private Partnerships: A Comparative Perspective.* Cheltenham, UK: Elgar Publishing, 2022.

Vickrey, William S. "Congestion Theory and Transport Investment." *American
Economic Review* 59, no. 2 (1969): 251–60.

Villa, Demetrius. "92% of Americans Support High Speed Rail." American Rail
Club. June 3, 2015. https://www.linkedin.com/pulse/92-americans-support
-high-speed-rail-demetrius-villa/.

Vogels, Emily A. "Millennials Stand out for Their Technology Use, but Older
Generations Also Embrace Digital Life." Pew Research Center. September 9,
2019. https://www.pewresearch.org/fact-tank/2019/09/09/us-generations
-technology-use/.

Vranich, Joseph. *Derailed: What Went Wrong and What to Do about America's
Passenger Trains.* New York: St. Martin's Press, 1997.

Vranich, Joseph, and Edward L. Hudgins. "Help Passenger Rail by Privatizing Amtrak." Cato Institute. November 1, 2001. https://www.cato.org/policy-analysis
/help-passenger-rail-privatizing-amtrak.

Wahba, Sadek. "Accelerating Sustainable Infrastructure: An Investor's Perspective." McKinsey & Company. September 16, 2021. https://www.mckinsey.com
/capabilities/operations/our-insights/accelerating-sustainable-infrastructure
-an-investors-perspective.

———. "Americans and Infrastructure: Results of a National Survey (Released
November 2022)." New York University Development Research Institute.
November 2022. https://static1.squarespace.com/static/5605cc76e4b0829832

a5boa4/t/64b16da4fcd58c734866db82/1689349541119/AMERICANS+AND
+INFRASTRUCTURE_RESULTS+OF+A+NATIONAL+SURVEY+
%28Released+November+2022%29.pdf.

———. "Americans and Infrastructure: Results of a National Survey (Released
September 2021)." New York University Development Research Institute.
September 2021. https://static1.squarespace.com/static/5605cc76e4b08298
32a5boa4/t/64b16ddeod8c4f7a3cf66847/1689349598785/AMERICANS
+AND+INFRASTRUCTURE_RESULTS+OF+A+NATIONAL+SURVEY+
%28Released+September+2021%29.pdf.

———. "Chicagoans and Infrastructure Survey, 2023." New York University Development Research Institute. 2023. https://static1.squarespace.com/static
/5605cc76e4b0829832a5boa4/t/64d352e50dddd8603dad9eb8/1691570917882
/Chicagoans+and+Infrastructure+2023.pdf.

———. "Commentary: Pension Funds Can Launch a New Infrastructure Era."
Pensions & Investments. June 2, 2021. https://www.pionline.com/industry
-voices/commentary-pension-funds-can-launch-new-infrastructure-era.

———. "Estimation of Causal Effects in Observational Studies: Applications to
Training Programs and Labor Migration Decisions." PhD diss., Harvard University, 1996.

———. "The Future of U.S. Infrastructure: Proposals for Progress." *Journal of Applied Corporate Finance* 23, no. 3 (2011): 92–98.

———. "Integrating Infrastructure in U.S. Domestic and Foreign Policy: Lessons
from China." Wilson Center. September 1, 2021. https://www.wilsoncenter.org
/article/integrating-infrastructure-us-domestic-and-foreign-policy-lessons
-china.

———. *Measuring Risk-Adjusted Returns for Infrastructure Assets.* I Squared Capital, 2021.

———. "US Infra Funding Needs More Than Just a Tax Hike." Infrastructure Investor. March 15, 2021. https://www.infrastructureinvestor.com/sadek-wahba-us
-infra-funding-needs-more-than-just-a-tax-hike/.

"Warner, Blunt, Colleagues Reintroduce Bipartisan Bill to Improve Nation's Infrastructure." Mark Warner, US Senate. April 29, 2021. https://www.warner.senate
.gov/public/index.cfm/2021/4/warner-blunt-colleagues-reintroduce-bipartisan
-bill-to-improve-nation-s-infrastructure.

"Waterborne Disease in the United States." US Centers for Disease Control. January 4, 2023. https://www.cdc.gov/healthywater/surveillance/burden/index
.html.

"Weaponizing the Belt and Road Initiative." Asia Society Policy Institute. September 8, 2020. https://asiasociety.org/policy-institute/weaponizing-belt-and
-road-initiative.

"A Whole New LGA Nears Completion." A New LGA. Accessed December 6,
2022. https://www.anewlga.com/.

"William Bingham." University of Pennsylvania Archives and Records Center. Accessed March 14, 2023. https://archives.upenn.edu/exhibits/penn-people /biography/william-bingham/.

"William Vickrey (1914–1996)." Department of Economics at Columbia University. Accessed December 31, 2023. https://econ.columbia.edu/faculty/in-memoriam /william-vickrey-1914-1996/#:~:text=Vickrey%20is%20othe%20father%20 of,the%20technology%20was%20not%20ready.

Williams, John Hoyt. *A Great and Shining Road: The Epic Story of the Transcontinental Railroad.* New York: Times Books, 1988.

Wind Market Reports: 2022 Edition. Office of Energy Efficiency & Renewable Energy. 2022. https://www.energy.gov/eere/wind/wind-market-reports-2022 -edition.

Winston, Clifford. *Gaining Ground: Markets Helping Government.* Washington, DC: Brookings Institution Press, 2021.

———. *Government Failure vs Market Failure: Microeconomics Research and Government Performance.* Washington, DC: AEI-Brookings Joint Center for Regulatory Studies, 2006.

———. *Last Exit: Privatization and Deregulation of the US Transportation System.* Washington, DC: Brookings Institution Press, 2010.

———. "On the Performance of the US Transportation System: Caution Ahead." *Journal of Economic Literature* 51, no. 3 (September 2013): 773–824.

Wiser, Ryan, Andrew Mills, Joachim Seel, Todd Levin, and Audun Botterud. "Impacts of Variable Renewable Energy on Bulk Power System Assets, Pricing, and Costs." Lawrence Berkely National Lab. November 2017. https:// eta-publications.lbl.gov/sites/default/files/lbnl_anl_impacts_of_variable _renewable_energy_final_0.pdf.

Wood, Frederic J. *The Turnpikes of New England.* Boston: Marshall Jones Company, 1909.

World Bank Group Support to Public Private Partnerships: Lessons from Experience in Client Countries, FY 02-12. Washington, DC: World Bank Group, 2015.

"World Development Indicators." World Bank. Accessed July 24, 2023. https:// databank.worldbank.org/source/world-development-indicators#.

"World of Change: Water Level in Lake Powell." NASA Earth Observatory. Accessed January 15, 2023. https://earthobservatory.nasa.gov/world-of-change /LakePowell.

Yescombe, E. R., and Edward Farquharson. *Public-Private Partnerships for Infrastructure: Principles of Policy and Finance.* 2nd ed. Oxford: Butterworth-Heinemann, 2018.

Yu, Au Loong, and Liu Danqing. "The Privatization of Water Supply in China." Business & Human Rights Centre. September 1, 2006. https://www.business -humanrights.org/en/latest-news/pdf-the-privatization-of-water-supply -in-china/.

Zhang, Guojing, Yongjian Liu, Jiang Liu, Shiyong Lan, and Jian Yang. "Causes and Statistical Characteristics of Bridge Failures: A Review." *Journal of Traffic and Transportation Engineering* 9, no. 3 (June 2022): 388–406.

Zhao, Jianfeng, Henry J. Liu, Peter E. D. Love, and David J. Greenwood. "Public-Private Partnerships: A Dynamic Discrete Choice Model for Road Projects." *Socio-Economic Planning Sciences* 82, pt. A (August 2022): 101227. https://doi .org/10.1016/j.seps.2022.101227.

Zheng, Xiaoting, Yi Jiang, and Craig Sugden. "People's Republic of China: Do Private Water Utilities Outperform State-Run Utilities?" Asia Development Bank. August 2016. https://www.adb.org/sites/default/files/publication/190682 /eawp-05.pdf.

Zwalf, Sebastian. "From Turnpikes to Toll Roads: A Short History of Government Policy for Privately Financed Public Infrastructure in Australia." *Journal of Economic Policy Reform* 25, no. 2 (2022): 103–20.

INDEX

ABOUT THE AUTHOR

Sadek Wahba is the founder and chairman of I Squared Capital, a global infrastructure investment firm. A former economist at the World Bank, Wahba has spent the last three decades in the financial sector, where he was voted global infrastructure personality of the decade by Private Equity International in 2019. Wahba earned a PhD in economics from Harvard University and is a published author, with one of his publications selected by MIT among its fifty most influential papers in the last fifty years. He is a member of the President's National Infrastructure Advisory Council, a member of the global advisory council of The Wilson Center, and a senior fellow at New York University's Development Research Institute. Wahba has two children and lives in Miami with his wife and his dog, Whiskey.